Family Demography

international union
for the scientific study
of population

The International Union for the Scientific Study of Population Problems was set up in 1928, with Dr Raymond Pearl as President. At that time the Union's main purpose was to promote international scientific co-operation to study the various aspects of population problems, through national committees and through its members themselves. In 1947 the International Union for the Scientific Study of Population (IUSSP) was reconstituted into its present form. It expanded its activities to:
- stimulate research on population
- develop interest in demographic matters among governments, national and international organizations, scientific bodies, and the general public
- foster relations between people involved in population studies
- disseminate scientific knowledge on population.

The principal ways through which the IUSSP currently achieves its aims are:
- organization of worldwide or regional conferences operations of Scientific Committees under the responsibility of the Council
- organization of training courses
- publication of conference proceedings and committee reports.

Demography can be defined by its field of study and its analytical methods. Accordingly, it can be regarded as the scientific study of human populations primarily with respect to their size, their structure, and their development. For reasons which are related to the history of the discipline, the demographic method is essentially inductive: progress in the knowledge results from the improvement of observation, the sophistication of measurement methods, the search for regularities and stable factors leading to the formulation of explanatory models. In conclusion, the three objectives of demographic analysis are to describe, measure, and analyse.

International Studies in Demography is the outcome of an agreement concluded by the IUSSP and the Oxford University Press. This joint series is expected to reflect the broad range of the Union's activities and, in the first instance, will be based on the seminars organized by the Union. The Editorial Board of the series is comprised of:

Family Demography
Methods and their Application

EDITORS:
JOHN BONGAARTS
THOMAS K. BURCH
KENNETH W. WACHTER

Clarendon Press · Oxford
1987

Oxford University Press, Walton Street, Oxford OX2 6DP

Oxford New York Toronto
Delhi Bombay Calcutta Madras Karachi
Petaling Jaya Singapore Hong Kong Tokyo
Nairobi Dar es Salaam Cape Town
Melbourne Auckland
and associated companies in
Beirut Berlin Ibadan Nicosia

Oxford is a trade mark of Oxford University Press

Published in the United States
by Oxford University Press, New York

British Library Cataloguing in Publication Data
Family demography: methods and their
application.——(International studies in
demography; 2)
1. Demography——Methodology   2. Family——Research
I. Bongaarts, John   II. Burch, Thomas
III. Wachter, Kenneth   IV. International
Union for the Scientific Study of Population
Series 306.8'5'072
HB849.4
ISBN 0-19-829501-4

Library of Congress Cataloging in Publication Data
Family demography.
Papers prepared by the Committee on Family Demography
and Life Cycle, Council of the International Union for
Scientific Study of Population and discussed and revised
at the Council's workshop, December 1984.
Includes index.
1. Family demography——Congresses. 2. Life cycle,
Human——Congresses. I. Bongaarts, John, 1945-
II. Burch, Thomas K. III. Wachter, Kenneth W.
IV. International Union for the Scientific Study of
Population. Committee on Family Demography and Life
Cycle.
HQ759.98.F36 1987   306.8'5   86-31182
ISBN 0-19-829501-4

Set by Colset Private Limited, Singapore
Printed in Great Britain
at the University Printing House, Oxford
by David Stanford
Printer to the University

Preface

In February 1982 the Council of the International Union for the Scientific Study of Population (IUSSP) established a Scientific Committee on Family Demography and the Life Cycle with the mandate to promote research in the emerging subdiscipline of family demography and to give it visability within the scientific community. The fact that the committee was the first on this topic in the history of the IUSSP reflected the rapidly growing interest in family demography as well as its relative neglect by demographers in the past.

The committee gave highest priority to the preparation of a state-of-the-art volume on family demography. The existing literature is scattered in journals and conference proceedings. Overviews of the field are scarcely to be found. Although demographic textbooks usually cover fertility and related family building processes in detail, they either ignore the broad field of family and household demography entirely or dismiss it in short paragraphs. This situation needs to be remedied.

Although it is still much too early for a comprehensive treatment of social and economic determinants and consequences of family size and structure, the methodology of family and life cycle studies has already reached an advanced state, suited for summary in a volume like the present effort.

Prominent researchers were invited to prepare papers in each of the major areas on which research had been focused: measurement and estimation, the family life cycle, multistate life tables, kin models, and household projection. The aim was to provide the reader with highlights of past work and of promising recent research. The drafts of these papers were discussed at length during a workshop at the Population Council in December 1984. Following the workshop, each of the papers was revised extensively to reflect insights gained during the discussion and to incorporate revisions suggested by the editors. The present volume is the outcome of this process. We hope it will benefit not only demographers, but also students of the family in a wide range of disciplines, including sociology, economics, anthropology, and history.

After the New York workshop, the committee turned its attention from method to substance, and organized a conference on the Later States of the Family Life Cycle. The conference, co-sponsored by the IUSSP and the German Association for the Scientific Study of Population, met in Berlin in September 1984, and readers of the present volume will probably also be interested in work emerging from that meeting.

· We thank the authors who spent many hours preparing and revising their contributions. We are especially grateful to the Population Council which co-sponsored the workshop and provided the facilities and logistical support to make this meeting a successful one. We gratefully acknowledge, finally, the efficient assistance provided throughout the project by Marc Lebrun and Virginia Gonzaga of the IUSSP.

John Bongaarts, Thomas Burch, and Kenneth Wachter
1986

Contents

List of Figures

Part I

Introduction

1 Form and Substance in Family Demography

NATHAN KEYFITZ
International Institute for Applied Systems Analysis (IIASA), Laxenburg, Austria

The Italian statistician Barberi complained about the lack of statistical data on the family, and attributed it to the lack of theoretical study of the family as such (*in quanto tale*) as against its individual components (Barberi, 1958). A statistical agency could not usefully collect data concerning an entity whose essential features had not been brought out by theoretical analysis.

On the other hand, the United Nations (1963) says the opposite — that the lack of theory is due to the lack of statistical information: 'The paucity of demographic studies of families and households is due largely to the lack of pertinent census and survey data'.

This is the classical problem of the direction of causation that dogs all social science. Both contentions are in some degree right. Theory and data influence each other reciprocally, and the absence of one is a handicap to the other. But an underlying factor operates to hamper both — as John Bongaarts tells us (introduction to chapter 10): the complexity of the subject makes it difficult both to gather data and to develop rational understanding.

Thus at the meta-level of the discussion of family demography, i.e., before we get into the subject proper, there lies a problem: does A cause B (Barberi), does B cause A (United Nations), or are both A and B caused by C (Bongaarts)? The methods provided in this book help to organize — i.e., reduce the complexity of — the subject, contribute to methodology for analysis, and, by making use of what data are in existence, encourage the production of more data.

The choice of unit for demographic (as for any other) analysis depends on the problem to be solved. For forecasts of total population, of the future labour force, of the pension burden, it has seemed sufficient to work with the individual, and often without characterizing each individual beyond age and sex. One supposes that individuals give rise to other individuals over the course of time in a renewal process, irrespective of marriage or co-residence; individuals are discrete from birth; they live their separate lives, reproduce, and die. There could well be a hidden individualistic ideology underlying the standard demographic practice, though such an assertion is impossible to prove.

One direction of improvement has been to consider the marriage and reproduction of the two sexes jointly, but an authentic two-sex model is stubbornly non-linear, and none of the attempts to deal with it analytically can be regarded as wholly satisfactory. Kendall (1949) and Goodman (1953) provide solutions, but with the strong assumption of dominance by one sex; most population projections also assume dominance, which means they are essentially one-sex models. Norman Ryder (Chapter 6) believes we can do better, and the coming years may well see some advance on this front.

Recognizing families is even harder than recognizing the joint effect of the two sexes on marriage and reproduction, and no one ought to hope for closed form solutions to the analogue for the family of Lotka's renewal equation for individuals. Families do produce families in successive gene-rations in an authentic renewal process, but even the formulation of this process is difficult. Yet the need is there, and approximations are more than welcome. This book provides various approaches to the formal demography of the family, none pretending to analytical completeness, but each making a large contribution based on one simplification or another. The art lies in knowing what to leave out of the model.

Especially useful is the way of tracing the effects of birth, death, marriage, and divorce proposed by Brass (1983). In the real world these are indeed proximate determinants; in the paper world of analysis and model building they are inputs to the representation of family formation and dissolution. Brass's way of doing family demography is to select a 'marker' and to suppose a certain rate at which others attach themselves to this marker. One can imagine a girl born, sooner or later getting married — i.e., having a spouse attached — then having a child, then another child, then being divorced, etc. Alternatively, one could start the process on the male side and proceed similarly to the construction and ultimately the dissolution of the family unit. Related approaches are found in a number of chapters in this volume.

If year-by-year probabilities of vital events are given, there can in principle be no difficulty in constructing arithmetically the expected conglomeration of persons that cluster about each individual designated a marker. The parti-cular nuclear family in question is created, goes through a certain evolution, then disappears. Perhaps the children leave home, and one of the spouses dies; perhaps there are no children, and the couple divorce; there are many possibilities.

One can go from the formation of the family and the counting of its expected members at various stages to analysis of attributes. Given the prob-ability of an individual's being in the labour force at a given moment, of being at school, of being pregnant, of being retired, one can go on to fill out the picture of the family, either on the basis of expected values (macrosimu-lation) or by an individual family application of probabilities followed through to the various possible outcomes (microsimulation).

Beyond kinship is the question of co-residence. We may ask not only what is the number of children expected to have been born to a woman of 55 and the number still alive, but also the number still living in the same household with her. Family demography includes both kinship and co-residence. Long before many such factors are taken into account one has to abandon attempts to obtain analytic solutions, but simulation models can give good approximations.

Continuance of Earlier Work

It is an advantage of the present volume that many of the authors have available a stock of earlier work, concerned with individual demography, that they can exploit to develop methods and propositions for family demography. Samuel Preston refers to a recent series of articles by himself and Ansley Coale relating flow and inventory data, in effect generalizing the Lotka theory by allowing the parameters to vary.

If we have two censuses, for example, separated by 10 years, we can estimate the probability of surviving 10 years for persons aged 25 at the first census by either (*a*) taking the ratio of persons aged 35 at the later census divided by the number aged 25 at the earlier, making what allowance we can for migration, or (*b*) taking the ratio of those aged 35 to those aged 25 at either census and using the censuses to estimate the rate of increase at the ages in question; with zero increase the age distribution of either census is identical with the life table survivorship. Preston and Coale develop the latter approach, and Preston shows how the method is applicable to contingencies other than death, and how it can be extended to allow for several decrements so that it is suitable for finding the probability of survivorship of a marriage in the face of divorce conditional on both parties living. The method can give probabilities and expected times of residence in the several states, with relative insensitivity to errors and gaps in the data.

Simulation

Kenneth Wachter has been working with microsimulation programs for at least a dozen years, and his chapter shows the procedures at their best. Microsimulation can handle complex hypotheses. Whatever time sequence of births, whatever age-specific rates of marriage and of childbearing, whatever rates of dissolution that can be specified can be fed in, and a 'census' taken periodically (in the core of the computer — the only place where the exact count of a population is possible!) to see to what cross-sectional distribution they have led. It is true, as Brass says, that analytical models contribute more (than microsimulation) to an understanding of the factors which matter in the overall process, but simulation is needed to get numbers out when analytic equations prove intractable.

As an example of questions that can only be approached with simulation one recalls the study (Kunstadter, Westoff, and Stephan, 1963) of cross-cousin marriage: where marriage of a man with his mother's brother's daughter is the preferred form, what proportion of the population will be able to enjoy this ideal marriage? (They found less than 40 per cent, as against the 100 per cent that would be possible in a deterministic model.) If the bride is to be within a certain age difference from the groom, and under other practical constraints, there is no possibility of an analytic solution, and only simulation as described by Wachter and Smith will serve.

If the data come in the form of real censuses, then a process of experimentation can be undertaken to ascertain the trajectory of inputs that would produce those censuses, and presumably a best-fitting set could be found. Wachter and his colleagues have developed simulation programs that bring this within reach, and an extension of their methods could add to the armoury of devices available for filling gaps in data. Finding an algorithm that would be efficient enough to provide answers in reasonable time would present problems, but these need not be beyond solution. The 'inverse problem' (i.e. inferring the time-path of inputs from the cross-section of outputs) was approached by Goldman (1978), who infers the rate at which a population has been increasing from a census of younger and older sisters, and McDaniel and Hammel (1984) develop this further.

Kenneth Wachter and Eugene Hammel have developed what is perhaps the most realistic microsimulation model for tracking out a population of individuals, in effect creating random genealogies. Their simulation package is applied by Jaxk Reeves to the study of kinship.

James Smith describes the key features of the algorithm that constitutes the heart of the CAMSIM program for simulating genealogies. In the language that has developed in such work, this is an 'open' model, in that when women are followed and the toss of the random numbers assigns them a mate, the mate is always there; the SOCSIM model of Hammel and Wachter, which is 'closed', considers marriage as requiring a bride and a groom simultaneously from the limited stock of those available and is therefore suitable for investigating the two-sex problem. The closed model is far more difficult to program, and Smith is able to avoid its complexities for his purposes.

Norman Ryder refers to an earlier paper in which he studied family relations, among other purposes to determine the effect on the family of a decline in mortality without a decline in fertility. He viewed the net reproduction rate in terms of a cycle beginning not with the birth of a child and proceeding to the birth of a child in the next generation, as in the usual formulation, but rather as starting with marriage and proceeding through childbirth to the subsequent marriage of the child. The renewal feature permits starting the analysis of the cycle at a number of points, and it is good to have experiments starting at points other than birth. Availability of data will often dictate the choice among the several ways of formulating the renewal cycle.

Continuing to illustrate how the contributions to the present volume are enriched by the previous work of its authors, Thomas Pullum takes up issues in the mathematical theory of kinship. He discusses the use of anthropological data in elucidating alternative ways of defining the family — as a certain kin group wherever located, or as a certain residence group — and reviews the mathematical formulas that he has had a major part in developing.

Frans Willekens extends to the family his earlier work developed in individual multistate demography. Once in possession of various transition probabilities — say, the chance within a one-year period that a single person will become married, that a married person will become divorced, etc. — the use of matrices permits remarkably simple formulas for calculating such probabilities as that a woman married at age 32 will be alive and widowed 37 years later at age 69. Not only probabilities but the expected length of residence in the various states can be calculated from the viewpoint of a person at a given age and in a given state.

Gustav Feichtinger develops, without the use of matrices, formulas for the several sorts of probabilities — the chance of surviving in the single state from age 15 onward; the chance of a marriage being dissolved by death; the mean age at widowhood; in short, the whole set of probabilities associated with the processes of marriage, reproduction, and death. Recognition of parity permits a precise way of dealing with the reproduction of cohorts. The model is deterministic, a restriction that is justified by the intention of applying the formulas to large populations, in which the random variation is swamped by non-random factors. Divorce is less frequent in Austria than it is in most other western countries, which is presumably the reason why the Feichtinger models can neglect it. In some other countries divorce is more than comparable with death as a dissolver of marriages. In order to keep the formulas simple, Feichtinger excludes mortality of children, supposes that all children stay at home 18 years, and disregards remarriage of widows and widowers.

With somewhat the same objective as Feichtinger, Thomas Espenshade calculates marriage probabilities; but instead of using actuarial type decrement formulas for the several probabilities he handles the arithmetic by means of a matrix, in fact using computer programs developed by Frans Willekens and Andrei Roger that take account of divorce and remarriage. The perspective is intermediate between individual demography and family demography, in that these authors follow women through their marital careers. The difference between this and following marriages as such may not be as great as it sounds, in that both can take account of divorce, remarriage, childbearing, etc. The comments of Norman Ryder, who favours consideration of the couple rather than of either sex by itself, elucidate the trade-off between the simplicity of the one-sex versus the richness and difficulty of the two-sex analysis.

Sandra Hofferth carries the analysis further, still using the Willekens and Rogers computer programs. The living arrangements of children, and particularly their being with one or with two parents, are her special interest in this chapter. She finds that 31 per cent of the childhood of white children and 59 per cent of the childhood of black children can be expected to be spent with one parent. This is arrived at by using a realistic projection for the future, and contrasts with the 14 and 50 per cent derived from the synthetic cohorts of 1950–79.

Thomas Burch *et al.* do some effective work with an indirectly standardized headship index based on specific headship rates. The headship rate is the reciprocal of the household size — it is the proportion of the total population that are heads. Burch compares the headship rates of several countries. The rate for India is well below that for the United States, and the procedure applied tells us the factors that bring this about.

Widows and Widowers

The writers by no means exhaust the possibilities of analysis for answering some of the questions about the family. Kingsley Davis suggests that divorce increases because people live longer; a couple can stand one another for only so many years. A model could tell us how much of present divorce is attributable to greater longevity.

Longevity is greater than in the past, but the number of widows and widowers depends on the timing and variance of death rates more than on their overall level. If the ages of bride and groom at marriage are the same, and males and females are subject to the same life table, then according to present mortality trends widowhood would diminish. This follows from the narrowing variance of hazard rates over most of this century. But higher age at marriage of men, and especially the superior survivorship of women, introduces a strong element of asymmetry that makes the number of widows far greater than the number of widowers. And for determining the number living alone, the asymmetry is greatly affected by the process of divorce and remarriage as men replace their original spouses with younger ones. One may speculate on the kind of equilibrium condition that would be arrived at if the disposition of divorced men of 40 to remarry became generalized, while divorced women remained unmarried after 40.

How Much Realism?

A question suggested by the present volume is how much realism one wants or can obtain in the models. At one end of the spectrum we have the work of Gustav Feichtinger, who omits divorce and concentrates on the process of couple formation and dissolution by death, what he calls the potential of married life together. One would go on to incorporate the sequence of birth rates at successive ages of the couples, divorce rates, the fraction attending school or in the labour force at each age. One could determine the fraction of the aged who have living and working offspring. Beyond this are incomes of the family members and their pattern of expenditures, housing arrangements, etc.

To be completely realistic and take account of everything at once is hardly the object. Suppose it were possible to make a simulation that corresponded exactly with what occurs, with all the variables of the real world operating; one would not have a simulation at all, but would be simply reproducing the entity simulated. If one could go that far in the direction of realism, one would have a multiplicity of 'empirical' data, but then one would have to start from the beginning to make simpler models in order to draw understandable conclusions.

In short, simulation and analytical models are alike in that they do not replace direct observation of the population but do something quite different: they find what the population relations, and the family effects of changes in the input variables, would be if everything omitted were held constant.

Forecasting Households and Houses

A prime use of family demography is forecasting, for instance of the number of houses, and houses of each kind, or at least of each size, that will be needed over the next century. Whether to guide the market or to aid government planning, such forecasts are the more important the more the family and household constitution of the population is changing. And never has the household constitution of nations and of localities changed so rapidly as in recent decades. Births have been subject to wide swings that make even the forecast of total population hazardous; and to unpredictable swings in total population is added unpredictable household formation, as young people, old people, and middle-aged people who are divorced increasingly live alone. At one time children remained in their parents' homes until they married and formed households of their own that lasted for the lifetime of the couple. No longer can we draw from the past assured knowledge of how finely the population will be split into households. The splintering of the population into smaller household groups, of which persons living alone are the most common type, seems to be an enduring feature of industrialized countries, and the rate at which it will occur is not easy to forecast.

Thus on the one hand the splintering of the family makes it essential to know the future distribution so that the housing supply can be adjusted to the population to be housed, while, on the other hand, the same splintering makes forecasting more difficult than ever. Not infrequently, the changing circumstances which make forecasting difficult also make forecasting more essential. John Bongaarts's family status life tables, Ingvar Holmberg's flow model, and the innovative methods of John Pitkin and George Masnick will be of value to all those who have to make or use such forecasts.

The headship index method (i.e., analysis of the ratio of households to population) is developed in the chapters by Shigemi Kono, by Pitkin and Masnick, and most particularly by Burch. The decomposition of the headship index could be further developed to tell us how much of the increase that is occurring is due to fewer babies, how much to children leaving home earlier, and how much to divorce.

Embarrassments For Family Demography

It is worth summarizing the four kinds of difficulty that stand in the way of concise expressions and crisp results in family demography.

1. The many types of family groups. Classical demography concerns individuals supposed homogeneous within age and sex groups, and its widespread use is due to the extensive conclusions and applications that can be made despite its gross simplifications. It has clear implications for pensions, for how crowded the schools will be, for the rate at which workers in offices and factories will be promoted.

As for family groups there are not only many types at a given moment, but also rapid changes from one to another. A couple with two children has a third child, or is divorced and the children live with the mother. Even the bare presentation of data, let alone models, is handicapped by this multiplicity of types; no one is satisfied for long with census breakdowns as published.

2. Heterogeneity. The easiest kind of analysis assumes that all members of a group can be taken to have identical transition probabilities, as in the usual life table. Yet we know that even for mortality people have different degrees of frailty or robustness at a given age, and it makes a good deal of difference to expectation of life and other functions how heterogeneous the populations are, as Vaupel and Yashin (1983), Manton (1981), and their coworkers have shown. Heterogeneity is even greater in divorce, for most ages a larger reason for family dissolution than death. Everyone dies once, but some individuals marry and divorce many times, others never divorce. The problem has been faced in migration studies under the heading of the mover-stayer model.

The usual marriage table as published assumes that all couples have the same chance of breaking up. But suppose that underlying the statistics is a condition in which a large fraction of the population marries only once and stays married for life, while a small fraction marries and divorces many times. No one can tell whether the underlying population is homogeneous or not from the way that statistics are usually presented, in which first and later marriages are not distinguished. If there is much heterogeneity then the obvious interpretation of the marriage table, giving, say, 40 per cent probability that a given marriage will end in divorce, is wholly invalid. To separate all couples according to the order of marriage, as Charlotte Höhn wishes us to do, is of course desirable, and a recent version of the US Current Population Survey has done just that.

3. Lack of independence. An awkwardness for model building is the correlation that often exists between the demographic inputs. Thus model building is much more feasible if one can assume that the families of high fertility have the same mortality as those of low fertility. It is hard to take account of intercorrelations among the inputs, yet we can be sure that these exist, both because there are class differences in the several inputs — the poor have more children *and* die younger — and because even without such third variables as social class there could well be direct causal relations between the inputs.

4. Non-marriage. Especially awkward is the weakening of marriage. In many parts of the world, for instance Latin America, couples have long lived together without formal marriage. Common-law marriage may well be equivalent to formal legal marriage in many ways, but it is much less easily measured. With formal marriage, requiring a formal divorce for its termination, at least the nominal situation can be reported to enumerators, boundaries are sharp, and the census-taker's work is straightforward.

In recent years informal cohabitation has spread from Latin America to North America and Europe. Some couples live together as a preliminary to marriage, a kind of trial, some to save on rent, with no intention to remain together once the convenience of both partners is no longer served by the living arrangement. 'My roommate moved out,' said one young woman to me. 'He got a job in St. Louis. Now the apartment is too expensive for me, and I have to move.' We have a continuum from lifetime registered marriage to temporary arrangements for economizing on rent. Which of these should be counted as stable unions, i.e. as families?

Our authors cope as well as they can with such difficulties.

Form and Substance

So far I have discussed only methods, and methods, that is to say the formal side, are what the book is about. But from the point of view of someone who is not a professional demographer, but engaged in the construction industry, say, and who just wants to know what the future constitution of households will be, or one who is planning old-age security and wants to know what kind of family help those over 85 can count on to supplement state-supplied assistance, all this will be preparation rather than substance. Such a prelude aids other demographers, who may make forecasts or draw conclusions. The following brief paragraphs are intended to justify the effort that has gone into elaborating the methods presented here, by noting some of the substantive problems to whose solution they can contribute.

The Substance of the Matter

An earlier overview by Bongaarts (1983), which has served as a guide to the authors here, and which is in some respects the inspiration of the project, mentions substance at several points. For instance he refers to Lansing and Kish (1957), who show that 'for several variables, including home ownership, income, and the purchase of consumer durables, the family cycle state explains more of the total variation than age'. He does not cover the social and economic determinants and consequences of family and household structure, but with him I am sure that the study of these will be facilitated by the development of the formal parts.

Other questions arise that require further data for their answering. What kinds of social skills, what qualities of personality does it take for two people to share a household? We know little about whether living alone, say for the elderly, is due to a wish for independence or to the incapacity to get along with another person. In so far as living alone is the wish of the individual, does it correspond to a partial disengagement from life? Is seeking such disengagement a part of the explanation of high divorce rates? To what extent do friends and relatives take the place of a spouse for the person who lives alone?

When families were large the older children could help with the rearing of the younger ones. Not only did that introduce them to general adult responsibilities at an early age, but it gave them an apprenticeship in childrearing that was helpful when they in turn had children. An only child lacks both the observation of a mother and father raising children and exercise in helping them. That creates a great demand for 'how-to-do-it' books for parents, but books are an imperfect substitute for apprenticeship.

Because children in the small family have little opportunity to observe childraising, this comes to seem a mysterious art, and when only children grow up they have little confidence in their ability to exercise it. That childraising ceases to be a routine matter discourages couples from having children, or from having more than one or two. Such a circular mechanism operating from one generation to the next can help explain continued low fertility in the framework of family demography. (Of course there are many other factors operating to continue the small family, from women's careers to old-age security provided by the state.)

Whether the scarcity of children permits mothers to take outside jobs or their taking outside jobs causes them to have fewer children we do not know, but in either case mothers who work create a demand for outside help, and a large child-care industry, described by Easterlin (1982), comes into being.

There may be less demand for teachers as the school-attending cohorts contract, but there is more need for pre-school help of various kinds as mothers continue their move into the labour force and single-parent families increase. The demand for pre-school help due to wives going out to work more than offsets the fact that there are fewer children.

It is largely the high rate of marital dissolution by divorce that is responsible for the growing proportion of children being raised by one parent rather than two. The effects of this on discipline, on school attendance and dropping out, and on other circumstances surrounding the child are not yet known, and even more uncertain is the effect on the character and disposition of the adult that the child will become.

In the two-parent families where the mother is away all day, or where there is only one parent present who necessarily works outside the home, keeping the children occupied is a main problem. The extreme case is one child alone, but even two or three may not be satisfied to play together unsupervised for long periods. In such cases the solution is to automate: have television provide child care. In one survey children two to five years of age were reported as watching television 31.4 hours per week; the number of hours diminished with age, down to female teenagers who watched only (!) 23.4 hours (Easterlin, 1982). We may well have here the major determinant of the culture of the next generation.

A host of other problems are raised at the far end of life. Co-residence of the extended family has greatly diminished, especially since social security was introduced. What family statistics as now compiled do not tell us is the extent to which the adult sibling members of the family seek to live 'together' in the sense of being in the same city with grandparents nearby. Some data are available to show the tendency to reside in the same neighbourhood, though diminishingly in the same home.

If there is one characteristic on which present youth prides itself, and that sets it apart from its elders, it is informality, the ability to enter immediately into direct human relations with others, untrammelled by traditional forms of address and unobstructed by institutional constraints. In European languages this shows itself in addressing even strangers with 'tu' or 'du'; in English by first-naming. Titles are dispensed with, even between students and teachers, as placing an unnecessary barrier between individuals. It is a merit to be perfectly frank in discourse, to dispense with the restraints on self-expression that hampered earlier generations. Social forms in the wider world come more and more to resemble the familiar styles hitherto confined to the intimate ambience of the family.

And yet this spontaneity in untrammelled human relations has accompanied a diminishing proportion who live with a spouse. Single-member households in the USA were 4 per cent of all households in 1790, 7 per cent in 1940; today they are 25 per cent. More than a million divorces per year testify to the inability or unwillingness of couples to stay together.

One possible explanation is that the immediate informality gets in the way of human relations in the longer term. Previous generations protected individuals with multiple forms of restraint. In traditional societies couples do not share all information; even today surveys in less developed countries show that couples often cannot bring themselves to discuss birth control. The restrictions on discussion provide a kind of privacy to each within the home, which is lacking when everything is up for frank comment. It is possible that the various traditional restraints within the family, including those that kept the couple in some degree apart from one another in their daily rounds, helped to hold them together over the years.

This is only one explanation of the increase in separate living. Perhaps people have always wanted to live in separate households, while only now have incomes become high enough for this to be affordable. Perhaps they always lived with kin in the past because kin were available; now families are small and hence kin so few that there are often none available with whom to live. Perhaps there has been a change in tastes and people now prefer separate living, where before they preferred to live together. This last sounds like the sort of explanation after the fact that is not very helpful in the absence of some measure of taste independent of the living together it professes to explain.

Thomas Burch (1985) does somewhat better than this in attributing the decline of the larger household to the decline in the division of labour. If husband, wife, and unmarried daughter live together, but all three have jobs, and all do about the same amount of housework, then they cannot be seen as having separate niches within the home, and they might as well live separately. They would lose some economy of scale in cooking meals, etc., but this may well be insufficient to offset the gain of privacy if they separate. The Burch hypothesis is just what the field of family demography needs — an axis along which methodologies can be applied to ascertain the quantitative effect of what may be called the niche hypothesis.

Issues concerned with the solidarity of the family arise when people live separately — not only how many contemporaneously living kin there are as a result of current rates of birth, death, and divorce, but the extent to which they are a mutually assisting group, both in routine matters and in crises. How the costly and impersonal services funded by the state — hospital care for minor ailments, for example — can be provided better and less expensively by the family is a key issue. As the costs of public provision for the old and disabled rise higher, and the facilities are increasingly seen as unsatisfactory, family sociology and demography will inevitably be expected to give answers to these questions.

Solidarity in the Family and the State

Since the 1930s we have steadily shifted the responsibility for the old, the disabled, the poor, and, in considerable measure, for the education of children, from the family, the religious community, and the local neighbourhood to the state. Whether impelled in the first place by the decline of family solidarity or by some other more positive force of individuals seeking freedom and independence from their relatives, the shift has been almost universally supported; only encrusted conservatives opposed the advance of the welfare state. The solidarity of the national state has seemed sufficiently strong to handle all burdens.

In the 1980s has come the realization that the state too has its limits. One need no longer be a reactionary to see that relieving the family of the care of the old and disabled is related to the immediate political interest of important actors, and that these may have pushed the expansion of the state farther than is sustainable in the long run. A part of the interest in family demography lies in the question whether some backtracking will be possible. We may have come to the limit of what the state can do; can we have the family reassume some of its former obligations?

This realization does not apply to the financial aspects alone, but to the human and moral aspects as well. Quite aside from costs (and these are often very high), the sort of care that is provided by nursing homes and other institutions is not equivalent to what the family at its best can give. Perhaps financial incentives can be devised strong enough to strengthen the family as a resource for the old. Care as such is not the province of family demography, but at least it can say something about the existence and proximity of family members who are potential care-givers.

I repeat that these are questions not taken up in the chapters that follow, but they are examples of the substantive issues in the background that give those chapters their interest and importance.

References

Barberi, B. (1958), *Elementi di statistica economica*, Torino.

Bongaarts, J. (1983), 'The Formal Demography of Families and Households: An Overview', *IUSSP Newsletter* No. 17: 27–42.

Brass, W. (1983), 'The Formal Demography of the Family: An Overview of the Proximate Determinants', In: *The Family. British Society for Population Studies (OPCS) Occasional Paper*, No. 31, Office of Population Censuses and Surveys [OPCS], London: 37–49.

Burch, T. K. (1979), 'Household and Family Demography: A Bibliographic Essay', *Population Index* 43: 173–95.

—— (1985), 'Changing Age–Sex Roles and Household Crowding: A Theoretical Note', *Proceedings, International Population Conference, Florence 1985*, Liege: IUSSP, 3: 253–61.

Easterlin, R. A. (1982), 'The Changing Circumstances of Child-rearing', *Journal of Communication* 32, 3: 86–98.

Goldman, Noreen (1978), 'Estimating the Intrinsic Rate of Increase from the Average Numbers of Younger and Older Sisters', *Demography* 15: 499–507.

Goodman, L.A. (1953), 'Population growth of the sexes' *Biometrics*, IX: 212–25.

Goodman, L. A., N. Keyfitz, and T. W. Pullum (1974), 'Family Formation and the Frequency of Various Kinship Relationships', *Theoretical Population Biology* 5: 1–27.

Kendall, D.G. (1949), 'Stochastic Processes and Population Growth', *Journal of the Royal Statistical Society*, B, XI: 230–64.

Keyfitz, N. (1984), *Applied Mathematical Demography*, 2nd Edition, Springer-Verlag, New York.

Kunstadter, P., C. Westoff, and F. F. Stephan (1963), 'Demographic Variability and Preferential Marriage Patterns', *American Journal of Physical Anthropology*, New Series 21: 511–19.

Lansing and Kish (1957), 'Family Cycle as the Independent Variable', *American Sociological Review* 28: 86–96.

Manton, K. G., E. Stallard, and J. W. Vaupel (1981), 'Methods for Comparing the Mortality Experience of Heterogeneous Populations', *Demography* 18: 389–410.

McDaniel, C. K., and E. A. Hammel (1984), 'A Kin-based Measure of r and an Evaluation of its Effectiveness', *Demography* 21: 41–51.

United Nations (1963), *Determinants and Consequences of Population Trends*, United Nations, New York.

Vaupel, J. W., and A. I. Yashin (1983), 'The Deviant Dynamics of Death in Heterogeneous Populations', Research Report RR-83-1, International Institute for Applied Systems Analysis, Laxenburg, Austria.

Part II

Measurement and Estimation

2 Measures of Household Composition and Headship Based on Aggregate Routine Census Data*

THOMAS K. BURCH, SHIVA S. HALLI, ASHOK K. MADAN, KAUSAR
THOMAS and LOKKY WAI

*Population Studies Centre and Department of Sociology University of Western Ontario
London, Ontario, Canada*

---

1 Introduction

The historical and comparative study of household structure has long been
hampered by the lack of large series of comparable data. In the UN's *Determinants and Consequences* (1973a) we read:

> The paucity of demographic studies of families and households is due largely to the
> lack of pertinent census and survey data. The concept of the headship rate is a key to
> modern methods of projecting the number of families and households and it may be
> a good indicator of the degree of family doubling-up or of the degree of nucleari-
> zation. However, aside from the developed countries, only certain Latin American
> countries, India and Singapore have so far provided census tabulations of heads of
> families and households classified by sex and age. Furthermore, because most of
> these countries have collected sex-age-specific headship data only recently, in many
> cases only since the 1960 round of censuses, it is not possible to undertake historical
> analysis of changes in headship rates and of their effects on average size of families
> and households (p. 364).

The situation has not changed radically since, although available series of
age–sex-specific headship rates have become larger and more representative
geographically (see UN, 1981).

Lacking ideal data, what can be done with census materials that are widely
available? More concretely, what can be said about changes and differences
in household composition using routine aggregate census data on number
of households and on the population classified by age, sex, and marital
status?

* Research for this chapter was performed under grants from the Social Sciences and Humanities
Research Council of Canada (#410-80-0717-R2) and the US National Institute of Child Health and
Human Development — Center for Population Research (#5R01HD 15004-02). We are indebted to
Marilyn McQuillan and Fran McGillvary for assistance with data transcription and preparation. As
usual, the Social Science Computing Laboratory at Western has provided excellent assistance at
many stages of our work; we particularly acknowledge the help of Doug Link. Our colleagues Fred
Evers, Paul Maxim, Ed Grabb, and Tom Wonnacott have helped clarify some statistical issues.
Veronica D'Souza has typed several versions of the manuscript with skill and patience.

This chapter attempts to answer these questions by exploring several measures based on such data. It consists of two main sections. The second section describes two indirectly standardized headship indices: I_H (see Burch, 1980), which standardizes for age and sex; and I'_H, which standardizes as well for marital status. It also discusses the decomposition of these and related indices into components reflecting the separate contributions to 'overall headship' of the two sexes, or of persons of different marital statuses.

The third section examines several simple ratios that have been used or proposed for the study of household structure, for example, average household size (or its inverse the 'crude headship rate'), adults per household, and married persons per household. These ratios are examined in the context of a decomposition of the 'crude headship rate'. The use of these simple ratios as proxies for more complex measures such as I_H or I'_H is explored. Finally, decomposition is used to study the sources of variation in average household size.

For purposes of methodological exposition, we make several assumptions. Among the most important are the following:

1. We assume that the systematic analysis of data on households (residential units) is worthwhile, despite their inherent inability to tell us anything about broader, non-residential family or kinship structures. The value of household data has been questioned (see Caldwell, 1976) but we agree with Irene Taeuber (1971) that '. . . the fact that the abundant data of census and survey do not permit all types of analyses of kinship structures and dynamics is not an argument for their discard' (p. 42).

2. We assume that census concepts of *household* generally are comparable from one time and place to another. This assumption is valid for the vast majority of population censuses, although problems arise for particular cases (see Burch, 1967, pp. 356–58); the assumption may be most problematic for Tropical Africa.

3. In working with age–sex-specific headship rates, we have not modified the traditional convention of assigning headship to the male in husband–wife households.

4. We have not resolved the problem of faulty data on marital status, especially in Latin America (but also in highly developed societies, where non-marital cohabitation has become more common). In practice, we either assume the data are accurate or eliminate questionable cases from consideration.

2 Standardized Indices of Household Headship

2.1 The Index I_H

I_H is a ratio of actual households to expected households, where the expected number is the number that would exist if a set of standard age–sex-specific headship rates were to apply to the actual age–sex distribution of the population. The formula, using vector notation and dot products, is

$$I_H = \frac{H}{\hat{H}} = \frac{H}{\mathbf{c} \cdot \mathbf{p}} \tag{2.1}$$

where H = actual number of households

$\hat{H}$ = expected number of households

$\mathbf{c}$ = vector of standard headship rates by age and sex

$\mathbf{p}$ = vector of actual population by age and sex

(Note: Using the more traditional summation notation, the denominator of this equation would be

$$\sum_{i=1}^{n} \sum_{j=1}^{2} \mathbf{c}_{ij}\, \mathbf{p}_{ij}$$

where the summation is over 2 sexes and n age groups. In other words a dot product of two vectors is equivalent to the sum of their term by term products.)

I_H is indirectly standardized for age and sex.

2.1.1 Choice of Standard Rates. In traditional standardization, the choice of standard rates is a central problem. Common practice has been to use rates from one of the populations being compared, or rates from a similar population. The use of maximum rates was popularized by Coale in connection with his fertility indices (Coale, 1969). An advantage of using maximum rates is that values of the resulting index will be less than 1.0, so that they are easier to interpret relative to that convenient reference point.

For his fertility indices, Coale chose as standard the age-specific fertility rates for married Hutterite women early in this century, who had the highest total marital fertility rate ever reliably observed. The analogue for headship would be a set of age-specific headship rates for married males for some highly developed society like Sweden or Germany. For deriving summary measures of headship *standardized* for sex and/or marital status, however, the use of a single set of standard rates across all sub-groups does not work. It is necessary to use appropriate rates specific for sex and marital status (but see below Section 2.5).

In the case of headship rates specific for sex, a suitable maximum set is difficult to find since female rates tend to be highest in the Caribbean and male rates in Northern and Western Europe. For rates specific for marital status as well, the problem is even more difficult.

In the present chapter, we have abandoned the notion of maximum rates and used age–sex and (see below) age–sex–marital status-specific rates for Sweden (1960), which are high for males but only moderately high for females. Note that the resulting indices may legitimately exceed 1.0, and that for individual populations represented in both series, I_H values are different from those presented in Burch (1980). Finally, we have tried to assess the effects of using different standards by means of a sensitivity analysis (see Section 2.4 below).

2.1.2 Choice of Lower Age Limit. The adult population has been defined using a lower age limit of 15 years. Some may object that this is too low, especially for developed nations, where the age at marriage and the proportion of children attending high school both are relatively high. For comparative purposes, however, the choice of a lower age limit makes little difference. For the series in Burch (1980), for example, the correlation between indices calculated with a lower age limit of 15 and with a lower limit of 20 was + 0.99. This insensitivity of the results to the choice of the lower age limit is due primarily to the lower headship rate for the earliest age group.

2.1.3 Interpreting I_H. I_H is a global measure of the tendency of adults in a population to head their own households rather than to live in households headed by other adults, or, the tendency toward separate rather than joint residence — Kuznets (1978) has called it the 'jointness or apartness' of adults or 'JAA factor'. Included under this general concept, however, are several distinct patterns of behaviour:

1. the residence of unmarried adults in the parental home;
2. the residence of young married couples in the parental home, as in the classic extended family;
3. the tendency of spouses or quasi-spouses to co-reside;
4. the tendency of unmarried persons — siblings, aunts, nephews, etc. to live with kin rather than by themselves;
5. the tendency of elderly parents to live with their adult children;
6. the prevalence of domestic service and of boarding and lodging.

Another way of stating this characteristic of I_H is that it reflects the behaviour of adults of all ages, both sexes, and all marital status categories. This raises the question whether variation in I_H is being 'driven' by some of these categories more than others. Analysis of a relevant series shows that I_H tends to be moderately highly correlated with specific headship rates for all age-sex categories, with r generally between + 0.5 and + 0.7. There is a hint of higher correlations among younger (<35) women and among older (>65) men and women. But overall the results confirm that I_H is tapping a broad behavioural tendency toward separate living.

The global character of I_H just described is inherent in the data on which it is based, namely, simple counts of total households. This makes the measure widely applicable — indeed to almost any population census — but raises problems of interpretation. The most serious one relates to the level of female headship rates. Concretely, I_H can assume high levels because headship rates are generally high across all age–sex categories (as in Sweden), or because headship rates are unusually high among females (as in Guadeloupe). And there is nothing in the index itself which can distinguish the two cases. Similar problems, although less apparent, may arise with respect to persons of different marital statuses.

Where data on household heads are classified by sex or by marital status, the problem can be solved by means of decomposing I_H and related measures into separate indices for each sex or marital status (see below, Section 2.5).

I_H also may be interpreted as an inverse measure of household composition or complexity, where this is conceptualized in terms of the number of adults per household. For substantive contexts where it is more natural to use this approach, one can use the reciprocal of I_H so long as one recalls that it is a purely relative number.

2.2 I'_H — Standardizing for Marital Status

Where data on age, sex, *and* marital status compositon of a population are available, a headship index that indirectly standardizes for marital status can be computed by a straightforward extension of the above.

2.2.1 Headship and Marital Status. The actual number of household heads in a population is a function of: *a*) actual age–sex–marital status-specific headship rates; and *b*) the population distribution by age, sex, and marital status. Thus variation in I_H may be due to differences or changes in marital status composition as well as to differences or changes in household formation behaviour within age–sex–marital status categories.

The effects of marital status composition on I_H can be described more specifically, based on an examination of some typical age–sex–marital status-specific headship rates (see UN, 1973a, p. 351):

a) The highest rates occur for married *couples*. But by past census conventions, in husband–wife households the husband is considered the head, so that when rates are presented separately by sex, married males have the highest rates, married females the lowest — usually close to zero.

b) Single (never-married) persons of both sexes have low headship rates, though not as low as for married females.

c) Rates for widowed, divorced and separated persons generally are intermediate to those for the single and for married males.

2.2.2 Calculating I'_H. By a straightforward extension of equation (2.1) above, we can compute an index of headship standardized for marital status. The formula is

$$I'_H = H/\hat{H}' \qquad (2.2)$$

where $\hat{H}'$ refers to the number of households (heads) expected if actual persons in the various age–sex–marital status categories were to experience some standard age–sex–marital status-specific headship rates. The formula for $\hat{H}'$ is

$$\hat{H}' = c' \cdot p' \tag{2.2a}$$

where c' = a vector of standard age–sex–marital status-specific headship rates and p' = a vector of actual population by age, sex, and marital status.

In computing I'_H, the same issues relating to the choice of standard rates arise as were discussed above in Section 2.1.1. For this paper, the standard rates used are from Sweden (1960). Some evidence on the sensitivity of I'_H to different standard rates is given in Section 2.4 below.

2.3 Illustrative Results

Table 2.1 presents illustrative results for world regions and sub-regions, and for selected individual nations. These are from a series for 75 nations of one million population or more, at the latest date for which data on numbers of households and on marital status by age and sex were available in the UN *Demographic Yearbook*. Data for regions and sub-regions are unweighted averages of indices for constituent countries.

In terms of I_H, reflecting headship net of age and sex composition, Asia shows the lowest level, as might be expected given its reputation for extended family systems. North America and Africa have the highest indices. Europe, Latin America, and Oceania (Australia and New Zealand) have similar, intermediate values. In terms of I'_H, reflecting headship with control also for marital status, the rankings by region are roughly the same, with Africa moving into the intermediate group.

Regional figures mask a good bit of sub-regional variation. Sub-Saharan Africa has unusually high values; indeed, its I_H value of 1.14 is the highest of any sub-region; its I'_H value of .99 is tied for the lead with North America. The meaning of this result is not clear, but the following possible explanations must be considered:

1. The high values may be a statistical artifact, based on the non-comparability of African census and survey concepts of *household* with those used in other parts of the world.
2. They may reflect generally high rates of household formation related to the ease of construction of separate dwellings (Caldwell, 1976) due to low population densities, warm climate, and ready availability of building materials.
3. They may reflect relatively high rates of female headship (cf. the Caribbean), associated with polygamy, consensual unions, and high rates of marital instability.

In Asia, the lowest headship rates by far are found in Middle South Asia (containing India, Pakistan, Nepal, Iran, Sri Lanka). I_H is relatively low for

Table 2.1 I_H and I'_H values and their differences for regions, sub-regions and selected individual nations, various recent dates

A. Region and Sub-Regions	I_H	I'_H	Difference
Africa	1.07	.94	.13
Northern	.99	.88	.11
Sub-Saharan	1.14	.99	.15
Asia	.92	.83	.09
S.W.	.93	.84	.09
Middle So.	.86	.76	.10
Southeast	.96	.84	.12
East	.90	.88	.02
Europe	1.00	.94	.06
Northern	1.02	.98	.04
Western	1.03	.98	.05
Eastern	1.04	.95	.09
Southern	.90	.85	.05
North America	1.06	.99	.07
Latin America	.99	.92	.07
Middle	1.01	.92	.09
Caribbean	1.01	.97	.04
Tropical So.	1.00	.92	.08
Temperate So.	.92	.88	.04
Oceania	.99	.94	.05
B. Selected individual nations	I_H	I'_H	Difference
Africa			
Morocco	.97	.84	.13
Niger	1.21	.99	.22
Asia			
India	.81	.67	.14
Indonesia	1.06	.86	.20
Japan	.92	.88	.04
Turkey	.84	.72	.12
Hong Kong	.90	.95	−.05
Europe			
Sweden	1.09	1.09	.00
Germany	1.11	1.02	.09
Ireland	.85	.87	−.02
Spain	.88	.86	.02
Albania	.83	.74	.09
Latin America			
Dominican Republic	1.07	1.08	−.01
Mexico	1.13	1.00	.13
Argentina	.92	.85	.07
North America			
U.S.	1.10	1.00	.10
Canada	1.01	.97	.04
Oceania			
Australia	1.00	.94	.06

East Asia (Hong Kong, Japan, South Korea), but when marital status is controlled, its index is the highest in Asia. That is, headship is relatively high, given the considerable delay of marriage in these populations.

Northern, Western, and Eastern Europe have broadly similar headship indices, although the value for Eastern Europe is slightly lower than the other two sub-regions when a control for marital status is introduced. Southern Europe has low values, comparable to those for East Asia, in a striking demonstration of the reality of a distinctive 'Mediterranean' family system.

In Latin America, distinctively low values of both indices are found for Temperate South America (Argentina, Chile, Uruguay), in what is probably a reflection of the Southern European pattern just noted. Values for the Caribbean are somewhat high (especially I'_H), perhaps reflecting unusually high rates of female headship associated with the prevalence of consensual unions. I'_H values for Latin America generally, however, must be treated with caution due to frequent unreliability of data on marital status.

Values for Australia and New Zealand are similar to those for Europe.

Data for individual nations show even greater variation. The differences in I_H values between Albania and Sweden in Europe or between India and Indonesia in Asia are almost as great as the difference between the highest and lowest values for the series taken as a whole. And Argentina has values closer to Japan than to most other parts of Latin America or to Europe.

The distinctive merit of I_H and I'_H as demographic measures is that they can capture this kind of variation, and help to break down prevailing stereotypes of Asian versus European or Western patterns, stereotypes often based on data for only a few nations from each region.

2.3.1 Relative Size of I_H and I'_H The last column of Table 2.1 shows the differences between I_H and I'_H. I'_H is generally lower, that is, the headship index drops with control for marital status. The number of expected households is larger when calculated using separate marital status categories and marital status-specific rates, than when using total population in each age–sex category and average rates across marital status categories. This is related to the fact that headship rates among married males are considerably higher than for all males, especially in the younger age groups (where the absolute numbers of persons tend to be large), and that headship rates for single, widowed, and divorced females are higher than those for total females. Where the proportions married for males, or the proportions single, widowed or divorced for females are high, $\hat{H}'$ will tend to be higher than $\hat{H}$, and I'_H lower than I_H.

2.4 Sensitivity of I_H and I'_H to Choice of Standard Rates

The illustrative data presented so far have used standard rates from Sweden,

Table 2.2 Correlations between I'_H and I_H values computed using various standard rates: for international series and US States in 1900 and 1970

		International	US 1900	US 1970
I'_H	Sweden	.971	.973	.870
I_H	Sweden and Japan	.976	.995	.918
	Sweden and Argentina	.924	.978	.792
	Sweden and Guadeloupe	.990	.984	.990
	Japan and Argentina	.982	.993	.965
	Japan and Guadeloupe	.944	.964	.878
	Argentina and Guadeloupe	.870	.927	.734

1960. How much difference in results would it make if other standard rates were chosen, especially other rates with a pattern sharply different from that for Sweden? To provide a preliminary answer to this question, we have re-run I_H using standard rates from Japan (1965), Guadeloupe (1961), and Argentina (1960) and I'_H using Japanese rates (marital status-specific rates for Guadeloupe or Argentina are not available). Japan represents an Asian pattern of headship, with notably low rates for single, widowed, and divorced females. Guadeloupe represents a Caribbean pattern with unusually high rates for females generally. Argentina has unusually low female rates relative to those of males.

The basic results are presented in Table 2.2 for three different empirical series. In comparing indices using Japanese and Swedish rates, we find correlations of $+0.97$ or higher for our contemporary international series of 75 nations and for the US states in 1900, satisfactory levels for the broad comparative or historical studies for which I_H and I'_H are best suited. For the US states in 1970, the correlation is somewhat lower, but still in the neighbourhood of $+0.90$.

We would expect less consistency in results with rates from Guadeloupe or Argentina since these represent extreme patterns. Table 2.2 presents results for comparisons among I_H using all four sets of standard rates. Most of the correlations are greater than $+0.90$, with those falling below that value involving either Argentina or Guadeloupe, our extreme cases. The lowest value ($r = +0.73$) involves both.

Our conclusion is that for broad international comparative purposes, the choice of any non-extreme set of standard rates will yield satisfactory results. For studies of specific nations or regions which are thought to have distinctive patterns of headship, the choice of standard rates should reflect this fact.

2.5 Decomposing Headship Indexes

As noted above, a limitation of I_H and I'_H is their global character, the fact that they summarize behaviour across both sexes, all adult ages, and all marital status categories, and thus fail to reveal different sources of variation in the index. For example, the indices cannot distinguish between situations in which headship is high in general (e.g., Sweden) from those where it is particularly high for women (e.g., Guadeloupe). Where data allow, it will be useful to decompose such summary indices into separate components reflecting headship among males and females, among persons of different marital status categories, or both.

The decomposition procedures require, in addition to an age, sex, marital status distribution of the population, a classification of households by sex and/or marital status of head (but not by age). Thus, there will be many populations for which summary indices such as I_H and I'_H can be calculated (from data on total number of households/heads) but for which decomposition will not be possible, due to a lack of any further classifications of households/heads by sex or marital status. If, on the other hand, household heads are classified by *age* as well as by sex and marital status, then summary measures of age–sex–marital status-specific headship rates can be calculated directly, and the indirect standardization procedures described here are unnecessary.

Several different approaches to this decomposition are possible depending on which summary index and which standard rates are used. There is no unique correct procedure. For example, either I_H or I'_H can be decomposed using age–sex or age–sex–marital status-specific headship rates as standards. A more useful approach, in our view, is to start with a summary index, say I^*_H, that is unstandardized for sex or marital status (i.e., is standardized for age only). The decomposition by sex and marital status of a summary index already standardized for those compositional factors seems to us to work at cross-purposes. In theory, indices relating to the contribution of factors controlled through standardization should have little variance. In practice, the numerical results can be hard to interpret and even misleading.

A precedent for our recommended procedure is Coale's (1969) decomposition of I_f, the index of overall fertility, into three components reflecting marital fertility, non-marital fertility, and proportion married. In this procedure, one set of standard rates, those for married Hutterite women, was used throughout. For example, the standard rates for married women are applied to the actual population of non-married women in computing the index of non-marital fertility, I_h. The advantage of this procedure is that it yields fertility indices of the right relative magnitudes — I_h (non-marital fertility) is typically very low relative to I_g (marital fertility). In the alternate procedure of applying 'appropriate' standard specific rates to each specific sub-group, this advantage is lost. In the case of fertility, non-marital fertility indices might often be higher than marital. In the case of headship, the headship index for non-married males could be higher than for married males, a potentially misleading result. Indices for a particular sub-group could be compared across populations, but the proper proportionality among the indices would be lost. Using the recommended procedure, indices can be compared both across and within populations.

We illustrate the procedure with a decomposition of I^*_H by sex and marital status simultaneously. Simpler decompositions, by sex only or by marital status only, should be obvious. The proof of the identity is omitted due to space limitations, but is straightforward.

We use vector notation as being simpler and more compact (summation signs and age indexes can be omitted). The subscripts m and f are used for male and female; the superscripts m and n are used for married and non-married.

H^m_m = actual number of households headed by married males
H^m_f = actual number of households headed by married females
H^n_m = actual number of households headed by non-married males
H^n_f = actual number of households headed by non-married females
$\mathbf{p}$ = vector of actual adult population by age
$\mathbf{p}^m_m$ = vector of actual married male population by age
$\mathbf{p}^m_f, \mathbf{p}^n_m, \mathbf{p}^n_f$ = similar vectors for married females and non-married males and females
$\mathbf{c}$ = a vector of standard headship rates by age, specifically, standard rates for married males.

The decomposition formula is:

$$I^*_H = K_m (I^m_m J^m_m + [1 - I^m_m] J^n_m) + (1 - K_m)(I^m_f J^m_f + [1 + I^m_f] J^n_f)$$

(2.3)

$$I^*_H = \frac{H}{\mathbf{c} \cdot (\mathbf{p}^m_m + \mathbf{p}^n_m + \mathbf{p}^m_f + \mathbf{p}^n_f)} = \frac{H}{\mathbf{c} \cdot \mathbf{p}}$$

(2.4)

$$J^m_m = \frac{H^m_m}{\mathbf{c} \cdot \mathbf{p}^m_m} \quad \text{index of headship for married males}$$

(2.5a)

$$J^n_m = \frac{H^n_m}{\mathbf{c} \cdot \mathbf{p}^n_m} \quad \text{index of headship for non-married males}$$

(2.5b)

$$J^m_f = \frac{H^m_f}{\mathbf{c} \cdot \mathbf{p}^m_f} \quad \text{index of headship for married females}$$

(2.5c)

$$J^n_f = \frac{H^n_f}{\mathbf{c} \cdot \mathbf{p}^n_f} \quad \text{index of headship for non-married females}$$

(2.5d)

$$I^m_m = \frac{\mathbf{c} \cdot \mathbf{p}^m_m}{\mathbf{c} \cdot \mathbf{p}_m} \quad \text{index of proportion married for males}$$

(2.6a)

$$I_f^m = \frac{c \cdot p_f^m}{c \cdot p_f} \text{ index of proportion married for females} \qquad (2.6b)$$

$$K_m = \frac{c \cdot p_m}{c \cdot p} \text{ index of proportion male} \qquad (2.7)$$

Using as standard age-specific headship rates for married males in Sweden (1960), we obtain the following illustrative results:

	Canada (1971)	Japan (1965)
I_H^*	.422	.333
J_m^m	.974	.864
J_m^n	.189	.136
J_f^m	.033	.021
J_f^n	.333	.174
I_m^m	.665	.637
I_f^m	.649	.592
K_m	.496	.484

These results show that, net of age composition, headship in Canada is about one-third higher than in Japan. This is the result of higher headship rates in all four sex–marital status categories in Canada, and to somewhat higher proportions married for both sexes. Sex composition is not an important factor in this particular comparison.

It is interesting to note that headship rates for non-married females are higher than for non-married males, in both countries, but particularly in Canada. This is a reflection mainly of higher headship rates among widowed and divorced females than among males of similar marital statuses (although this relationship is not uniform across all age groups in all populations). The relatively small contribution of females to overall headship (.043 out of .333 for Japan and .070 out of .422 for Canada) is related to the use of conventional data on household heads, which for married couples attributes headship to the male.

3 Simple Ratios of Household Size and Composition

Past studies of household composition and related phenomena such as headship and living alone have often used simple ratios. Examples include: average household size or P/H, where P = total population, H = number of households; adult headship rate or H/A, where A = adult population (UN, 1973b); adults per household or A/H, the reciprocal of the adult headship rate (Burch, 1970; Parish and Schwartz, 1972; Kuznets, 1978); 'marital units per household', where marital units = the sum of married couples and widowed and divorced persons (Parish and Schwartz, 1972); households per married male or H/M_m (Dandekar and Unde, 1967).

With the exception of Parish and Schwartz, who related their ratios to measures based on more detailed census data, there has been little evaluation of these measures. It has been apparent for some time that average household size (or its inverse, H/P, the 'crude headship rate') is not generally a good measure of household composition insofar as it reflects the relative number of children (who are not at risk of household headship). Similarly, it is possible that ratios of adults per household or married persons per household might also be unduly influenced by compositional changes or differences.

An advantage of such ratios, apart from their conceptual attractiveness, is that they can be computed easily from data readily at hand. The amount of data retrieval and entry is trivial, for example, compared to that required for the computation of I_H and I'_H. At issue is whether the simpler measures can do an adequate job of measurement, at least in broad-ranging exploratory studies.

The present section examines some of these simple ratios in the context of a decomposition of H/P, the crude headship rate. First the decomposition is presented; then, illustrative data are presented to examine the empirical relations of various simple ratios among one another and with I_H and I'_H. The exercise is also of interest in exploring the components of variation in average household size.

3.1 Decomposing The Crude Headship Rate (H/P)

Let:

H = number of households
A = number of adults, say, persons over 15 years old
M = number of currently married persons
A_m = number of adult males
P = total population

Then
$$H/P = (H/M)(M/A_m)(A_m/A)(A/P) \tag{2.8}$$

that is, the crude headship rate can be expressed as the product of (1) a measure of the prevalence of headship among married persons; (2) the prevalence of marriage; (3) sex composition of the adult population; (4) age composition of the total population.

It should be noted that H/M is not an exposure type measure or a true proportion, since non-married persons can and do head households, and thus contribute to H. The notion of relating the number of households to the number of married persons derives from conceptualizations of family/household extension in terms of the number of married or ever-married persons per household, however, and from this perspective H/M makes sense as a descriptive measure.

Many variations on these expressions are possible. For example, following Parish and Schwartz (1972), the number of 'marital units' (*U*) or more simply, the total number of ever-married persons can be substituted for *M*. Also, M_m can be substituted for *M*, that is, the number of married males rather than the total of married males and married females (Dandekar and Unde, 1967). H/M_m is then a ratio of households to married males, and M_m/A_m is simply the proportion of adult males who are married. The resulting expression

$$H/P = (H/M_m)\,(M_m/A_m)\,(A_m/A)\,(A/P) \qquad (2.9)$$

is perhaps the simplest and most straightforward of the various possibilities presented above. This is so partly because M_m/A_m is a true proportion of males married, and partly because H/M_m relates to the traditional notion that married males, as opposed to unmarried persons or females, tend to head households. In areas of the traditional patriarchal extended family (e.g., India), one would expect H/M_m to be less than one; in areas where single persons, including young adults, tend to form households (e.g., Northern and Western Europe and North America), or where many women head households (e.g., the Caribbean), one would expect a ratio greater than one. A disadvantage is that this treatment tends to ignore women and to perpetuate traditional and partly fictional notions of headship.

The first term of equations 2.8 and 2.9 can be further decomposed into a ratio of actual to expected households (*H/EH*) and a ratio of expected households to married persons or married males (*EH/M* or EH/M_m). If expected households are defined as in the formula for I'_H (see equation 2a), then *H/P* can be expressed as a product of I'_H and terms representing an 'expected headship rate' ($\hat{H}'/M_m$), nuptiality, and sex and age composition.

3.2 Illustrative Results

Table 2.3 gives several of these simple ratios for selected nations from our international series, repeating the I_H and I'_H values from Table 2.1 above.

We note that the 'crude headship rate' (*H/P*) is highest (approximately 0.3 or greater) in developed countries. This result is partly a function of age composition as reflected by *A/P*, but also reflects generally higher headship as indicated by a variety of ratios (or their inverses): H/M_m, the inverse of *U/H*, I_H, and I'_H.

The variation in the adult sex ratio, captured by A_m/A, is relatively small, and has little effect on variation in *H/P*. Variation in marital status, on the other hand, clearly is important: compare Niger or Indonesia with Ireland or Dominican Republic.

Although the consistency among various measures of headship/complexity is far from perfect (see Section 3.2.1) it is of interest to note that by any measure India, Turkey, and Albania rank lowest in headship (highest in

Table 2.3 Decomposition of H/P, selected nations

Region and Nation	Ratios									
	H/P	H/M_m	MM/A_m	A_m/A	A/P	A/H	P/H	U/H	I_H	I'_H
Africa:										
Morocco (1971)	.18	1.09	.65	.49	.53	2.9	5.5	1.2	.97	.84
Niger (1960)	.24	1.16	.77	.47	.58	2.4	4.1	1.1	1.21	.99
Asia:										
India (1971	.18	.83	.71	.52	.58	3.3	5.6	1.5	.81	.67
Indonesia (1961)	.22	1.10	.80	.46	.55	2.5	4.6	1.2	1.06	.86
Japan (1975)	.28	1.13	.67	.49	.76	2.7	3.6	1.1	.92	.88
Turkey (1965)	.18	.86	.70	.50	.58	3.3	5.6	1.4	.84	.72
Hong Kong	.22	1.21	.56	.51	.64	3.0	4.6	1.0	.90	.95
Europe:										
Sweden (1970)	.38	1.58	.61	.50	.79	2.1	2.6	0.9	1.09	1.09
West Germany (1970)	.36	1.44	.70	.46	.77	2.1	2.8	1.0	1.11	1.02
Ireland (1971)	.24	1.41	.50	.50	.69	2.8	4.1	0.9	.85	.87
Spain (1970)	.26	1.18	.63	.48	.72	2.8	3.8	1.1	.88	.86
Albania (1960)	.18	.98	.61	.51	.60	3.3	5.5	1.4	.83	.74
Latin America:										
Dominican Republic (1970)	.19	1.51	.48	.50	.52	2.8	5.3	0.8	1.07	1.08
Mexico (1970)	.20	1.27	.61	.49	.54	2.6	4.9	1.0	1.13	1.00
Argentina (1970)	.26	1.27	.60	.49	.70	2.7	3.9	1.0	.92	.85
North America:										
U.S. (1970)	.31	1.38	.66	.48	.71	2.3	3.2	1.0	1.10	1.00
Canada (1971)	.28	1.24	.65	.50	.70	2.5	3.6	1.0	1.01	.97
Oceania:										
Australia	.29	1.26	.65	.50	.71	2.5	3.5	1.1	1.00	.94

Definitions:

H/P: ratio of households to total population
H/M_m: ratio of households to married males
M_m/A_m: proportion of adult males currently married
A_m/A: proportion of adults who are males
A/P: population of total population who are adults i.e., over 15
A/H: number of adults per household
P/H: average household size
U/H: number of marital units per household
I_H: index of overall headship
I'_H: index of overall headship standardized for marital status

complexity); Sweden, West Germany, Dominican Republic, and Niger are generally high.

3.2.1 Simple Ratios as Proxies for I_H and I'_H As noted above, it would be convenient were one of the simple ratios able to measure headship propensities (net of compositional factors such as age, sex and marital status) as well as I_H or I'_H. In stating the issue in these terms, we are implicitly assuming that the latter indices are superior, insofar as they control for composition.

Table 2.4 presents correlation matrices for a variety of simple ratios and the two indirectly standardized indices for our international series, and for the US states in 1900 and 1970. In addition to the full international series, we also have run correlations excluding observations for Africa and Latin America. As noted above, the headship indices for Africa may be unduly high; for Latin America (and perhaps for Africa also) marital status data are suspect (the number of persons married is apt to be under-reported). Inclusion of indices involving marital status data for these regions may be introducing large measurement errors.

This analysis is a reminder that relationships among different measures which are thought of as tapping the same underlying dimension (and thus as potential proxies for one another) can be situation-specific. In the present case, there are appreciable differences in relationships as one moves from contemporary international data to sub-national data for the US in 1900 to the US in 1970. The differences could be even greater were one to study series relating to minor civil divisions, cities, and so forth. The measure of choice in a particular empirical analysis clearly is a matter for judgement.

Nonetheless, of the four 'quick ratios' that might serve as proxies for I'_H or I_H (H/A, H/U, H/M, H/M_m), H/A generally seems to work the best. With respect to I_H, it is most highly correlated in each of the four sets of data. In the two US series, it also is most highly correlated with I'_H; in the international series, especially that excluding Latin America and Africa, it comes close to the highest correlation. As a proxy for I_H, H/M appears to be a second choice; for I'_H, perhaps H/U.

The above result with respect to H/A is somewhat counter-intuitive, since, as noted above, there are conceptual grounds for relating households to married persons or ever-married persons or to married males. There is also a sense in which a ratio such as H/M_m may seem to be more refined than H/A. The resolution of the problem is related to the observation made earlier that H/M_m, H/U and H/M are not true exposure-type rates — persons exposed to headship are excluded from the denominator. Whatever other deficiencies it may have in terms of failure to take account of marital status or the age distribution of adults, H/A at least relates headship to the population at risk of that status, namely, all adults.

Figure 2.1 provides some additional data on this issue. Of five measures for Canada for the period 1871–1981, most of them capture the major

Table 2.4 Correlation matrices of simple ratios, I_H and I'_H: international series and US States, 1900 and 1970

A. International series (total):

	I'_H	I_H	H/P	H/A	H/U	H/M
I'_H						
I_H	.84					
H/P	.61	.44				
H/A	.78	.74	.89			
H/U	.79	.48	.39	.44		
H/M	.84	.58	.73	.74	.79	
H/M_m	.89	.64	.66	.71	.85	.97

B. International series (excluding Latin America and Africa)

	I'_H	I_H	H/P	H/A	H/U	H/M
I'_H						
I_H	.87					
H/P	.86	.76				
H/A	.91	.89	.95			
H/U	.92	.66	.78	.78		
H/M	.93	.78	.89	.89	.93	
H/M_m	.92	.75	.87	.87	.94	.99

C. US States, 1970:

	I'_H	I_H	H/P	H/A	H/U	H/M
I'_H						
I_H	.76					
H/P	.58	.37				
H/A	.80	.58	.90			
H/U	.76	.46	.42	.48		
H/M	.70	.56	.63	.62	.88	
H/M_m	.68	.55	.63	.61	.87	.99

D. US States, 1900:

	I'_H	I_H	H/P	H/A	H/U	H/M
I'_H						
I_H	.65					
H/P	-.16	-.46				
H/A	.86	.58	.26			
H/U	.73	.02	.18	.62		
H/M	.42	-.05	.46	.55	.79	
H/M_m	.52	.16	.36	.64	.75	.97

features of trends in household headship, viz., virtual stability or only slight decline from the turn of the century to World War II, with sharp rises thereafter. The exception is H/P, which rises more or less continuously (due to long-term fertility decline), although it too shows an upturn in the last two decades or so.

A practical implication of these results is that for broad comparative and historical studies (especially those of an exploratory nature), simple ratios

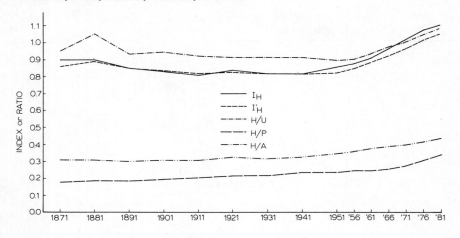

Figure 2.1 Headship indices and simple ratios, Canada, 1871–1981

Data for Figure 2.1

	I_H	I'_H	H/U	H/P	H/A
1981	1.12	1.06	1.09	.34	.44
1976	1.08	1.02	1.05	.31	.42
1971	1.02	.97	1.01	.28	.40
1966	.97	.93	.98	.26	.39
1961	.92	.89	.94	.25	.38
1956	.88	.85	.91	.25	.36
1951	.86	.83	.90	.24	.35
1941	.82	.82	.92	.24	.33
1931	.82	.82	.92	.22	.32
1921	.84	.83	.92	.22	.33
1911	.81	.82	.93	.21	.31
1901	.83	.84	.95	.20	.30
1891	.85	.85	.94	.19	.30
1881	.90	.89	1.05	.19	.31
1871	.90	.86	.95	.18	.31

such as households per adults (H/A) may be used with the expectation that they will capture strong patterns of difference or change in propensities to headship. For more definitive or refined studies, the extra effort of indirect standardization involved in I_H and I'_H would seem to be justified.

3.2.2 *Components of Variation in H/P* The decomposition formulas in Section 3.1 lead naturally to an investigation of the relative importance of various components of H/P to its overall variation, following methods set forth in Duncan (1966). Based on our assumption that I'_H is the best measure of headship net of age, sex, and marital status, we have concentrated on the following decomposition:

$$H/P = (I'_H) (\hat{H}'/M_m) (M_m/A_m) (A_m/A) (A/P),$$

where $I'_H = \dfrac{H}{\hat{H}'}$ and $\hat{H}'$ refers to expected households.

Since $\hat{H}'/M_m$ does not have any very direct interpretation, however, and since there are statistical advantages in working with a non-identity (notably, tests of significance and R^2 make sense), we prefer the model that drops $\hat{H}'/M_m$. Path diagrams for this model (using the log of all variables) were constructed for the international series (including and excluding Latin America and Africa) and for the US cross-sections in 1900 and 1970. The factor A/P, measuring gross age composition, bears the strongest relation to H/P, followed by I'_H, measuring propensity to head households. M_m/A_m, our measure of proportions married runs a poor third; A_m/A, a measure of the sex composition of adult population, is relatively unimportant in all contexts. Figure 2.2, giving the results for the international series (exclusive of Africa and Latin America), is representative of all four path diagrams.

4 Concluding Comments

1. I_H and I'_H have a useful role to play in studying variation in the propensity of adults to form separate households, among nations, within nations by sub-areas, and over time. Their chief merit lies in their wide applicability to almost any modern population census. But they also indirectly standardize for age, sex, and marital status composition, and such standardization is often necessary. Results are reasonably insensitive to the choice of standard rates.

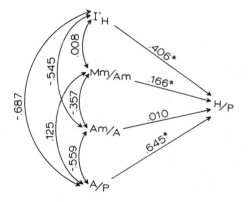

Figure 2.2 Path analysis: components of variation in H/P for international series (excluding Latin America and Africa)**
$N = 49$; $R^2 = .983$

* Significant at .01 level
** Estimated model is:
$\log(H/P) = \log(I'_H) + \log(M_m/A_m) + \log(A_M/A) + \log(A/P)$

The major weakness of I_H and I'_H is their global character, in particular their inability to distinguish situations where headship is generally high from those where female headship is particularly high. Where household heads are classified by sex, this problem is easily overcome by decomposition.

2. Simple indices such as the ratio of adults to households seem to work surprisingly well in a variety of circumstances as proxies for I_H or I'_H. For reasons of economy, they might be used in exploratory studies, especially studies of regional variation within nations over time; with strong patterns or trends identified, more detailed work can proceed using the more refined indices.

3. The reason why simple indices work reasonably well is that most of the variation in average household size is due to variation in the proportion of adults in the population (age composition) and in adult headship. With gross variation in age composition controlled (as with the ratio of adults to households), much of the remaining variation is due to adult household formation behaviour, and is captured by simple ratios relating to adults.

4. In the nature of the case, the measurement system discussed here helps paint only a broad picture of variation in some aspects of household structure. There is no substitute for more detailed analyses based on micro-data — whether contemporary censuses or surveys, past census manuscripts, or integrated sets of data for specific localities. For the complete picture, both macro and micro perspectives are essential.

References

Burch, T. K. (1967), 'The Size and Structure of Families: A Comparative Analysis of Census Data', *American Sociological Review* 32, 347–63.

—— (1970), 'Some Demographic Determinants of Average Household Size: An Analytical Approach', *Demography* 7, 61–9.

—— (1980), 'The Index of Overall Headship: A Simple Measure of Household Complexity Standardized for Age and Sex', *Demography* 17, 25–37.

Caldwell, J. C. (1976), 'Toward A Restatement of Demographic Transition Theory', *Population and Development Review* 2, 321–66.

Coale, A. J. (1969), 'The Decline of Fertility in Europe from the French Revolution to World War II', in S. J. Behrman, Leslie Corsa, Jr., and Ronald Freedman (eds.), *Fertility and Family Planning: A World View*. The University of Michigan Press, Ann Arbor.

Dandekar, K., and D. B. Unde. (1967), 'Inter-state and Intra-state Differentials in Household Formation Rates', in A. Bose (ed.), *Patterns of Population Change in India, 1951–61*. Allied Publishers, Bombay.

Duncan, O. D. (1966), 'Path Analysis: Sociological Examples', *American Journal of Sociology* 72, 1–16.

Kuznets, S. (1978), 'Size and Age Structure of Family Households: Exploratory Comparisons', *Population and Development Review* 4, 187–223.

Parish, W. L., Jr., and M. Schwartz (1972), 'Household Complexity in Nineteenth Century France', *American Sociological Review* 37, 154–73.

Taeuber, I. B. (1971), Change and Transition in Family Structures, In *The Family in Transition* (Fogarty International Center Proceedings No. 3), pp. 35–97, Government Printing Office, Washington.

United Nations (1973a), *The Determinants and Consequences of Population Trends*, United Nations, New York.

—— (1973b), *Manuals on Methods of Estimating Population. Manual VII: Methods of Projecting Households and Families*. United Nations, New York.

—— (1981), *Estimates and Projections of the Number of Households by Country, 1975–2000*. ESA/P/WP.73. Population Division, United Nations, New York.

3 Estimation of Certain Measures in Family Demography Based upon Generalized Stable Population Relations*

SAMUEL H. PRESTON
Population Studies Center, University of Pennsylvania, U S A

A good deal of family demography is concerned with studying the distribution of time spent in various states. The unit of analysis is either an individual or a relationship. Common questions asked at the individual level concern how long an individual spends in various marital categories, usually from a starting point of birth, age 15, or of entrance into a particular category. The individual is viewed as being subject to the risks of leaving a particular state. The risks under study may include all of those encountered in reality, or only a subset of those risks. The individual may also be permitted to reenter certain states (e.g., currently married), depending on the analytic question being asked. Many related processes can also be studied through the same schema, such as the process of leaving home, having a first birth, having the last child leave home, and so on.

The same approach is also used to study a particular relationship. These relationships include those established biologically (e.g., mother and child), those established socially (e.g., husband and wife), or some combination of the two (e.g., a nuclear family). Again, those relations can be viewed as being subject to all or only some of the risks that a relationship actually encounters. Unlike the analysis of individuals, the analysis of relationships does not (normally) permit reentry. Biological relations, once terminated by death (their only risk of dissolution), obviously cannot be reentered. Social relations can often be reentered, but the frequency of reentry is normally so low that analysis is not fruitful.

The amount of time spent in a state is typically registed in years of duration; when the state is only entered at birth, age is a perfect proxy for duration and is often used as a substitute. When studying relationships, duration is always the indexing variable, since the partners to a relationship normally have different ages.[1]

* I would like to thank Michael Strong for discussion and programming related to this paper and James Weed for supplying unpublished data without which several key tables could not have been produced. The work was supported by a grant from the Ford Foundation.
[1] Some processes can be studied with equal facility from the point of view of a relationship or of an individual. For example, the survivorship of a mother–child relationship can also be studied by

A final distinction is useful. The family related processes examined can pertain to actual cohorts of persons or of relationships or to synthetic cohorts. This distinction is well known throughout demography. If the problem is to track the behavior of an actual cohort, the solution is normally simply to count events occurring to that cohort. Conceptual problems are not difficult, but data availability often places rigid constraints on what can be accomplished. In the case of synthetic cohorts, the common question asked is what *would* happen to a cohort if it were subjected for all of its lifetime to the transition risks that were recorded during a particular time period. To this hypothetical question, solutions require more than simply counting. Assumptions must usually be made about how observed occurrence/exposure rates in a period relate to underlying probabilities for a cohort. These assumptions are not normally problematic and results are not particularly sensitive to choices made among reasonable alternatives.

Data constraints encountered in constructing period measures for recent years are usually less serious than in the case of real cohorts, since data systems normally improve. Some of the requisite data are derived from censuses and vital statistics, and others can be gleaned from increasingly abundant longitudinal surveys. But for many, if not most, desired calculations, the data are still deficient in type or detail. Data on flows into and out of various states are particularly problematic. In this paper we show how newly established theorems permit the calculation of certain desired measures even when flow data are missing. We will deal only with period measures pertaining to synthetic cohorts.

The different types of processes examined in family demography correspond to conventional distinctions in demographic and actuarial literature between single decrement, multiple decrement, associated single decrement, and increment-decrement processes. We will consider each of these cases in turn, utilizing the new theorems to provide a mathematical representation of the process in a population and a formula that can be used for estimation. The type of data required for implementing the estimation formula is discussed. Examples are presented in several instances.

Mathematical Background

Let us begin with a brief review of the mathematics of the processes. We will deal first with the simplest process, the single decrement or conventional life table process. Suppose we begin with a cohort that numbers $N(0)$ persons at birth. Now suppose that this cohort is subjected to a single force of decre-

---

asking how long the child will live as a non-orphan or how long the mother will remain alive with a surviving child. In all these cases, remaining in a state is subject to the dual risks of death of mother and death of child, and there is no reason why answers would differ. In other instances, however, the distinction is useful. For example, the expected length of time spent alive after first marrying (an individual-level concept) is quite different from the expected duration of first marriage (a relationship).

ment function of intensity $\mu(x)$ at age x. Designate the number of survivors in the cohort at age x as $N(x)$. Our definition of $\mu(x)$ is that

$$\mu(x) = \frac{\dfrac{-d\,N(x)}{N(x)}}{dx} = \frac{-d\,\ln N(x)}{dx} \tag{3.1}$$

Thus, $\mu(x)$ is the proportionate change in $N(x)$ per unit change in x as changes in x get smaller and smaller. x is usually measured in years. Integrating both sides of equation (3.1) from age 0 to some specific age a and taking antilogs gives

$$N(a) = N(0)e^{-\int_0^a \mu(x)\,dx} \tag{3.2}$$

This formula and its derivation are well known (see, for example, Keyfitz, 1977). The definition of $N(a)$ — survivors of the single decrement process — of course depends upon the particular application. In the conventional life-table (where $N(a)$ is usually designated 1_a), $N(a)$ is simply the number of persons at age a who have survived the risk of death from all causes combined at all prior ages. In other analyses it may be the number of persons who remain alive in the single state at age a. While the latter appears to be a multiple decrement process because single persons are exposed to the risks of both death and marriage, the point is that both risks can be treated as though they are combined into one force of mortality function in the conventional life table. It is almost always possible to break a particular decrement into components (deaths by cause, marriages by type, divorces by grounds, etc.); treating something as a single decrement process is usually a matter of analytic convenience. If explicit recognition is to be given to different types of decrement, it is customary to treat the different decrements as additive, so that

$$\mu(x) = \mu^1(x) + \mu^2(x) + \ldots \mu^n(x) \tag{3.3}$$

where $\mu^i(x)$ is the force of decrement from decrement i at age x and n is the total number of decrements recognized. The additivity of the decrements is sometimes thought to be an assumption that is subject to empirical verification. However, it is simply an accounting identity: each decrement comes with a label (e.g. death, marriage) and the set of labels is mutually exclusive and exhaustive. The rate of change of a cohort with age is simply the sum of changes from these mutually exclusive and exhaustive various sources of decrement that we have labelled.

Substituting (3.3) into (3.2), we have

$$N(a) = N(0)e^{-\int_0^a [\mu^1(x) + \mu^2(x) + \ldots \mu^n(x)]dx} \tag{3.4}$$

A population at any point in time is composed of many cohorts.[2] Let us

---

[2] The following three paragraphs are a summary of parts of Preston and Coale (1982).

designate the number of persons aged x at time t as $N(x, t)$. Each cohort aged x at time t is subject to a force of decrement function from all causes combined, $\mu(x, t)$. This function is, as before, the (negative of the) proportionate change in the size of the cohort per unit of age (and time) as the units get smaller and smaller:

$$-\mu(x,t) = \lim_{dx \to 0} \frac{\ln N(x + dx, t + dt) - \ln N(x,t)}{dx}$$

But this definition of $-\mu(x,t)$ is simply the total differential of the $\ln N(x,t)$ function. By a standard theorem in multivariate calculus, this differential is the sum of the two partial derivatives (assuming their existence and continuity):

$$-\mu(x,t) = \frac{\partial \ln N(x,t)}{\partial t} + \frac{\partial \ln N(x,t)}{\partial x}$$

The first term on the right hand side is simply $r(x,t)$, the growth rate of the population aged a at time t. Making this substitution and rearranging we have

$$\frac{\partial \ln N(x,t)}{\partial x} = -\mu(x,t) - r(x,t)$$

Integrating both sides between specific ages 0 and a and taking exponentials gives

$$N(a,t) = N(0,t)e^{-\int_0^a [\mu(x,t) + r(x,t)]dx} \tag{3.5}$$

Equation (3.5) is identical in form to equation (3.4), which described relations among the numbers of persons reaching two ages in a *cohort* subject to multiple decrements. Equation (3.5), however, pertains to a *population* at a moment in time; one of the 'decrements' in this case is $r(x,t)$, the contemporaneous age-specific growth rate function. What the equation says very simply is that $r(x,t)$ affects a population's age structure in exactly the same way that a certain decrement affects numbers at various ages in a cohort subject to multiple decrements.

The major concern of this paper is to find ways of drawing out the implications of various $\mu(x,t)$ functions (period decrement functions) for family-related processes. Equation (3.5) provides a very convenient analytic starting point for a wide variety of applications. These applications would be academic, however, if data did not exist to estimate the various functions. Fortunately, the data for utilizing this equation are considerably more abundant than other forms of data for studying the processes.

Single Decrement Processes

When all forms of decrement are to be combined into one, equation (3.5) presents a very straightforward way of constructing a single decrement table. Isolating the term in $\mu(x,t)$, we have

$$e^{-\int_0^a \mu(x,t)da} = \frac{N(a,t)}{N(0,t)} \; e_0^{\int_0^a r(x,t)dt} \tag{3.6}$$

The term on the left hand side is simply $p(a,t)$, the probability of survival to age a under the period risk function, $\mu(x,t)$. From this function, all other functions of interest in the period decrement table can be derived. This $p(a,t)$ function can be empirically evaluated in one of two ways. One is through occurrence–exposure rates for the decrement itself at time t, which requires knowing the number of event occurences by age (or duration) and the distribution of population at risk by age (or duration). The other is from two cross-sectional observations of the distribution of population at risk by age (or duration), which will supply estimates of $N(a,t)$ and of $r(x,t)$ for the period between the observations. In this sense, a second cross-sectional observation on the age distribution of the population is a substitute for the flow data. If both flow data and a second observation of the age distribution are available, then the system is over-determined. The identity in (3.6) can then be used to check the consistency of data and to iron out irregularities.

The substitutability between a second cross-section and flow data is perhaps the key insight pertinent to estimation that is provided by the new equations. This insight is surely not totally fresh. For more than a half century, actuaries and demographers have been comparing successive censuses to try to infer the amount of mortality during the intercensal period. Equation (3.6) just makes the basis for such operations more explicit and, by its simplicity, provides insights into many other kinds of processes that can be similarly approached.

In one sense the message of equation (3.6) is profoundly simple: the age (or duration) distribution of a population would be identical to that of a stationary population produced by the current decrement function if no growth were occurring (i.e., if $r(x,t)$'s were zero at all ages). It is population growth that distorts the current age distribution relative to what it would be under current decrement rates; all that is necessary to reveal that underlying distribution is to adjust the current age distribution for the observed growth.

Equation (3.6) pertains at a particular point in time, t, and age, a. But observations always occur over discrete time and age intervals. This rude fact is no less pertinent to occurrence–exposure rates than to rates derived from successive cross-sections, and the solutions are in principle no different. There seem to be two reasonable and generally satisfactory solutions in the present case. Derivation of solutions are available from the author on request. Both result in equations of the form (when data are in 5-year intervals)

$$_5L_a \cong \frac{_5N_a\, e^{S(a+2.5)}}{N(0)}, \text{ where}$$

$_5L_a$ = person-years lived between ages a and a + 5 according to the decrement function pertaining during the period of observation, with radix of one;

$S(a)$ = sum of observed age-specific growth rates up to age a;

$_5N_a$ = number of persons or person-years lived in the age interval a to a + 5;

$N(0)$ = number of entrances into the defined state during the period of observation.

In the case utilized here, $_5N_a$ is estimated as the geometric mean of persons alive in the age interval a to a + 5 at the first and second observations; $N(0)$ is estimated as the mean annual number of entrances between observations.

Table 3.1 presents a table of marriage survivorship for first marriages according to attrition rates for such marriages in the United States between 1975 and 1980. The attrition rates are implicit, being inferred from cross-sections of intact first marriages by duration for the US at the beginning and end of the period. The radix of the table is the mean annual number of first marriages between June 1975 and June 1980, the survey dates. This figure is necessary only for l_0 and e_0; survivors to and life expectancy at ages starting with one can be estimated directly from the two cross-sections.[3] The table shows a very reasonable survivorship (l_x) curve, although in two instances it rises from one duration to the next (but by less than 0.5 per cent). A provocative feature of the table is that the life expectancy of a marriage changes very little during the first twelve or so years of marriage.

It is clear, especially in the $_2L_x$ function, that results are affected to some extent by digit preference (there are too many marriages at a 5 and 10 years duration and too few at 13; there are also too few at duration zero, probably reflecting a tendency to round duration upwards to one year for infant marriages). These problems are not as serious for conventional approaches, where problems of age and duration misreporting are at least partially offsetting because they affect both numerator and denominator of decrement rates. Nevertheless, misreporting should not have a large effect on the main product of the indirect exercises, the life expectancy column, since persons who misreport duration presumably show up in most instances at a reported duration close to their real one. To construct a first marriage table by duration normally requires the distribution of first marriages by duration, divorces by duration of first marriages, and death rates by duration of first marriage. The latter are probably not available directly in any country and

---

[3] The l_x estimator is $\frac{1}{2}(_1L_x + _1L_{x-1})$ when adjacent duration groups are 1 year wide; $1/10$ $(_5L_x + _5L_{x-5})$ when they are 5 years wide; and $1/20\,(_{10}L_x + _{10}L_{x+10})$ when they are 10 years wide. These formulas assume linearity of the l_x function in the interval. In this application we are clearly assuming that net migration rates of marriages by age are zero.

Table 3.1   Life Table for first marriages in the United States corresponding to decrement rates (from divorce and death of partners) in 1975–80, estimated from cross-sectional surveys of intact first marriages by duration in 1975 and 1980.

Duration of Marriage a to $a+z$	Number of Females Married Once, by Duration, in[a] 1975 (1)	1980 (2)	$\bar{N}_a$ (3) $= [(1) \times (2)]^{\frac{1}{2}}$	$_z\bar{r}_a = \dfrac{\ln\left[\frac{(2)}{(1)}\right]}{5}$ (4)	Cumulation of growth rates to midpoint of interval $S\left(a+\frac{z}{2}\right)$ (5)	Person-years lived by marriages in interval (6) $=(3)\times {}^z L_a \times \exp[(5)]$	Number of marriages surviving to a l_a (7)	Person-years lived in marriage above duration T_a (8)	Life expectancy of a marriage surviving to a e^o_a (9)
0	1428	1395	1411	−.00468	−.00234	1408	1534[b]	43219	28.17
1	1448	1432	1440	−.00222	−.00579	1431	1420	41811	29.44
2	1457	1411	1434	−.00642	−.01011	1420	1425	40380	28.34
3	1436	1246	1338	−.02838	−.02751	1302	1361	38960	28.63
4	1315	1288	1301	−.00415	−.04378	1245	1274	37658	29.56
5	1462	1242	1348	−.03262	−.06216	1267	1256	36413	28.99
6	1383	1180	1277	−.03175	−.09435	1162	1214	35146	28.95
7	1258	1317	1287	.00917	−.10564	1158	1160	33984	29.30
8	1104	1217	1159	.01949	−.09131	1058	1108	32826	29.63
9	1020	1161	1088	.02590	−.06861	1016	1037	31768	30.63
10	1039	1143	1090	.01908	−.04612	1041	1029	30752	29.89
11	975	1118	1044	.02737	−.02289	1020	1030	28711	28.84
12	943	1071	1005	.02546	.00352	1009	1015	28691	28.27
13	943	908	925	−.00756	.01247	937	973	27682	28.45
14	954	1022	987	.01377	.01558	1002	969	26745	27.60
15	4477	4477	4477	0	.02246	4579	959	25743	26.84
20	4424	4200	4311	−.01039	−.00352	4296	888	21164	23.83
25	4712	3984	4333	−.03357	−.11342	3868	816	16868	20.67
30	6475	7553	6993	.03080	−.04334	6696	743	13000	17.50
40	3277	3621	3448	.01996	.21046	4256	548	6304	11.50
50	1351	1343	1347	−.00119	.30431	1826	304	2048	6.74
60	170	167	168	−.00356	.28056	222	102	222	2.18

[a] Source: Unpublished tabulations supplied by James Weed of the U.S. Bureau of Census based on Current Population Survey. The 1980 survey data covered ages only up to 74. Intact first marriages of women 75+ were estimated by adopting the same number and duration distribution as for women 75+ in 1975. These were only 1.9 per cent of all intact first marriages in 1975.

[b] Derived from official vital statistics published by the National Center for Health Statistics for the inter-survey period from June 1975 to June 1980. Total female marriages are assumed to be distributed by marriage order in the same proportions as in those reporting on marriage order. U.S. Bureau of Census, *Statistical Abstract of the United States 1982–83*; U.S. National Center for Health Statistics, *Monthly Vital Statistics Report* Vol. 32(5) Supplement. August 18, 1983.

would have to be estimated, which is quite a complicated process (and usually involves the assumption that death rates are independent of marital status). The most recent marriage tables constructed in this fashion for the US were done by the National Center for Health Statistics (1980). The first marriage decrement table in that source for the 1975 period is similar in configuration to that in Table 3.2, but life expectancy in the first 15 years of marriage is in the range of 25 to 27 years rather than 26 to 31 years as in Table 3.1. The difference is mainly attributable to survivorship at high durations; the difference in $p(10)$ is only between .670 in Table 3.2 and .673 in the NCHS volume. It is possible that durations are grossly exaggerated in Table 3.1, but we find it equally likely that the 'official' tables have overestimated the mortality of married persons by assigning to them the mortality of all persons, thus spuriously shortening the life expectancy of a marriage. It is unlikely that differences in time periods covered could account for the difference in results since marital dissolution rates were not declining during 1975–80.

The same exercise was repeated for females in second and higher order marriages (not shown). The contrast in marital survivorship is quite distinct, with the life expectancy of a second marriage being only about 50–60 per cent of that of a first marriage at almost all durations. Agreement with an 'official' life table for 1975 marriages (NCHS, 1980) is very close, so that whatever cause has produced the 2-year or so discrepancy in life expectancy for first marriages does not seem to be operative for higher-order marriages. There is little concrete information on the survivorship of second marriage; this information from two cross-sections of higher-order marriages by duration can be a valuable supplement to existing data sources.

Associated Single Decrement Processes

A common type of question in family demography is 'what would happen if only a certain subset decrement were operating on the population at risk?' Perhaps the most frequent question of this sort is 'at what ages would single people marry if they were not exposed to mortality?' The answer to this question sometimes takes the form of a gross nuptiality table, a device which dates back at least to Kuczynski (1935). In 1953, Hajnal demonstrated how such a table could be constructed from a single cross-sectional observation on proportions married by age, provided that one were willing to assume that rates of death and net migration by age had been the same for the single population as for the ever-married, and that rates of marriage for the population had been constant. If marriage rates had not been constant, then the table constructed from the cross-section would be an amorphous amalgam of rates in an ill-defined past, with the proportion married at older ages a product of earlier nuptiality regimes than the proportion at younger ages.

With two cross-sectional observations and the new equations, one can eliminate the time indeterminacy and construct a table that refers explicitly to the period between observations. In order to be as thorough as possible in demonstrating this, let us insert a migration term in the appropriate place in equation (3.5):

$$N(a,t) = N(0,t)e^{-\int_0^a r(x,t)dx}\, e^{-\int_0^a h(x,t)dx}\, p(a,t) \tag{3.7}$$

where $h(x,t)$ is the rate of net out-migration at age x, time t.

An equivalent expression exists for the single population at time t. It is only necessary to recognize that this population is subject to an additional force of decrement, embodied in the rate of first marriage for the single population aged a at time t, $n(a,t)$. Denoting other variables pertaining to the single population with subscript s,

$$S(a,t) = N(0,t)e^{-\int_0^a r_s(x,t)dx}\, e^{-\int_0^a h_s(x,t)dx}\, p_s(a,t)e^{-\int_0^a n(x,t)dx} \tag{3.8}$$

Let us now assume that

$p(a,t) = p_s(a,t)$ for all a; and
$h(x,t) = h_s(x,t)$ for all x.

These are Hajnal's assumptions of no differential mortality or migration by marital status. Unlike Hajnal's case, however, they do not require that there have been no differential mortality or migration by marital status over the preceding 35 years, only that there be no current differentials at time t. With these assumptions, the proportions single at age a will be

$$s(a,t) = \frac{S(a,t)}{N(a,t)} = e^{-\int_0^a [r(x,t) - r_s(x,t)]dx}\, e^{-\int_0^a n(x,t)dx} \tag{3.9}$$

Equation (3.9) expresses the proportion single at age a, time t in terms of current age-specific nuptiality conditions, $n(x,t)$, and the difference between age-specific growth rates of the total population and the single population.

The object of period gross marriage tables is to express the proportions surviving in the single state exclusively in terms of the force of nuptiality function currently prevailing, $n(x,t)$. For a cohort all of whose members are single at age 15, the proportion remaining single at age a according to the period nuptiality function is

$$\Pi(a,t) = e^{-\int_{15}^a n(x,t)dx}\quad a \geq 15.$$

But from (3.9) it is clear that

$$\Pi(a,t) = e^{-\int_{15}^a n(x,t)dx} = s(a,t)e^{-\int_{15}^a [r_s(x,t) - r(x,t)]dx} \tag{3.10}$$
$$= s(a,t)e^{-\int_{15}^a r_D(x,t)dx}$$

where $r_D(x,t)$ is the growth rate of the proportion single at age x, time t. Since equation (3.10) requires only proportions single, it permits estimation based on comparisons of a census and a survey.

Equation (3.10) pertains to an associated single decrement process in which nuptiality alone acts to decrement the single population. Other decrements have been eliminated from consideration by dealing with proportions in a state and by making the assumption that the forces of decrement from 'other' causes are the same for persons in the state of interest and for those in other states. Equation (3.10) thus provides a way of correcting the observed proportions single, $s(a,t)$, so that they represent what those proportions would be if they were determined exclusively by period nuptiality conditions. The correction factor simply involves the difference in age-specific growth rates between the single and the total population. If that difference is zero at all ages, then $\Pi(a,t) = s(a,t)$ and Hajnal's procedure would yield unbiased results.

In effect, the $r_s(x-t) - r(x,t)$ correction factor is adjusting for whatever changes have occurred in nuptiality. If there have been no changes, then the growth rate of the single population will necessarily equal the growth rate of the total population at a particular age. The growth rates will be identical because constant nuptiality over time will produce constant proportions single by age. Regardless of what these proportions are, the single and total populations must be growing by the same factor at a particular age. If, however, nuptiality has been declining then the growth rate of the single population will exceed that of the total population. In this case, the correction factor will be greater than unity: $s(a,t)$ will understate $\Pi(a,t)$. The reason is obviously that the current proportion single, $s(a,t)$, is a product of the higher nuptiality conditions that applied in the past, whereas $\Pi(a,t)$ expresses only current nuptiality conditions.

To demonstrate the use and usefulness of the adjustment procedure, we have performed a simulation based upon the following assumptions:

1. First marriage rates among the single population were constant for 35 years before the first census. These rates were

Age interval	Annual first-marriage rates per person
15–19	.08
20–24	.14
25–29	.10
30–34	.06
35–39	.04
40–44	.02
45–49	.02
50–54	.02

2. Each of these first-marriage rates declines continuously at a constant proportionate rate during the 10 years after the first census. The annual rate of decline is .05. For example, after 10 years the rate at age 15–19 is

.08 .exp $\{10(-.05)\}$ = .04852, and the rate at age 20–24 is .14.exp $\{10(-.05)\}$ = .08491. A second census is taken 10 years after the first. The mean rate of nuptiality during the 10-year period can be found by integrating each $n(a,t)$ rate over the 10-year period.

3. There is no differential mortality or migration by marital status.

Figure 3.1 shows the proportions single at the first and the second census that result from these assumptions. It also shows the proportion single in a gross nuptiality table based upon the mean intercensal rates of marriage. Obviously, the two censuses do not (in general) bound the proportion single based upon intercensal experience. Beyond age 26, the intercensal nuptiality table contains a higher proportion single than does either census. The reason is simply that proportions single beyond age 25 are functions not only of nuptiality during the intercensal period but also of the higher nuptiality conditions that preceded the first census. By age 50, 15.7 per cent of persons in the intercensal table are still single, versus 10.0 and 10.5 per cent in the two censuses. Clearly, neither census, nor any simple combination of the two, will provide a reliable indication of intercensal nuptiality conditions.

Table 3.2 presents the proportions single in 5-year age groups in the three situations. The population within each 5-year age interval is assumed to be evenly distributed by age. Also shown is the 'adjusted' proportion single, derived by multiplying the geometric mean of proportions single in the two censuses at ages a to $a+5$ by exp $\{5.\Sigma_{15}^{a-5} \, {}_5r_{Dx} + 2.5 \, {}_5r_{Da}\}$ where ${}_5r_{Dx}$ is the

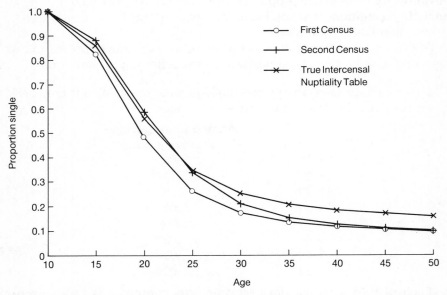

Figure 3.1 Proportions single by age in two censuses and in marriage table corresponding to average intercensal marriage rates

Table 3.2 Proportions single by age and certain other nuptiality indicators simulation of nuptiality declining from steady state

Age interval	First census	Second census	True intercensal nuptiality table	Average annual growth rate of proportion single	Exponential of sum of growth rates to midpoint of interval	Geometric mean of proportions single in two censuses	Estimated proportion single based on intercensal experience
	(1)	(2)	(3)	(4)	(5)	(6) = $\sqrt{(1)(2)}$	(7) = (6) × (5)
15–19	.8246	.8810	.8582	.00661	1.0167	.8523	.8666
20–24	.4828	.5881	.5618	.01973	1.0859	.5329	.5786
25–29	.2622	.3378	.3480	.02533	1.2154	.2976	.3617
30–34	.1745	.2109	.2529	.01895	1.3576	.1918	.2606
35–39	.1356	.1529	.2075	.01201	1.4669	.1440	.2115
40–44	.1165	.1254	.1842	.00736	1.5397	.1209	.1861
45–49	.1054	.1102	.1703	.00445	1.5858	.1078	.1709
50–54	.0954	.0996	.1574	.00431	1.6209	.0975	.1580
Proportion single at age 50	.1004	.1049	.1639				.1645
Person-years lived in single state per person before age 50							
50	25.51	27.03	27.91				28.18
SMAM	22.77	24.34	23.59				23.88

growth rate in the proportion single at ages x to $x+5$. This adjustment clearly works quite well. The maximum error in proportions single of .014 occurs at age 25–29, and 6 of the 8 estimates are in error by less than .01 from the proportion single in the true intercensal table. The proportion marrying by age 50 is in error by only .0006.

Expected person-years lived in the single state before age 50 is 27.91 in the true table and 28.18 in the estimated table. The error of +0.27 years contrasts with error of −2.40 years and −0.88 years in the first and second census, respectively. The adjusted SMAM is in error by +0.29 years, versus −0.82 and +0.75 years in the two censuses. Note that in this case the mean of the two censal SMAM's is very nearly correct; however, this result does not invariably apply. SMAM is more robust to changing nuptiality than are either person-years lived in the single state or proportions remaining single at age 50, because errors in these latter two measures will always be in the same direction. Since SMAM involves a ratio of the two, the errors will be partially offsetting.

In any event, the total volume of single years lived, and the proportion marrying by age 50, is much more accurately rendered by the adjustment procedure than by either census or by any simple combination of them. It should be noted that use of the arithmetic mean, rather than the geometric mean, as the basis for adjustment made very little difference, resulting in exactly the same proportion ever-marrying and a SMAM of 23.93 versus 23.88.

The availability of this new procedure for inferring nuptiality conditions, and the importance of nuptiality in developing countries, has led us to make an extensive application of the procedure. Table 3.3 applies the intercensal procedure to males and females in a wide variety of countries. Evidence of the biases from using a single cross-sectional observation is not hard to find. In the large majority of cases, the value of expected years of single life lived before age 50 based on intercensal experience lies outside of the range of values calculated directly from the cross-sections. For example, the rapid reduction in female marriage in Thailand between 1970 and 1975 yields the following values:

	Expected years lived single before age 50	Expected proportion single at age 50	SMAM
Based on 1970 Census cross-section	22.74	.028	21.96
Based on 1975 WFS cross-section	23.45	.036	22.46
Based on 1970–75 inter-observation conditions	24.52	0.81	22.29

The second observation underestimates years of single life by more than a year, and the expected proportion single at age 50 is less than half its

Table 3.3. Expected years lived in the single state by age 50, percent single at age 50, and singulate mean age at marriage in gross nuptiality tables computed from cross–sectional observations. Selected countries

Country	Year	Males Years single	% Single (age 50)	SMAM	Females Years single	% Single (age 50)	SMAM
Kenya	1969	26.87	6.15	25.35	20.09	2.90	19.20
	1979	26.75	5.05	25.51	20.92	2.18	20.28
	1969–79	26.74	4.46	25.66	21.23	3.58	20.16
Liberia	1962	27.79	6.40	26.27	18.58	1.96	17.96
	1974	28.20	6.80	26.61	20.13	2.79	19.27
	1962–74	28.30	7.09	26.64	20.63	6.96	18.44
Egypt	1960	26.71	2.05	26.22	20.63	1.24	20.26
	1976	27.79	3.96	26.87	22.83	4.18	21.65
	1960–76	27.69	5.04	26.50	23.00	11.71	19.41
Jordan	1961	25.64	3.50	24.75	21.21	2.79	20.39
	1976	26.38	0.87	26.18	21.97	1.57	21.53
	1961–76	26.29	0.61	26.14	21.90	1.58	21.45
Kuwait	1965	27.82	4.69	26.72	19.81	2.47	19.05
	1975	27.17	3.34	26.38	21.41	3.16	20.48
	1965–75	27.12	1.99	26.65	22.02	5.57	20.37
Libya	1954	27.43	3.53	26.61	19.59	1.32	19.18
	1973	24.94	1.35	24.60	18.88	0.49	18.73
	1954–73	25.31	0.56	25.18	19.01	0.25	18.93
Morocco	1960	24.79	2.56	24.12	18.09	1.66	17.55
	1971	25.71	2.94	24.98	19.89	2.48	19.12
	1960–71	25.85	4.31	24.76	20.20	6.93	17.98
Syria	1960	26.91	4.38	25.85	20.99	2.70	20.19
	1970	26.56	2.71	25.91	21.41	2.52	20.67
	1960–70	26.46	1.47	26.21	21.51	2.99	20.63
Tunisia	1966	27.80	3.44	27.01	21.32	1.54	20.87
	1975	27.80	2.89	27.14	22.99	1.54	22.57
	1966–75	27.83	2.01	27.37	23.42	3.09	22.57
Turkey	1965	23.89	2.10	23.34	20.01	1.47	19.56
	1975	24.13	1.84	23.64	20.92	1.61	20.45
	1965–75	24.17	1.92	23.66	21.19	3.79	20.06
Bangladesh	1974	24.27	1.05	23.99	16.52	0.33	16.41
	1976	24.19	0.69	24.01	16.81	0.25	16.73
	1974–76	24.16	0.06	24.14	17.52	0.00	17.52
India	1961	22.87	3.26	21.95	17.00	0.49	16.84
	1971	23.46	2.85	22.69	17.82	0.43	17.68
	1961–71	23.59	2.82	22.82	17.76	0.49	17.60
S. Korea	1966	26.73	0.13	26.70	22.85	0.09	22.83
	1974	27.09	0.35	27.01	23.23	0.44	23.11
	1966–74	27.10	0.84	26.90	23.26	2.03	22.71
Nepal	1971	21.56	1.52	21.12	17.70	0.74	17.46
	1976	21.12	1.10	20.80	17.41	0.76	17.16
	1971–76	20.91	0.12	20.88	17.27	0.09	17.24
Pakistan	1968	26.21	2.83	25.51	19.88	0.98	19.58
	1975	26.10	3.09	25.33	20.02	0.45	19.88
	1968–75	26.04	2.46	25.44	20.44	1.61	19.96

Table 3.3   *continued*

Country	Year	Males Years single	Males % Single (age 50)	Males SMAM	Females Years single	Females % Single (age 50)	Females SMAM
Philippines	1970	26.28	3.48	25.43	24.74	7.00	22.83
	1978	26.84	3.65	25.97	25.62	5.20	24.28
	1970–78	27.09	4.40	26.03	26.31	6.35	24.71
Singapore	1957	27.85	7.54	26.04	22.06	5.79	20.34
	1970	29.07	5.72	27.80	25.18	3.61	24.25
	1957–70	29.29	7.51	27.60	25.88	9.25	23.42
Sri Lanka	1971	29.77	7.75	28.07	24.63	4.30	23.50
	1975	29.79	5.45	28.62	25.54	2.05	25.03
	1971–75	29.96	3.15	29.31	27.41	2.35	26.87
Thailand	1970	25.49	3.16	24.69	22.74	2.78	21.96
	1975	25.30	2.12	24.76	23.45	3.61	22.46
	1970–75	25.17	1.13	24.89	24.52	8.05	22.29
Costa Rica	1963	28.36	11.84	25.45	26.06	16.59	21.30
	1973	27.97	10.63	25.35	26.06	15.34	21.73
	1963–73	27.87	8.92	25.70	26.18	14.11	22.27
Cuba	1953	30.46	18.56	26.01	25.45	12.20	22.04
	1970	27.38	15.01	23.38	22.65	10.38	19.48
	1953–70	27.14	9.25	24.81	22.41	5.23	20.89
Guatemala	1964	26.61	10.85	23.77	23.59	15.27	18.82
	1973	25.76	7.97	23.66	23.24	11.64	19.72
	1964–73	25.44	4.76	24.21	23.19	8.59	20.67
Mexico	1970	26.01	6.42	24.36	23.36	7.53	21.19
	1976	25.41	4.05	24.37	22.98	4.65	21.66
	1970–76	25.13	2.02	24.62	22.82	2.29	22.19
Panama	1970	27.72	11.61	24.79	22.56	7.19	20.43
	1976	27.24	6.86	25.57	22.52	3.30	21.59
	1970–76	27.00	3.17	26.25	22.69	0.94	22.43
Puerto Rico	1960	26.81	8.67	24.61	23.15	5.53	21.58
	1970	26.50	9.55	24.02	23.99	6.67	22.14
	1960–70	26.33	8.10	24.24	24.44	11.18	21.22
Argentina	1960	30.11	14.12	26.84	26.72	13.39	23.12
	1970	29.33	12.36	26.41	26.20	11.50	23.11
	1960–70	29.00	10.39	26.57	26.03	8.92	23.68
Chile	1952	30.12	13.49	27.02	27.90	16.01	23.69
	1970	28.34	10.85	25.70	26.87	12.95	23.42
	1952–70	28.34	8.00	26.45	26.82	10.86	23.99
Colombia	1964	29.74	13.76	26.51	26.78	19.23	21.25
	1973	29.03	11.50	26.30	26.71	15.35	22.49
	1963–73	28.73	8.79	26.68	26.94	14.04	23.17
Ecuador	1962	27.58	9.90	25.12	25.08	14.93	20.71
	1974	27.38	9.61	24.97	24.57	11.58	21.24
	1962–74	27.30	8.75	25.13	24.45	9.25	21.85
Guyana	1960	29.35	17.01	25.11	26.45	21.17	20.13
	1970	28.91	16.44	24.76	26.24	16.59	21.51
	1960–70	28.66	13.05	25.46	26.29	13.11	22.71

'correct' value based upon nuptiality conditions of 1970–75. The situation is analogous to water running into a pool. If the water entering the pool is hotter than the water already in the pool, then two observations on the pool's temperature will show the water to be getting warmer, but in neither case will the temperature be as warm as that of the water entering the pool. The procedure described here obviously converts the two observations into an estimate of the temperature of the water entering the pool. Note that the biases again offset one another in calculation of SMAM, which fails altogether to register the large change in marriage intensity under conditions of rapid change. Especially when fertility implications are of central concern, expected years of single life seems far more salient than SMAM.

One word of caution: intercensal nuptiality calculations are probably more vulnerable to data error than are calculations using either census alone, simply because the intercensal procedures are based upon first differences, whose values can change substantially even when one element changes only slightly. Errors are particularly likely when observations are closely spaced.

Multiple Decrement Processes

Almost all states of interest in family demography have more than one mode of exit. At times, it is convenient to ignore the multiplicity of exit routes, but at other times they need to be recognized. The basic advance offered by the new procedures for multiple decrement analysis results from the principle enunciated earlier that a second cross-sectional observation can substitute for flow data. When more than one type of flow is to be studied, the second cross-sectional observation on duration in a state can substitute for one flow (presumably one in which data are missing or otherwise impaired), or for all flows combined, as illustrated earlier. If data on only one decrement are available, then the second cross-section can also substitute for all other decrements combined.

The mathematics are exceedingly simple. Multiply both sides of equation (3.5) by $\mu_1(a)$, the force of decrement from the first decrement:

$$N(a)\mu_1(a) = N(0)e^{\int_0^a r(x)dx} p(a) \mu_1(a).$$

We will designate $N(a)\mu_1(a)$ as $D_1(a)$, the number of decrements of type 1 age a in the population. The number of decrements at age a in the multiple decrement life table with radix one at age a is $p(a)\mu_1(a) = d_1(a)$. So the number of decrements from source 1 in the multiple decrement life table is simply

$$d_1(a) = \frac{D_1(a)\, e^{\int_0^a r(x)dx}}{N(0)} \tag{3.13}$$

To use equation (3.13) it is not necessary to know anything directly about other decrements. In a stationary population, $r(x) = 0$ at all x and equation (3.1) becomes even simpler.

The probability that someone entering the state will eventually exit via decrement 1 is found simply by integrating equation (3.13) over all durations from zero to infinity.

This simplicity of mathematical relations suggests that the new equations could well prove useful in family demography. To illustrate their potential utility we compute the decrements from divorce in a marriage table for the US in 1975–80 in Table 3.4. What is needed to apply equation (3.13) are divorces by duration, available from US vital statistics, and two cross-sectional observations on the number of marriages by duration. No mortality information is used; the activity of mortality is inferred from the inability of divorces combined with population growth to account for the decline in marriages with duration.

The application appears to be highly successful, judging from a comparison with an 'official' table for a slightly earlier time period when divorce rates were slightly lower. The computed probability that a marriage will end in divorce, .520, is close to that in the earlier table, .496. Furthermore, the two duration patterns of divorce are extremely similar to one another, with the $d_1(a)$ function always being slightly higher in the present application. The divergence grows in proportionate terms at the high durations, which is consistent with our earlier position that the official tables may have underestimated the number of very longevous marriages by applying too high a set a death rates. The differences, however, are small.

Not all applications of equation (3.13) were successful. Attempts to estimate the proportion of a birth cohort who will ever marry in the US based on first marriages and the growth rate of the single population between 1977 and 1979 resulted in a figure of 1.00 for females and .98 for males, both doubtless too high. What appears to have happened is that substantial migration into the single population occurred during the period, which was not accounted for in computation. Some of this migration was international (both legal and illegal) but other appears to have been a social 'migration' of the previously married into the single category. Some people evidently preferred to report themselves as single even though they were previously married, a tendency documented elsewhere (Preston and McDonald, 1979). This tendency raised the r_x function relative to what it should have been and thus inflated the $d_1(a)$ estimates. A similar result occurred in an application to Taiwan, 1975–80. This problem can be turned into an advantage for certain applications in which the aim is to uncover errors in data. The basic equations of the system are the age-specific equivalents of the balancing equation of population growth, wherein a change in population size is ascribed to birth, death, and migration. Violations of identities must, of course, be attributed to errors in variables.

Table 3.4 Computation of the probability that a marriage will end in divorce at various durations, US 1975–1980.

Duration of Marriage a to a + z	Estimated Number of Divorces by Duration, June 1975 –June 1980[a]	Growth Rate in Number of Intact Marriages, June 1975–June 1980[b]	Sum of Growth Rates from Duration Zero to Mid-point of Interval	Probability that a Marriage Just Contracted Will End in Divorce at Stated Durations Under Death and Divorce Rates of 1975–1980[c]	Probability that a Marriage will End in Divorce in Complete Marriage Life Table for 1976–1977[d]
	(1)	(2)	(3)	(4)	
0	251 888	.00603	.00301	.0225	.0220
1	458 995	.01270	.01238	.0414	.0409
2	506 574	.00558	.02152	.0461	.0454
3	506 574	–.01319	.01772	.0460	.0440
4	464 592	.01300	.01762	.0422	.0397
5	405 819	–.02505	.01160	.0366	.0348
6	352 642	–.01454	–.00820	.0312	.0308
7	323 460	.01799	–.00647	.0278	.0273
8	265 881	.02607	.01556	.0241	.0234
9	229 497	.01948	.03833	.0213	.0207
10–14	766 858	.01649	.08930	.0747	.0736
15–19	442 202	–.00164	.12642	.0447	.0416
20–24	299 466	–.01092	.09502	.0294	.0260
25–29	179 120	–.03556	–.02118	.0156	.0143
30+	156 730	.02494	.13932	.0160	.0125
				Sum = .520	Sum = .496

[a] Estimated by applying divorce distribution by duration of marriage in 1977–1978 in Divorce Registration Area to total number of divorces in US between June 1975 and June 1980. Sources: National Center for Health Statistics, *Monthly Vital Statistics*, Vol. 32(3) Supplement, June 27, 1983; National Center for Health Statistics, *Vital Statistics of the United States*, Vol. III, Marriage and Divorce, 1977 and 1978.
[b] Computed from unpublished data.
[c] Col (1) × exp [Col 3] ÷ N(0). N(0) is the total number of marriages between June 1975 and June 1980, or 11,218,2400.
[d] James A. Weed (1980), 'National Estimates of Marriage Dissolution and Survivorship' National Center for Health Statistics, *Vital and Health Statistics*, Series 3, No. 19.

Increment–Decrement Processes

The major application of the new system of equations to increment–decrement processes would appear to lie in the estimation of a particular increment or decrement function in the absence of any direct information on the increment or decrement itself. With this function estimated, a complete increment–decrement table could then be constructed by conventional means (e.g., see Land and Rogers, 1982). In this case the new equations are providing only an input to an estimation process, rather than a final, closed-form estimation equation itself.

Let us suppose that our interest is in constructing an increment–decrement life table for the currently married and currently non-married states and that no information is available on the number of deaths by age and marital status. The number of non-married people aged a at time t will equal

$$NM(a,t) = NM(0,t)\, e^{-\int_0^a [r_{NM}(x,t) - \mu_{NM}(x,t) - m(x,t) + d(x,t)]\, dx} \qquad (3.14)$$

where
$r_{NM}(x,t)$ = growth rate of the non-married population at age x, time t

$\mu_{NM}(x,t)$ = death rate of the non-married population aged x at time t

$m(x,t)$ = rate of marriage for the non-married at age x, time t

$d(x,t)$ = rate of increase of the non-married population resulting from divorce at age x, time t

It is clearly possible to manipulate equation 3.14 in such a way as to isolate the term in exp $\{-\mu_{NM}(x,t)\}$ on one side, to solve for the value of this expression at repeated ages, and then take logs to solve for the $\mu_{NM}(x,t)$ function itself. Measurement error is likely to be very large in individual values of $\mu_{NM}(x,t)$, so that some kind of parameterization of the risk function is likely to prove useful. A one-parameter logit transformation of risk functions can be introduced into such a system in a way that results in a simple linear equation whose slope is the requisite parameter in the one-parameter system (Preston, 1983). One potential application of this system is for identifying the flow functions by which household heads or 'markers' are constituted or deposed. From this identification, one may produce an increment–decrement table for household heads, or combine the flow functions with a set of age-specific growth rates to represent mean household size in a population. Note that specifying an age-specific growth rate function is tantamount to specifying an age structure.

Alternative sets of identities for increment–decrement processes that use the numbers of increments and decrements, rather than their rates, can be found in Preston and Coale (1982). These can also be used to establish the values of a particular flow function or, where complete data are available, to test data consistency.

Summary

This chapter presents new mathematical expressions for indices frequently encountered in family demography. These indices pertain to the survival of individuals in a defined social state or relationship. They include such functions as the likelihood of marrying, the expected duration of marriage, and the chance that a marriage will end in divorce.

The new expressions are based upon a recent generalization of stable population relations. They suggest ways of estimating parameters that were not previously obvious. In general the estimation proceeds by substituting a second cross-sectional observation on the age — or duration — distribution of a population for certain flow data. These expressions are then applied to data and their utility for estimation is assessed. Estimation of the singulate mean age at marriage and of marital survivorship functions appear to be promising applications of these procedures.

Appendix

DERIVATION OF DISCRETE APPROXIMATIONS USED FOR ESTIMATION

The basic text equation (3.5) that relates age distributions, growth rates, and decrement rates is expressed in continuous terms. For estimation purposes, it is necessary to develop a procedure for dealing with the observations that are in discrete ages and time periods.

There are two relatively straightforward approaches to this problem. One is to recognize that, since equation (3.5) applies at any time, it applies at any pair of times. Suppose that we have observations on the age distribution of the population at time T_1 and at time T_2. We write out equation (3.5) for both dates and multiply the two equations together:

$$\frac{N(a,T_1) \cdot N(a,T_2)}{N(0,T_1) \cdot N(0,T_2)} \ e^{\int_0^a [r(x,T_1) + r(x,T_2)]dx} = e^{-\int_0^a [\mu(x,T_1) + \mu(x,T_2)]dx}$$

Now raising each term to the power ½, we have

$$\frac{\overline{N}(a)}{\overline{N}(0)} \ e^{\int_0^a \overline{r}(x)dx} = \overline{p}(a),\qquad(3.A.1)$$

where
- $\overline{N}(a)$ = geometric mean of population at age a at T_1 and T_2.
- $\overline{r}(x)$ = arithmetic mean of growth rates at age x at T_1 and T_2.
- $\overline{p}(a)$ = probability of survival to age a for a person exposed to the arithmetic mean of decrement functions at T_1 and T_2.

It seems reasonable to estimate the arithmetic mean of growth rates at the beginning and end of the period as the arithmetic mean of growth rates at age x throughout the period:

$$\overline{r}(x) \cong \frac{\displaystyle\int_{T_1}^{T_2} r(x,t)dt}{T_2 - T_1} = \ln \frac{\left[\dfrac{N(x,T_2)}{N(x,T_1)}\right]}{T_2 - T_1}\qquad(3.A.2)$$

This approximation will be exact if growth rates are constant or change linearly during the period, or in certain other circumstances. Ages can be made discrete by summing equation (3.6) over the appropriate age intervals (say, 5 years wide).[1]

$$\frac{\sum_{y}^{y+5} \overline{N}(a) \, e^{\int_0^a \overline{r}(x)dx}}{\overline{N}(0)} = \int_{y}^{y+5} \overline{p}(a)da, \text{ or}$$

$$\frac{{}_5\overline{N}_y \, e^{S(y+2.5)}}{\overline{N}(0)} \cong \int_{y}^{y+5} \overline{p}(a)da = {}_5L_y \tag{3.A.3}$$

where $\quad {}_5\overline{N}_y = [{}_5N_y(T_1) \cdot {}_5N_a(T_2)]^{1/2}$

$$S(y + 2.5) = 5 \sum_{A=0}^{y-5} {}_5r_a + 2.5 \, {}_5r_y, \text{ and}$$

${}_5L_y$ = person years lived in a life table based on $\overline{p}(a)$ between ages y and $y+5$, with radix of unity.

The life table that will be constructed from equation (3.A.1) is, to state the obvious, technically appropriate to the average force of decrement conditions at the beginning and end of the period. One suspects that this average will usually be close to that for the period as a whole.

The second way of proceeding to make equation (3.6) discrete is to assume that the age-specific growth rate, $r(x,t)$, is constant at $\overline{r}(x)$ during the period of observation from T_1 to T_2. Then from (3.6),

$$\int_{T_1}^{T_2} N(a,t)dt = e^{-\int_0^a \overline{r}(x)dx} \int_{T_1}^{T_2} N(0,t) \, p(a,t)dt$$

Dividing both sides by $\int_{T_1}^{T_2} N(0,t)dt \, [T_2 - T_1]$, we have

$$\frac{\overline{\overline{N}}(a)}{\overline{\overline{N}}(0)} = e^{\int_0^a \overline{r}(x)dx} \, \overline{\overline{p}}(a), \text{ where} \tag{3.A.4}$$

$\overline{\overline{N}}(a)$ = mean population alive at age a between T_1 and T_2; by assumptions this is equal to $[N(a,T_1) - N(a,T_1)]/r(T_2-T_1)$ unless $r=0$, in which case $\overline{N}(a) = N(a,T_1) = N(a,T_2)$.

$\overline{\overline{p}}(a)$ = weighted mean of functions that prevailed during the period, where the weight is supplied by the $N(0,t)$ function.

$\overline{r}(x)$ was already defined in equation (3.8). Ages can be made discrete in the same fashion as above, so that

$$\frac{{}_5\overline{\overline{N}}_y \, e^{S(y+2.5)}}{\overline{\overline{N}}(0)} = {}_5L_y \tag{3.A.5}$$

Equation (3.A.5) is very similar to equation (3.A.3) except that the survivorship function, ${}_5L_y$, is a weighted average over the period instead of an average of begin-

---

[1] While it is not in general the case that the geometric mean of two sums will equal the sum of geometric means of individual components as implied in the formula for ${}_5\overline{N}_y$, experimentation with 5-year age intervals over 10-year time periods under a situation with rapid population growth indicates no difference to six significant digits.

ning and end period conditions, and $_5\overline{N}_y$ is an arithmetic mean of person years lived at ages y to $y+5$, rather than a geometric mean. There is no question that (3.A.5) achieves broader temporal coverage than (3.A.3), but at the expense of making a more restrictive assumption that the $r(x,t)$ function is constant for all x.

Which of these formulations is preferable? Surely (3.A.5) is preferred if the assumption of constant age-specific growth rates is tenable, but the only time that we can be assured of its reasonableness is when the population is stable. A virtue of (3.A.3) is that it collapses to familiar cohort-specific identities when the period of age and time are equal. To show this, imagine that we have taken censuses at 5-year intervals. Express equation 3.A.3 for successive 5-year intervals and divide the two equations:

$$\frac{_5L_y}{_5L_{y-5}} = \frac{_5\overline{N}_y\, e^{S(y+2.5)}}{_5\overline{N}_{y-5}\, e^{S(y-2.5)}} \tag{3.A.6}$$

Making the substitutions described above, we have

$$\frac{_5L_y}{_5L_{y-5}} = \frac{[_5N_y\,(T_1)\cdot {_5}N_y(T_1+5)]^{\frac{1}{2}}\, e^{5\sum_0^{y-5} {_5}r_a + 2.5{_5}r_{y-5}}}{[_5N_{y-5}\,(T_1)\cdot {_5}N_{y-5}\,(T_1+5)]^{\frac{1}{2}}\; \exp\left\{5\sum_0^{y-5} {_5}r_a + 2.5{_5}r_{y-5}\right\}}$$

Now squaring both sides and recognizing that

$$_5N_y(T_1)\exp\{5{_5}r_y\} = {_5}N_y(T_1+5) \text{ and that}$$
$$_5N_{y-5}(T_1+5)\exp\{-5{_5}r_{y-5}\} = {_5}N_{y-5}(T_1)$$

and finally taking square roots, we have

$$\frac{_5L_y}{_5L_{y-5}} = \frac{_5N_y\,(T_1+5)}{_5N_{y-5}\,(T_1)} \tag{3.A.7}$$

Equation (3.A.7) shows that the value of the decrement function estimated through the apparently unrelated equation (3.A.3) is identical to the cohort survival ratio through the same interval when the age span and time span are of equal length. This result lends a reassuring concreteness to the estimation procedure. Nevertheless, it should be noted that the cohort in question occupies only one-half of the lexis diagram for ages $y-5$ to $y+5$ during the interval T to $T+5$ (and only three-quarters of the area from $y-2.5$ to $y+2.5$), so that the cohort survival ratio could, under unusual circumstances, be a misleading indicator of mortality conditions in the age–time interval.

Data needed

For applying equation (3.5) in either of its guises (3.A.3 or 3.A.5), the only data absolutely required are observations on $N(a,t)$ at two points in time. From this information, assuming that we use equation (3.A.3), $_5\overline{N}_a$ and $_5\overline{r}_a$ can be readily constructed. These functions in turn are sufficient to compute ratios of $_5L_x$ functions for successive intervals via (3.A.6). However, the resulting life table will lack a radix without information on $\overline{N}(0)$. The most appealing way to compute $\overline{N}(0)$ (or $\overline{\overline{N}}(0)$) is simply to count all of the entrances into the defined state that occur between T_1 and T_2 and divide by (T_2-T_1).

If data are not available on $\overline{N}(0)$, a life table based on the single decrement at issue can still be constructed, but it must start with a higher age for which the radix (the number of persons passing the age boundary during the interval) can be estimated. There are several ways to perform this estimation. If the observations are separated by 5 years and age intervals are 5 years wide, persons reaching age y in the interval are all aged $y - 5$ to y at the outset and y to $y + 5$ at the end so that the number entrances into the population in the age interval $y + $ can be inferred by averaging the size of the cohort at these two points. More generally, it seems to be adequate to assume that

$$1_x = \frac{{}_5L_x + {}_5L_{x-5}}{10}.$$

This assumption, combined with the estimation system based on (3.A.5), produced a life expectancy for Swedish females, 1966–70, that was within 1 per cent of the 'observed' value (based on vital statistics) at all ages from 5 to 60 (Preston and Bennett, 1983). Ansley Coale has experimented with alternative interpolation procedures that can be expected in general to produce more accurate results.

When data on $\overline{N}(0)$ are missing and an estimate of the life table from age 0 is sought, it is possible to introduce a model life table system and to solve simultaneously for $\overline{N}(0)$ and the intensity of the decrement process (see Preston, 1983, for examples when the decrement is mortality from all causes). If the model decrement system is a Brass-type one parameter logit transformation, a simple analytic solution is available. Such model systems are rare in family demography although their utility could be considerable.

References

Agarwala, S. N. (1957), 'The Age at Marriage in India', *Population Index*, Vol. 23, April:96–107.

Brass, William and E. A. Bamboye (1981), 'The Time-Location of Reports of Survivorship: Estimates for Maternal and Paternal Orphanhood and Ever-Widowed', London School of Hygiene and Tropical Medicine, Centre for Population Studies Working Paper No. 81–1.

Hajnal, John (1953), 'Age at Marriage and Proportion Marrying', *Population Studies*, Vol. 7:111–36.

Keyfitz, Nathan (1968), *Introduction to the Mathematics of Population*, Addison–Wesley, Reading, Mass.

Kuszynski, Robert (1935), *The Measurement of Population Growth*, Sidgwick and Jackson, London.

Land, Kenneth C. and Andrei Rogers (1982), *Multidimensional Mathematical Demography*, Academic Press, New York.

Preston, Samuel H. and Ansley J. Coale (1982), 'Age Structure, Growth, Attrition and Accession: A New Synthesis', *Population Index*, Vol. 48(2):217–59.

—— and J. McDonald (1979), 'Incidence of Divorce Among Cohorts of American Marriages Contracted Since the Civil War', *Demography*, Vol. 16(1):1–26.

Ryder, Norman (1975), 'Models of Family Demography', United Nations Ad Hoc Group of Experts on Demographic Models, New York, December.

—— (1978), 'Methods in Measuring the Family Life Cycle', *IUSSP International Population Conference, Mexico 1977*, Proceedings, 219–26.

United States, National Center for Health Statistics (1980), *National Estimates of Marriage Dissolution and Survivorship: United States*, Vital and Health Statistics, Series 3(19).

Part III

The Family Life Cycle

4 The Family Life Cycle: Needed Extensions of the Concept

CHARLOTTE HÖHN

Federal Institute for Population Research Wiesbaden, Federal Republic of Germany

1 The classical concept of the family life cycle

1.1 Introduction

The concept of the family life cycle brings together and synthesizes several central topics in demography: nuptiality, fertility, and mortality. This concept seems to respond to Le Bras's criticism of many demographic studies. When he writes that 'married life punctuated by marriage and divorce, procreative life marked by births, and life itself ending in death are three chapters of demography, whereas these events are all experienced in families' (Le Bras, 1979, 52), he invites the development of a more integrated approach to these events, in fact a *family* demography.

The family life cycle concept is a step in this direction. but in its classical form it is not complete; it does not cover all family types nor the life courses of all individuals. Classical family life cycle studies neglect single-parent or childless families, as well as never-married individuals, whether living together or alone. Core demographic events like divorce, remarriage, and migration typically are not included in the family life cycle, while events not traditionally studied in demography (like the home-leaving of adult children) have been added.

Over the years several authors have expressed high expectations for life cycle measures. Lansing and Kish (1957) and Bogue (1969, 385) argue that family life cycle stage is a more important concept than age, since it has greater explanatory power for behaviour. Hill and Rogers state (1964) that the development of individual roles both inside and outside the family are determined more by life cycle events than by age as such. Ryder (1978, 220) suggests the life cycle model as an appropriate context for understanding most demographic events:

The family as an aggregate has non-demographic properties which strongly influence the occurrence of demographic events to its individual members, e.g., the place of residence, the kind of housing, the family income, the aggregate participation in the labour force. More difficult to measure but probably more salient is the structure of role relationships within the family, such as the relative rights and responsibilities of males *vis-à-vis* females, and of the senior *vis-à-vis* the junior generation.

The family life cycle concept is thus a standard part of population studies, and one with promise of further fruitful applications. But the classic concept has its limitations; some of which have led to a number of necessary and useful modifications in its use. We review these in Part 1 before entering into a broader critique of the concept and technique in Part 2 (see also Höhn, 1982). How well these limitations and criticisms are dealt with will determine the ultimate place of the family life cycle in demographic analysis.

The classical or original concept[1] divides the history of a nuclear family, from marriage to the dissolution by death of the surviving spouse, into six phases. The father of the classical concept is Paul C. Glick, with Sorokin, Zimmermann and Galpin (1931) and Loomis and Hamilton (1936) commonly cited as predecessors. In his first essay in 1947, Glick defined the beginning and the end of each of the six phases using median age of husband or wife at seven events (see Table 4.1).[2] Glick continued to use these indicators in his research, although he gave revised methods for their computation in later publications (1955, 1957, 1964, 1977).

As simple and as convincing as the concept of the family life cycle is at first glance, it poses many methodological problems. Glick himself dealt with

Table 4.1   Basic model of nuclear family life cycle

Phases of Family Life Cycle		Events characterizing Respective Phases	
		Beginning	End
I	Formation	marriage	birth of first child
II	Extension	birth of first child	birth of last child
III	Completed extension	birth of last child	first child leaves home
IV	Contraction	first child leaves home of parents	last child leaves home of parents
V	Completed contraction	last child has left home of parents	first spouse dies
VI	Dissolution	first spouse dies	death of survivor (extinction)

[1] We call it the classical concept because it has served as the basis for differentiation into more than six phases (see e.g. Hill, Duvall, Rodgers) and for generalization to other types of families than the nuclear type, and also to distinguish life-cycle analysis from more recent studies of marriage, fertility, mortality, and marriage dissolution, that is to say of components of the family life cycle, using multistate life table techniques (see for example A. Rodgers, Schoen and Urton, Schwarz), or micro-simulation (see for instance Bongaarts, Steger, Wachter/Hammel/Laslett). These authors generally do not consider their studies as 'family life cycle' analysis although they could be so classified, if their output is cast in family life cycle form.

[2] Glick's phases were recently given names by a study group of the WHO (Statistical Indices, 1976). The events marking the beginning and end of each phase are the same as those of Glick, except that 'marriage of children' is replaced by 'leaving home' (see Table 4.1).

many of these over the years, and so we will follow the development of his work.

1.2 Problems of measurement

To calculate an average or median *age at first marriage* is a simple statistical exercise provided the data distinguish first and later marriages. But there are problems of meaning with the resulting figure. For one thing, not all first marriages remain intact; and age at marriage is not independent of the risk of divorce later on. Since the classical family life cycle concept assumes stable marriages, perhaps this should be taken into consideration right from the beginning by calculating age at first marriage only for those neither divorced nor widowed before the end of reproductive life span. More generally, to what extent should age at first marriage be calculated separately for groups homogeneous with respect to later events?

Another problem is the ambiguity of the term *first marriage*. Is it first marriage to the individual 'marker' of the study only or also to his/her partner? Most analyses treat men and women as isolated individuals neglecting characteristics of their spouse or of the marriage as such. Most current population statistics, of course, involve individual rather than family-oriented tabulations and empirical research in family demography is sharply limited by this statistical practice.

If, in response to the two problems just noted, we compute age at first marriage only for stable marriages where *both* spouses were single prior to marriage, we would achieve maximum homogeneity. But we also would be discarding a non-negligible part of all marriages: all remarriages for one or both partners and all first marriages broken by divorce or death before age 50 of the wife. We are no longer studying all families; our findings lose generality.

In his book *American Families* (1957) Glick finds differences in age at first marriage of women married only once and of those remarried (56–57). Nevertheless he refrains from forming two separate groups. He calculates age at first marriage for all first marriages irrespective of previous marital status and eventual stability of the marriage. But he adds: 'If research is undertaken in this area it would be better to prepare various models of the family life cycle according to age at remarriage and previous marital status of the husband and wife' (Glick, 1957, 70). In 1977 Glick published data limited to the family life cycle of women in stable first marriages. Glick is aware that non-stable marriages and remarriages are becoming more frequent (Norton and Glick, 1976), and suggests further investigation into various types of family life cycles disrupted by divorce (1977, 12). Norton (1983) has pursued this line of analysis.

After discussing only the first event in the family life cycle we see the basis for defining more than one type of cycle, in fact three: those involving pure first marriages, pure remarriages, and 'mixed' marriages (one spouse marrying for the first time, the other remarrying).

The next phase in the classical family life cycle begins with the *birth of the first child*. If a marriage remains childless, however, the cycle collapses to two phases instead of six. The first phase ends with the death of one spouse, followed by the second and last phase up to the death of the other spouse. Glick excludes childless women in his latest analysis (1977, 5), which increases homogeneity, but reduces representativeness. The analysis no longer applies to all families, which conventionally include married couples without children.

The measurement of age at birth of first child raises statistical problems that are characteristic of life cycle analyses. Does one use medians or means? Does one try to measure age at a given event directly (for example, in the case at hand, from the age distribution of first births), or indirectly, by adding to age at marriage the calculated interval from marriage to first birth? A more detailed discussion of these issues is given in the next chapter by Feichtinger.

In traditional life cycle analysis, measures of dispersion are rare (but see Glick, 1957, and Glick and Parke, 1965), giving a misleading impression of neatly separated events and clear-cut phases. Glick and Parke (1965) give data on quartiles which amply illustrate the extent of variation, especially when the group under study is not homogeneous.

The second life cycle event, then, can be used to distinguish marriages with or without children. Combining this criterion with that based on marriage stability leads logically to six (2 × 3) types of family life cycle.

In our opinion, the trickiest problem in life cycle analysis is the calculation of *age at birth of the last child*. Ryder comments humorously: 'On top of these problems, so familiar to the fertility analyst, there is the conundrum of which child may be the last child — something many parents would like to know' (1978, 224). This information cannot be obtained from current vital statistics. Birth order, of course, is available. But this is of no use for studies of the family life cycle. It is unsatisfactory to use age at birth of children with highest rank order, or to interpolate age of mother at the average completed family size, because these measures are so unrepresentative of the experience of very small families. Suppose completed family size is one child; then ages at first birth and at last birth are identical. The number of phases is reduced to four. Unfortunately, we will need averages for heterogeneous populations with a variety of family sizes. A correct measurement of the interval between first and second birth should consider only women with at least two births (Feichtinger, 1979, 99–100). In general, family life cycles should be computed separately for women or couples having different numbers of children.

The only adequate solution to this problem is to use birth histories of women with completed fertility. Such biographical data, from either a longitudinal or a retrospective survey, however, should not be limited to a birth history. They should contain all data required to analyse the family life cycle. The problem of which is the last child makes it obvious that biographical data are needed. But we should note also that the delimitation of homogeneous groups of *stable* marriages requires the same approach. How else can we know whether a new marriage is destined to remain intact?

The disadvantage of biographical data is the time lag. Attempts to circumvent this regarding the 'last child' have involved asking women about their desire to have further children and their intentions about timing. Glick makes use of such intentions, and believes 'that the data provide reasonably reliable indications about the average size of completed family that women will have during the next decade or two' (1977, 5). The reliability of birth intentions for such estimates and forecasts is still strongly debated. Nobody would ask the newly-wed whether and when they might divorce or will die. So the need for biographical data *ex post* is obvious.

If the problem of estimating age at birth of the last child is tricky, the situation concerning age when *children leave home* is desolate. Statistical data are scarce and in general must be obtained in biographical surveys. The lack of data concerning the age of parents at the home-leaving stage of children (also called *launching* or *passage*) does not bother analysts who assume that marriage and home-leaving occur simultaneously. One simply adds current mean age at first marriage to the average age at birth (of first or last child). This has been Glick's procedure 'in the absence of a more plausible hypothesis' (1957, 67). He is aware, however, that a growing percentage of younger generations does not marry. 'During more recent times an increasing proportion of young adults have been leaving home before they marry, but a long series of statistics to demonstrate this well recognized fact is not available' (Glick, 1977, 8).

A simple solution to the problem of measurement of launching has been suggested: 'To estimate the end of phase III (completed extension) 18 years are added to the average age of the mother at the birth of the first child, since this was considered to be approximately the age from which a child can support itself' (Herberger, 1982, 40). But such a solution would not seem adequate, based on existing empirical evidence, e.g. the Australian data (Young, 1982) or some evaluations of the German census 1970 (Schwarz, 1979). Young reports a decline in the age at marriage, and an even lower age of leaving home for other reasons, like education, a job or independence. She also reminds us that daughters marry earlier than sons. Schwarz finds that German mothers are surprisingly old by the time all children have left home. For mothers with only one child the median age is 51, while for mothers of two, three, and four children, the median ages are 55, 58, and 60 respectively.

We should strengthen efforts to collect data on this phase of the family life cycle. There seem to be large cross-national differences, and considerable change over time. The 'empty nest' period is one of the most interesting from a sociological and psychological point of view.

In the latest stages of the life cycle, a common mistake is to compute the *age at death of spouses* (age at widowhood of the wife, or the husband) by adding to the age at first marriage of the wife or the husband the further life expectancy of the husband or wife (Herberger, 1978), even though it has been made quite clear by Myers (1959) that such a calculation is misleading. Adding age at marriage of women and life expectation of men leads to an age at widowhood without correction for mortality of women (see Feichtinger, 1979, 101–6 and in chapter 5). These two indicators can be derived from life tables; biographical data are not required. Life tables by marital status are preferable but general life tables usually are sufficiently reliable.

1.3 The indispensable cohort approach

We have already noted that for measuring life cycle events, biographical data are needed in order to define reasonably homogeneous groups as regards marriage and fertility. Arguments for longitudinal data go beyond these considerations, however, and extend to recognition of the cohort approach as indispensable for understanding demographic change. A slackening of nuptiality, a decline in fertility, a change in birth intervals, new patterns of leaving home — these simply cannot be grasped using only cross-sectional data.

Glick always understood that the family life cycle tended to change over time. If he adopted the cross-sectional approach in his earlier studies, he did so in a comparative-static way, giving hypothetical family life cycles for periods very far apart. As soon as longitudinal data were available Glick published them (with Parke, 1965), after having emphasized the need for the cohort approach one year before: 'Families, as separate entities, are in a continuous process of change throughout their existence. Moreover, patterns of family behavior in modern societies, and in societies which are becoming modern, are likewise in a process of change over the decades. So, the life cycle of family behavior is variable in two aspects' (Glick, 1964, 324). Landmark studies using the cohort approach to the family life cycle also are found in Uhlenberg (1969 and 1974) and R. Hill (1970 and 1977). Unfortunately the cohort approach is neglected in the chapter on 'Households and Families' UN (1973), though the article by Glick and Parke (1965) is quoted. At least a hint that cross-sectional analysis (lacking more suitable data) might be better than no international comparison at all would have been appropriate. Such a pragmatic attitude, however, can lead to crude work (see e.g. Herberger, 1978). Since demographic change takes place everywhere, cross-sectional studies should be avoided whenever possible.

More and better biographical data are necessary not only for correct measurement but for a better understanding of change.

2 Critique of the concept

2.1 Restriction to nuclear family

The classical family life cycle applies only to the nuclear family, that is the two-generation family without further relatives or other non-related members of household (Höhn, 1982; Federal Institute/WHO, 1982). 'Perhaps more important is the basic premise behind the family life cycle approach which is that real families have beginnings and ends. The extended family system often does not have this restriction; in principle, such families are immortal' (Browning and Herberger, 1978, 16). Therefore a different approach has to be adopted to show transitions from, say, the extended to the nuclear family type and vice versa. A rare example of a new approach can be found in Concepción and Landa-Jocano (1975, 258). In Collver's study of India (1963) and Morioka's of Japan (1967), we find examples of the classical family life cycle applied to societies where the extended family type still exists. Collver criticizes his own attempt to fit the model of the family life cycle (for nuclear families) to India when he writes:

In the Indian villages . . . the cycle is a continuous flow, with little to mark off the transition from one stage to another . . . The concept of stages is inadequate to describe this situation in which early marriage, prolonged childbearing and early death combine to run the stages together, or to obscure entirely the final stage in which a couple go on living after the marriage of their last child (Collver, 1963, 86 and 87).

The final publication of the WHO Working Group on *Health and the Family Life Cycle* contains a number of case studies demonstrating the need to find a family life cycle concept for family types other than the nuclear family (Federal Institute, 1982). A broad field for systematic research remains.

2.2 Restriction to stable marriages

The classical family life cycle concept, as already mentioned, does not allow for divorce, though calculations of average age at marriage do not in fact always exclude marriages that will end in divorce. Though there are country-specific differences — see for the USA Weed (1980) and for West Germany Höhn (1980, 361) — the percentages of marriages ending in divorce are far from negligible, and calculations that ignore divorce are suspect.

Neglecting divorce is not compensated for by a separate consideration of age at remarriage. The easiest solution is to exclude remarriages entirely (see Glick, 1977), but if the family life cycle is supposed to portray all families, if it is to be more than the life cycle of pure first marriages, then indeed remarriages have to be dealt with.

A completely unresolved problem is that of children affected by divorce or death of their parents and the incomplete families they live in. We could show that in the 1966 marriage cohort in the Federal Republic of Germany, after a marriage duration of 14.5 years, 13.2 per cent of surviving children born to this cohort had already become orphans by death (4.8 per cent) or divorce (8.4 per cent) of parents (Höhn, 1982, 64–6). Traditional family life cycle measures do not reflect these important changes. One-parent families are always neglected. Trost criticizes this fact sharply:

The one-parent families are excluded, since they do not fit the existing family life cycles. All three types of one-parent families are non-fits: those resulting from divorce, those resulting from the death of one or the other spouse and those that never have been knitted into a marriage group (the unmarried mother and father with children). The first two of these families have belonged to the family life cycle but have been removed from it at the time of dissolution (Trost, 1977; 469).

Infant and child mortality and migration are similarly neglected. The classical concept thus does not cover all families. It focuses on stable marriages (sometimes excluding childless marriages), neglecting divorces, incomplete families and remarriages. The family life cycle is therefore a partial concept.

2.3 The normative touch

Despite its partial character, classical family life cycle measures seem to describe 'the family' because their limitations are not obvious. On the contrary, the family life cycle seems to present in concise and plausible form the normal course of family life. Some authors note that the typical sequence is not only statistically average but culturally prescribed.

The model should also be normative in the sense that it should reflect marriage and the subsequent sequence of phases which are not only culturally sanctioned but also encouraged by strong social pressures for conformity. Persons born into diverse cultures willingly marry and then remain in the marital union throughout the phases of the family life cycle until death. In other words, traversing the family life cycle is seen as appropriate behavior for virtually everyone (Browning and Herberger, 1978, 15).

The family life cycle 'preferred for and by females' is defined by Uhlenberg as follows: 'We accept a female as following the preferred life cycle if, when she arrives at age 50, she has married, borne at least one child, and still has her first marriage intact. Any variation from this particular life style is considered deviant' (1974, 285). In the same article Uhlenberg finds that 20 per cent of younger marriages are unstable and that leads him to 'the prediction that, instead of increasing uniformity, we now have increasing deviance from the preferred pattern' (Uhlenberg, 1974, 288). This deviance may, however, be transformed by remarriage to a 'modified preferred' life cycle.

Lables like 'deviant' in contrast to 'normal' and 'conventional', and expressions like 'barren' for 'childless', 'active' for 'with minor children', and 'mature' for families in the empty nest phase (Priest, 1982) run the risk of seeming to give the author's — rather than a given society's — approval or disapproval to certain modes of behaviour. Some have warned of the danger of family life cycle analyses becoming normative in this further sense. 'All that remains is the ideal family: father, mother and children, all united, all surviving' (Le Bras, 1979, 52). 'The concept of family life cycle is harmless *per se*. However, the use made of this concept is not always harmless. The concept might steer the research into wrong channels, or put blinds on the researcher, or, when used as an educational tool, act as an conserving agent' (Trost, 1977, 468).

3 Towards a concept of life courses

3.1 Reasons to enlarge the concept

It should be clear that a single 'family life cycle' is not enough to cover all families. With effort and good will, however, the normative touch can be avoided, and divorces, childless families, one-parent-families, and remarriages can be given adequate consideration. But even this would not be enough. The family life cycle (implicitly) claims to be a general, all-encompassing population model. It assumes universal marriage, and where that condition is approximated, of course, the whole population is studied. If the concept is to retain its universality under new demographic circumstances (decreasing nuptiality, increasing consensual unions), however, a new system of life courses will have to be conceptualized. *Family* life cycles (several types) will be part of such a larger system, but only a part.

The decline of first marriage has been well documented (see for example Glick and Parke, 1977 for the USA and Höhn, 1976 for the Federal Republic of Germany). In the Federal Republic of Germany 10–20 per cent of the younger generation might never marry (Höhn, Mammey, and Schwarz, 1980) and hence never enter their own *family* life cycle. In their youth, however, they belonged to a family.

By definition, the individual is brought into being as a member of the junior generation of a nuclear family, called in the sociological literature his or her family of orientation. The first phase of life is exposure to the competing risks of death and passage. Subsequently, although the typical sequence involves early movement into what is called the individual's family of procreation, many individuals remain solo, and many others move back and forth between solo and familial residence throughout their lives (Ryder, 1978, 223).

These transitions require identification of many more types of life courses compared to the one or more family life cycles on which attention has previously focused. 'It would be premature and, at the present time, quite foolish to try to develop a single model of life-cycle events' (Sweet, 1977, 366). But a rough typology of life courses can and should be attempted.

3.2 Some examples of life-course analysis

Life course analysis is never simple.

Not only are there sets of interrelated processes that tend to be sequenced in a particular way, as the members of a population live through their lives, but these processes interrelate with one another . . . People . . . live in continuous time, and decisions about marrying, working, having and educating children, moving, divorcing, and the like are interdependent events (Sweet, 1977, 366).

There is a first rough concept of the life cycle using age brackets (Bogue, 1969, 163) following popular belief about phases of life (see also the diagram by Epinal, described in Höhn, 1982, 89–90). A more sophisticated model is Uhlenberg's (1969) (adopted also by Feichtinger and Hansluwka, 1977) distinguishing the following life cycle types:

1.   Abbreviated: die before age 20
2.   Spinster: survive to 20, never marry
3.   Barren: marry, remain childless
4.   Dying mother: have children, die before age 55
4a. Motherless-child producing: husband survives to 57
4b. Orphan producing: husband dies before he is 57
5.   Widowed mother: have children, survive to 55, husband dies before he is 57
6.   Typical: survive to 20, marry, have children, survive with husband alive to age 55.

This concept was later revised by Uhlenberg to consider divorce and remarriage, so that type would be sub-divided into 'preferred' and 'modified preferred' (the life course of the remarried).

An interesting approach is presented by Priest (1982, 65–88) by means of a flow chart showing the classical family life cycle, but also other paths, such as the life courses of the childless couple, of the one-parent family (by death, divorce or separation) and the possibility of remarriage. A reinterpretation of 'marriage' would allow for beginning of a family life cycle by entering a consensual union. The never-married are not considered, but could easily be added.

3.3 Outline of a typology

A typology of life courses would contain as a very important element a set of family life cycles. These are not totally separate, however; they are in fact defined in terms of interdependent life cycles of individuals.

In applying the life-course perspective to marriage and the family unit, we begin with the interdependent life histories of their members; . . . A life-course framework views the family unit in terms of mutually contingent careers, their differentiating characteristics and problems of management. It facilitates study of divergent or non-conventional family patterns, as well as the conventional, by working with the life histories of individuals (Elder, 1978, 29 and 30).

Needless to repeat that biographical data are required.

The attempt at completeness should not lead to consideration of all possible life courses or all possible types of family life cycles. Then individual personal life histories would be the outcome because, finally, particularities would triumph over common traits. Case studies (however interesting or important they may be for psychoanalysis) are not the objective. A certain grouping, a generalization, a typology — not too rough and not too detailed — is the objective. But as Table 4.2 illustrates, even a few of the distinctions discussed above lead very quickly to as many as 10 distinct types of family cycles. Combining marriages and consensual unions helps reduce the number of types. The key issue, however, is comparable behaviour. Should marriage and consensual unions be found empirically to differ in important respects, they might have to be treated separately.

Table 4.2 A rough typology of life courses

	Pure first marriages, stable	Pure remarriages, stable	Mixed marriages, stable	Unstable marriages, no remarriage	Never married
Childless	1	2	3	4	5
With children	6	7	8	9	10

Note: Marriages include consensual unions.

A typology allowing for differentiation by number of children would certainly be more satisfying, as explained earlier, but this turns out to be quite complicated. How does one deal with children from a previous union? Either children are counted per woman or per marriage. We prefer the latter version because it seems more adequate for family demography. For remarriage, ages at marriage, and at birth of further children very probably are different for those with children from a prior marriage. If we include all these variants and allow, "parit" levels, we now have 40 kinds of life cycles (Table 4.3). Even to reduce this to 24 requires collapsing number of children into broad categories (0, 1, 2 +).

From Table 4.3 we understand that only the classical family life cycle is easily analysed in terms of family size. For all other types, the very notion of completed family size defies easy operationalization. One recommendation

Table 4.3 Suggested typology of life courses

Number of children in given life course	Pure first marriages, stable	Pure remarriages, stable	Mixed marriages, stable	Unstable marriages, no remarriage	Never married
0	1	2a 2b	3a 3b	4a 4b	5
1	6	7a 7b	8a 8b	9a 9b	10
2	11	12a 12b	13a 13b	14a 14b	15
3	16	18a 18b	19a 19b	20a 20b	21
4 and over	17	22a 22b	23a 23b	24a 24b	25

Note: Marriages include consensual unions.
a: without children from prior union
b: with children from prior union

would be to describe remarriages (type 12a and 12b) as follows (x = required; — = not required):

Indicator	Type 12a	Type 12b
Age at first marriage	x	x
Age at first birth prior to remarriage	—	x
Age at last birth prior to remarriage	—	x
Age at marital dissolution	x	x
Age at remarriage	x	x
Age at first birth in remarriage	x	x
Age at last birth in remarriage	x	x
Age at launching of any first child	x	x
Age at launching of the last child	x	x
Age at death of spouse	x	x
Age at death	x	x
Average number of children prior to remarriage	—	x
Average number of children in remarriage	x	x
Average number of children	x	x
% of cohort	x	x

Similar descriptions could be given for other types of life courses. These indicators have to be gathered for each generation of women and men; otherwise comparisons are not possible, and changes between generations cannot be shown. The complexity of such an evaluation is obvious.

Such a set of life courses, defined in terms of ages at events, should be complemented by the percentage following a given type. This weighting of life courses reveals major changes or differences in family life styles. This type of analysis meets the needs of family demography which, as explained by Glick (1964, 324) is variable in two aspects, change within cycles, and changes in the prevalence of different types of cycles.

For practical work 24 types are too many. To reduce the number, a first step would be to look at the percentage of a cohort following each type. Extremely rare life courses may be eliminated, while similar ones with small numbers may be combined (combinations of mixed marriages will in most cases be appropriate). Only the most important life courses should be analysed.

A possible reduction might focus on the following 12:

Pure first marriages, stable
  without children
  with one child
  with two children
  with three and more children

Pure remarriages and mixed marriages, stable, without children from prior union
  without children in current marriage
  with children in current marriage

Pure remarriages and mixed marriages, stable, with children from prior union (indicating average number)
  without children in current marriage
  with children in current marriage

Unstable marriages, no remarriage
  without children
  with children

Never married
  without children
  with children.

We believe that a further reduction would conceal important differences in behaviour, although clearly this is an empirical not a purely logical question.

4 Conclusion

The classical concept of the family life cycle is a partial approach to family demography. It applies to stable first marriages of the nuclear family type only. Measures such as age at first marriage, birth of the first and the last child, and age at launching of children have to be derived from biographical data. This is necessary not only for methodological reasons but also because the longitudinal approach is needed to fully capture demographic change.

The partial concept of the family life cycle has to be enlarged to a concept of life courses. Otherwise unstable marriages, incomplete families, and remarriages would be neglected, along with never married persons with or without children.

A typology of a maximum of 40 and a minimum of 12 life courses is suggested. Biographical data for cohorts should be gathered to use this enlarged concept of life courses for a meaningful analysis of change in the pattern and choice of different family life cycles and related life courses.

References

Bogue, D. J. (1969), *Principles of Demography*, John Wiley, New York.

Bongaarts, J. (1982), 'Simulation of the Family Life Cycle', *International Population Conference, Manila 1981*, Vol. 3, IUSSP, Liège, 399–416.

Boongaarts, J. (1983), 'The Formal Demography of Families and Households: An Overview', *IUSSP Newsletter* No 17, 27–42.

Browning, H. and L. Herberger, (1978), 'The Normative Life Cycle of the Nuclear Family', *Health and the Family*, WHO, Geneva, 13–20.

Collver, A. (1963), 'The Family Cycle in India and the United States', *American Sociological Review*, 28, 1, 86–96.

Concepción, M. and F. Landa-Jocano, (1975), 'Demographic Factors Influencing the Family Cycle', in *The Population Debate: Dimensions and Perspectives*, Vol. II, United Nations, 252–62.

Cuisenier, J. (ed.) (1977), *Le cycle de la vie familiale dans les sociétés européennes*, Mouton, Paris.

Duvall, E. M. (1962), *Family Development*, Lippincott, Philadelphia, (1st edn. 1957–5th edn. 1977).

Elder, G. H. Jr., (1978), 'Family History and the Life Course', in T. K. Hareven (ed.) *Transitions. The Family and the Life Course in Historical Perspective*, Academic Press, New York, 17–64.

Federal Institute for Population Research/WHO (eds.) (1982), *Health and the Family Life Cycle*, WHO, Geneva.

Feichtinger, G. (1979), *Demographische Analyse und populationsdynamische Modelle. Grundzüge der Bevölkerungsmathematik*, Springer, Vienna, New York.

Feichtinger, G. and H. Hansluwka, (1977), 'The Impact of Mortality on the Life Cycle of the Family in Austria', *Zeitschrift für Bevölkerungswissenschaft*, 4, 51–79.

Glick, P. C. (1947), 'The Family Cycle', *American Sociological Review*, 12, 2, 164–74.

—— (1955), 'The Life Cycle of the Family', *Marriage and Family Living*, 17, 1, 3–9.

—— (1957), *American Families*, John Wiley, New York.

—— (1964), 'Demographic Analysis of Family Data', in H. T. Christensen (ed.) *Handbook of Marriage and the Family*, Rand McNally, Chicago, 300–34.

—— (1977), 'Updating the Life Cycle of the Family', *Journal of Marriage and the Family*, 39, 1, 5–13.

—— and A. J. Norton, (1973), 'Perspectives on the Recent Upturn in Divorce and Remarriage', *Demography*, 10, 3, 301–14.

—— —— (1977), 'Marrying, Divorcing and Living Together in the US Today', *Population Bulletin*, 32, October, 1–39.

Glick, P. C. and R., Parke Jr., (1965), 'New Approaches in Studying the Life Cycle of the Family', *Demography*, 2, 187–202.

Henry, L. (1954), 'Intervalles entre naissances', *Population*, 9, 4, 759–61.

Herberger, L. (1978), 'Contemporary Demographic Patterns', in *Health and the Family*, WHO (ed.), WHO, Geneva, 21–71.

Herberger, L. (1982), 'The Population Census as Source for Family Life Cycle Data', in *Health and the Family Life Cycle*, Federal Institute for Population Research/WHO (eds.), WHO, Geneva, 37–63.

Hill, R. (1970), *Family Development in Three Generations*, Schenkman, Cambridge, Mass.

—— (1977), 'Social Theory and Family Development', in J. Cuisenier (ed.) *Le cycle de la vie familiale*, Mouton, Paris, 9–38.

—— and R. Rodgers, (1964), 'The Developmental Approach', in H. T. Christensen (ed.) *Handbook of Marriage and the Family*, Rand McNally, Chicago, 171–211.

Höhn, Ch. (1980), 'Rechtliche und demographische Einflüsse auf die Entwicklung der Ehescheidungen seit 1946', *Zeitschrift für Bevölkerungswissenschaft*, 3/4, 335–71.

—— (1982), *Der Familienzyklus — Zur Notwendigkeit einer Konzepterweiterung*, Schrifte-nreihe des Bundesinstituts für Bevölkerungsforschung, Vol. 12, Boldt, Boppard.

—— U. Mammey, and K. Schwarz, (1980), 'Die demographische Lage in der Bundesrepublik Deutschland', *Zeitschrift für Bevölkerungswissenschaft*, 2, 141–225.

Lansing, J. B. and L. Kish, (1957), 'Family Life Cycle as an Independent Variable', *American Sociological Review*, 22, 512–19.

Le Bras, H. (1979), *Child and Family. Demographic Developments in the OECD Countries*, OECD, Paris.

Loomis, C. P. and H. H. Hamilton, (1936), 'Family Life Cycle Analysis', *Social Forces*, 15, December, 225–31.

Morioka, K. (1967), 'Life Cycle Patterns in Japan, China and the United States', *Journal of Marriage and the Family*, 29, August, 595–606.

Myers, R. J. (1959), 'Statistical Measures in the Marital Life Cycle of Men and Women', in *International Population Conference Vienna*, 1959, Christoph Reissner's Sons, Vienna, 229–33.

Norton, A. J. (1983), 'Family Life Cycle: 1980', *Journal of Marriage and the Family*, 45, 2, 267–75.

Norton, A. J. and P. C. Glick, (1976), 'Marital Instability: Past, Present and Future', *Journal and Social Issues*, 32, 1, 5–20.

Priest, G. E. (1982), *Operationalizing the Family Life-cycle Concept within the Context of United Nations Recommendations for the 1980 Census*, Federal Institute for Population Research/WHO (eds.), 65–88.

Rodgers, A. (1982), 'Parameterized Multistate Population Dynamics', IIASA Working Paper WP-82-125, IIASA, Laxenburg.

Rodgers, R. H. (1964), 'Toward a Theory of Family Development', *Journal of Marriage and the Family*, 26, 262–270.

—— (1977), 'The Family Life Cycle Concept: Past, Present and Future', in J. Cuisenier (ed.) *Le cycle de la vie familiale*, Mouton, Paris, 39–57.

Ryder, N. B. (1978), 'Methods in Measuring the Family Life Cycle', in *International Population Conference Mexico 1977*, Vol. 4, Liège, 219–26.

Schoen, R. (1975), 'Constructing Increment–Decrement Life Tables', *Demography*, 12, May, 313–24.

Schoen, R. and W. Urton, (1977), 'Marriage, Divorce and Mortality', in *International Population Conference Mexico 1977*, Vol. 1, IUSSP, Liège, 311–32.

Schwarz, K. (1979), 'Ehen im April 1977 nach dem Einkommen des Mannes', *Wirtschaft und Statistik*, 3, 170–4.

Sorokin, P. A., C. C. Zimmermann, and C. J. Galpin, (1931), *A Systematic Source Book in Rural Sociology*, Vol. II, University of Minnesota Press, Minneapolis.

Statistical Indices of Family Health (1976): Report of a WHO Study Group, *Technical Report Series* 587, WHO, Geneva.

Statistisches Bundesamt (1969), *Lebenslauf einer Generation* (aufgrund von Tafelberechnungen 1960/62), (by Schwarz, K.), Fachserie A, Bevölkerung und Kultur, Reihe 2, Natürliche Bevölkerungsbewegung, Sonderbeitrag, Kohlhammer, Stuttgart, Mainz.

Steger, A. (1980), *Haushalte und Familien bis zum Jahr 2000*, Schriftenreihe/Sonderforschungsbereich 3 of the Universities of Frankfurt and Mannheim, Mikroanalytische Grundlagen der Gesellschaftspolitik, Vol. 3, Campus, Frankfurt/Main.

Trost, J. (1977), 'The Family Life Cycle: A Problematic Approach', in J. Cuisenier (ed.) *Le cycle de vie familiale*, Mouton, Paris.

Uhlenberg, P. R. (1969), 'A Study of Cohort Life Cycles: Cohorts of Native Born Massachusetts Women, 1830–1920', *Population Studies*, 23, 3, 407–20.

—— (1974), 'Cohort Variations in Family Life Cycle Experiences of US Females', *Journal of Marriage and the Family*, 36, 2, 284–92.

United Nations (1973), *The Determinants and Consequences of Population Trends: New Summary of Findings on Interaction of Demographic, Economic and Social Factors*, Vol. 1, Population Studies, No. 50 St/SOA/SER.A/50, UN, Department of Economic and Social Affairs, New York.

United Nations (ed.) (1975), *The Population Debate: Dimensions and Perspectives; Papers of the World Population Conference Bucarest, 1974*, Vol. II, UN, New York.

Wachter, K. H., E. A. Hammel, and P. Laslett, (1978), *Statistical Studies of the Historical Social Structure*, Academic Press, New York.

Weed, J. A. (1980), 'National Estimates of Marriage Dissolution and Survivorship: United States', *Vital and Health Statistics*, Series 3, Analytical Studies, 19.

WHO (ed.) (1978), *Health and the Family*, WHO, Geneva.

Young, C. M. (1977), *The Family Life Cycle*, Australian Family Formation Project Monograph No. 6, The Australian National University Press, Canberra.

—— (1982), 'Mortality and the Family Life Cycle in Australia', in *Health and the Family Life Cycle*, Federal Institute of Population Research, WHO, eds., 431–80.

5 The Statistical Measurement of the Family Life Cycle*

GUSTAV FEICHTINGER

Technical University, Vienna, Austria

Introduction

The previous chapter noted that a central focus of research in family demography is the measurement of the family life cycle. The purpose of the present chapter is to summarize a methodological framework by which the *timing and the structure of the family life cycle* can be estimated.

An obvious way to investigate the family life cycle is to follow up a marriage cohort with respect to all relevant changes of characteristics (births, death of the spouse, divorce etc.). Through the registration of events and the duration between them, estimates of statistical measures describing the process can be obtained. Based on these statistics a mathematical model of the family life cycle is to be developed. Such a model has certain advantages. First, it enables us to study the influences of vital processes on the life cycle. Moreover, a formal model allows to calculate a complete description of the life cycle process on the basis of partial informations. Finally, using a mathematical framework helps to avoid dangerous pitfalls in the measurement of the family life cycle patterns.

There are many possibilities to calculate erroneous measures of the intensity and the tempo of the life cycle, and indeed some of these mistakes occur in the literature. Let us mention two examples of wrong estimates. Firstly, it is obviously not correct to calculate the average period of widowhood as the difference of the (further) life expectancies of wife and husband (see also Myers, 1959). Secondly, and more important, the differences between successive means of ages or durations are meaningless, since the succession of averages applies to a continually changing set of persons. It is, for example, not correct to determine the mean duration of marriage at first birth as the difference between the age at first (legal) birth and the age at marriage, sinc both ages refer to different universes of persons.

A basic conceptual framework of the nuclear family is the six phase model (described in Chapter 4 by Höhn) and going back to Paul Glick (see, e.g., Glick and Parke, 1965). Our main objective is to derive correct estimates for

* For helpful remarks and suggestions I am grateful to Wolfgang Lutz, Richard Gisser, and Alois Haslinger.

time pattern and the structure of such a life cycle. However, the *limitations* of the above model should be stressed. First, to simplify the analysis divorce and remarriage is excluded from consideration. Second, the model assumes that there is no child mortality and a fixed age at departure (marriage) of children from home. Third, the life cycle concept is restricted to births, i.e. the distribution of families according to their *surviving* children is not considered here (cf. Höhn, 1982, 67).

Thus, although the simplified family life cycle concept as used in the following is highly questionable, it provides a starting point to study demographic processes in the family on a cohort basis. We should, however, keep in mind, that for a more detailed analysis more sophisticated models must be constructed. The multistate life table analysis described by Willekens in Chapter 7 provides a suitable framework to analyse such models.

This chapter is organized as follows. In Section 1 some possibilities of measurement of the *first marriage* phenomenon are briefly discussed. Moreover, it contains a full analysis of the impact of *mortality* on the life cycle of the family. Here we deal with (dissolution specific) marriage duration, probabilities and periods of widowhood, and their dependence on survival rates. The third section provides some ideas on how to include *fertility* into the life cycle concept on a parity-specific basis. Finally, some concluding remarks, e.g. on divorce, remarriage etc., are made and some extensions of the basic model are mentioned. All analytical expressions are illustrated by Austrian data.

1 Marriage and Widowhood

1.1 The Basic Model

Men and women are born and get married, or eventually die single. Neglecting divorce as a cause of marital dissolution, a marriage persists until the death of one of the spouses. To measure the timing and the intensity of marriage and widowhood, a simple basic model is used (see Figure 5.1) where the life cycle is followed up until the death of the surviving spouse. Divorces and remarriages are — at this stage of the work — not taken into account.

1.2 Family Formation: First Marriage

The basic instruments for analysing the first marriage phenomenon are nuptiality tables. Since there is a wellknown literature on this subject (see, e.g., Shryock and Siegel, 1976, Feichtinger, 1979), the description of decrement tables for single persons is omitted. However, for most countries, nuptiality tables are rarely calculated. In what follows, we shall show how cohort nuptiality can be assessed by using only age specific proportions of

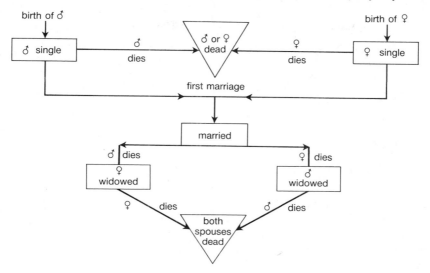

Figure 5.1 State diagram of a basic model for the nuptiality/marriage dissolution/widowhood process

Explanation: Transient states are distinguished by rectangles, absorbing ones by triangles. Direct transitions between states are marked by arrows and demographic events which cause these transitions; ō denotes the husband and ♀ his wife.

Source: Feichtinger and Hansluwka (1977).

single persons. Starting from a sufficiently long series of successive census data on age, sex and marital status, Hajnal (1953) and Ryder (1961) have calculated the *Proportion Ever Married* by a limit age, say 50, and the *Mean Age at first Marriage* for marriages occurring by age 50. The first quantity measures the quantum (intensity) of nuptiality and is abbreviated as PEM, whereas the second one provides an indicator for the (average) timing of first marriage (denoted as MAM).

Given successive censuses for a country, appropriate intercensal interpolations were used for obtaining quinquennial proportions single in five year age groups. Let $_5 s_{5a}(t)$ be the proportion single in age group $(5a, 5a + 5)$ at time t ($a = 2, 3, \ldots$); then the survival probability for single persons from one five year age group to the next for the time interval $t = (t, t + 5)$ may be found by

$$_5 P_{5a}(\bar{t}) = {_5 s_{5a + 5}}(t + 5)/{_5 s_{5a}}(t).$$

This computation rests on the assumption that movements of the cohort attributable to mortality and migration do not affect the proportions single, an assumption usually not distorting inferences to any substantial degree.

With these survival probabilities it is possible to compute PEM and MAM in the following manner. The proportion single in age group $(5a, 5a + 5)$ for the birth cohort born in $\bar{t}$ is provided by cumulating the $_5P_{5a}$'s by cohorts:

$$_5S_{5a}(\bar{t}) = {}_5P_{10}\overline{(t+15)}......{}_5P_{5(a-1)}\overline{(t+5a)}.$$

From these probabilities to survive in the single state one proceeds to calculating

$$A(\bar{t}) = {}_5S_{15}(\bar{t}) + ... + {}_5S_{45}(\bar{t}), \text{ and } B(\bar{t}) = {}_5S_{45}(\bar{t}) + {}_5S_{50}(\bar{t})$$

and finally one obtains

$$PEM(\bar{t}) = \frac{2-B(\bar{t})}{2}, \quad MAM(\bar{t}) = 10\frac{3+A(\bar{t})-5B(\bar{t})}{2-B(\bar{t})}. \quad (5.1)$$

Following Ryder (1961) the measures for the last cohorts are calculated on the assumption that the age-specific experience beyond 1970 is identical to that observed in 1965–70. Therefore the results for recent cohorts presented in Table 5.1 are more or less artificial.

Table 5.1   Indices of cohort nuptiality for Austria: PEM (in %) and MAM (in years)

Birth period	Females		Males	
	PEM	MAM	PEM	MAM
1880–1885	82.9	27.3	88.1	30.6
1885–1890	82.7	27.2	88.8	30.4
1890–1895	83.3	27.3	89.5	30.4
1895–1900	84.9	27.6	90.4	30.5
1900–1905	86.2	27.6	90.9	30.6
1905–1910	87.2	27.3	91.6	30.2
1910–1915	88.2	26.7	92.5	29.4
1915–1920	88.7	25.5	93.2	28.6
1920–1925	88.9	25.1	93.6	27.8
1925–1930	89.9	24.5	93.5	27.1
1930–1935	91.4	24.0	93.3	26.8
1935–1940	92.5	23.6	93.5	26.6
1940–1945	93.5	23.1	93.9	26.2
1945–1950	94.3	22.6	94.3	25.9

Source: Feichtinger and Hansluwka (1977).

Using the age/sex-specific marital status classification of the Austrian censuses from 1880 until 1971, Table 5.1 is obtained.

The results provide further evidence for the observation made by Hajnal, Ryder, and others that for both sexes PEM has been rising markedly and that MAM has been falling to a substantial extent. The interpretation of the last birth cohorts requires reservations since their nuptiality experience is still not completed. There is a high positive correlation between the female and the male MAM. We further observe an increase of PEM with decreasing MAM for males and females, respectively.

1.3 Family Dissolution: Widowhood

1.3.1 Dissolution Probabilities and Mean Duration of Marriage

Let u be the age of the groom and v the age of the bride at first marriage. Let further x denote the marriage duration in completed years. Following Feichtinger and Hansluwka (1977) we define an (u, v, x)-marriage as a couple marrying with u and v years, respectively, whose marriage lasts x years at the time of observation. Excluding divorce as a cause of dissolution, a (u, v, x)-marriage has three possibilities during the marriage duration interval $x- = (x, x + 1)$, namely (a) to be dissolved by death of the husband or (b) of his wife or (c) to survive at least until duration $x + 1$.

We generally assume that the husband and his wife are independently exposed to the risk of mortality. Moreover we suppose that mortality is independent of the family status. The life table functions for females are denoted as usual by l_a, d_a, L_a, e°_a, whereas those for males are indicated by a stroke: l'_a, d'_a, L'_a, $e^{\circ'}_a$.

To calculate the probability of (i) we have to add the probabilities of the event that the husband dies in x- and his wife survives (at least) until $x + 1$ and of the event that both partners die in x- but the husband before his wife. Assuming that this occurs in approximately half of the cases the probability of (i) is given by

$$\frac{d'_{u+x}}{l'_{u+x}} \frac{l_{v+x+1}}{l_{v+x}} + \frac{1}{2} \frac{d'_{u+x}}{l'_{u+x}} \frac{d_{v+x}}{l_{v+x}} = \frac{d'_{u+x}}{l'_{u+x}} \frac{L_{v+x}}{l_{v+x}}. \tag{5.2}$$

A proof of the formulas for the dissolution probabilities is given in the theory of competing risks (see Feichtinger, 1979, Sect. 2.5).

Because of independence of female and male mortality the joint survival probability of a $(u, v, 0)$-couple to marriage duration x is $(l'_{u+x}/l'_u)(l_{v+x}/l_v)$. From this probability for a $(u, v, 0)$-marriage to be dissolved eventually by death of the husband can be calculated as

$$P_1 = \sum d'_{u+x} L_{v+x} / l'_u l_v, \tag{5.3}$$

where here and in the following the summation runs from $x = 0$ to $\min(w' - u, w - v)$, w' and w denoting the maximal age in the life table for males and females, respectively. Analogous to (5.3) the proportion of husbands who survive their wives is given by

$$P_2 = \sum L'_{u+x} d_{v+x} / l'_u l_v. \tag{5.4}$$

The conditional average potential[1] marriage duration given that the wife survives the husband is given by

$$M_1 = \sum [(x + 1/2) d'_{u+x} l_{v+x+1} + (x + 1/3) d'_{u+x} d_{v+x}/2] / \sum d'_{u+x} L_{v+x}. \tag{5.5}$$

---

[1] Since divorce is excluded as a dissolution cause, we may speak of 'potential' marriage duration.

The mean potential duration of marriage under the condition that the wife dies first is given by

$$M_2 = \sum [(x + 1/2)l'_{u+x+1}d_{v+x} + (x + 1/3)d'_{u+x}d_{v+x}/2]/ \sum L'_{u+x}d_{v+x}. \quad (5.6)$$

The mean potential duration of marriage is obtained as weighted arithmetic mean of M_1 and M_2, the eventual marriage dissolution probabilities being the weights:

$$M = \frac{1}{l'_u l_v} \sum [(x + 1/2)d'_{u+x}l_{v+x+1} + l'_{u+x+1}d_{v+x}) + (x + 1/3)d'_{u+x}d_{v+x}] \quad (5.7)$$

$$= \frac{1}{l'_u l_v} \left[\sum l'_{u+x}l_{v+x} - \tfrac{1}{6} \sum d'_{u+x}d_{v+x} \right] - \tfrac{1}{2}.$$

Since divorce is disregarded, the mean potential marriage duration M is equal to the further joint expectation of life, i.e. the average time a u years old man can expect to live *jointly* with his wife v years old.

1.3.2 Periods of Widowhood The measurement of the period of widowhood is by no means unique. There are four different indicators of the mean duration of widowhood depending on information on the duration and the dissolution of the marriage. More precisely, we should also speak of 'potential' duration of widowhood because divorce is not taken into account.

First, the average duration of widowhood of a wife (husband) whose husband (wife) dies at a marriage duration of $v + x (u + x)$ years is given by her (his) further life expectancy $e°_{v+x} (e'_{u+x})$. Note that this measure refers to the time of the death of the other spouse.

Secondly, at the time of marriage the mean duration of widowhood of a v years old woman under the condition that her husband dies first is to be ascertained as

$$W_1 = \sum [(1/2 + e°_{v+x+1})d'_{u+x}l_{v+x+1} + d'_{u+x}d_{v+x}/6]/ \sum d'_{u+x}L_{v+x}. \quad (5.8)$$

If the husband dies in x- but his wife survives to $x + 1$, the mean duration of widowhood is half a year in x- plus $e°_{v+x+1}$ years starting at $v + x + 1$. If both partners die in x-, the mean period of widowhood is $1/3$ year. Since the husband dies in x- before his wife dying also in x- with probability $d'_{u+x}d_{v+x}/2$ we obtain (5.8). Similarly, we have for the mean period of conditional widowerhood

$$W_2 = \sum [(1/2 + e°'_{u+x+1})l'_{u+x+1}d_{v+x} + d'_{u+x}d_{v+x}/6] \sum L'_{u+x}d_{v+x}. \quad (5.9)$$

Clearly, the mean age at widow(er)hood is provided by

$$v + M_1, u + M_2, \quad (5.10)$$

respectively. From this we can determine the surviving partner's mean age at death by adding the mean period of conditional widow(er)hood:

$$\text{Surviving partner's} \atop \text{mean age at death} = \begin{cases} v + M_1 + W_1 & \text{if the husband dies first} \quad (5.11) \\ u + M_2 + W_2 & \text{if the wife dies first} \quad (5.12) \end{cases}$$

Thirdly, there is a second possibility to measure the duration of widowhood at the time of marriage. If we have no information which spouse dies first the average period the woman of a $(u, v, 0)$-couple can expect to survive as widow is obtained as weighted mean,

$$\overline{W}_1 = W_1 P_1 + 0.P_2 = \frac{1}{l'_u l_v} \sum [(1/2 + e^\circ_{v+x+1}) d'_{u+x} l_{v+x+1} + d'_{u+x} d_{v+x}/6].$$

$$(5.13)$$

Symmetrically, the mean (absolute) duration of widowerhood is given by

$$\overline{W}_2 = 0.P_1 + W_2 P_2 = \frac{1}{l'_u l_v} \sum [(1/2 + e^{\circ'}_{u+x+1}) l'_{u+x+1} d_{v+x} + d'_{u+x} d_{v+x}/6].$$

$$(5.14)$$

$\overline{W}_1$ and $\overline{W}_2$ have an intuitively appealing relationship with the mean duration of marriage, M, and the life expectancies at the time of marriage ($e^{\circ'}_u$ and e°_v):

$$e^\circ_v = M + \overline{W}_1, \; e^{\circ'}_u = M + \overline{W}_2. \qquad (5.15)$$

A proof is given in Feichtinger (1977); see also Chiang and Chiang (1982).

Finally, the expected duration of widowhood at the time of marriage can be calculated as *weighted* sum of the mean periods of conditional widowhood of the wife and husband, where the weights are the proportion of wives (or husbands) who survive their spouse:

$$W = W_1 P_1 + W_2 P_2$$

$$= \frac{1}{l'_u l_v} \sum \left[\left(\tfrac{1}{2} + e^\circ_{v+x+1} \right) d'_{u+x} l_{v+x+1} + \left(\tfrac{1}{2} + e^\circ_{u+x+1} \right) l'_{u+x+1} d_{v+x} \right.$$

$$\left. + \tfrac{1}{3} d'_{u+x} d_{v+x} \right]. \qquad (5.16)$$

Using (5.8), (5.9) and (5.10), respectively, the mean duration of widowhood W may also be written as

$$W = \overline{W}_1 + \overline{W}_2 = e^{\circ'}_u + e^\circ_v - 2M. \qquad (5.17)$$

It is intuitively clear that the average duration of the family life cycle, *FLC*, is equal to the mean duration of marriage, M, plus the expected duration of widowhood. Which among the various periods of widowhood should be used to estimate the duration *FLC*? Since W defined in (5.16) is the weighted mean of all possible periods of widowhood that either the husband or the wife of a married couple may experience during their lifetime, with the corresponding probabilities used as weights, the conceptually correct period of widowhood is the duration of widowhood, W, and we have

$$FLC = M + W. \tag{5.18}$$

Using (5.17) and writing M in the appealing form $\overset{\circ}{e}_{uv}$ (further joint life expectation of a $(u, v, 0)$–couple) we obtain from (5.18)

$$FLC = \overset{\circ}{e}''_u + \overset{\circ}{e}_v - \overset{\circ}{e}_{uv}. \tag{5.19}$$

1.3.3 Numerical illustration The indicators of the family life cycle based on life tables and mean ages at marriage are illustrated by Austrian data and a selected birth cohort in Table 5.2.

Table 5.2   Measures of the marriage/marital dissolution part of the family life cycle for an Austrian cohort born between 1920 and 1930

Indicator	Wife		Husband
Mean age at first marriage (v, u)	25		28
Further expectation of life at marriage	51.9		42.3
Probability to survive the spouse	0.73		0.27
M_1		38.9	
M_2		38.7	
M		38.8	
Mean age at widow(er)hood $(v + M_1, u + M_2)$	63.9		66.7
Mean period of conditional widow(er)hood (W_1, W_2)	17.9		12.7
Surviving partner's mean age at death	81.8		79.4
Mean period of absolute widow(er)hood $(\overline{W}_1, \overline{W}_2)$	13.0		3.5
Expected duration of widowhood (W)		16.5	
Expected duration of the family life cycle $(M + W)$		55.3	

Source: Feichtinger and Hansluwka (1977).

Since the cohort life tabels available for Austria have been calculated by a rather primitive procedure, the computation of the corresponding measures yields only crude estimations. Our aim is primarily, however, to provide a conceptual clarification of the calculation of statistical measures for the family life cycle rather than an exact picture of the underlying demographic processes.

The 'wrong' calculation of the average period of widowhood by means of $\overset{\circ}{e}_v - \overset{\circ}{e}''_u$ mentioned by Myers (1959) yields 9.6 years being different from the other indicators measuring the duration of widowhood adequately. Similarly, the expectation of life of the husband at the time of marriage is sometimes added to the age of the wife for calculating the age at which the wife will become widow: $v + \overset{\circ}{e}''_u$. For the cohort considered, this procedure gives $25 + 42.3 = 67.3$ years which is quite different from the correct mean age at widowhood of a 25-year-old bride, namely 63.9 years. Note that $v + \overset{\circ}{e}''_u$ is meaningless since it includes deaths of husbands whose wives had pre-deceased them, with the wives' ages taken as what they would have been if death had not previously occurred (Myers, 1959).

The dissolution behaviour of further Austrian cohorts is described in Feichtinger and Hansluwka (1977). Summarizing we can say that the historical decrease in mortality has had a decisive influence on the tempo and the quantum of marriage dissolution as well as on patterns of widowhood. The joint life expectation of the partners has increased enormously, and widowhood now occurs at a substantially later age. The proportion of marriages dissolved by death of husband as well as the surviving spouse's mean age at death both have increased considerably.

1.4 Structure of the Life Cycle with Respect to Marriage and Death

Until now we have considered the time of the family life cycle process, especially with respect to mortality and nuptiality. The succession of demographic events in women's lives produces different patterns of family cycles. By putting together various events and the timing of these events in a predetermined way it is possible to define cycle patterns. To assess the structure of the family life cycle one may calculate the distribution of women who experience any cycle of given classification.

We compute the distribution of families according to states occupied at age fifty (after that age first marriages are very rare and the reproductive process is completed) using a special classification; however, it should be borne in mind that this classification does not really constitute a genuine classification of family life cycles, but rather portrays the marriage cycles as a basis for studying reproductive performance as evidenced by its limitation to age 50, say, as cut-off point:

woman dies before age 15 (non-marriage abbreviated cycle)
woman survives to age 50 but never marries (non-marriage celibate cycle)
she marries but dies before age 50 (incomplete marriage cycle)
she marries, survives to age 50 but is divorced or widowed (truncated marriage cycle)
she survives to age 50 and is married (completed marriage cycle).

To assess time trends in the family life cycle structure of the Austrian population Feichtinger and Hansluwka (1977) have used cohort life tables and the marital status classification of past censuses. Thus decennial birth cohorts are followed up and their members are classified by marital status. This can be done by transforming age-specific rates of marital status from successive censuses into cohort data. Although the method is admittedly crude (e.g. the migration component is neglected and mortality is assumed to be independent of marital status) some qualitative assessments of the structure of the assumed family life cycle patterns are possible. Assuming that age-specific proportions of statuses beyond 1971 are identical with those observed in 1971, the following crude orientation has been calculated, permitting a first insight into changing patterns of marriage cycles.

Birth cohorts of l_0 women are reduced at each age according to the mortality schedule and the nuptiality experience corresponding to the

Table 5.3　Distribution (in percentages) of women according to marriage cycle stages for some Austrian birth cohorts between 1870 and 1970

Time	Early death			Survivors to age 50			
	Less than age 15	Less than age 50		Disrupted marriage		Currently married	Never married
		Never married	Ever married	Widowed	Divorced		
1870	42.1	6.3	9.1	6.0	0.9	28.1	7.5
1890	36.3	5.1	7.1	7.5	1.4	34.0	8.7
1910	27.7	2.9	4.7	9.9	2.8	43.9	8.0
1930	13.4	1.2	3.6	11.0	4.5	57.5	8.8
1950	7.2	0.6	2.8	12.0	4.9	62.8	9.7
1970	3.9	0.5	1.9	12.6	5.1	65.9	10.1

Source: Feichtinger and Hansluwka (1977).

various periods. Although some studies indicate that death rates are higher for single than married women, the mortality risk is assumed to be equal regardless of marital status because of the lack of an adequate statistical data basis.

Thus, the female data for calculating the numbers in Table 5.3 are as follows: abridged decennial cohort life tables from 1870 to 1970, age-specific rates of marital status in five year age groups in five year calendar intervals from 1890 to 1970.

Let 1_a denote the survivors at age a for an arbitrary birth cohort, and s_a the proportion single in the age group $(a, a + 5)$ for $a = 0, 5, 10, \ldots, 50$. Applying these proportions to the stock of survivors the number of single persons at age a is obtained:

$$l_a^* = 1_a s_a.$$

This yields the number of ever-married survivors as

$$1_a^{em} = 1_a - 1_a^*.$$

Since the population of ever-married females consists of currently married, widowed, and divorced survivors, the currently married survivors 1_a can be determined by

$$1_a^{cm} = 1_a^{em} - 1_a^w - 1_a^d.$$

Herein the number of widows and divorced surviving females at age a is given by

$$1_a^w = 1_a^{em}\omega_a \text{ and } 1_a^d = 1_a^{em}\delta_a,$$

with age-specific proportions widowed and divorced, ω_a and δ_a, respectively. By using this approach it is possible to calculate the family status of survivors at age 50. Thus the last four columns of Table 5.3 are provided by

$$l_{50}^w = l_{50}^{em}\omega_{50}, \quad l_{50}^d = l_{50}^{em}\delta_{50}, \quad l_{50}^{em} = l_{50}^{em} - l_{50}^w - l_{50}^d, \quad l_{50}^* = l_{50}s_{50}$$
$$\text{with } l_{50}^{em} = l_{50} - l_{50}^*.$$

Clearly, the first column is given by $l_0 - l_{15}$, and the sum of the second and third by $l_{15} - l_{50}$. To ascertain column 2 and 3 of Table 5.3 separately, namely the females dying single between 15 and 50, and those dying ever married in the same age interval, the probability of first marriage, $_5p_a^m$, during the 5-year interval $(a, a + 5)$ is needed. Omitting the details for the estimation procedure of $_5p_a^m$ we refer to Feichtinger and Hansluwka (1977, 65–6); see also Kantrow (1976). Defining $_5p_a$ as the 5-year probability of dying in the age interval $(a, a + 5)$ assumed to be independent of marital status, we may conclude that the number of females dying single between age 15 and 50 is yielded by

$$\sum_{a=15}^{45} l_a^* \cdot {}_5q_a(1 - {}_5p_a^m/2),$$

and the females dying ever married in the age interval (15, 50) are then provided by

$$\sum_{a=15}^{45} (l_a^{em} \cdot {}_5q_a + l_a^* \cdot {}_5p_a^m \cdot {}_5q_a/2).$$

The sum of both these expressions is $l_{15} - l_{50}$ as it should be.

By calculating the probability of various events occurring from one age to the next (i.e. probabilities of first marriage, of widowhood and divorce) it is possible to assess the timing of structural changes of the family life cycle as well as the pace. By the age of 50 the same numbers of women may have experienced one special family cycle but they could have arrived at this point through different amounts of time in the successive stages of the family life cycle.

2 Family Extension: Fertility

In the fertility sector of the family life cycle the reproductive behaviour of (marriage) cohorts of women is analysed. To draw an undisturbed picture of pure fertility, the competing risks (mortality, divorce, migration) must be eliminated.

2.1 Parity-specific Reproduction by Duration of Marriage

The purpose of this section is to measure legitimate fertility classified by birth order. More specifically, our aim is to study the speed with which the family is built within the *first marriage*. However, there is no necessity to restrict the following analysis to a first marriage model. With appropriately defined variables the formulas derived below can also apply to an *ever-married* group of women or even to a birth cohort (with marriage defined as parity 0). Moreover, the analysis of Section 2.1 could apply to real as well to synthetic cohorts.

Let us assume that for a cohort of women marrying at a given age the following information is given:

(i) the parity distribution at marriage,
(ii) the rate of legitimate live births, tabulated by duration of marriage x and birth order i, denoted by $b_i(x)$, i.e. the number of births divided by the number of women at risk.

Note that in the following, x can refer to the duration of marriage either in completed or in exact years. Following Farid (1974) we consider only live births. A married woman is able to have only one child in any one year, i.e. a multiple birth is counted as one birth.

Assume that a marriage cohort of l_0 women is exposed to the reproductive behaviour as described by (i), (ii). Let us follow them through their reproductive period by classifying them according to their parity in steps of one year. Considering five parity classes $i = 0, 1, 2, 3, 4$ and more, the distribution for any given marriage duration, x say, is defined by the vector

$$\mathbf{d}(x) = (d_0(x), \ldots, d_4(x)),$$

where $d_i(x)$ is the number of women at exact duration x with i children, and x runs from zero to x_m such that $v + x_m$ is the age at the end of the reproductive period. Since mortality and migration are excluded, it holds that

$$l_0 = \sum_{i=0}^{4} d_i(x)$$

To determine $\mathbf{d}(x+1)$ from $\mathbf{d}(x)$ we introduce the so-called birth order probabilities $\pi_{i+1}(x)$ which are defined as probabilities that a woman of parity i at exact duration x has a birth in the year $x\text{-} = (x, x + 1)$ of marriage:

Defining the matrix $\Pi(x)$ of transition probabilities as

$$\Pi(x) = \begin{vmatrix} 1 - \pi_1(x) & \pi_1(x) & 0 & 0 & 0 \\ 0 & 1 - \pi_2(x) & \pi_2(x) & 0 & 0 \\ 0 & 0 & 1 - \pi_3(x) & \pi_3(x) & 0 \\ 0 & 0 & 0 & 1 - \pi_4(x) & \pi_4(x) \\ 0 & 0 & 0 & 0 & 1 \end{vmatrix}$$

the parity distributions at successive marriage durations are recursively connected as follows

$$\mathbf{d}(x+1) = \mathbf{d}(x)\Pi(x). \tag{5.20}$$

Starting from an initial parity distribution $\mathbf{d}(0)$ and applying successively (5.20) we finally obtain the completed parity distribution $\mathbf{d} = (d_0, \ldots, d_4)$ at the maximal duration of marriage, i.e. $d_i = d_i(x_m)$.

Note that d_i denotes the number of women in the cohort who stop child-bearing after the i-th live birth, i.e. who have the completed parity i. From l_0 and d_i we derive the function l_i by

$$l_{i+1} = l_i - d_i,$$

representing the number of women out of the original l_0 persons who have i live births.

To calculate the parity-specific and marriage duration-dependent prob-abilities $\pi_{i+1}(x)$ we use the information available in (ii) and obtain

$$\pi_{i+1}(x) = \frac{b_{i+1}(x)l_0}{d_i(x)} \tag{5.21}$$

(see Farid, 1974, and Haslinger and Feichtinger, 1978, for more detailed explanations of this procedure).

For a given marriage duration the marriage duration-specific parity progression ratio, $p_i(x)$, is defined as the proportion of women of parity i who have ever progressed to parity $i + 1$ by the given duration. It is easily seen that

$$p_i(x) = \frac{\sum\limits_{j \geq i+1} d_j(x)}{\sum\limits_{j \geq i} d_j(x)}$$

for all x and i.

The mean length of the interval between marriage and all i-th births may be calculated as

$$x_i = \sum_{x=0}^{x_m} (x + 1/2)b_i(x) / \sum_{x=0}^{x_m} b_i(x). \tag{5.22}$$

Note that x denotes here the number of years of completed marriage duration running from 0 to the $w - v$.

To assess the global fertility, i.e. aggregated over parity, we simply set

$$b(x) = \sum_i b_i(x). \tag{5.23}$$

Then, the average number of births is given by

$$TFR = \sum_x b(x). \tag{5.24}$$

Note that (5.24) may be also denoted as the total fertility rate within first marriage. It measures the quantum of pure legitimate fertility. It is easy to see that TFR is the expected value of the completed parity distribution $\mathbf{d} = (d_i)$:[2]

$$\text{TFR} = \frac{1}{l_0} \sum_i \text{id}_i. \tag{5.25}$$

Furthermore

$$\bar{x} = \sum_x (x + 1/2)b(x)/\Sigma b(x), \tag{5.26}$$

provides an indicator of the global average duration of marriage at birth of all children under the assumption that the risk of mortality and divorce has been eliminated.

Clearly, it is now possible to measure the intensity of marital fertility at a specific parity i by

$$\text{TFR}_i = \sum_x b_i(x). \tag{5.27}$$

Obviously, we have $\text{TFR} = \sum_i \text{TFR}_i$. It holds that $\text{TFR}_i = \frac{1}{l_0} \sum_{j \geq i} d_j$, and

$$p_i = \text{TFR}_{i+1}/\text{TFR}_i \tag{5.28}$$

for all $i = 0, 1, \ldots, 4$. Moreover, we have $\text{TFR} = \sum_i \text{TFR}_i =$

$\frac{1}{l_0} \sum_i \sum_{j \geq i} d_j = \frac{1}{l_0} \sum_i \text{id}_i$, and $\text{TFR} = p_0 + p_0 p_1 + p_0 p_1 p_2 + p_0 p_1 p_2 p_3$.

Furthermore, the mean family size of fertile women is computed by dividing the mean family size of all women of the cohort by the parity progression ratio, i.e. by the probability that a woman has at least one child: TFR/p_0.

Finally, the speed of the reproductive career may be described by cumulating the fertility rates over varying marriage durations, i.e. we define

$$\text{TFR}_i(y) = \sum_{x=0}^{y} b_i(x), \quad \text{TFR}(y) = \sum_{x=0}^{y} b(x). \tag{5.29}$$

To illustrate the measurement of the tempo of fertility as indicated we use data of the Austrian microcensus. In June 1976 a one per cent sample of the

---

[2] Note that (5.25) is only accurate for infinite maximal parity. For a finite number (here: five) of parity cases, formula (5.25) slightly underestimates the true total fertility rate. The numerical difference is negligible.

ever married female population between 16 and 60 years (i.e. 20 000 women) was interviewed on their number of children and the birth dates (fertility histories). It can be shown (see, e.g., Feichtinger, 1979, Chap. 2.6 for details) that such *retrospective* data describe the *pure* fertility pattern, i.e. the reproductive behaviour which is *not* disturbed by divorce and mortality of the husband. However, as is well known, these disturbing demographic phenomena are eliminated in a retrospective framework only if mortality and divorce are *not selective* with respect to fertility, an assumption which is satisfied only approximately.

To obtain a specific picture of marital fertility we take into consideration only the fertility of ever-married women in their first marriage. Finally, it is convenient to follow up marriage sub-cohorts according to the age of women at marriage. For simplicity, premarital births have been omitted, i.e. $d(0) = (1, 0, 0, 0, 0)$. We have selected the female cohort of first marriages in 1951/55 with the age at marriage between 20 and 24.

Since births of an order higher than four are not shown in Table 5.4, for larger duration x $b(x)$ is slightly greater than $\sum_i b_i(x)$. The sums of the columns in Table 5.4 are the parity-specific total marital fertility rates, TFR_i.

Table 5.4 Parity-specific fertility rates by duration of marriage (per 1000 women in the respective duration of marriage) of the first marriage cohort 1951/55 of Austrian women (age at marriage 20–24)

Marriage duration (in completed years)	Parity				
	1	2	3	4	All births
0	406	0	0	0	406
1	185	73	0	0	257
2	74	105	10	0	189
3	63	122	37	3	225
4	40	75	52	13	180
5	42	63	47	15	171
6	21	71	32	19	153
7	20	31	29	10	102
8	6	31	32	25	114
9	3	55	33	12	121
10	3	11	22	18	73
11	6	14	21	22	86
12	8	7	15	13	56
13	3	7	13	9	44
14	0	5	8	10	45
15	1	4	5	1	30
16	0	0	6	6	19
17	0	0	3	5	24
18	1	2	1	3	14
19	0	1	3	3	11
Total	882	677	369	187	2320

Source: Feichtinger (1979). Computed by A. Haslinger from data of the Austrian microcensus of June 1976.

According to (5.28) they can be used to determine the (completed) parity progression ratios yielding

$$p_0 = 0.88, \; p_1 = 0.77, \; p_2 = 0.54, \; p_3 = 0.51.$$

From Table 5.4 we obtain according to (5.21) the birth order probabilities. Hence, according to (5.20) we successively get the parity distributions (see Table 5.5).

Table 5.5   Parity distributions according to duration of marriage for the first marriage cohort 1951/55 of Austrian women (age at marriage 20–24)

Marriage duration (in exact years)	Parity				
	0	1	2	3	4 and more
0	1000	0	0	0	0
1	594	406	0	0	0
2	410	518	73	0	0
3	335	487	168	10	0
4	272	428	253	44	3
5	231	394	275	84	16
6	189	373	290	116	30
7	168	323	330	130	49
8	148	312	331	149	60
9	142	288	330	155	85
14	118	216	322	184	159
19	116	208	311	181	184
20	116	206	309	182	187

Source: Feichtinger (1979).

Using Table 5.4 from (5.22) and (5.26) we obtain for the average marriage duration at birth of order i

$$x_1 = 2.3, \; x_2 = 5.4, \; x_3 = 7.9, \; x_4 = 10.0; \; \overline{x} = 5.5.$$

Furthermore, Table 5.6 shows the parity progression ratios for some selected durations of marriage.

Table 5.6   Marriage duration-specific parity progression ratios for the first marriage cohort 1951/55 of Austrian women (age at marriage 20–24)

Marriage duration (in exact years)	Parity			
	0	1	2	3
1	406	0	0	0
3	665	267	57	0
5	769	487	266	156
7	832	611	352	276
9	858	664	421	353
14	882	754	515	465
19	884	765	540	504
20	884	767	544	508

Source: Feichtinger (1979).

2.2 Measurement of Birth Intervals

It was mentioned before that for calculating unbiased birth intervals we may not simply take the differences between x_{i+1} and x_i, because x_i includes births of women that will not experience an additional birth. The correct method to calculate the mean birth interval t_i is as follows:

$$t_i = x_{i+1} - x_i^{i+1},\qquad\qquad(5.30)$$

where $i = 1, \ldots, m$ ($t_0 = x_1$; m denotes the highest parity class 'm and more births'). x_i^{i+1} stands for the mean duration of marriage at birth of order i for women *who experience at least one additional birth*. To derive this quantity we must have information on the reproductive career of a woman after her i-th birth, thus restricting this kind of analysis to *cohort* tables.

A more detailed analysis of the timing of the life cycle's reproductive part uses an additional variable $x_{i,j}$ which is explained as the mean duration of marriage of the i-th birth of those d_j women whose completed parity is j ($j = i, i + 1, \ldots, m$), (see also Rückert, 1975). Moreover, $x_{0,j} = 0$ for each j. According to this definition we have

$$x_i = \sum_{j=i}^{m} \frac{d_j}{l_i} x_{i,j}\qquad\qquad(5.31)$$

(see also Chiang and van den Berg, 1982; Feichtinger and Lutz, 1983). The weights are the probabilities that a woman in parity i will end up with j children. x_i^{i+1} can be expressed in terms of the $x_{i,j}$ by

$$x_i^{i+1} = \sum_{j=i+1}^{m} \frac{d_j}{l_{i+1}} x_{i,j}.\qquad\qquad(5.32)$$

By combining (5.30), (5.31) and (5.32) we obtain

$$t_i = \sum_{j=i+1}^{m} \frac{d_j}{l_{i+1}} (x_{i+1,j} - x_{i,j}) = x_{i+1} - \sum_{j=i+1}^{m} \frac{d_j}{l_{i+1}} x_{i,j}.\qquad(5.33)$$

Moreover, it is easily seen that $x_i^{i+1} < x_i < x_{i,i}$

Table 5.7 presents the mean duration of marriage at the i-th birth by completed parity for the first marriage cohort 1951/55 of Austrian women.[3]

Table 5.7 illustrates the fact that for each fixed i $x_{i,j}$ decreases with increasing final parity j. Empirically the $x_{i,j}$ can be estimated from birth histories of women already beyond reproductive age.

---

[3] Note the slightly changed universe with respect to Tables 5.4, 5.5 and 5.6. In Table 5.7 all ever-married women of the first marriage cohort are included without regard to divorce or widowhood. Moreover, all marital births are included, i.e. the fertility of remarriages is taken into consideration. Finally, the age at marriage has not been specified as in Tables 5.4–5.6.

Table 5.7   Mean duration of marriage at the i-th birth[1] by completed parity j ($x_{i,j}$) for the first marriage cohort 1951/55 of Austrian women[2]

Birth order i	Completed parity							Mean duration of marriage at i-th birth x_i
	0	1	2	3	4	5	6	
1		3.8	1.9	1.5	1.3	1.1	0.7	2.2
2			6.8	5.0	3.8	3.3	2.7	5.4
3				9.8	7.0	5.7	4.6	8.0
4					11.8	9.5	7.0	10.0
5						13.5	9.5	11.4
6							13.0	13.0
Completed marital parity distribution $100(d_i/l_0)$	14.4	23.1	28.5	17.4	8.5	4.1	3.9	100.0

[1] Only marital births are included
[2] All women of the first marriage cohort are included without regard to marital disruptions
Source: Microcensus June 1981 for Austria.
Calculation: W. Lutz.

This refined analysis of timing allows to quantify the magnitude of the error that is made when using the naive (wrong) estimator $t_i^* = x_{i+1} - x_i$ for calculating birth intervals.

Table 5.8 shows that error seems to be substantial.

Table 5.8   Calculation of birth intervals according to

i	correct formula t_i	wrong formula t_i^*	difference $t_i - t_i^*$
1	3.8	3.2	0.6
2	3.8	2.6	1.2
3	3.9	2.0	1.9
4	3.2	1.4	1.8
5	3.7	1.6	2.1

Another timing variable which is of special interest for the analysis of the family life cycle is the mean duration of marriage at last birth. It can be calculated as a weighted average of the conditional mean durations $x_{i,i}$ indicating duration at i-th birth *if it is the last one:*

$$x_1 + \epsilon_1 = \sum_{i=1}^{m} \frac{d_i}{l_1} x_{i,i} \qquad (5.34)$$

(see also Feichtinger, 1978, Feichtinger and Lutz, 1983). Thus the mean interval from the first to the last birth is

$$\epsilon_1 = \sum_{i=1}^{m} \frac{d_i}{l_1} (x_{i,i} - x_{1,i}) = \sum_{i=1}^{m} \frac{d_i}{l_1} x_{i,i} - x_1. \qquad (5.35)$$

For the first marriage cohort considered the application of formula (5.35) and Table 5.7 yields the following mean duration from the first to the last birth:

$$\epsilon_1 = 5.5 \text{ years.}$$

3 Concluding Remarks and Extensions

By combining the mortality and the fertility sector we obtain the time pattern of the family life cycle sketched in Figure 5.2

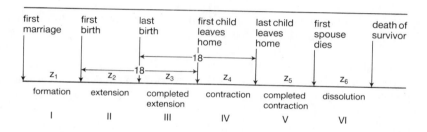

Figure 5.2 Time framework of a normal sequence of states in the family life cycle

Defining z_i as the mean duration of phase n ($n = $ I, . . ., IV; see Figure 5.2) we get according to (5.35), (5.7), (5.17)

$$z_1 = x_1, z_2 = \epsilon_1, z_3 = 18\text{-}\epsilon_1, z_4 = \epsilon_1, z_5 = M\text{-}x_1\text{-}\epsilon_1\text{-}18, z_6 = W.$$

According to (5.18) the total expected length of the family life cycle (in this basic model) is given by

$$\sum_{i=1}^{6} z_i = FLC = M + W.$$

For the birth cohort of Austrian females born between 1920 and 1930, and a corresponding first marriage cohort considered (1951/55) the following time pattern of the cycle is obtained (in years).

$$M = 38.3, W = 16.5, FLC = 55.3, v = 24,$$
$$z_1 = 2.3, z_2 = 5.5, z_3 = 12.5, z_4 = 5.5, z_5 = 13.0, z_6 = 16.5.$$

Using (life) table methods we have tried to draw a picture of the family life cycle of a birth cohort and a related first marriage cohort.

For this we have calculated the size and the composition of the family life cycle at different points in the cycle and the timing of various demographic events. Our primary aim was to provide sound calculation procedures for estimating various indicators of the tempo and the quantum of the life cycle. The derived formulas enable us to see how the constituting demographic processes (nuptiality, fertility and mortality) influence the family life cycle.

Let us briefly summarize the restrictive assumptions which we have made to obtain statistical estimations of the life cycle indicators.

First, divorce as cause of marriage dissolution and remarriage is not taken into consideration in the basic model. It would, however, be not very difficult to include divorce as dissolution cause of marriage. The corresponding scheme would be a marriage dissolution table (see, e.g., Feichtinger, 1979, Chap. 2.7). Second, and more important, it should be borne in mind that it has been assumed that there is no child mortality and that each child stays at home 18 years. Third, remarriage is excluded from consideration.

A further drawback is that the number and distribution of currently living children are not included in the basic model. Thus, the jointly lived years of the parents and their children being the basis for a correct estimation of the time-dependent size of the family (see Ryder, 1975) cannot be calculated. It should be mentioned that Höhn (1982) has tried to investigate the family structures (marriages by number of surviving children) according to the duration of marriage.

Finally, let us stress the importance of life table methods to assess the timing and quantum of the life cycle. More specifically, in this field a stochastic process framework would be suitable. The degree of mathematical sophistication of a formal model should depend on the aim of the study to be carried out and on the nature and the quality of the available data. Thus, the selection of the type of model must be a compromise between the questions to be answered by the model on the one hand and the availability of statistical data on the other. As pointed out by a series of authors the approach most convenient from a mathematical point of view for demographic models at the individual level is a stochastic process framework. The life table approach can be interpreted as a statistical estimation procedure for the random process concept behind it; see, e.g., Feichtinger (1971). The usual procedure to describe the demographic processes through means often only provides an insufficient picture of the variability of demographic behaviour. To assess the variability of the phenomena not only expected values but also variances and covariances should be calculated (cf. also Ryder, 1976).

References

Chiang, C. L., and B.J. van den Berg (1982), 'A Fertility Table for the Analysis of Human Reproduction', *Mathematical Biosciences* 62, 237–51.
Chiang, C. L. and R. Chiang (1982), 'The Family Life Cycle Revisited', in: *Health*

and the Family Life Cycle: Selected Studies on the Interaction between Mortality, the Family and its Life Cycle, Federal Institute for Population Research, Wiesbaden, and World Health Organization, Geneva, 89–101.

Farid, S. M. (1974), *The Current Tempo of Fertility in England and Wales*, Studies on Medical and Population Subjects No. 27, Office of Population Censuses and Surveys, London: Her Majesty's Stationery Office.

Feichtinger, G. (1971), *Stochastische Modelle demographischer Prozesse*. Lecture Notes in Operations Research and Mathematical Systems, Vol. 44, Springer, Berlin.

—— (1977), 'Methodische Probleme der Familienlebenszyklus-Statistik', in *Quantitatie Wirtschaftsforschung, Festschrift zum 60. Geburtstag W. Krelles*, Mohr, Tübingen, 171–183.

—— (1978), 'Cohort Trends in the Timing of the Family Life Cycle in Austria and West Germany', *Zeitschrift für Bevölkerungswissenschaft*, 2, 149–59.

—— (1979), *Demographische Analyse und populationsdynamische Modelle: Grundzüge der Bevölkerungsmathematik*, Springer, Vienna.

—— and H. Hansluwka (1977), 'The Impact of Mortality on the Life Cycle of the Family in Austria', *Zeitschrift für Bevölkerungswissenschaft*, 4, 51–79.

—— and W. Lutz (1983), 'Eine Fruchtbarkeitstafel auf Paritätsbasis', *Zeitschrift für Bevölkerungswissenschaft*, 3, 363–76.

Glick, P. C. and R. Parke, Jr. (1965), 'New Approaches in Studying the Life Cycle of the Family', *Demography*, 2, 187–202.

Hajnal, J. (1953), 'Age at Marriage and Proportion Marrying', *Population Studies*, 7, 111–36.

Haslinger, A. and G. Feichtinger (1978), *Analyse der Fertilitätsentwicklung in Österreich nach Heiratskohorten*, Schriftenreihe des Institute für Demographie der Österreichischen Akademie der Wissenschaften, Vol. 5, Vienna.

Höhn, C. (1982), *Der Familienzyklus — Zur Notwendigkeit einer Konzepterweiterung*, Boldt, Boppard am Rhein.

Kantrow, L. (1976), 'The Family Life Cycle as a Conceptual Framework: Methodological Issues and Problems', Background Report Prepared for UN/WHO — *Meeting on Family Life Cycle Methodology*, 16–18 November 1976, New York.

Myers, R. J. (1959), 'Statistical Measures in the Marital Life Cycle of Men and Women', in *Proceedings of the IUSSP Conference, Vienna*, 229–33.

Rückert, G,-R. (1975), 'Zur Bedeutung der Veränderungen der Geburtenabstände in der Bundesrepublik Deutschland', *Zeitschrift für Bevölkerungswissenschaft*, 1, 85–93.

Ryder, N. B. (1963), Measures of Recent Nuptiality in the Western World, *Proceedings of the IUSSP International Population Conference New York 1961*. Vol. 2, 293–301.

—— (1976), 'Methods in Measuring the Family Life Cycle', Session 2.2 of the Mexico Conference of the International Union for the Scientific Study of Population, *Newsletter No. 5*, 25–26, also appeared in *Proceedings of the International Population Conference Mexico 1977*, IUSSP (ed.), Vol. 4 (1978), Ordina, Liège, 219–226.

Shryock, H. S. and J. S. Siegel and Associates (Condensed edn. by E. G. Stockwell) (1976), *The Methods and Materials of Demography*, Academic Press, New York.

6 Reconsideration of a Model of Family Demography

NORMAN B. RYDER

Office of Population Research, Princeton, New Jersey, USA.

1 Introduction

Some years ago, I presented a macro-simulation model designed to pursue demographic analysis from a familial rather than individual perspective. (Ryder, 1975). Perhaps because of the novelty of the approach for that time, in a context of growing interest in family histories, the paper elicited more than the usual attention. Here I propose to reappraise that work, not at all to revisit the scene of a past triumph, but rather to identify what now seem to be major defects in the construction, and to suggest directions for their resolution.

The central purpose was to determine some demographic consequences, for family dimensions, of a decline in mortality without a decline in fertility. The format was an examination of appropriate parameters at the beginning, middle and end of a stylized demographic transition. The first of these, called inefficient equilibrium, was based on survival functions from a model life table representing high mortality, with fertility just sufficient for replacement in that context. In the second, called disequilibrium, survival was increased substantially but fertility remained the same as before. The end of the transition was efficient equilibrium, with low mortality and replacement fertility.

The main outputs of the model were based on the history of a typical family exposed to the predicated levels of fertility and mortality; the history was displayed in terms of the person-years spent by the various family members individually, and the joint person-years for various relational pairs among them, in successive phases of the history. To identify a beginning and end for the history, I defined a family as beginning with marriage and persisting so long as the couple survived and the wife was still of reproductive age, or so long as at least one parent and child survived with the child still in the family. Although I added to the list of common vital events the passage of the child out of the family at a specified young adult age, I failed to exploit that as an independent variable because I made it identical to the child's age at marriage, serving merely to signify that marriage was neolocal.

The one innovation in model inputs which might have deserved to be called familial rather than individual demography was a reformulation of the net reproduction rate. Conventionally that is a product-sum of age-specific fertility and survival for females. I partitioned the survival function into survival of parents subsequent to marriage, and survival of child from birth to marriage, because families begin at marriage whereas individuals begin at birth, and because the history of a family is based on a temporal alignment of the survival experience of parents and children. I also said: 'In order to distribute fertility over the course of the family life cycle, it has been decided to work with successive marital durations rather than ages, since the former seems a more appropriate temporal variable for family analysis.' Although the idea has merit, my execution there negated the possible advantages of the shift. Since I fixed the age of females at marriage at 20, there was merely a coding distinction between age and marital duration.

One virtue of partitioning was to make clear the general unacceptability of female survival as an appropriate element in the net reproduction rate. Since a woman needs a spouse for reproduction, the conventional practice of using individual female survival is appropriate only if all widows were to remarry immediately upon widowhood. With the polar opposite of this assumption — that no widows remarry — the proper value is joint survival of wives and husbands. Although the gross reproduction rate is often called a pure measure of fertility, it is pure only if there is complete remarriage. Otherwise a change in (male) mortality means a change in the proportion of females married and thus, *ceteris paribus*, a change in fertility. With high mortality, joint survival is much lower than individual survival, and its slope is much steeper. Because I assumed no remarriage of widows, my disequilibrium model had a very high growth rate.

The most important flaw in the work was my failure to take advantage of the construction which partitioned fertility into marriage and marital fertility, and address the important question of how much marriage there would be. My assumption was that there would be the same number of brides and grooms at the stipulated ages of marriage, regardless of the consequences of demographic change. One such consequence is an age distribution which yields insufficient grooms for brides, and accordingly less growth than inferred. One might, nevertheless, surmise that an unanswered question about numbers of marriages would not vitiate the outputs from family histories, since they are marriage-specific, but it does, as will be shown in Section 2.

Another aspect of the model, in the spirit of simplification, which had unfortunate consequences, was the assumption of no remarriage. It is not inconceivable that all women would be able to marry at the specified age, if widowers as well as bachelors were eligible as their spouses. And once remarriage is introduced, important distinctions arise between fertility from a female and from a male perspective, with repercussions for the shape of the family history. This too is adumbrated in Section 2. The lost opportunity can be indicated from another direction. Males as well as females play a role in the reproductive process, and family demography should consider that. Although the calculations in my model were based on separate male and female survival functions, fertility was treated in the conventional mono-sexual fashion, with no possibility, given the fixed age at marriage for males and females, of independent variation by gender. The sole effect of assuming a different (higher) age at marriage for males than for females was to use a somewhat higher level of male mortality than otherwise.

Differential marriage and remarriage by gender also plays hob with the answer I proposed for the question of the probability of an heir (a son surviving to marriage age). That was the only question for which I made an assumption about the parity distribution (an aspect of family modelling I now consider indispensable). But the answer I then sought no longer seems interesting. There are many important questions of intergenerational relationships attracting theoretical attention currently, concerning fathers and adult sons, and sons as a source for support of widows. (Ryder, 1983.) The outputs required to address such questions need to be addressed separately from male and female perspectives, and answers in the form of probabilities are much less useful than calculations of joint survival of the respective relatives on an age-specific basis. I have a further note on the subject in Section 4 of this chapter.

Failure to incorporate parity as an intrinsic element of the model was the most egregious example of the impoverishment of possible outputs of a family model by focusing solely on mean values. For example, the result in the previous paper which attracted the most attention was a calculation based on the age distribution of family person-years, in which age was used to distinguish net consumer and net producer years by the arbitrary assumption that a child shifted from the former to the latter status at age 15. My presentation of average values not only concealed the rapidly changing ratio of consumers to producers over the course of the family life cycle but also vitiated the possibility of determining the proportion of families which would by demographic happenstance become grossly imbalanced in that ratio, to the point that their economic viability would be in question. This is one aspect of the third major flaw in my model: the failure to consider what would happen in a population to those individuals bereft of a support structure by the exigencies of their family history and clearly dependent on the basis of their young or old ages. I consider this kind of question in the third section of the present chapter. Clearly one cannot address such questions effectively without maintaining a sense of the distribution of families by size and composition throughout their histories.

In summary, the major respects in which my original manuscript was flawed as an effort at family demography were the formation of families by marriage and remarriage, the consequences of the family histories which end with dependent individuals, and the absence of variance in family histories. These are the topics of the three following sections of the present chapter.

Furthermore, those who read the original paper closely may have been bothered by somewhat cryptic resolutions of particular empirical questions. They were approximations devised to keep calculations within the bounds of what could be (and was) done by hand, with explanations framed to keep the presentation on a non-technical level. In the light of the major amendments required, I do not think it worthwhile to rationalize those exercises here.

2 The Marriage Market

The conventional focus on female fertility in population models tempts one to avoid the thickets of marriage. Fertility may be partitioned into proportion married and marital fertility. Since growth causes change in the relative numbers of any groups differentiated by age — such as brides and grooms — the implication is that it also produces change in the proportions married. To assume fixed age-specific fertility is tantamount to assuming change in marital fertility (to the degree required to accommodate whatever happens to proportion married because of the modification of the age–gender distribution). That is not what is ordinarily considered to be fixed reproductive behaviour.

The problem is complicated still further by incorporating remarriage in the model. If marital dissolution is restricted to that caused by mortality, the level of survival clearly has something to do with the supply of widows and widowers in the marriage market, in the aggregate, and by age. If mortality is assumed to change, it is likely that the population structure by age and marital status also changes, in ways relevant for fertility.

The problem I intend to investigate here is the dependence of proportion married on the marriage market, specifically the relative supply of bachelors and widowers, spinsters and widows, based on a set of rules concerning formation of unions of the four possible kinds by marital status. Recognizing the difficulty of formulating credible rules, I have taken the following considerations into account. Empirically, most societies at inefficient equilibrium have early and nearly universal marriage for both bachelors and spinsters, with the age at marriage higher for bachelors than for spinsters. Remarriage of widows is much less likely than remarriage of widowers. Unlimited remarriage is unlikely because marriage is costly. Nevertheless, given the range of cultural variability in such matters, the best that can be claimed for the example which follows is that it exemplifies the importance of considering the question of marriage rules and patterns.

We specified the age of bachelors and spinsters at marriage as 25 and 15. We assumed that the number of marriages occurring would be maximized, within the constraint of availability of spouses. It was further specified that men preferred spinsters to widows, but that women had no preference for men by marital status. We set upper age limits of 65 and 25 on the nubility of widowers and widows, and an upper limit of two marriages per person, over the course of a lifetime. The model is monogamous, and divorce is excluded.

Following the lead of the previous manuscript, the first example is an inefficient equilibrium with female expectation of life at birth 25 (specifically the West level 3 model life tables from Coale et al., 1983). Since we know the ages of spouses in bachelor/spinster unions, these life tables permit us to calculate a joint survival function, determining *inter alia* the proportion of those marriages ending in a nubile widower (say w), and the proportion ending in a nubile widow (say x).

Suppose there are B bachelors and they all marry. (The contingency if this is not feasible is considered below.) Those marriages produce Bw widowers who, since there is no preference by women for bachelors or widowers, also all marry, so that the total number of marriages is $B(1 + w)$.

Suppose there are S spinsters. If there are more spinsters than bachelors and widowers combined, all marriages involve spinsters but some spinsters remain unmarried. There would be two classes of marriage, numbering B and Bw respectively. If there are fewer spinsters than bachelors and widowers combined, all spinsters as well as some widows would marry. Let the proportion of bachelors (and thus of widowers) who marry spinsters be p. It follows that $pB(1 + w) = S$, giving an equation $p = S/(B(1 + w))$.

Since all S spinsters marry in those circumstances, and spinster marriages produce x widows each, the total supply of women for marriage is $S(1 + x)$. The condition that all bachelors and widowers marry is that the number of bachelors and widowers be less than the number of spinsters and widows. Because male mortality is ordinarily higher than female mortality at each age, and because the male age at marriage is ordinarily higher than the female age at marriage, this condition generally holds unless there is a severe restriction on the nubility of widows. Otherwise the constraint on the number of marriages would be the number of women rather than the number of men in the market. In such circumstances, let the proportion of bachelors and widowers who marry be m. The total number of bachelor and widower unions would be $BM(1 + m(1 + w))$, and that must equal $S(1 + x)$. That gives a quadratic which can be solved for m. In short, the relative numbers in the different categories in the market in one or another situation pose no special difficulty with the proposed rules.

Using l_x values from the life tables, there are 48 732 spinsters at 15, and $40\ 201*1.05 = 42\ 211$ bachelors at 25. The joint survival function for bachelor–spinster unions gives $w = 0.35$ nubile widowers. Then the proportion of bachelors marrying spinsters (using the above formula) is $p = 0.8539$. Thus we can determine the numbers in each of the four classes of union. The survival function for bachelor–spinster unions also indicates mean ages of 40 for nubile widowers and 20 for nubile widows, so that joint survival can be calculated for all classes of union, and thus the numbers of women married in each reproductive age. We posited relative marital fertility for the quinquennial age groups from 15 to 45 at 0.20, 0.23, 0.21, 0.18,

Table 6.1   Reproduction parameters for three models

	Inefficient Equilibrium	Disequilibrium Spinster age 15	Disequilibrium Spinster age 20
Growth rate	0.0000	0.0240	0.0202
Net reproduction rate			
male	1.00	2.50	2.11
female	1.00	1.87	1.80
Generation length			
male	38.2	39.2	37.4
female	25.3	26.1	29.1
Mean marital parity			
male	4.85	5.86	4.94
female	4.21	5.10	4.24
Parity standard deviation			
male	3.28	4.23	3.99
female	2.71	3.18	2.76

0.12, 0.06 respectively (values which are arbitrary but not unreasonable). To satisfy the condition that the population is stationary, the sum over the four classes of union of the products (marriages)*(proportion married)*(marital fertility) must equal the size of the life table birth cohort, 205 000. This determines the absolute levels of marital fertility (1.1542 times the relative values). Those values are held fixed in the two following examples.

With these data we can calculate the mean marital parity for women and for men. The results are shown in Table 6.1. Since all spinsters and bachelors marry, the difference between their values reflects the difference in their numbers (48 732 spinsters and 42 211 bachelors) since the output for each is the same, 205 000 births. Although parity is not part of these calculations, one can estimate the standard deviation of marital parity as follows. Since the mean age of fertility for women marrying at 15 is 25.33, the mean marital duration is 10.33; the standard deviation of age (and duration) is 6.66. Assuming that the coefficient of variation is the same for parity as for duration, the estimate of the standard deviation of marital parity for women is 2.71. A comparable calculation gives a standard deviation of marital parity for men of 3.28. This measure is relevant for such inferences as the proportion with no child or no son, since such proportions tend to vary directly with the mean but inversely with the standard deviation. Clearly consideration of the marriage market emphasizes the importance of distinguishing the male and female perspectives on these important questions. As a final point, the length of generation where there is replacement is the first moment by age of the net fertility function. For males and females the values are respectively 38.2 and 25.3. These too are important aspects of the family life cycle.

The second marriage market to be examined is that of disequilibrium, with the female expectation of life at birth increased to 60 (West level 17 in the Coale *et al.* models) but with fertility remaining at the inefficient equilibrium level. More precisely that means that marital fertility remains the same, and the marriage rules remain the same (but not necessarily age-specific fertility). There are 87 584 bachelors at age 25, and the joint survival function for bachelor–spinster unions indicates 0.16 as the proportion of nubile widowers generated by such unions. The number of spinsters at age 15 is 88 013, but that number must be inflated by e^{cr}, where r is the rate of growth and c is the average distance in age (and thus in cohort) between spinsters and their spouses. The surmise (which proves to be correct) is that there will be more spinsters than bachelors and widowers combined, so that there are only the two classes of spinster union. From the bachelor–spinster survival function, we derive the mean age of nubile widowers (48) and use that to develop a survival function for widower–spinster unions. The proportion married from these two functions, and the prescribed levels of marital fertility, determine the mean net fertility for bachelor unions (5.2) and for widower unions (4.2); their weighted sum, divided by 205 000, gives the male net reproduction rate, 2.50. In a growing population, the generation length can be estimated from the first and second moments by age of the net fertility function. Here the male generation length is 39.2 and thus the intrinsic rate of natural increase is 0.0240. (Note, for comparison, that a comparable procedure based on fixity of age-specific fertility would have yielded an intrinsic rate of natural increase of 0.0284.)

In order to derive the female counterparts of these measures, it is necessary to view the market from the female perspective. The 88 013 spinsters confront 87 584*exp(-10r) bachelors from the cohort of ten years earlier, and 87 584*0.16*exp(-33r) widowers from the cohort of 33 years earlier. The intrinsic rate of natural increase, r, is necessarily the same for females and for males, so that its value here is 0.0240. The upshot for females is a net reproduction rate of 1.87 and a generation length of 26.1. Following the same procedures as outlined above, the mean and standard deviation of marital parity are 5.86 and 4.23 for males, and 5.10 and 3.18 for females. Moreover, in considering the parity distribution of children from the standpoint of all females, a most important element of this particular example is that 14.4 percent of spinsters never marry.

The third marriage market to be considered is a consequence of the consideration that an outcome in which one spinster in seven never married may be considered undesirable from various viewpoints. That outcome can be changed by raising the age at marriage for females or by lowering the age at marriage for males. Since population growth is an unlikely context in which to expect a lower age at marriage for males, we consider the former option: the marriage rules are changed in one respect only, raising the age of spinster at marriage to 20. Under such circumstances it turns out that there are more than enough bachelors and widowers to permit all spinsters to marry.

Determining the relative magnitudes of the four marriage classes is complicated in this situation. Where $r = 0$, the formula for the proportion of bachelors marrying spinsters is $p = S/(B + Bw)$, where S is the number spinsters and B and Bw the numbers of bachelors and widowers. Where r is not zero, the number of spinsters must be inflated by $exp(ar)$, where a is the age difference between bachelors and spinsters at marriage, and the number of widowers must be deflated by $exp(-br)$, where b is the age difference between widowers and bachelors at marriage. With the formula for p modified in those respects, the numbers of marriages become pB bachelor–spinster, pwB widower–spinster, $(1-p)B$ bachelor–widow, and $(1-p)wB$ widower–widow. The joint survival function for bachelor–spinster unions gives mean ages of nubile widows and widowers, so that the same functions can be calculated for the other classes of union. As above, this leads to an expression for the net reproduction rate as the ratio of the product-sum (as before) to 205 000, but in this case it is an implicit expression for r to be solved by successive approximation. The result is $r = 0.0202$, with a net reproduction rate of 2.11 and a length of generation 37.4, for the male cohort.

From the female standpoint, the distribution of unions by classes as specified above for males must be adjusted as follows: unions involving spinsters must be weighted by $exp(-ar)$ and unions involving widowers by $exp(-br)$, in each case to reflect the cohort difference between the spouses. Since the value of r is known from the male calculations, the rest of the procedure is straightforward. The results are reported in Table 6.1.

Consider the findings in that table by way of summary. The growth rate consequent upon an increase in survival, with fixed marital fertility and no change in marriage rules, is 2.4 percent (and one-seventh of the spinsters remain unmarried). If, to avoid that level of spinsterhood, the female age at first marriage is raised from 15 to 20, the objective is accomplished but the growth rate is reduced to 2.0 percent. What is happening is indicated by the components of r: the female net reproduction rate changes little — because there is a trade-off between some spinsters remaining unmarried throughout their entire reproductive lives and all spinsters waiting five years to begin their reproductive lives — but the generation length increases considerably, bringing down the growth rate. Clearly population growth can be quite sensitive to marriage strategy.

In the second place, there are major differences, typically concealed in an individual-oriented model, between maternity and paternity. The gender differences are marked with respect to every parameter in Table 1 (except for the mandatory identity of the intrinsic rate of natural increase). Such differences are relevant for the family life cycle in both quantitative and temporal respects, and perhaps especially for integenerational relationships, such as that between fathers and sons as the latter become adults, and between mothers and sons as the former approach widowed dependency. It should be emphasized that the account has not considered the possible effect of age of male on fertility, independently of age of female, a neglected subject in fertility research.

Another kind of output from the same models which suggests interesting inferences is the distribution of adult life (above age 15) by marital status, for the female and male cohorts. (The cross-sectional outcomes are also available and useful, but their configuration reflects the obvious age-distribution consequences of different growth rates; our purpose here is to focus on the marriage market consequences of the results, in abstraction from that well-known relationship.) The results are shown in Table 6.2.

For the males, the decline of mortality from high to moderately low has the consequence of increasing the proportion of adult life spent in the married state, relative to premarital time; the proportion of male life spent in widowhood is small, and little affected by mortality level or marriage strategy. Incidentally, the small magnitude of the proportion of male life spent in widowhood shows that modifications of the marriage market which would expand the definition of nubility for a widower, or permit multiple remarriage by widowers, would have little effect on the outputs of the model.

For females, the proportion of life spent in the married state decreases substantially, when the same marriage rules are maintained, and increases only a little, should the age of spinsters at marriage be increased. The proportion of life spent in widowhood is very large, but it is reduced substantially by mortality decline. The most striking aspect of the results in Table 6.2 is the large role played in these societies by the premarital male and the post-marital female. These are counterparts, since the primary cause of each is the circumstance that males marry at a later age than females (and, somewhat more subtle, widowers are much more likely to remarry than widows). Without much prompting from anthropological accounts, the demography indicated in Table 2 suggests immediately two points of importance for such societies: given the magnitude of the labour force contributions of premarital males, what are the respective claims of the father and the son to that

Table 6.2   Percentage distribution of adult life (ages 15 +) for male and female cohorts, in three models.

	Inefficient Equilibrium	Disequilibrium	
		Spinster age 15	Spinster age 20
Male			
single	28.9	19.6	19.6
married	67.4	77.6	76.9
widowed	3.8	2.7	3.5
Female			
single		14.4	9.4
married	63.8	57.5	65.1
widowed	36.2	28.0	25.5

product; given the incidence of widows, do they have sons to provide them with social support?

The preceding account is open to criticism on several levels. The effort is crude in the sense that means are frequently used when distributions would be more appropriate, as in the collapsing of the age distribution of widowers into its mean in order to derive joint survival functions for unions involving widowers. Although I doubt that the outcomes would be much affected by more refined calculations, there is no technical difficulty in achieving such a refinement. Similarly accommodation of the disequilibrium marriage rules in the face of excessive spinsterhood is likely to occur through a mixture of modifications of established custom rather than in one direction only. One may also question the appropriateness of the particular marriage rules selected. Yet the procedure is adaptable to various formulations of rules. The characteristics of any marriage market that are relevant for determining the allocations of marriages by the categories of the respective spouses (including age and perhaps other considerations as well as marital status) are that there be a ranking for each gender of the preference for categories of the other. With a clear specification of those preference structures, perhaps derivative from ethnographic accounts, the joint distribution of marriages by category can be accomplished.

The problem unaddressed is whether one can, in the absence of such ethnographic prescriptions, discern from the configuration of marriages specific for male and female characteristics, and from the frequency of such characteristics in those males and females eligible for marriage, the principles followed in forming those unions. My impression is that the problem, stated in those terms, is insoluble.

On the other hand, it does seem feasible to adapt to the two-gender situation those procedures followed in expressing occurrences to individuals relative to specific characteristics of those individuals. The so-called two-sex or two-gender problem is a special case of the more general problem of specification of exposure to risk of joint events of any kind, involving more than one individual, where the individuals are unequal in numbers. Marriage is a joint event, occurring to an individual male and an individual female. The males in such unions are selected from a set of males, and the females from a set of females; the sizes of the two sets are generally unequal. From male and female perspectives, there is the same numerator but different denominators. Any model specifying, *inter alia*, a fixed value for one of these ratios is in effect specifying a fixed relationship between the two denominators, ordinarily contradictory to whatever relationship between those values is given by other components of the model. The most notorious by-product of this problem arises in the stable population model. Although there is no logical basis for preferring males or females as the basis of the stable model, the outcome in terms of the growth rate is ordinarily different, an evidently illogical result demonstrating the fundamental flaw of using a monosexual basis for a bisexual behaviour pattern.

Consider how the concept of exposure to risk is used with an individual event. When one has two sets of unequal size, each of which has a subset of interest, the calculation of the proportion of each set in that subset is a pre-analytic device for abstracting the scale from the account of sources of difference, on the elementary (but sometimes incorrect) assumption that scale is irrelevant to the incidence of the phenomenon or, if relevant, will take a less mechanical approach to detect. The same principle underlies the occurrence/exposure ratio, except that exposure is ordinarily two-dimensional, embracing multiplicatively both persons and time, each dimension handled in the same way with respect to scale. We abstract from the time consideration in this account because it involves no difference in principle. The sense of the procedure is that, of all the various modifications of exposure which may produce a change in occurrences, one follows a formula for abstracting from the merely arithmetical consequences of scale, leaving all other considerations relative to the way in which scale was removed. One chooses to ignore the uninteresting proposition that an increase of k per cent in exposure produces an increase of k per cent in occurrences, *ceteris paribus*, and focuses thenceforth, in the analysis proper, on the respects in which all other things are not equal.

Consider a joint event in this light. M marriages occur as a consequence of the interaction of B bachelors and S spinsters. Since one of each is required for the event to occur, the scale should evidently be responsive to the size of the smaller of B and S. The total number of possible pairings is the product of B and S; in some form, that should play a part in the specification of scale. Suppose that S is the smaller and B the bigger of the two. Thinking of S as the maximum number of occurrences, it seems arithmetically appropriate that the approximation to the maximum would depend on the relative sizes of B and S. One convenient way to express this notion would be to multiply S by $B/(B + S)$. That gives $BS/(B + S)$ which, since it is symmetrical in B and S, relieves one of the question of which of the two is smaller. Note also that, if both B and S were increased by k per cent, the exposure, so measured, would be increased by k per cent, satisfying the primitive sense of how scale operates.

The proposed expression is one-half the harmonic mean of B and S. (If used as a denominator for M, the result is the sum of M/B and M/S.) I proposed this approach to the marriage market in a paper at the 1960 meetings of the Population Association of America, unfortunately not submitted for publication. Alternatives are discussed in the large literature on the question.

The measure has a role to play in analysis and in model construction. The intent in the former is to engage in pre-analysis, abstracting from an empirical situation the uninteresting arithmetical consequences of scale before beginning the study of the interesting residuals. Here we are more concerned with its role in models. A model is a system of structures of exposure, and of occurrences (structure-transforming events) generated by exposure, in which the program consists of a specification of processes (relationships between exposure structures and occurrences). Processes take two forms: How do occurrences depend on exposure, and how does exposure depend on occurrences? Any specification of the form of a relationship between structure-changing events, like marriage, and exposure structures, like the numbers of bachelors and spinsters, provides the necessary programmatic instruction in one or the other direction. The operation of the model is designed to demonstrate the structural consequences of variation in one or more processes, with the rest held fixed.

The algorithm implicit in the occurrence–exposure ratio proposed resolves the two-gender problem, since the process from the standpoint of the female is dependent on the male as well as the female structure, and similarly for the male standpoint. (In the models outlined above, the rate of growth is the same regardless of which gender is the basis for its derivation.) The form of the occurrence–exposure ratio proposed is not intended in any sense to convey the richness of possibilities provided by sociocultural variations in family formation, or by individual preferences with respect to various male and female criteria, but merely to set the stage for that examination.

Given data on the frequency of eligible males by class, say $B(i)$, and eligible females by class, say $S(j)$, and on the consequent $M(i, j)$ marriages, the proposal is to calculate ratios $R(i, j) = M(i, j)*(B(i) + S(j))/(B(i)* S(j))$. Then the beginning of analysis, *sensu stricto*, would be the configuration $R(i, j)$. The relative values of $B(i)$ and $S(j)$ would remain of interest in considering the directions in which to proceed to explain the $R(i, j)$ surface, because only the scale has been removed.

3 Residential Considerations

From a standpoint of distinctive issues involved in modelling, it seems to me that the field of family demography has three divisions: the marriage market, the family history, and what might perhaps be called the adoption market. The last of these is discussed in this section. The broader dimensions of the subject are kinship and residence, with family as their intersection. Both a kinship group and a residence group may be thought of as a population, because boundaries can be drawn to determine who is and is not a member of the group (with very considerable cultural variation for both), and each type of group has a mode of addition to membership to compensate for attrition, and thus a history unlimited by the lifetime of any particular individual member (Ryder, 1964). In principle, then, one can regard such groups as candidates for demographic enquiry.

Residential and kinship groups have distinctive characteristics based on substantive considerations which have methodological consequences. The proposition to be advanced here is that the residential group is much less amenable to a demographic approach than the kinship group. A residential group is known as a household. It is distinguished by the circumstance that the members share in those activities concerned with their day-to-day survival, principally the provision of food and shelter. A kinship group, to the contrary, shares in those activities concerned with the long-term survival of the group, not only as a concrete membership but also as an institutional structure.

Households are interesting objects commercially. Moreover, there are ample data on household composition because the residence is the most common unit of data collection. Household membership, in and of itself, may carry little meaning for temporal commitment: additions to and subtractions from membership may occur without official or societal notice. Although residence histories are often collected, they are complex and unresponsive to the concept of exposure to risk. Perhaps the most promising key to the analysis of households is to think of them as firms, in an economic sense, changing in size and composition in response to considerations of production and consumption. Consider the common observation that large and complex households are uncommon even in societies characterized by high fertility and extended family ideals. This may be because, when demographic processes yield households which are too large or too small, there is redistribution among households to eliminate the deviant cases, by processes outside the reach of demographic analysis.

The family is a household or part of a household. Were the membership of a family based solely on the events of birth, marriage, and so forth, its composition, in consequence of the exigencies of death and passage, might be inadequate to the requirements of day-to-day self-sufficiency. Were such episodes transitory, the problem could be resolved by transfer of resources into the household, by kith or kin. But the longer and more severe the resource imbalance, the more likely that there will be either the immigration of productive persons from outside the household or the outmigration of nonproductive persons from inside the household, the limiting case being disappearance of the household. The counterpart of problems posed by insufficient numbers of producers, or by a composition not lending itself to an advantageous division of labour, is the problem of shortage of non-human resources, or of social control, posed by too many members in productive ages. Again the stage is set for a resolution of the problem by subtracting members through outmigration (presumably conditional on the viability of the household so attenuated).

While there are political aspects to day-to-day survival, implicit in the notion that shelter includes protection, the predominant orientation of household membership is joint production and consumption. One may expect additions to and subtractions from household membership on economic criteria. Exposure to the risk of occurrence of such events is different in kind from exposure to risk of birth and death and marriage. Each such solution involves cooperation among the members of more than one household. The particular solution depends on the array of available alternatives outside the household. (In this sense it is parallel to the marriage market.)

A parallel to interest in household data, together with a rich supply of such data, is the profusion of information for small politico-geographic units in a nation. These are imporant subjects for administrators, and the organization of the census guarantees the supply of data in that form. But the combination of practical interest and richness of information does not suffice to create an intellectually promising field for application of the methods and models with which the demographer is familiar. A like kind of problem is encountered in the study of immigration.

Kinship relations are either conjugal or consanguineal, i.e. formed by the events of marriage or birth. Those events imply prolonged coresidence for the parties concerned, are fraught with significance for all members of the kinship group, are closely governed by rules, and are recorded or remembered for their significance. In short, the kinship group is the kind of population most clearly adaptable to the models of demographers.

Given the demographer's interest in socially identified events, and in the occupancy of long-term statuses as the consequence of such events, it seems to me to be a sensible strategy for the demographer to restrict his household concerns to family members, committed over the long run to obligations of a diffuse kind, maintained in such commitments by social control, and symbolized by the formality with which such relationships are formed and dissolved. I recommend that the demographer make as his primary objective the fiction of the family as a closed population, entered only by marriage or birth, and exited from by passage or divorce or death. The cost of such a restriction is that the workings of the model will pose but not answer the problem of what happens to those net consumers, young and old, who are the products of family histories, and clearly need a household location for day-to-day survival. Problems of their redistribution would not seem to be responsive to demographic modes of thought.

Two processes intrinsic to family demography are not part of individual demography: fusion and fission. Fusion and fission are changes in the distribution of persons by households, other than by change in the number of persons as a consequence of birth or death. Fusion is the formation of one unit out of two, and fission the formation of two units out of one. In short, they are residential recombinations. The motivation for fusion and fission lies in the characteristics of households, specifically their composition with respect to economic properties. Those properties are concerned with the balance of production and consumption, each dependent on the age distribution of the group. Productivity is also dependent on the division of labour (by gender as well as age), on nonhuman resources, and on the solidarity of the unit with respect to the administrative challenges posed by its size and shape. Demographic analysis of such redistributive events is particularly difficult because such relevant questions as whether there are too many or too few persons, or whether co-residence is required for cooperative endeavours, or whether a particular kind of work can or cannot be performed by a person of a particular age or gender, are not at all categorical.

Confining attention to the residential rearrangements of kin, fusion may be conjugal or consanguineal. In either case, the fusion may involve an individual, or the member of a pre-existing family group. Conjugal fusion is marriage; consanguineal fusion often involves orphan children adopted by kin, or dependent seniors moving in with kin. Similarly fission may be conjugal or consanguineal. In the former case, the divorce may mean the separation of two individuals, or one individual from a family, or the separation of two family groups. The most important institutionalized case of consanguineal fission is the passage of the young adult out of his or her parents' home, often simultaneously with marriage. But consanguineal fission may also occur in the case of two brothers and their families, members of their father's household so long as he (or his wife) survives, but separate units thereafter. Consanguineal fissions and fusions are interesting because they involve different generations. Accordingly their quantitative character is responsive to a situation of population growth, in which the relative sizes of age groups, and thus generations, change.

The important distinction between fissions and fusions as classes of event is that the relevant characteristics of fissions may be reasonably confined to characteristics of members of the unit experiencing that event, whereas every case of fusion involves the matching of persons or groups, and is thus conditional on the properties of the population viewed in the aggregate. In the case of conjugal fusion (marriage and remarriage), the well-defined nature of exposure to risk, even though it is a joint event, makes it a possible albeit challenging subject for demographic modelling, whereas consanguineal fusion seems to be too varied and inchoate in possibilities to permit a simple and credible resolution. This is not how I initially perceived the problem. It had seemed to me that one could draw a fruitful analogy between the two-gender problem in the marriage market, and the problem of matching, say, orphan children with the kin of their dead parents. That would suggest that the problem be framed first by identifying the shape of the 'adoption' market, in terms of the number of eligible adopters and adoptees. The following enquiry was one reason I was disabused of that simplistic motion.

Consider a patrilineal kinship system in a replacement population (but with variance in net reproductivity). For example, assume that 25 per cent of fathers are replaced by no sons, 50 per cent by one son, and 25 per cent by two sons. The size of the population, and thus the number of males, is fixed over time, but the number of patrilines (names) becomes smaller with each generation, since some of the fraternities have no sons in the next generation. It follows that the mean size of surviving fraternity increases (without limit). Following the selected example, it may be shown that, if $q_1 = 0.25$, and $q_{i+1} = q_i p_i$, where $p_i = 1 - q_i$, then, if each name is represented at the beginning by one male (mean fraternity size one), the proportion of the original fraternities surviving after t generations is the product of p_i over $i = 1, t$. After five generations, the mean fraternity size is 2.5, and, with each successive five generations, it becomes 3.9, 5.2, 6.5, 7.8, 9.1, 10.4. Thus, after 35 generations (something like a millenium) fewer than ten per cent (the reciprocal of 10.4) of the original names have survived.

From a technical standpoint, this poses the interesting quandary that a closed population which is stationary does not yield any convergence towards a fixed distribution of population by kin groups. That gives an arbitrary character to any specified kin distribution. A relatively short time in historical terms suffices to produce large enough fraternities, on average, that cases of orphans without appropriate kin to adopt them would be very small. (Realistically, the extinction of patrilines is probably checked by the subterfuge of adopting a son-in-law and giving him the name that would otherwise vanish.)

The 'adoption' market arises as the end-product of family histories, and is concerned especially with the residential redistribution among kin of dependent junior and senior individuals. In some respects the technical problems of consanguineal fusion are isomorphic with those of conjugal fusion, but residential redistribution, even within a kinship framework, and the matching of such individuals with particular other families, is based on non-demographic parameters in large part. Like questions of household size in general, the subject, in my judgement, lies outside the reach of demographers.

4 Family Histories

Prior to the concept of a family history, one requires a definition of a family. The United Nations recommendation, that a family is constituted of co-resident kin (by blood or marriage), seems to me too broad from a substantive standpoint and to unwieldy from a standpoint of demographic methodology. I propose defining a family as two or more persons, each of which is either married to, a parent of, or a child of, another member of the co-resident group. The parent/child relationship would reflect social as well as genealogical reality, just as the conjugal relationship would not require official or religious sanction. The critical test for inclusion, in my judgement, is the sense of temporal commitment in the relationship, so that it focuses attention on salient social patterning of this particular kind, and also makes demographic modelling feasible and useful. The intent of my proposal is to exclude those kin relationships which may be formed and dissolved, in a residential sense, solely for the transitory convenience of sharing a household.

The concept of a family history implies a record with a clear operational definition of a beginning and an end to the life of a particular family. The problem is that those termini depend on the perspective of the particular individual or relationship being considered. Given a particular problem, to which the calculation of the dimensions of a family history was relevant, it is likely that the nature of the problem would provide a clear answer to how to define the beginning and end of a family. But if the ambition is to develop a product adaptable to many purposes, the question of definition must remain unanswered.

My recommendation would be to frame the accounting scheme in terms of marriage histories. A marriage history would begin with a marriage, and end with the earlier of two possible outcomes: remarriage of one of the parties to the original marriage, or the disappearance of the family (in the sense that it no longer contained either a married couple or a parent–child pair). As a footnote, since a family is a network of conjugal and/or consanguineal pairs, it follows logically that a family can be formed either by marriage or by birth. Accordingly, a special kind of 'marriage' history would be initiated by the birth of a child to a woman without a husband.

With marriage histories as units, it would be necessary, to be able to create family histories in one or another sense, to specify the family status of the parties to each marriage. Either or both may be continuing co-residence with their family of procreation, or one of them may be continuing co-residence with their family of orientation. In the former instance, the event is remarriage for at least one of the spouses; in the latter instance, one would have a patrilocal or matrilocal marriage.

A comprehensive model of a population would need to include not only marriage histories (as segments of family histories) but also individual histories. The sense of the definition of an individual would not in this case be a one-person household, but rather a person who did not share a household with either a spouse or a parent or a child. Thus two siblings who happened to be living together for the time being would be considered as two individuals.

Within a marriage history, the minimal events to be recorded would be those which change the size of the family. Given the definition of the family, these may be classified as the formation or dissolution of conjugal or consanguineal (parent/child) relationships. A marriage history would end with the remarriage of one of the original couple, whereas a new marriage history would be initiated if a co-resident child of the original couple were to marry, and the marriage were patrilocal or matrilocal. In the event of a neolocal marriage of a child, the implication is that the marriage would be preceded by the child's passage into the status of individual. Conjugal dissolution, as a consequence of the death or divorce or separation of one of a couple, would subtract a member from the family.

Consanguineal formation is typically the birth of a child to the original couple, but there are also two kinds of consanguineal formation by adoption. One is the adoption of a child; the other is the rejoining of a parent of the original couple in his or her family of procreation. Consanguineal dissolution is the death or passage of a child, or the death of a sole surviving parent.

With respect to the exposure to risk of such events, there are three distinct classes. The first of these, marriage (and remarriage), has been discussed in Section 2. The second concerns those events, the exposure to risk of which can reasonably be defined in terms of the characteristics of the members of the family concerned. Although much of the exposure to risk would follow conventional individual demography, such as age and gender, it would be desirable, in the spirit of family demography, to consider the extent to which the behaviour concerned may be affected by considerations of family structure. One example would be mortality as a function of marital status and presence of children. Another would be fertility as a function of number of living co-resident children.

The third class of event concerns what was termed in Section 3 consanguineal fission and fusion. The commonplace case of the former is passage from childhood to adulthood, accompanied by residence change. But consanguineal fission can also occur as a consequence of the attrition of viability in a family, because of the loss of members or because of their ageing. The counterpart of that is the process of consanguineal fusion (junior and senior adoption). Rather than consider this set of questions as a problem of matching in a market (as with marriage), I would suggest that the generation of evidently dependent individuals (because they are very young or very old) as outcomes of family histories be treated from a modelling standpoint as a problem of allocation of such individuals to existing families, either randomly, or on the basis of such considerations as the ages of the adults and the number of children in the prospective receiving families.

The form of record is principally constrained by the considerable number of possible classes of family, as required for one or another purpose. My view of a minimum system of accounts would be a classification of married couples by ages at marriage, and a family roster, conducted at each quinquennial duration, of numbers of children by marital duration of birth. Aside from the consequences of ageing, the transition probabilities from one duration to the next would be those prescribing a transformation of the family configuration by number and class of members. (Among the evident variables in such an accounting scheme, the most expendable if the detail should prove excessive would, in my judgement, be gender.)

The principal difference between this accounting scheme and the one employed in my previous manuscript would be the systematic inclusion of parity in particular, and the retention of the distribution of families by size and structure in general. The values of joint person-years for any particular relationship pair would be an immediate by-product of the quinquennial roster of families by structure. Such joint person-years calculations seem preferable to probability calculations for answering questions like whether there is an heir, since probabilities are dependent for interpretation on the precise specifications of the relevant denominator and numerator, and provide point averages where joint exposure over successive intervals of time would be more useful.

As a methodological postscript, I prefer to use macro-simulation rather than micro-simulation in family demography models. In a summary of the characteristics of those approaches, Bongaarts (1983) emphasized the distinction that the former was deterministic and the latter probabilistic. His case against the latter was that, with a small number of individuals in the simulated population (necessarily small because of computer costs), aggregate results have substantial sampling error. (If one is interested in populations which may in fact be empirically small, that vice would be a virtue.)

In a deterministic model, the rate at which events occur is exactly determined by specified input variables. But the same would be true of the probabilistic model, in the limit. The essential difference, in my judgement, is not so much the role of chance as it is the circumstance that micro-simulation yields distributions of possible outcomes, whereas deterministic models often suppress the distributions underlying at least some of the parameters in the effort to avoid the complexity of multidimensional distributional arrays.

If the desired product is macro-analytic in form, the issue when one chooses to collapse a distribution into a value without variance (such as a mean) is the extent to which the macroanalytic outputs are distorted relative to their values if variance were retained. Yet if the ignoring of variance could lead one astray, it does not follow that the only alternative to the mean is the distribution *in toto*. Macro-analytic outputs are often insensitive to distributional nuances beyond those conveyed by the first and second (and sometimes the third) moments. My experience suggests that the consequences of distributional variation can often be accommodated in a parsimonious fashion, for example by splitting the relevant group into one-half with the value of the mean plus one standard deviation, and one-half with the value of the mean minus one standard deviation.

Quite apart from technical considerations, my preference for macro-analytic simulation reflects a sociological stance. I think of populations as manifesting in their aggregate behaviour something more than the arithmetical summarization of assemblages of evidence about individuals. That something reflects the presence of organizing principles of life within the popuation, principles more or less accepted by individuals as conditions of membership. For me this is the proximate motivation for the study of families rather than individuals as the operant units of demographic behaviour. Moreover, computer simulation is a congenial setting for analysis in this mode because of the isomorphism between programmed instructions for allocating transitions of individuals as a function of their characteristics as members of aggregates like the family and the kinship group and the surrounding culture, on the one hand, and those systems of socialization and social control which operate to achieve preferred patterns of behaviour by the members of socio-cultural collectivities, on the other.

Earlier in this account I suggsted that the status of households as units of data collection and thereby as rich stores of data did not suffice to make them self-evident elements in a conceptual sense for the conduct of demographic analysis (although the substantive implications of co-residence suggest alternative approaches for which they would be suitable elements). I am inclined, in the same spirit, to propose that, despite the status of individuals as the immediate sources of information about nuptiality and marital fertility, for example, such a circumstance does not constitute them as the self-evident elements in a conceptual sense for analysing patterns of nuptiality and marital fertility. (Given the prevailing winds of professional opinion, this is heresy or, more charitably, a devil's advocate view.) I believe that we have much to learn about aggregate patterns of demographic behaviour as functions of collective properties of the sociocultural systems which provide populations with their identities, recognizing of course that the manifestations of such collective influences in the behaviour of any individual will necessarily reflect characteristics particular to him or her as well as those of the groups with which he or she is associated.

In brief, and in summary, my enthusiasm for family demography as an alternative to individual demography (and not simply as a by-product of it) is akin to my preference for macro-analysis as an alternative to micro-analysis (and not merely as a simplified approximation to it for the sake of convenience and cost). Demographers have always been concerned with the aggregate consequences of behaviour. I think it is now time to begin the challenging task of applying demographic skills to the study of the aggregate determinants of behaviour.

References

Bongaarts, J., (1983), 'The Formal Demography of Families and Households: An Overview', in International Union for the Scientific Study of Population, *Newsletter* No. 17, pp. 27–42.
Coale, A., P. Demeny and B. Vaughan, (1983), *Regional Model Life Tables and Stable Populations*, Revised edition, Academic Press.
Ryder, N. B., (1960), 'Bisexual Marriage Rates', Paper presented at the annual meetings of the Population Association of America.
—— (1964), 'Notes on the Concept of a Population', *American Journal of Sociology* 59(5): 447–63.
—— (1975), 'Reproductive Behaviour and the Family Life Cycle', United Nations, Department of Economic and Social Affairs, *The Population Debate:*

Dimensions and Perspectives, Volume II, pp. 278–88.

—— (1983), 'Fertility and family structure', United Nations, Department of International Economic and Social Affairs, *Population Bulletin of the United Nations* No. 15, pp. 15–34.

Part IV

Multistate Life Tables

7 The Marital Status Life Table

FRANS WILLEKENS

Netherlands Interdisciplinary Demographic Institute (NIDI), The Hague, The Netherlands

1 Introduction

Keyfitz (1979, p. 191) points out that much of sociology and practically all of demography deals with transitions of people from one state at a certain moment to another state: alive to dead, single to married, married to divorced, employed to unemployed, region of residence i to region of residence j, etc. The states may define subpopulations (e.g. married population) and/or stages of life. The structure of a population at a given point in time or the stage reached by a person is the outcome of transitions made in previous time periods. Some of the transitions can be experienced only once, whereas other transitions can be repeated. Some transitions may prevent particular types of transitions or may make further transitions possible. Any transition may be defined by the state before and the state after the transition.

To study transitions and the states connected by transitions, demographers have traditionally used the life table. The life table translates a set of age-specific transition rates or probabilities into measures we are more familiar with and which picture the demographic consequences of a set of rates or probabilities: duration, frequency, and population size. The life table may be approached from two different perspectives. The first views the life table as a description of the life course or life history of members of a fictitious cohort, the demographic experience of which is represented by a set of transition probabilities. It will be referred to as the *life history perspective*. The second approach views the life table as a description of a population that is consistent with a set of transition probabilities and a hypothetical cohort size. The perspective will be denoted as the *population perspective*. In the population that is being considered to translate a set of transition probabilities into more familiar measures, the number of deaths per unit time interval is assumed to be equal to the number of births, hence the population is stationary. The life table may therefore be viewed as a table presenting characteristics of a stationary population.

The life history perspective is a micro-perspective since it focuses on events and statuses at the individual level. The description of a life history however does not depend on the availability of individual level data and micro data. Aggregate transition probabilities are adequate to describe the life histories of members of a homogeneous population. Individuals are distinguished by a limited set of attributes only and individuals with identical attributes cannot be distinguished. Each combination of attributes defines a particular state. By changing attributes, a person moves to a different state. In most life table analyses, cohort members have identical attributes at the outset but they differentiate as they age because of transitions made. The life history perspective is also a longitudinal perspective. It focuses on the life course development of cohort members (intra-cohort development). This perspective is therefore analytically equivalent to the one adopted in life (family) cycle analysis as proposed by Glick (1947, 1977) and life course analysis as proposed by Elder (1974, 1978, 1981, 508–13). The potential of life table methods for the correct estimation of life cycle measures was demonstrated by Feichtinger (chapter 5 in this volume). The potential for life course analysis was stressed by Espenshade and Braun (1982).

The population perspective is a macro-perspective. It focuses on the composition of a population, i.e. on the number of people in each of the population categories that are defined by a set of predefined attributes. The population composition expresses the state of the demographic system. The population perspective is also a cross-sectional perspective since the state of the system is considered at a given point in time. Note that the stationarity assumption present in life table analyses implies a state of the system, which remains constant.

Under conditions of stationarity, an important relation holds: there is a perfect correspondence between individual life histories and population characteristics (see also Preston, 1982). In a stationary population the results obtained by a micro- and longitudinal analysis are completely consistent with results obtained by a macro- and cross-sectional study. The stationary population and the associated life table provides therefore an appropriate instrument for a better understanding of the demographic meaning of a set of transition probabilities.

When people make transitions and enter new states, they may adopt new behavioural patterns. For instance, women entering motherhood may change their behaviour with respect to fertility, labour force participation, time budgeting etc. To fully appreciate the consequences of transitions, members of a cohort should be followed after transitions have occurred; they may return to the original state or more on to another state. For instance, never married persons may get married; after marriage, some may divorce and remarry. Classical single and multiple decrement life table models are useful to investigate the decrements from each state separately. But decrements of one state are often increments to another state. To keep track of members of a cohort as they move between different stages of life or different population categories, the classical models are inadequate. Instead of a set of independent life tables for each category of interest, a single life table is needed that integrates all categories. Such a life table is a multistate life table.

The integrated life table analysis of a population decomposed by marital status received much attention in recent years. Originally, the focus was on methodological issues. The issues may be divided into two sets. The first is related to the estimation of transition probabilities from the data. The second is related to the calculation of statistics showing the demographic consequences of a set of transition probabilities.

The problem of estimating transition probabilities from the data was addressed extensively by Schoen and Nelson (1974), Schoen (1975), Rogers and Ledent (1976), Rees and Wilson (1977), Schoen and Land (1979), Ledent (1980, 1982), Ledent and Rees (1980, 1986), and Land and Schoen (1982). In the tradition of demographic analysis, the transition probabilities were derived from accounting equations relating population stock and flow data. The accounting perspective was complemented by a probabilistic perspective. In it, the transition probabilities are derived from a probabilistic model, postulated to describe the underlying continuous stochastic process, of which the data are realizations and the parameters of which must be estimated from these data. The probabilistic perspective was adopted by Hoem (1977), Hoem and Funck Jensen (1982) and Nour and Suchindran (1983). The underlying probability structure is taken to be that of a Markov process.

Research on the demographic consequences of a set of transition rates and probabilities led to the multistate life table and to the multistate projection and stable population models. Whereas a life table describes the evolution of a fictitious group of people who experienced the same event during a given period of time (life history perspective), a projection model pictures the evolution of an actual group of people present at a given point in time. Several life table statistics are independent of the size and composition of the initial group of people and several statistics derived from the projection model are independent of the initial population (stable population measures). The multistate life table, projection and stable population models were developed by Rogers in the sixties and early seventies (Rogers, 1966, 1973, 1975). By adopting matrix notation and matrix algebra, Rogers was able to generalize the classical models of mathematical demography to multistate populations. Some of the further developments of the multistate models are documented in Willekens and Rogers (1978) and Rogers and Willekens (1986).

Some of the life course questions that the multistate marital status life table is able to answer are:

What is the probability of marriage ending in a divorce?

What is the probability of being married at age 30?

How long will a person, widowed at the age of 25, wait on the average before remarriage? What is the probability of never remarrying?

How many years has a divorcee of age 40 already been divorced on the average?

In recent years, the methodological research has been complemented by considerable applied research. We limit ourselves to research related to marriage and family. The multistate life table model was adopted to study marital status patterns in Sweden (Schoen and Urton, 1977, 1979), the United States (Krishnamoorthy, 1979; Espenshade, 1983a, 1983b; Espenshade and Braun, 1982; Hofferth, 1982, 1985; Espenshade; chapter 8 in this volume and Hofferth, chapter 9 in this volume), Belgium (Willekens *et al.*, 1982; Wijewickrema, *et al.*, 1983; Schoen and Woodrow, 1984), The Netherlands (Koesoebjono, 1981; Storm, 1982; CBS, 1983) and Australia (Krishnamoorthy, 1982). Schoen and Baj (1983) compared marital status patterns in the United States, Belgium, England and Wales, Sweden and Switzerland for male and female birth cohorts born from 1808 through 1945. In several of these applications, the computer program LIFEINDEC was used or was adapted for use (Willekens, 1979). Schoen's computer program is given in Schoen and Urton (1979). As part of the applied research, demographic indicators were developed to summarize the experience of a multistate life table population. Some of the indicators are reformulations of measures that are traditionally used to describe marital status patterns.

The life table measures that describe, either prospectively or retrospectively, life histories of members of a synthetic cohort may be grouped into four types: measures of probability or proportion, duration measures, size measures and frequency measures. Each of these measures may be unconditional or conditional upon the status (marital status) at the age for which the measure is calculated from the set of transition probabilities (reference age). Unconditional measures, which will be referred to as *population-based* measures, describe the life history of an average person of a given age, irrespective of the persons' marital status at that age. *Marital-status based measures* depend on the marital status of the person for which the measure is calculated. The population-based and the status-based measures serve different purposes. For instance, if one is interested in the number of years that a person irrespective of marital status may expect to live in marriage, the population-based measure is appropriate. However, if the interest is in the years of married life remaining to a married individual, the marital status-based measure will be more appropriate. In this chapter, population-based measures are presented first. Their calculation requires a level of mathematical sophistication which is considerably less than the derivation of status-based measures. Status-based measures require matrix inversion. Before we review the different life-table measures, a brief description is given of the identification and measurement of life histories and the estimation of transition probabilities from the data.

2 Identification and measurement of life histories

The multistate life table may be viewed as describing the life histories from birth or a given age y (reference age) to death of members of a synthetic cohort. This perspective, which is well suited for life course analysis, as Espenshade and Braun (1982, 1027) observed, will be followed in this chapter. For the presentation of life histories we draw not only on the traditional demographic literature but also on the more recent literature on event history analysis, in particular Tuma and Hannan (1984).

The first step in any multistate demographic analysis is the identification of the states an individual may occupy. In this chapter we consider four marital states:

1. single
2. married
3. widowed
4. divorced

To these states, the state of dead is added. Espenshade and Hofferth in this volume distinguish additional marital status categories: first marriages, remarriages, separated after first marriage and separated after second or higher order marriage. Bongaarts in chapter 10 in this volume distinguishes, in additon to marital states, fecundity status and parity. The set of states a person may occupy is called the *state space* and the number of states (N) is the size of the state space.

The life history of an individual from birth or age y to death may be described by a variable $Y(x, t)$, representing the state a person occupies at exact seniority x and time t. The seniority is the time elapsed since age y, the age at which the event occurred that started the process (event-origin). Since we selected birth as the event-origin, the seniority variable is age.[1] The variable $Y(x, t)$ can take on a finite number of distinct values $(1, 2, 3, \ldots N)$ and is therefore a qualitative variable. For instance, $Y(x, t) = 2$ if the person with exact age x is married at time t. Note that the knowledge of x and t implies the knowledge of the date of birth. Changes in $Y(x, t)$ are referred to as *events*. Marriage, divorce, widowhood, and death are the events of interest in this chapter.

The life history may be displayed graphically. One way of showing the marital history is presented by Tuma and Hannan (1984, 46). Another graphic display of the marital history is the Lexis diagram (Figure 7.1). In the Lexis diagram, the horizontal axis represents time (historical or calender time) and the vertical axis gives the person's seniority. The events are

---

[1] The methodology presented in this chapter is independent of the event-origin selected. The event-origin defines the duration variable. In applied research, the selection of the event-origin should be based on substantive knowledge. For instance, if the focus is on events which depend on duration of marriage, rather than on age, marriage should be selected as the event-origin.

denoted on the lifeline of individual *b* by A (marriage), B (divorce), C (remarriage), and D (death). The Lexis diagram is attractive for demographic analysis because of its focus on both seniority and historical time dependence of events. From now on, we will only use age as the seniority variable.

The drawing of individual life lines and the exact location of the events on the life line requires a continuous time observation. Continuous time observation is frequently not available to the demographer and the exact time of an event remains unknown. Instead, the time interval in which an event occurs is recorded (discrete-time observation). A consequence of discrete time observation is that the location of an event on the life line is only known approximately. Not the point on the line, but the segment is identified. We will refer to data which are grouped over time as *grouped data*. These data are fundamentally different from event data which are grouped over individuals, yielding data for the population as a whole or for population categories. Data grouped over individuals will be referred to as *aggregate or population level data*.

Consider Figure 7.1. The Lexis diagram shows three life lines (*a, b* and *c*).

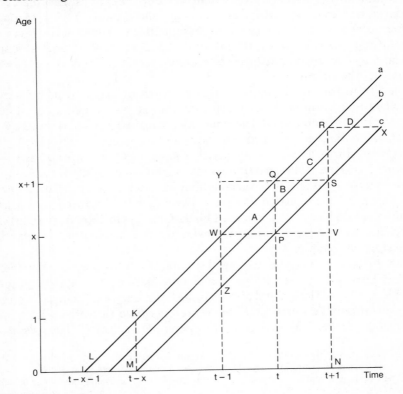

Figure 7.1 Lexis diagram

On life line *b*, four events are shown (A, B, C and D). The figure shows an age interval $(x, x + 1)$, a time interval $(t, t + 1)$ and a cohort inter-val $(t - x - 1, t - x)$. The cohort consists of the group of people who experienced the initial event in the time period from $t - x - 1$ to $t - x$. By fixing two of the three component intervals, the observation interval is fixed.

The issues involved in measuring the timing of events may be illustrated in a Lexis diagram. Two questions are of prime importance:

1. How is time (age) measured?
2. When is time (age) measured?

If discrete time intervals are considered, it is important to note *when* age is measured. It may be measured at any point of the interval. Consider inter-vals of one year length. Age is measured either at the exact time of the event, at the end of the year or at the beginning of the year. The measurement of age in completed years at the end of the interval is common in retrospective surveys. It is equivalent to measuring seniority in period difference, which is the difference obtained by subtracting the year of occurrence of the initial event from the year of occurrence of the event under study. The measure-ment of age at the beginning of the year is equivalent to the measurement of the year of birth. A person born between $t - x - 1$ and $t - x$ is at time t between x and $x + 1$ years old, i.e. of age x in completed years.

The measurement of the timing of events in completed time units (discrete time) implies the definition of *observation period* or interval. The observa-tion period is the period during which the events are recorded. In the Lexis diagram, the observation period refers to the segment of the life line for which events are recorded. Events on parts of the life line not included in the segment remain invisible.

The ways of fixing the observation period lead to different observational plans. They may be illustrated with reference to Figure 7.1. In this chapter, we present only a few possible observational plans. For a more elaborate typology of observational plans that are commonly used to record demo-graphic events, the reader is referred to Willekens (1984).

If we assume that the observation period is of a fixed length (one year, say), four observational plans may be distinguished.

a. Cohort (cohort–age) observation:
  A cohort observational plan records for a person experiencing an event the cohort to which the person belongs (or equivalently the age at the beginning or end of the observation interval) and the age in completed years at the time of the event (parallelogram WQSP in Figure 7.1). The observation interval extends over two calender years.

b. Period–cohort observation:
  A period–cohort observational plan records the calender year in which the event occurs as well as the cohort to which the person belongs

(parallelogram PQRS in Figure 7.1). The observation interval covers two age classes.

c. Period (period–age) observation:
A period observational plan records the calender year in which an event occurs as well as the age of the person in completed years at the time of the event (square PVSQ in Figure 7.1). The observation interval covers two cohorts.

d. Age–period–cohort observation:
This observational plan records for a person experiencing an event the calender year in which the event occurs, the year of birth of the person and his/her age in completed years at the time of the event (triangle PQS in Figure 7.1). The observation interval covers only one cohort, one age and one calender year. The data that are recorded by an age–period–cohort observational plan are commonly referred to as doubly classified data.

The ways in which the observation period is fixed affects the analysis of the event data and in particular the estimation of the transition probabilities. The transition probabilities, from which all measures that are relevant in life-table analysis are derived, must be estimated from the data. The data available to the demographers are generally grouped data. The grouping necessarily affects the type of transition probabilities that can be estimated.

3 Estimation of transition probabilities

With each observational plan is associated a type of transition probability that can directly be derived from the data (empirical measures). The type of probabilities may very well differ from the types used in demographic models such as the life table and the projection models (model measures). Consequently, with each demographic model may be associated an ideal observational plan which assures complete consistency between the model measures and the empirical measures. For life table analysis, the ideal observational plan is the cohort (cohort–age) observational plan, since the life table provides information on the status of cohort members at consecutive exact ages. For population projection, the period–cohort observational plan is the ideal one, since the projection model provides information on the status of cohort members at consecutive exact historical times.

The estimation of life table transition probabilities from cohort–age data is straightforward. In this chapter, we assume that cohort–age data are available. The estimation of life table transition probabilities from other types of data is discussed in Willekens (1984).

In this section we present formulas to estimate life table or cohort transition probabilities. We assume that we are given for each member of a birth cohort the number of events of a particular type occurring during age intervals of one year. In addition we assume that we have no data on individual attributes except cohort membership and state occupied.

The transition probabilities are derived in three steps. In the first step, the distribution of the cohort members among the states at each age $x + 1$ is written as a function of the distribution at age x and the events between ages x and $x + 1$. The flow equation results in an accounting equation. In this chapter, it is assumed that the population system is closed to migration. Introduction of emigration does however not complicate the estimation. Emigration, like death, may be viewed as a passage to an absorbing state. In the second step, occurrence–exposure rates are derived from the data. An occurrence–exposure rate is the ratio between the number of events during a given time period and/or age interval and the person-years lived during the interval. The calculation of occurrence–exposure rates raises two issues. First, differences in the measurement of the number of events lead to different types of occurrence–exposure rates (Pressat, 1969; Hoem, 1971). Second, except for data available on a complete, continuous-time observation of all events, the person-years lived during an interval by the population at risk cannot be determined exactly. Grouped data require an assumption about the distribution of the events over the interval or an equivalent assumption. In the third step, transition probabilities are derived from the occurrence–exposure rates. The three steps, considered by Land and Schoen (1982) for the estimation of increment–decrement life-table models can be translated into the steps presented above.

In a cohort observational plan, events or transitions are recorded by age in completed years and by year of birth of the person experiencing the event or transition. The flow equation relates the number of persons occupying a given state at eact age $x + 1$ (lifelines crossing the segment QS in the Lexis diagram) to the number of persons occupying the same state at exact age x (lifelines crossing WP) and the events that occurred between the two exact ages (parallelogram WQSP). This flow equation is identical to the equation proposed by Schoen (1975), and later adopted by others. It is an appropriate point of departure for life-table analysis since it applies to members of a particular cohort. The equation is as follows:

$$k_i(x + 1) = k_i(x) - D_i(x) - \sum_{j \neq i} O_{ij}(x) + \sum_{k \neq i} O_{ki}(x), \qquad (7.1)$$

where $k_i(x)$ is the number of cohort members who reach exact age x in state i, $D_i(x)$ is the number of cohort members who die in state i between the exact ages x and $x + 1$, and $O_{ij}(x)$ is the number of transfers from state i to state j between the ages x and $x + 1$, experienced by the same cohort. Note that i is the state that a cohort member occupies at the moment the event in question (death, transfer) occurs. It is not necessarily the state at exact age x.

The cohort occurrence–exposure rates are:

Mortality rate:

$$d_i(x) = D_i(x)/L_i(x). \tag{7.2}$$

Mobility rate (rate of transfer):

$$m_{ij}(x) = O_{ij}(x)/L_i(x). \tag{7.3}$$

with $L_i(x)$ being the number of person-years that members of the cohort at risk can experience the event of interest.

To calculate $L_i(x)$ from the data, an assumption is needed about the distribution of the events over the observation interval (parallelogram WQSP). Equivalently, assumptions may be formulated for intensities of occurrence or for the local behaviour of the survival function. The assumption of uniform distribution of the events over the observation interval and of births of cohort members over the interval $t - x - 1$ to $t - x$ leads to a piecewise linear survival function and to a simple linear model of the person-years lived:

$$L_i(x) = \tfrac{1}{2}[k_i(x) - k_i(x + 1)]. \tag{7.4}$$

Because the observation interval is one year, the person-years lived are equal to the average size of the population at risk. This population can be considered either as $k_i(x + \tfrac{1}{2})$ (the number of people at exact age $x + \tfrac{1}{2}$) and represented in the Lexis diagram by the number of lifelines crossing the horizontal line at age $x + \tfrac{1}{2}$, or as $L_i(x)$ (the number of people in age group x to $x + 1$) and represented by the number of lifelines crossing the vertical line PQ.

A combination of (7.1) to (7.4) gives the following flow equation:

$$k_i(x + 1) = k_i(x) - \tfrac{1}{2}d_i(x)\,[k_i(x) + k_i(x + 1)]$$
$$- \tfrac{1}{2}\sum_{j \neq 1} m_{ij}(x)\,[k_i(x) + k_i(x + 1)]$$
$$+ \tfrac{1}{2}\sum_{k \neq i} m_{ki}(x)\,[k_k(x) + k_k(x + 1)]$$

from which we obtain the following expression:

$$[1 + \tfrac{1}{2}d_i(x) + \tfrac{1}{2}\sum_{j \neq i} m_{ij}(x)\,]k_i(x + 1) - \tfrac{1}{2}\sum_{k \neq i} m_{ki}(x)k_k(x + 1) =$$
$$[1 - \tfrac{1}{2}d_i(x) - \tfrac{1}{2}\sum_{j \neq i} m_{ij}(x)\,]k_i(x) + \tfrac{1}{2}\sum_{k \neq i} m_{ki}(x)\,k_k(x). \tag{7.5}$$

This summation over j and k is for all values $j \neq i$ and $k \neq i$.

This equation may be written for all i and the system of equations may be expressed in matrix terms:

$$[\mathbf{I} + \tfrac{1}{2}\mathbf{m}(x)]\,\mathbf{k}(x + 1) = [\mathbf{I} - \tfrac{1}{2}\mathbf{m}(x)]\,\mathbf{k}(x) \tag{7.6}$$

where

$$\mathbf{m}(x) = \begin{bmatrix} m_{11}(x) & -m_{21}(x) & \ldots & -m_{N1}(x) \\ -m_{12}(x) & m_{22}(x) & \ldots & -m_{N2}(x) \\ \vdots & \vdots & & \\ -m_{1N}(x) & -m_{2N}(x) & \ldots & m_{NN}(x) \end{bmatrix}, \tag{7.7}$$

with $m_{ii}(x) = d_i(x) + \sum_{j \neq i} m_{ij}(x)$.

From (7.5) follows the equation that originally was developed by Rogers and Ledent (1976):

$$\mathbf{k}(x + 1) = [\mathbf{I} + \tfrac{1}{2}\mathbf{m}(x)]^{-1}[\mathbf{I} - \tfrac{1}{2}\mathbf{m}(x)]\,\mathbf{k}(x). \tag{7.8}$$

When we define the model $\mathbf{k}(x + 1) = \mathbf{p}(x)\,\mathbf{k}(x)$, the matrix of transition probabilities is:

$$\mathbf{p}(x) = [\mathbf{I} + \tfrac{1}{2}\mathbf{m}(x)]^{-1}[\mathbf{I} - \tfrac{1}{2}\mathbf{m}(x)], \tag{7.9}$$

where $\mathbf{m}(x)$ is a matrix of cohort rates and where an element $p_{ij}(x)$ of $\mathbf{p}(x)$ denotes the probability that a person of exact age x in state i will be in state j exactly one year later (i.e. at age $x + 1$). The configuration of the $\mathbf{p}(x)$ matrix is similar to that of $\mathbf{m}(x)$.

The methods for estimating rates and probabilities are based on the following premises:

1. The available data are population-level (aggregate) data: number of events or transitions in a subpopulation in discrete observation intervals.

2. The events are evenly distributed over the observation interval. The duration of exposure can therefore be estimated by a simple linear function of the population at the beginning and at the end of the interval. Note however that this assumption imbedded in equation (7.9) may result in negative transition probabilities if the time unit selected is excessively large in comparison with the frequency with which the events occur. Hoem and Funck Jensen (1982) and Nour and Suchindran (1984) suggest to circumvent the problem by replacing (7.9) by an exponential expression, since an exponential can never yield negative values of transition probabilities. This approach however does not really solve the problem of selecting an optimal time unit for the measurement and study of related events. For instance, divorce occurs on average 3 months after separation. A year is therefore too crude a time unit to study the relation between separation and divorce. If the year is however selected as the time unit, negative probabilities may be a consequence.

3. The transition probabilities are calculated from the occurrence–exposure rates following the accounting approach.

4. The rates and probabilities only depend on the seniority (age) of the person and the state occupied at the beginning of the interval. Within

each age-state category, perfect homogeneity is postulated implying that the rates and probabilities do not depend on the durations in the state or on any other omitted heterogeneity of the population.

Attempts to cope with the limitations inherent to the approach for estimating transition probabilities presented above are discussed in Willekens, 1984.

4 Population-Based life table measures

4.1 Probability calculations

To derive the life-table statistics, we are given a set of age-specific transition probabilities $p_{ij}(x)$ and the distribution of the birth cohort among the states. For some measures we also need the occurrence–exposure rates $m_{ij}(x)$. In the life history perspective, the transition probabilities are transformed into sojourn times in each state and number of transitions during a given period. In interpreting these measures, one should keep in mind the restrictions imposed on the $p_{ij}(x)$. Recall that $p_{ij}(x)$ is a conditional probability, which depends only on the state i occupied at age x and is independent of the prior life history, of the covariates (except age) of the person at the time of transition and of the context in which the transition takes place.

In order to determine the life-table measures, we need to derive, from the $p_{ij}(x)$, probabilities that relate to any interval between two exact ages, a reference age, y say, and another age, x say. Three types of probabilities are distinguished: survival probabilities, state probabilities and (y, x)-transition probabilities. The probabilities are closely linked and can easily be calculated once the $p_{ij}(x)$ values are known. The survival probability is a probability of surviving from a reference age y to another age x. The survival probability may be dependent on the state occupied at the reference age. The state probability is the probability that a person of the reference age y occupies a given state at age x. The state probability is always independent of the state at the reference age. The transition probability is the probability that a person of reference age y and occupying a given state at that age occupies another given state at age x. The transition probability is always origin-state-specific. To distinguish between the transition probabilities referring to the interval from y to x and the transition probabilities over unit intervals, $p_{ij}(x)$, we denote the first probabilities as (y, x)-transition probabilities. A similar distinction is made by Tuma and Hannan (1984, 51), who refer to the survival probability as the survivor function.

The probabilities are defined for intervals between two exact ages, a reference age, and an age denoting the end of the interval. Probabilities may be conditional on the state occupied at the reference age, such as the transition probabilities. Probabilities that are status-specific are referred to as status-based probabilities. Probabilities that are independent of the state occupied at the reference age, such as the state probabilities, are said to be population-based. In general, the reference age is zero (age at birth). Population-based probabilities are presented in this section. Status-based probabilities are presented in Section 5.

a. Survival probabilities The common definition of a survival probability is the probability that a person survives from birth to a given age x. This probability is population-based. We denote the population-based survival probability by $l(x)$.

The survival probabilities may be derived from the $p_{ij}(x)$. The probability of surviving the unit interval from birth to age h is

$$l(h) = \sum_{i,j} p_{ij}(0)\, l_i(0),$$

$$= \sum_{i} p_{i+}(0)\, l_i(0). \tag{7.10}$$

where $l_i(0)$ denotes the probability that the state occupied at birth (reference age 0) is the state i. The survival probability $l(x)$ is:

$$l(x) = \sum_{i} p_{i+}(x - h)\, l_i(x - h), \tag{7.11}$$

where $p_{i+}(x - h) = \sum_{j} p_{ij}(x - h)$.

Under conditions of no mortality, $p_{i+}(x) = 1$. Under conditions of non-differential mortality, $p_{i+}(x)$ is independent of i, i.e. $p_{i+}(x) = p(x)$ for all i, and the survival probability at age x is:

$$l(x) = p(x - h)\, p(x - 2h) \dots p(0). \tag{7.12}$$

This expression is well known from the classical life table.

The probability of surviving from any other reference age y to age x may easily be calculated from the series $l(t)$, $t = 0, 1, \dots x$:

$$_y l(x) = l(x)/l(y) \tag{7.13}$$

The (y, x)-survival probability is the conditional probability of surviving to age x given that one survives to y.

b. State probabilities The state probability is the probability that a member of the birth cohort occupies a particular state i at exact age x. This population-based measure is denoted by $l_i(x)$. The state probability at birth, $l_i(0)$, has already been used above. The distribution among the states at time of birth is given exogenously. If marital states are considered, all children are single (state 1) at time of birth, e.g. $l_i(0) = 1$ for $i = 1$ and $l_i(0) = 0$ otherwise. A multistate life table constructed for a population which occupies only one state at birth is called a uniradix life table. Marital status life tables belong to the class of uniradix life tables.

In marital status analysis, a child remains single at least till the minimum legal age at marriage (γ). The state probabilities $l_i(x)$ are therefore zero for $x < \gamma$ except for the state of single, in which case the state probabilities and the survival probabilities coincide.

The state probability at age x is:

$$l_i(x) = \sum_k p_{ki}(x - h) l_k(x - h). \tag{7.14}$$

The sum $\sum_i l_i(x) = l_+(x)$ is a survival probability. In the absence of mortality $l_+(x) = 1$. If the equation is written for all i, a system of equations results which can compactly be represented by a vector equation

$$\mathbf{l}(x) = \mathbf{p}(x - h)\, \mathbf{l}(x - h), \tag{7.15}$$

with

$$\mathbf{l}(x) = \begin{bmatrix} l_1(x) \\ l_2(x) \\ \vdots \\ l_N(x) \end{bmatrix}$$

and N the number of marital states.

In the discussion thus far the reference age is 0 and the state probabilities refer to the interval from age 0 to age x. From these probabilities we may derive (y, x)-state probabilities for the interval from y to x. The probability that a person alive at age y occupies state i at age x, $_y l_i(x)$, is:

$$_y l_i(x) = l_i(x)/l_+(y), \tag{7.16}$$

where $l_+(y) = \sum_i l_i(y)$. From equation (7.16) we may note that the state probability $l_i(x)$ may be viewed as a product of two probabilities: a survival probability $l_+(x)$ and a (x, x)-state probability:

$$l_i(x) = l_+(x)\, _x l_i(x). \tag{7.17}$$

The (x, x)-state probability $_x l_i(x)$ denotes the probability of occupying state i at age x conditional on survival to age x.

4.2 Sojourn times in each state

The time spent in each state between two exact ages by a member of a cohort may be estimated from the probabilities. It is assumed that the events that occur in a unit interval are uniformly distributed over the interval and that the events are independent.

The average sojourn time in years spent in state i between ages x and $x + h$ by a 0-year-old cohort member may be approximated by the following expression:

$$L_i(x) = \tfrac{1}{2}h[l_i(x) + l_i(x + h)]. \tag{7.18}$$

The sojourn time $L_i(x)$ is estimated irrespective of the state occupied at exact age x at any prior age and is therefore a population-based measure. It is equal to the average state probability times of length of the interval. In general:

$$L(x) = \tfrac{1}{2}h[l(x) + l(x + h)] \qquad (7.19)$$
$$= \tfrac{1}{2}h[I + p(x)]l(x).$$

The sojourn time depends on two components: the probability of surviving from age 0 to age x and the average time spent in state i during the h-year interval following x by a person alive at exact age x. It is not necessary that state i is occupied at exact age x.

The number of years lived in state i beyond age x is equal to

$$T_i(x) = \sum_{t=x}^{z} L_i(t), \qquad (7.20)$$

where z denotes the highest age. The measure $T_i(x)$ depends on the $(0, x)$-survival probability and the time spent in each state beyond age x by a person who reaches x (irrespective of the state occupied at that age). The latter component is a life expectancy measure.

The population-based measure of life expectancy in state i at age x is:

$$e_i(x) = T_i(x)/l_+(x) \qquad (7.21)$$

where $l_+(x)$ is the probability of surviving to age x $[l_+(x) = \sum_i l_i(x)]$.

The total life expectancy is:

$$e_+ = \sum_i e_i(x)$$

and the proportion of the remaining lifetime to be spent in state i is $e_i(x)/e_+(x)$.

Note that in the life expectancy calculation, the reference age is moved from age 0 to age x by introducing the survival probability $l_+(x)$.

4.3 Number of moves and transitions

The multistate life table enables the estimation of the number of times an average person changes his/her marital status during a given period. If the number is less than one, it indicates the probability that a person changes his/her marital status. The number of times a member of the cohort may expect to move from state i to state j between exact ages x and $x + h$ is:

$$m_{ij}(x) L_i(x),$$

where $m_{ij}(x)$ is the cohort occurrence–exposure rate and $L_i(x)$ is the duration of exposure between ages x and $x + h$, irrespective of the state occupied at age x or at any prior age. The average number of moves made during a given interval may be greater than one. The lifetime number of (i, j)-moves is the net mobility rate:

$$NMR_{ij} = \sum_{x=0}^{z} m_{ij}(x) \, L_i(x), \tag{7.22}$$

where z is the highest age.

A person is said to have made a transition if he/she is in state i at the beginning of the interval (age x) and in state j at the end of the interval (age $x + h$). The number of transitions form i to j in the interval $(x, x + h)$ by a member of the cohort, irrespective of states occupied at ages below x, is

$$p_{ij}(x) \, l_i(x),$$

with $l_i(x)$ the $(0, x)$-state probability. The average number of (i, j)-moves per (i, j)-transition in the interval $(x, x + h)$ is

$$m_{ij}(x) \, L_i(x)/p_{ij}(x) \, l_i(x) = m_{ij}(x) \, [1 - \tfrac{1}{2} \sum_{k \neq i} p_{ik}(x)]/p_{ij}(x) \tag{7.23}$$

since $L_i(x) = \tfrac{1}{2}h \, [1 + p_{ii}(x)]l_i(x)$ and $p_{ii}(x) = 1 - \sum_{k \neq i} p_{ik}(x)$.

The number of (i, j)-moves per (i, j)-transition, averaged over the lifetime, is

$$\sum_{x} m_{ij}(x) \, L_i(x)/ \sum_{x} p_{ij}(x) \, l_i(x). \tag{7.24}$$

Several interesting indicators of marital change may be derived from the information on the number of moves. The average number of first marriages is NMR_{12}. It is equal to the proportion of persons ever marrying (recall that in a stationary population, there is perfect correspondence between the individual life cycle and the population characteristics). The proportion ever married among 50-year-old persons is equal to the average number of first marriages (cumulated value of first marriage frequencies) up to exact age 50 divided by the probability of surviving to age 50.

$$\sum_{x=0}^{50-h} m_{12}(x) \, L_1(x)/l_+(50),$$

This measure is calculated by Espenshade (1983b). It is also used in relational models of fertility (e.g. Trussell, Menken and Coale, 1982). The first marriage rate is obtained by dividing the number of first marriages by the number of person-years spent in single state:

$$NMR_{12}/e_1(0).$$

The mean age at first marriage is

$$\sum_{x=0}^{z} (x + \tfrac{1}{2}h) \, m_{12}(x) \, L_1(x)/NMR_{12}.$$

The proportion of first marriages in the total number of marriages is NMR_{12}/NMR_{+2}.

The probability that a marriage ends in a divorce is NMR_{23}/NMR_{+2} and in widowhood is NMR_{24}/NMR_{+2}. The expected duration of a marriage (marriage spell) is $e_2(0)/NMR_{+2}$. The expected duration of a divorce is $e_3(0)/NMR_{23}$.

5 Status-Based life table measures

The status-based life table measures depend on the state occupied at the reference age. Their estimation is only meaningful for reference ages at which at least two states are occupied. For ages at which all cohort members occupy the same state, status-based measures and population-based measures are equal. In marital status analysis, status-based measures may be estimated for ages higher than the minimum legal age at marriage, γ, since below that age everyone is single.

In status-based measures calculations, a reference age y is selected at which all marital states are occupied, i.e. no state is empty. The minimum reference age which satisfies this condition is generally only a few years more than the minimum legal age at marriage. The estimation of status-based life table measures relies heavily on (y, x)-transition probabilities.

5.1 Probability calculations

The (y, x)-transition probability is the probability of a particular change in state between two exact ages. By $_{ky}l_i(x)$, we denote the probability that a person in state k at age y is in state i at age x, i.e. $x - y$ years later $(x > y)$. For instance $_{1y}l_3(x)$ represents the probability that a person who is y years old and single will be divorced at age x. The transition probability $_{ky}l_i(x)$ may be thought of as the state probability at age x for the subcohort of persons who are in state k at age y (state probability conditional on status at age y).

The (y, x)-transition probabilities are a general class of probabilities that encompass the transition probabilities $p_{ij}(x)$ and the state probabilities. When: $x = y$, $_{ky}l_i(x) = 1$ for $i = k$ and $_{ky}l_i(x) = 0$ otherwise. When $x - y = h$, the unit time interval, $_{ky}l_i(x) = p_{ki}(y)$, and $_{ky}l_i(x) = p_{ki}(y)\,_{ky}l_k(y)$. In general we have:

$$_{ky}l_i(x) = \sum_j p_{ji}(x - h)\,_{ky}l_j(x - h). \tag{7.25}$$

When we write the equation for all k and i, the system of equations that results may compactly be written as a matrix equation:

$$_yl(x) = p(x - h)\,_yl(x - h), \tag{7.26}$$

or equivalently

$$_yl(x) = p(x - h)\, p(x - 2h) \ldots . p(y)\,_yl(y).$$

where the matrix of (y, x)-transition probabilities is:

$$_y\mathbf{l}(x) = \begin{bmatrix} {_{1y}l_1(x)} & {_{2y}l_1(x)} & \cdots & {_{Ny}l_1(x)} \\ {_{1y}l_2(x)} & {_{2y}l_2(x)} & \cdots & {_{Ny}l_2(x)} \\ \vdots & \vdots & & \vdots \\ {_{1y}l_N(x)} & {_{2y}l_N(x)} & \cdots & {_{Ny}l_N(x)} \end{bmatrix}, \tag{7.27}$$

A number of properties of the (y, x)-transition probability matrix are of interest:

1. For $y = x$, $_y\mathbf{l}(x)$ is an identity matrix, a diagonal matrix with ones on the diagonal.
2. For $x - y = h$, $_y\mathbf{l}(x) = \mathbf{p}(x)$, the matrix of transition probabilities for the unit interval. In other words, $p_{ij}(y)$ is an $(y, y + h)$-transition probability.
3. For y less than the minimum legal age at marriage, all elements of $_y\mathbf{l}(x)$ are zero except those in the first column.
4. For $y = 0$, the elements $_{iy}l_i(x)$ of the first column of $_y\mathbf{l}(x)$ are equal to the state probabilities $l_i(x)$. For y larger than 0 but smaller than γ, the elements $_{iy}l_i(x)$ are (y, x)-state probabilities.
5. The column sums of $_y\mathbf{l}(x)$ are (y, x)-survival probabilities for the various subcohorts. These conditional or status-based survival probabilities are:

$$_{ky}l_+(x) = \sum_i {_{ky}l_i(x)}. \tag{7.28}$$

6. The row sums of $_y\mathbf{l}(x)$, weighted by the state probabilities at age y yield the $(0, x)$-state probabilities:

$$l_i(x) = \sum_k l_k(y) \, _{ky}l_i(x)$$

and in general

$$\mathbf{l}(x) = {_y\mathbf{l}(x)} \, \mathbf{l}(y). \tag{7.29}$$

To obtain the (y, x)-state probabilities, the weights to be chosen are the (y, y)-state probabilities $_yl_i(y)$.

The interval from y to x may be divided into smaller intervals and the probability of transition over the (y, x)-interval may be expressed in terms of transition probabilities over successive smaller intervals:

$$_{ky}l_i(x) = \sum_j {_{ky}l_j(t)} \, _{jt}l_i(x) \tag{7.30}$$

with $y \leq t \leq x$. For all states combined, we may write

$$_y\mathbf{l}(x) = {_t\mathbf{l}(x)} \, _y\mathbf{l}(t) \tag{7.31}$$

The expressions may be used to derive the probability of transition over intervals of different length. Three cases are considered:

A. $y < \gamma$ and $t < \gamma$.

When both the ages y and t are below the minimum legal age at marriage, all cohort members of these ages are in a single state. The transition probabilities that are derived are therefore also state probabilities.

Equation (7.25) gives

$$_{1y}l_i(x) = {}_{1y}l_1(t) \, _{1t}l_i(x).$$

The probability that a y-year-old person occupies state i at age x is the product of a population-based (y, t)-survival probability, $_{1y}l_1(t)$, and a (t, x)-state probability, $_{1t}l_i(x)$.

B. $y < \gamma$ and $t \geq \gamma$

Equation (7.25) gives

$$_{1y}l_i(x) = \sum_j {}_{1y}l_j(t) \, _{jt}l_i(x). \tag{7.32}$$

The transition probabilities $_{1y}l_i(x)$ and $_{1y}l_j(t)$ are (y, x)- and (y, t)-state probabilities, respectively. By multiplying both sides of the equation by the survival probability $l(y)$, equation (7.32) may be rewritten as

$$l_i(x) = \sum_j l_j(t) \, _{jt}l_i(x). \tag{7.33}$$

The transition probability $_{jt}l_i(x)$ is conditional on the status occupied at age t. This status-based probability is determined by two population based measures. From (7.33)

$$_{jt}l_i(x) = l_i(x)/l_j(t). \tag{7.34}$$

The (t, x)-transition probability that a person of age t occupies state i at age x, irrespective of the state at age t is simply the (t, x)-state probability

$$_tl_i(x) = l_i(x)/l_+(t). \tag{7.35}$$

(compare with equation 7.16).

C. $y \geq \gamma$ and $t \geq \gamma$

When $y \geq \gamma$, the k-year-old members of the birth cohort are distributed among different states. For each subcohort of y-year-old persons in a given state, we may derive probabilities analogous to the ones presented in **B**. The probabilities may also be determined for all the states simultaneously. We assume that all states are occupied (non-empty) and that the matrices $_y\mathbf{l}(t)$ for $t > y$ are non-singular, i.e. have an inverse.

The matrix of (t, x)-transition probabilities that are conditional on surviving to age t and the state occupied at that age is, from (7.31)

$$_t\mathbf{l}(x) = {}_y\mathbf{l}(x) \, [_y\mathbf{l}(t)]^{-1} \tag{7.36}$$

The matrix of (t, x)-transition probabilities that are independent of the state at age t but depend on the state at age y is:

$$_t\bar{\mathbf{I}}(x) = {}_y\mathbf{l}(x) \, [{}_y\hat{\mathbf{I}}(t)]^{-1}, \qquad (7.37)$$

where $_y\hat{\mathbf{I}}(t)$ is a diagonal matrix with the (k, t)-survival probabilities $_{ky}l_+(t)$ on the diagonal.

5.2 Sojourn times in each state

The average sojourn time in years, spent in state i between ages x and $x + h$ by a person in state k at exact age x can be estimated by the expression:

$$\begin{aligned}_{kx}L_i(x) &= \tfrac{1}{2}h \, [_{kx}l_i(x) + {}_{kx}l_i(x + h)] \\ &= \tfrac{1}{2}h \, [1 + p_{ki}(x)], \end{aligned}$$

since $_{kx}l_i(x) = 0$ for all $i \neq k$. For $i = k$, $_{kx}l_i(x) = 1$. In general

$$_xL(x) = \tfrac{1}{2}h \, [\mathbf{I} + \mathbf{p}(x)]. \qquad (7.38)$$

The average number of years spent in each state between the ages x and $x + h$ by state at age $y(y \leq x)$ is:

$$\begin{aligned}_yL(x) &= \tfrac{1}{2}h \, [_y\mathbf{l}(x) + {}_y\mathbf{l}(x + h)]. \\ &= \tfrac{1}{2}h \, [\mathbf{I} + \mathbf{p}(x)] \, {}_y\mathbf{l}(x). \\ &= {}_xL(x) \, {}_y\mathbf{l}(x) \end{aligned} \qquad (7.39)$$

The number of years lived in state i beyond age x by a person in state k at age y is

$$_{ky}T_i(x) = \sum_{t=x}^{z} {}_{ky}L_i(t)$$

and, in general,

$$_yT(x) = \sum_{t=x}^{z} {}_yL(t), \qquad (7.40)$$

The life expectancy at age x by state at age $y(y < x)$:

$$_ye(x) = \frac{1}{_{ky}l_+(x)} \, {}_yT(x) \qquad (7.41)$$

with

$$_{ky}l_+ = \sum_i {}_{ky}l_i(x).$$

An element $_{ky}e_i(x)$ of $_ye(x)$ represents the number of years a person in state k at age y may expect to spend in state i beyond age x, given that he/she reaches age x. The configuration of the matrix $_ye(x)$ is similar to that of $_y\mathbf{l}(x)$. If at age y, all states are non-empty, equation (7.41) may be written as follows:

$$_ye(x) = {}_yT(x) \, [_y\hat{\mathbf{I}}(x)]^{-1}, \qquad (7.42)$$

where $_y\hat{\mathbf{I}}(x)$ is a diagonal matrix with the elements $_{ky}l_+(x)$ on the diagonal.

The life expectancy beyond age x by state at age x is a special case of (7.42), for which $_{kx}1_+(x) = 1$:

$$_xe(x) = {}_xT(x).$$

The life expectancy beyond age x by status at age x may also be calculated in a different way. Analogous to (7.39) we may write:

$$_yT(x) = {}_xT(x) {}_yI(x),$$

which gives

$$_xT(x) = {}_yT(x) [{}_yI(x)]^{-1}. \tag{7.43}$$

The expression requires that $_yI(x)$ is non-singular, which is generally the case if y is larger than the lowest age for which all marital states are non-empty (age 20, say).

5.3 Number of moves and transitions

The expected number of moves beyond age y by state at age y and by state of destination is:

$$_{ky}NMR_i = \sum_{x=y}^{z} \sum_{j} m_{ji}(x) \, {}_{ky}L_j(x),$$

and in matrix notation

$$_yNMR = \sum_{x=y}^{z} M(x) \, {}_yL(x), \tag{7.44}$$

where $_yL(x)$ has the same configuration as $_yI(x)$ in (7.27) and

$$M(x) = \begin{bmatrix} 0 & m_{21}(x) & \dots & m_{N1}(x) \\ m_{12}(x) & 0 & \dots & m_{N2}(x) \\ \vdots & \vdots & & \vdots \\ m_{1N}(x) & m_{2N}(x) & \dots & 0 \end{bmatrix}, \tag{7.45}$$

The indicators of marital change, reviewed above, may also be made state-dependent. For instance, the expected duration of marriage for a married person of age 20 is:

$$_{2,20}e_2(20)/_{2,20}NMR_2,$$

where the denominator is the number of times a married person of age 20 may expect to remarry during his/her remaining lifetime. The number of remarriages depends on the number of years spent in divorce and widowhood:

$$_{2,20}NMR_2 = \sum_{x=20}^{z} \sum_{i=3}^{4} m_{i2}(x) \, {}_{2,20}L_i(x).$$

6 Conclusion

Marital change and family formation and dissolution are transitions from one state of life to another. These transitions have been the subject of much research in demography, sociology, psychology, and economics. Two sets of questions prevail in the studies. The first set relates to the types of transitions, their likelihood of occurrence and their determinants. The second set emphasizes the consequences of these transitions on the individual, the household and society at large.

The estimation of transition probabilities from available data has always been an important topic of research in demography. A main issue is the delineation of the population at risk and the estimation of the average duration of exposure by the population at risk. The estimation of the duration of exposure gets especially complicated if a person in a population may move freely between a set of transient states, such as married, divorced, and widowhood. In such a multistate population with interstatus movement and with state-specific transition rates, the transition probabilities cannot be estimated independently of one another. Instead, they must be estimated simultaneously. The estimation of transition probabilities not only depends on the identification of the multistate population, but also on the type of data that are available, i.e. the observational plan. With each demographic model is associated a particular 'ideal' observational plan, which ensures exact correspondence of model probability measures and empirical probability measures. We asserted that the ideal observational plan for life table analysis is a cohort (cohort-age) observational plan.

The marital status life table is a point of departure for the analytical investigation of family formation and changes in family size and structure over the family life cycle. When members of the synthetic cohort, the life course of which is described by a marital status life table, are allowed to have children following some marital status-specific fertility pattern, a range of new questions about the consequences of the rates and probabilities may receive an answer. The first set of questions relates to the impact of patterns of marriage and marriage dissolution on fertility. Since the multistate life table model provides an integrated analytical framework for combining schedules of marital change and marital-status-specific mortality and fertility, the model may be used to evaluate the combined effect on different fertility measures of changes in several of the schedules. The second set of questions relates to family formation. The apparatus for an integrated analysis of marital change and family formation is the family status life table. Such a life table is presented by Bongaarts in chapter 10 in this volume.

References

CBS (Central Bureau of Statistics) (1983), 'Overlevingstafels naar burgerlijke staat' (life tables by marital status) in *Maandstatistiek van de Bevolking*, 31(10), The Hague, pp. 22–34.

Elder, G. H. Jr., (1974), *'Children of the Great Depression'*, University of Chicago Press, Chicago.

—— (1978), 'Family History and the Life Course', in T. K. Harevan (ed.) *Transitions: The Family and Life Course in Historical Perspective*, Academic Press, New York. pp. 17–64.

—— (1981), 'History and the Family: the Discovery of Complexity'. *Journal of Marriage and the Family*, 43, pp. 489–519.

Espenshade, T. J., (1983a), 'Marriage, Divorce and Remarriage from Retrospective Data: a Multiregional Approach', *Environment and Planning A* 15, pp. 1633–52.

—— (1983b), 'Black-White Differences in Marriage, Separation, Divorce and Remarriage', Paper presented at the annual meeting of the Population Association of America, Pittsburg, Pennsylvania, April 1983.

—— and R. Eisenberg Braun, (1982), 'Life Course Analysis and Multistate Demography: an Application to Marriage, Divorce and Remarriage', *Journal of Marriage and the Family*, 44, pp. 1025–36.

Glick, P. C., (1947), 'The Family Cycle', *American Sociological Review*, 12, pp. 164–74.

—— (1977), 'Updating the life cycle of the family', *Journal of Marriage and the Family*, 39, pp. 5–13.

Hoem, J., (1971), 'On the Interpretation of Certain Vital Rates as Averages of Underlying Forces of Transition', *Theoretical Population Biology*, 2, pp. 454–68.

—— (1977), 'A Markov Chain Model of Working Life Tables', *Scandinavian Actuarial Journal*, pp. 1–20.

—— and U. Funck Jensen, (1982), 'Multistate Life Table Methodology: a Probabilistic Critique', in K. C. Land and A. Rogers (eds.) *Multi-dimensional Mathematical Demography*, Academic Press, New York, pp. 155–264.

Hofferth, S. L., (1982), 'Children's Family Experience to Age 18: a Cohort Life Table Analysis', Paper presented at the annual meeting of the Population Association of America, San Diego, April 1982. (Title of revised paper: Social Change and Children's Life Course).

—— (1985), 'Updating Children's Life Course', *Journal of Marriage and the Family*, 47, pp. 93–115.

Keyfitz, N., (1979), 'Multidimensionality in Population Analysis'. *Sociological Methodology 1980*, Jossey-Bass Publ., San Franscisco, pp. 191–218.

Koesoebjono, S., (1981), 'Marital Status Life Tables of Female Population in the Netherlands, 1978: an Application of Multidimensional Demography', Working Paper No. 20, NIDI, Voorburg, Netherlands.

Krishnamoorthy, S., (1979), 'Classical Approach to Increment–decrement Life Tables: an Application to the Study of the Marital Status of United State Females, 1970', *Mathematical Biosciences*, 44, pp. 139–54.

—— (1982), 'Marital Status Life Tables for Australian Women, 1971', *Genus*, 38, pp. 97–117.

Land, K. C. and R. Schoen, (1982), 'Statistical Methods for Markov-generated

Increment–decrement Life Tables with Polynomial Gross Flow Functions', in K. C. Land and A. Rogers (eds.), *Multidimensional Mathematical Demography*. Academic Press, New York, pp. 265–346.

Ledent, J., (1980), 'Multistate (Increment–decrement) Life Tables: Movement versus Transition Perspective', *Environment and Planning*, A12, pp. 533–62.

—— (1982), 'Transition Probability Estimation in Increment–decrement Life Tables using Mobility Data', in K. C. Land and A. Rogers (eds.), *Multidimensional Mathematical Demography*, Academic Press, New York, pp. 347–84.

—— and Ph. Rees, (1980), 'Choices in the Construction of Multiregional Life Tables', Working Paper WP-80-173, IIASA, Laxenburg, Austria.

—— and Ph. Rees, (1986), 'Life Tables', Chapter 10 in A. Rogers and F. Willekens (eds.), *Migration and Settlement: a Multiregional Comparative Study*, Reidel Press, Dordrecht, The Netherlands.

Nour, E-S. and C. M. Suchindran, (1983), 'A General Formulation of the Life Table', *Mathematical Biosciences*, 63, pp. 241–52.

—— —— (1984), 'The Construction of Multistate Life Tables: Comments on the Article by Willekens *et al*', *Population Studies*, 38, pp. 325–28.

Pressat, R., (1969), '*L'Analyse démographique*', Presses Universitaires de France, Paris.

Preston, S. H., (1982), 'Relations between Individual Life Cycles and Population Characteristics', *American Sociological Review*, 47, pp. 253–64.

Rees, Ph. and A. G. Wilson, (1977), *Spatial Population Analysis*, Arnold, London.

Rogers, A., (1966), 'The Multiregional Matrix Growth Operator and the Stable Interregional Age Structure', *Demography*, 3, pp. 537–44.

—— (1973), 'The Multiregional Life Table', *The Journal of Mathematical Sociology*, 3, pp. 127–137.

—— (1975), *Introduction to Multiregional Mathematical Demography*, J. Wiley, New York.

—— and J. Ledent, (1976), 'Increment–decrement Life Tables: a Comment', *Demography*, 13, pp. 287–90.

—— and F. Willekens, (1986), *Migration and Settlement. A Multiregional Comparative Study*, Reidel Press, Dordrecht, The Netherlands.

Schoen, R., (1975), 'Constructing Increment–decrement Life Tables'. *Demography*, 12, pp. 313–24.

—— (1983), 'United States Marital Status Life Tables for Periods 1910–1975 and Cohorts Born 1888–1945'. Available from National Technical Information Service, Washington D C.

—— and J. Baj, (1983), 'Marriage and Divorce in five Western Countries'. Paper presented at the annual meeting of the Population Association of America, Pittsburg, Pa., April 1983.

—— and K. Land, (1979), 'A General Algorithm for Estimating a Markov-generated Increment–decrement Life Table with Applications to Marital-status Patterns'. *Journal of the American Statistical Association*, 74, pp. 761–76.

—— and V. E. Nelson, (1974), 'Marriage, Divorce and Mortality: a Life Table Analysis'. *Demography*, 11, pp. 267–90.

—— and W. Urton, (1977), 'Marriage, Divorce and Mortality: the Swedish Experience'. *Proceedings of the IUSSP General Conference*, Vol. I, Liège, pp. 311–32.

—— —— (1979), 'Marital Status Life Tables for Sweden: Years 1911–1973 and Cohorts born 1885–1889 to 1940–1944, National Central Bureau of Statistics, Stockholm, Urval No. 10.

—— and K. Woodrow, (1984) 'Marriage and Divorce in Twentieth-century Belgian Cohorts'. *Journal of Family History*, 9, pp. 88–103.

—— W. Urton, K. Woodrow and J. Baj, (1985), 'Marriage and Divorce in Twentieth Century American Cohorts', *Demography*, 22, 101–14.

Storm, R., (1982), 'Overlevingstafels. Een concept voor differentiate binnen een populatie'. (Life tables. A model for differentiation within a population): *Maandstatistiek van de Bevolking* (Central Bureau of Statistics, The Hague), No. 30(6), pp. 13–40.

Trussell, J., J. Menken and A. J. Coale, (1982), 'A General Model for Analyzing the Effect of Nuptiality on Fertility', in L. T. Ruzicka (ed.), *Nuptiality and Fertility*, IUSSP — Ordina Editions, Liège, pp. 7–27.

Tuma, N. B. and M. T. Hannan, (1984), *Social Dynamics. Models and Methods.* Academic Press, Orlando.

Wijewickrema *et al.*, (1984), 'Marital Status Trends in Belgium (1961–1977): Application of Multistate Analysis'. In 'Population and Family in the Low Countries', IV, Voorburg: Netherlands Interuniversity Demographic Institute (NIDI), and Brussels: Population and Family Study Centre. pp. 47–72.

Willekens, F. J., (1979), 'Computer Program for Increment–decrement (multistate) Life Table Analysis: a User's Manual to LIFEINDEC', Working Paper WP-79-102, IIASA, Laxenburg, Austria.

—— (1984), 'Multistate Life Table Analysis of Marriage and the Family', Working Paper, NIDI, Voorburg, The Netherlands.

—— and A. Rogers, (1978), 'Spatial Population Analysis, Methods and Computer Programs', Research Report RR-78-18, IIASA, Laxenburg, Austria.

—— I. Shah, J. M. Shah and P. Ramachandran, (1982), 'Multistate Analysis of Marital Status Life Tables: Theory and Application', *Population Studies*, 36, pp. 129–44.

Zeng Yi, (1985), 'Marriage and Marriage Dissolution in China. A Marital Status Life Table Analysis', Working Paper n° 57, NIDI, Voorburg, The Netherlands.

8 Marital Careers of American Women: A Cohort Life Table Analysis*

THOMAS J. ESPENSHADE

The Urban Institute, Washington, DC, USA

1 Introduction

Trends in the United States since 1960 in marriage, divorce, and remarriage and in marital and nonmarital fertility have revolutionized the size and composition of American families and households, contributing to a decline in average household size, to rapid growth in the number of single-parent families headed by women, and to a general reduction in economic welfare in many segments of the population. Since 1900 the median age at first marriage has moved in a slow, pendulum-like fashion, first falling to a low during the 1950s and then rising up to the present. From a level of 22.0 years in 1890, the female median age at first marriage fell to 20.5 in 1947 with only a slight reversal during the Depression, and then averaged 20.3 between 1949 and 1962. Following 1962 the trend reversed and rose to 20.9 in 1972 and further to 22.5 by 1982. The 1982 value for females is the highest since 1890. Men have exhibited a similar pattern. The median age at first marriage was 26.1 years in 1890, and it fell without interruption to an average of 22.7 between 1949 and 1962. By 1982, however, the median age for men had risen to 25.2, increasing by 1.7 years since 1975 (US Bureau of the Census, 1983).

The rise in the probability that a marriage will end in divorce is partly reflected in increases in the divorce ratio, the number of divorced persons per one thousand married persons with spouse present. In 1960 the US divorce ratio stood at 35, but by 1982 it had risen to 114, more than double its 1970 level of 47. Since 1960 the black divorce ratio has been roughly twice the value for whites, and blacks and whites in 1982 had ratios of 220 and 107, respectively (US Bureau of the Census, 1983). Moreover, the rapid increase in the number of divorced persons in relation to the widowed population is the only factor preventing a decline in the total remarriage rate. Statistics provided by Barbara Wilson at the National Center for Health Statistics

* This chapter draws on research supported by NICHD Contract No. NO1–HD–02849 from the Center for Population Research, US Department of Health and Human Services. Discussions with Sandra Hofferth and Douglas Wolf have contributed to this work. The careful programming of Thy Dao and the capable technical assistance of Bobbie Mathis and Tracy Ann Goodis are also gratefully acknowledged. The views expressed here are those of the author and do not necessarily reflect the opinions of the Urban Institute or any of its sponsors.

show that, for black and white women combined, the total remarriage rate in the Marriage Registration Area rose from 33.0 in 1963 to 38.3 by 1980. The remarriage rate for previously widowed women fell from 10.2 in 1963 to 9.3 in 1973, and then more sharply to 6.7 by 1980. For remarriages among the previously divorced women, the rate stood at 133.5 in 1963, remained relatively stable at 131.0 by 1973, and then fell to 91.3 by 1980.[1]

Trends in marital and nonmarital fertility have been equally spectacular. Between 1960 and 1981 the number of children born out of wedlock tripled, growing from 224 000 to 687 000 (National Center for Health Statistics, 1982, 1983). Recent increases have been greater among whites than blacks so that by 1981 there were more white nonmarital births than black. For the US Population, the proportion of all births that are nonmarital births (the illegitimacy ratio) rose from 5.3 per cent in 1960 to 18.9 per cent in 1981 (National Center for Health Statistics, 1983). Strong racial differences persist since the proportion of black children born to currently unmarried mothers was five times greater in 1981 than the proportion for white children (56.0 versus 11.6 per cent). Trends in marital and nonmarital fertility have been moving in opposite directions; marital fertility has been falling whereas nonmarital fertility rates have been going up. Between 1960 and 1978 the fertility rate of married women fell from 156.3 to 96.8 per thousand, while the rate for unmarried women rose from 21.6 to 26.2 per thousand (National Center for Health Statistics, 1982). This fact alone would have caused the illegitimacy ratio to rise in the absence of other changes. The trend away from marriage and the comparatively faster growth in the population of unmarried females naturally aggravated this increase.

Much of our information about the marital status of adults comes from cross-sectional representations of the population at a moment in time. While not inaccurate, these snapshot perspectives do not tell us all we would like to know. They do not, for example, convey information on the population's actual experience with divorce. Trends in the proportion currently divorced may understate the population's experience of divorce if a high divorce rate is accompanied by a high remarriage rate. Moreover, aggregate cross-sectional data cannot yield estimates of either the proportions of a typical lifetime spent in alternative marital status categories or the average duration of a marriage.

Going beyond *net* flow data, one would ideally like to have micro-level longitudinal data on the transitions or *gross* flows that individuals experience over their lifetimes between and among alternative statuses. These gross flow data provide the relevant inputs into the multidimensional life

[1] The total remarriage rate is the annual number of remarriages to previously divorced or widowed women per one thousand divorced or widowed females 14 years of age and older. Remarriage rates for either previously divorced or previously widowed women are calculated by restricting both numerator and denominator of the rate to either divorced or widowed persons. The total remarriage rate is a weighted average of remarriage rates following divorce and following widowhood where the weights are the number of currently divorced and currently widowed persons, respectively.

tables described by Willekens in the previous chapter. In this chapter we discuss and analyse data on the transitions that American adults make between different marital statuses over their lifetimes. The chapter has two purposes. The first is to illustrate an application of multidimensional life table methodology using data from the supplement to the June 1980 Current Population Survey conducted by the US Bureau of the Census. This survey contains retrospective information on the marital and fertility histories of a sample of the adult population. The second purpose of this chapter is to serve as a companion piece to the following chapter by Hofferth who analyses data on the transitions American children make between alternative family situations as a result of the marital and fertility behaviour of their parents. Viewing the two chapters together, we begin to develop a comprehensive understanding of how the marital behaviours of adults are played out in the living arrangements of their children. Throughout this chapter we will place an emphasis on differences in the experiences of the white and black populations.

The second section discusses the data and methods used in the analysis. The third presents our principal findings. Results are summarized and their implications are developed in the final section.

2 Data and Methods

Data

As part of the monthly Current Population Survey designed to gather employment and labour force statistics, the US Bureau of the Census in June of 1980 asked supplementary questions concerning the marital histories of every adult between the ages of 15 and 75 in the households that were sampled. Most women were also asked to recount their fertility history to an interviewer. In June 1980 the CPS sample included about 68 000 eligible households, selected at random from the US population. Of these, approximately 65 000 were actually interviewed. Marital histories were subsequently provided for 59 918 males and 65 744 females.

Individuals were asked to supply information on their date of birth and on the dates of entry into and exit from up to three marriages (their first two and their most recent). Dates were recorded in terms of both the year and the month of occurrence. If a marriage ended, persons were asked how it ended, whether in widowhood or divorce. And if a prior marriage was terminated by a divorce, respondents were asked a follow-up question about when they actually stopped living with their former spouse. The questionnaire therefore detected spells of separation prior to divorce, and it also ascertained whether a person was separated at the time of the interview. However, previous spells of separation that did not end in divorce but were reconciled by the spouses getting back together again were not identified.

Methods

Multidimensional life tables are used to highlight the significance of these marital history data. Marital status life tables containing single year of age data from birth to age 75 and over were constructed for successive birth cohorts of individuals drawn from six population subgroups: all females, white and black females separately, all males, and white and black males separately. Our analysis here is limited to the results of the marital status life tables for white and black females separately. Since marital history data were collected from individuals between the ages of 15 and 75 in June 1980, persons in the sample had to have been born between June of 1904 and June of 1965. We report on successive five-year birth cohorts beginning with women born between 1905 and 1909 and continuing through women born between 1940 and 1944.[2]

Figure 8.1 shows the conceptual framework used to organize the data. Seven marital status categories are identified, linked through eleven marital status transitions (shown by arrows). All individuals start off life in the never-married status. Most eventually marry, and some of these have their marriages disrupted by separation, divorce, or widowhood. Some individuals who reported that a prior marriage ended in divorce gave a date for the divorce that was the same as their date of separation (when they actually stopped living with their former spouse). These persons, who comprised a small minority of those who had ever divorced, were assumed to make a transition directly from married to divorced with no intervening spell of separation. In Figure 8.1, first marriages are treated separately from remarriages (2 + marriages), as are separations from a first marriage and from a remarriage. As previously noted, spells of separation that end in reconciliation are not detected by the June 1980 CPS questionnaire. Persons who experienced such spells would appear to the outside observer to have been continuously married. For this reason there is no return flow from separated to married. Finally, Figure 8.1 registers transitions among various states only for the population that is alive, but it is important to recognize that life table cohort members are always subject to the additional risk of dying — a risk that varies with age and with marital status.

To construct marital status life tables requires data inputs of two kinds: (1) age-specific transition rates for each of the eleven marital status transitions in Figure 8.1 and (2) age-specific death rates for each marital status category. Transition rates are derived from the marital history data by calculating age-specific occurrence–exposure rates that measure the number of occurrences of a particular type of transition in relation to the number of person-years of exposure to the risk of a transition of that type. For example, suppose we are interested in the transition from first marriage to first

---

[2] Results of a period marital status life table analysis covering the period 1940–80 are reported in Espenshade (1983).

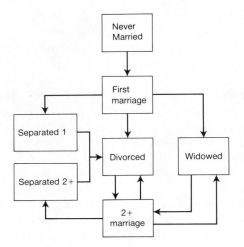

Figure 8.1 Marital status categories and transitions

separation at age 20 for white females born between 1905 and 1909. This rate is computed by dividing the cohort's (weighted) number of first separations at age 20 by its (weighted) number of person-years lived between exact ages 20 and 21 in the first marriage state. Similar calculations are performed for other ages (up to ages 75 and over) and for other transitions. To remove irregularities, single-year-of-age transition rate schedules were smoothed by taking a weighted three-year moving average where the weights consisted of the person-years of exposure in the denominators to the rates.

   To calculate cohort death rates by age and by marital status, cohort death rates for four marital statuses (single, married, divorced, and widowed) were first estimated by indirect standardization from death rates by age, race, sex, and marital status for 1940, 1949–51, and 1959–61 (National Center for Health Statistics, 1970). The same death rates were used for women in first marriages and in remarriages. It was also assumed that age-specific death rates for divorced women would characterize separated women, whether they were separated from a first marriage or from a remarriage.

   A problem posed by the attempt to derive marital status life tables for each five-year birth cohort up to 1940–44 is that, with the exception of women born between 1905 and 1909, other birth cohorts have no members who had reached age 75 by the time of the June 1980 survey. Two different approaches were combined to project the remaining cohort experience beyond 1980 for cohorts born between 1910–14 and 1940–44. First, it was assumed that mortality would not change after 1980. Accordingly, each cohort's death rates and the transition rates from first marriage to widowed and from remarried to widowed were used up to 1980, and beyond 1980 age-specific death rates and transition rates for the 1975–80 period were employed to project incomplete cohort experience. Each of the remaining nine marital status transitions is characterized by an age pattern that reaches a maximum prior to age 30 and then declines. To estimate the unobserved age-specific transition rates for these nine transitions, two-parameter declining exponential functions were fitted to those portions of the observed rate schedules where the rates were falling. Separate functions were estimated for each transition and for each birth cohort. These procedures mean that, problems of respondent recall aside, our estimates for the oldest birth cohorts should be most reliable because comparatively more of these cohorts' experiences would have been observed by 1980 and a smaller proportion would need to be projected. Graphs of age-specific marital status transition rates tend to show that, with the exception of the transition to widowhood, marital activity is largely confined to ages under 50. Only for the two most recent birth cohorts (1935–39 and 1940–44) was it necessary to estimate transition rates below age 50. No attempt was made to construct marital status life tables for cohorts born since 1945 since too much information from the critical years of marital status changes would have to be estimated.

Computer programs developed by Frans Willekens and Andrei Rogers (1978) were used to compute the marital status life tables. These programs generate a voluminous amount of output so that many of our results are presented with the aid of summary statistics generated from the life tables.

3 Results

First Marriage Patterns

A discussion of patterns of first marriage raises two questions: (1) how prevalent is marriage? and (2) for those who marry, at what age do they marry? Our data on these subjects are shown in Table 8.1. The prevalence of marriage can be measured by the percentage of life table cohort members surviving to age 50 who have married at some earlier point in their lives. For white females this figure is comparatively low for women reaching their prime marrying ages during the Depression, but it rises steadily up to 97 per cent for the 1930–34 cohort. A slight decline in this proportion is evident for women born since 1935, but the figure remains in excess of 96 per cent. Marriage is somewhat less prevalent among black females than among whites. The proportion ever marrying by age 50 fluctuates between 92 and 93 per cent for most cohorts born prior to 1935. Since 1935, however, this proportion has fallen to less than 90 per cent.

Trends in the proportion ever marrying are parallelled by data on age at first marriage. Following a mild increase for the 1910–14 cohort, the mean

Table 8.1   Patterns of first marriage, by race and birth cohort

Population	Mean age at first marriage ± one standard deviation	Percent ever-marrying by age 50	Percent of 20–24 year-olds in a stationary population never-married
White females			
1940–1944	21.2 ± 4.4	96.5	32.0
1935–1939	21.1 ± 4.4	96.4	31.4
1930–1934	21.3 ± 4.6	96.9	33.1
1925–1929	21.9 ± 5.0	95.7	38.0
1920–1924	22.4 ± 5.7	95.8	42.7
1915–1919	23.0 ± 5.7	94.6	48.9
1910–1914	23.5 ± 6.4	93.7	52.1
1905–1909	23.3 ± 6.5	93.1	49.1
Black females			
1940–1944	21.7 ± 5.7	89.9	39.0
1935–1939	21.7 ± 5.8	91.4	40.6
1930–1934	21.3 ± 4.8	93.4	37.6
1925–1929	21.6 ± 5.8	92.5	38.3
1920–1924	22.4 ± 6.0	92.6	45.2
1915–1919	22.7 ± 7.4	92.4	44.9
1910–1914	22.1 ± 6.8	92.7	42.1
1905–1909	22.9 ± 7.9	95.1	42.9

age at first marriage for white females declined steadily before bottoming out at 21.1 years with the 1935–39 cohort. Reductions in the mean age at marriage have not been as sharp for black females, and the data in Table 8.1 suggest that the reversal in this decline occurred somewhat earlier for blacks. Among women born near the beginning of this century, blacks married earlier than whites, but this propensity has shifted for women born since 1935. Table 8.1 also shows that, when the age at first marriage falls, marriages tend to be compressed into a smaller age range, and vice versa. The standard deviation of the age at first marriage is positively correlated with the mean.

The behaviour in a life table stationary population of the proportion of 20–24 year olds who have not yet married is influenced both by the proportion ever marrying and by the age at first marriage. Trends in this proportion follow closely those in the mean age at first marriage. Among white females, this proportion fell from close to 50 per cent to 31 per cent for the 1935–39 cohort. Declines were less pronounced for black females, and for the most recent cohorts, there were larger proportions of never-married 20–24 year-old black females than whites.

Marital Dissolution

Our discussion of marital dissolution is focused largely on the breakup of first marriages. First marriages can end in any one of four ways: (1) separation, (2) divorce with no prior spell of separation, (3) death of the husband, or (4) death of the wife. Data in Table 8.2 indicate the relative frequency of each type of termination for cohorts of American women. Most striking is the increasing frequency with which marriages end in separation. For white females this proportion increased from 10 to 44 per cent across the eight birth cohorts, and for black females the rise went from 20 per cent to 61 per cent. In the right-hand panel of Table 8.2 we have grouped the ways that marriages can end into two categories reflecting marital discord on the one hand and death to a spouse on the other. Most women born near the turn of the century could expect to live with their husbands until one of them died, but this expectation is no longer realistic. For white females born from 1940 to 1944, roughly half of all first marriages are projected to end through death and the remaining half through separation or divorce. The reversal is even more dramatic for black women. For the 1905–09 cohort, about one in every four marriages ended in separation or divorce, but this proportion has increased to nearly two out of three for the 1940–44 cohort.

Additional information on the dissolution of first marriages is contained in Table 8.3. Column 1 shows the probability that a separation is followed by a divorce. Our data do not capture separations followed by a reconciliation, but that not all separations end in divorce is explained by the fact that separated persons are also exposed to the risk of death and, depending upon the averge length of a separation, a nontrivial proportion may die before

Table 8.2   Types of marital dissolution from first marriage, by race and birth cohort

Population	Proportion of first marriages terminated by				Per cent terminated by	
	separation (1)	divorce[a] (2)	widowhood (3)	death (4)	separation or divorce (5)	widowhood or death (6)
White females						
1940–1944	0.439	0.032	0.380	0.149	47.1	52.9
1935–1939	0.402	0.034	0.404	0.160	43.6	56.4
1930–1934	0.257	0.042	0.501	0.201	29.8	70.2
1925–1929	0.217	0.030	0.538	0.215	24.7	75.3
1920–1924	0.192	0.032	0.552	0.224	22.3	77.7
1915–1919	0.151	0.026	0.585	0.238	17.7	82.3
1910–1914	0.128	0.027	0.596	0.249	15.6	84.4
1905–1909	0.100	0.022	0.585	0.293	12.2	87.8
Black females						
1940–1944	0.608	0.029	0.264	0.099	63.7	36.3
1935–1939	0.571	0.024	0.269	0.136	59.5	40.5
1930–1934	0.465	0.027	0.338	0.169	49.2	50.8
1925–1929	0.363	0.062	0.357	0.218	42.5	57.5
1920–1924	0.314	0.037	0.396	0.254	35.0	65.0
1915–1919	0.251	0.062	0.398	0.289	31.3	68.7
1910–1914	0.237	0.050	0.406	0.307	28.7	71.3
1905–1909	0.201	0.071	0.438	0.289	27.2	72.8

[a] For this fraction of first marriages, the separation and divorce occurred in the same month, so there is assumed to be no intervening spell of separation.

Table 8.3   Dimensions of separation and divorce following first marriage, by race and birth cohort

Population	Probability of			Average duration of separation
	Separation ending in divorce	marriage ending in separation or divorce	Marriage ending in divorce	
	(1)	(2)	(3)	(in years)
White females				
1940–1944	0.991	0.471	0.467	1.5
1935–1939	0.953	0.436	0.417	3.0
1930–1934	0.977	0.298	0.293	2.6
1925–1929	0.969	0.247	0.240	2.9
1920–1924	0.962	0.223	0.216	2.8
1915–1919	0.965	0.177	0.172	3.0
1910–1914	0.940	0.156	0.148	4.2
1905–1909	0.952	0.122	0.117	3.5
Black females				
1940–1944	0.748	0.637	0.484	12.7
1935–1939	0.594	0.595	0.363	17.4
1930–1934	0.554	0.492	0.285	18.3
1925–1929	0.642	0.425	0.295	16.6
1920–1924	0.705	0.350	0.258	12.8
1915–1919	0.717	0.313	0.242	13.0
1910–1914	0.797	0.287	0.239	9.7
1905–1909	0.864	0.272	0.245	7.0

divorcing. The proportion of white separated women who proceed to a divorce is consistently well above 90 per cent for all birth cohorts. By contrast, the proportion is much lower for black women primarily because black women spend a longer time separated than white women (see column 4 of Table 8.3). The probability of a first marriage ending in either separation or divorce (column 2) is simply the sum of columns 1 and 2 in Table 8.2. Black female marriages have consistently been more susceptible to this type of disruption than have white female marriages. However, if we consider the probability that a first marriage ends in divorce (column 3 of Table 8.3), blacks appear to be not so different from whites. For the 1940–44 birth cohort, for example, the probability of a first marriage ending in divorce is 0.47 for white females and 0.48 for black females.

The probability of a first marriage ending in divorce is computed by multiplying the probability of a marriage ending in a separation by the probability of a separation ending in divorce and adding the probability of a marriage ending directly in divorce. Black women have higher probabilities of their marriages ending in separation than do white women, but significantly lower probabilities of a separation ending in divorce. Thus when the probabilities are multiplied, some of the black-white differences disappear.

Remarriage

Selected indicators of remarriage are contained in Table 8.4. For the white female population, the secular increase in the probability that a marriage ends in divorce is reflected in the rising proportion of all marriages that are remarriages. For the 1905–09 cohort there were just 19 remarriages for every 100 first marriages, but for the most recent cohort this ratio is projected to reach 55 remarriages for every 100 first marriages. The total remarriage rate for white women has also risen steadily, more than doubling its value between the 1905–09 and 1940–44 cohorts.[3] This increase is not attributable to an increased probability of remarriage following divorce, which has remained relatively stable, or to a rise in the probability of remarriage following widowhood, which has shown no consistent time trend. Rather, the rise in the total remarriage rate has been caused (in a demographic sense) by an increase in the number of divorced women relative to widows and by the fact that remarriage rates following divorce are substantially higher than remarriage rates following widowhood.

Black females present a somewhat different picture. There is no evident trend in the proportion of all marriages that are remarriages. With the exception of the 1940–44 cohort, the number of remarriages per 100 first marriages has fluctuated between 25 and 36. In contrast to whites, the total remarriage rate for black women shows no substantial secular trend. Even though remarriage rates following divorce for black females are higher than remarriage rates following widowhood and despite the increased number of divorced black women, the decline in the remarriage rate following divorce is sufficient to prevent a sharp increase in the total remarriage rate.[4]

Combining Marital Spells from a Lifetime Perspective

In the remaining discussion marital experiences of successive birth cohorts are viewed over the entire lifetimes of individuals. To begin, consider the average duration of alternative marital spells shown in Table 8.5. The

---

[3] In Table 8.4 the total remarriage rate is derived by thinking of a life table as a stationary population. In particular, this rate is calculated as the total annual number of remarriages per 1000 divorced or widowed persons in a stationary population.

[4] The large differences between remarriage rates of divorced and widowed women in Table 8.4 are due to two factors. First, divorced women have higher age-specific remarriage rates than widowed women. For white females, for example, age-specific transition rates, when summed for ages 20 to 64 and averaged across all eight birth cohorts, are 44 per cent higher for the transition from divorced to remarried than from widowed to remarried. For black women, age-specific remarriage rates following divorce are on average 123 per cent higher than comparable rates following widowhood. Second, remarriage chances typically decline with age for both divorced and widowed women. Since widows are older than divorced females on average, this feature further depresses remarriage rates of widows. In the eight stationary populations corresponding to the eight cohort marital status life tables for white females, the average age of divorced individuals is 56.3 years compared to an average age of 68.8 for widows. Among blacks, the average ages are 52.6 and 63.6, respectively.

Table 8.4 Selected indicators of remarriage, by race and birth cohort

Population	Percent of all marriages that are		Number of marriages per person marrying	Total remarriage rate[a]	Remarriage rate following divorce[b]	Probability of remarriage following divorce[c]	Remarriage rate following widowhood[d]	Probability of remarriage following widowhood[e]
	first marriages	remarriages						
	(1)	(2)	(3)	(4)	(5)	(6)	(7)	(8)
White females								
1940–1944	64.7	35.3	1.55	31.9	62.6	0.741	9.5	0.138
1935–1939	70.2	29.8	1.42	24.7	40.1	0.567	9.4	0.141
1930–1934	73.9	26.1	1.35	23.1	57.3	0.693	6.3	0.097
1925–1929	75.9	24.1	1.32	21.8	58.2	0.703	8.2	0.122
1920–1924	79.4	20.6	1.26	18.3	43.8	0.595	9.3	0.139
1915–1919	79.2	20.8	1.26	19.1	53.2	0.673	10.1	0.149
1910–1914	81.5	18.5	1.23	16.8	53.0	0.685	9.4	0.142
1905–1909	84.0	16.0	1.19	14.7	58.2	0.715	8.1	0.129
Black females								
1940–1944	65.0	35.0	1.54	27.7	38.8	0.644	15.3	0.279
1935–1939	73.7	26.3	1.36	20.5	32.7	0.611	8.0	0.162
1930–1934	80.3	19.7	1.25	14.4	31.2	0.590	3.8	0.083
1925–1929	75.3	24.7	1.33	20.8	53.7	0.747	4.4	0.092
1920–1924	77.5	22.6	1.29	19.2	45.4	0.647	7.9	0.154
1915–1919	77.2	22.8	1.30	21.4	51.7	0.697	8.2	0.150
1910–1914	73.8	26.2	1.35	25.9	65.4	0.778	12.0	0.216
1905–1909	76.1	23.9	1.31	23.5	66.8	0.733	10.8	0.187

[a] Annual number of remarriages per 1000 divorced or widowed persons.
[b] Annual number of remarriages following divorce per 1000 divorced persons in a stationary population.
[c] Number of remarriages following divorce per divorce.
[d] Annual number of remarriages following widowhood per 1000 widowed persons in a stationary population.
[e] Number of remarriages following widowhood per widowing.

Table 8.5 Average duration (in years) of alternative marital spells, by race and birth cohort

Population	Never married	First marriage	Remarriage	All marriages	Separation after first marriage	Separation after remarriage	All separations	Divorce	Widowhood
White females									
1940–1944	22.4	30.0	16.7	25.3	1.5	2.0	1.6	11.8	14.6
1935–1939	22.1	32.2	14.8	27.1	3.0	1.9	2.7	14.1	14.9
1930–1934	21.8	35.2	16.1	30.2	2.7	1.7	2.3	12.1	15.3
1925–1929	22.4	35.5	17.7	31.2	2.9	2.0	2.6	12.1	14.9
1920–1924	22.3	35.7	19.7	32.4	2.8	3.6	2.9	13.6	14.9
1915–1919	23.3	35.6	18.1	31.9	3.0	3.1	3.0	12.7	14.7
1910–1914	23.2	35.1	19.8	32.2	4.2	5.9	4.5	12.9	15.2
1905–1909	23.2	36.1	19.8	33.5	3.5	2.5	3.4	12.3	16.0
Black females									
1940–1944	25.8	18.3	13.8	16.7	12.7	11.3	12.5	16.6	18.2
1935–1939	24.5	21.2	14.4	19.4	17.4	6.0	15.6	18.7	20.2
1930–1934	23.0	23.4	18.3	22.4	18.3	6.8	17.0	18.9	22.0
1925–1929	22.8	24.9	15.6	22.6	16.6	14.6	16.2	13.9	20.9
1920–1924	22.9	26.2	19.5	24.7	12.8	8.6	12.0	14.2	19.4
1915–1919	22.0	26.9	18.2	24.9	13.0	12.6	12.9	13.5	18.3
1910–1914	20.7	25.1	21.5	24.2	9.7	8.8	9.5	11.9	18.0
1905–1909	19.5	24.3	20.4	23.4	7.0	12.6	8.0	11.0	17.3

average amount of time spent in any marital status is defined only for individuals experiencing that marital status and is computed as the total number of person-years lived in a given marital status by the cohort over its entire lifetime divided by the number of times that marital status is entered. Several important differences between blacks and whites stand out. The average duration of a first marriage is noticeably higher for white females than for blacks. For white females the average is always above 30 years and is generally closer to 35 years with the exception of the last two birth cohorts in which the accelerating probability of marital disruption through separation and divorce is manifest. By contrast, the average duration of a first marriage for black women has been closer to 25 years, again with the exception of the two or three most recent cohorts in which it has fallen.

Black and white females also differ in terms of how long they spend separated. For white women born since 1920, the average length of a separation is less than three years, whereas for blacks it is in the teens. Similar differences, though not as large, show up when divorce and widowhood are considered. The average length of either type of spell is generally less for whites than for blacks. The picture that is beginning to emerge is one in which the average length of time spent married is greater for whites than for blacks, but the average length of time spend unmarried for blacks exceeds that for whites.[5]

A more succinct way to summarize a cohort's experience with marriage, separation, divorce, and remarriage is to decompose the cohort's life expectancy at birth into the number of years expected to be lived in each marital status category. This information is shown for white and black females in Tables 8.6 and 8.7, respectively. Concentrating first on white women, the declining age at first marriage is reflected in smaller proportions of one's lifetime spent in the never-married status. This trend can be expected to reverse for cohorts born since 1945, for whom a postponement

---

[5] There is an interesting relation between the average duration of never-married spells in Table 8.5 and the mean age at first marriage in Table 8.1. If we let A = the average duration in the never-married state, A_1 = the mean age at first marriage, A_2 = the mean age at death of all never-married persons, W_1 = the number of persons in a life table cohort who marry prior to death, and W_2 = the number of persons in a life table cohort who die in the never-married state, then

$$A = \frac{A_1 W_1 + A_2 W_2}{W_1 + W_2}.$$

There are several situations in which A and A_1 would be equal. For example, in a cohort free of mortality until age 50 and in which all women marry by age 50, $W_2 = 0$ and $A = A_1$. A circumstance that might be more plausible is one where $A_1 = A_2$, that is, where the mean age at first marriage equals the average age at death of never-married persons. If mortality is very high so there are many infant and childhood deaths, and if marriage is nearly universal among survivors, then A_2 will tend to be less than A_1 and A will be less than A_1. On the other hand, if mortality is relatively low and marriage does not approximate universality, then A_2 will exceed A_1 and A will be greater than A_1. Comparing measures of A and A_1 in Tables 8.5 and 8.1 for successive birth cohorts of black females provides a vivid illustration of these principles. For blacks, A_2 increased from 11.6 years in the 1905–09 cohort to 43.3 years for the 1940–44 cohort. For white females the increase is less, from 21.2 to 34.6 for the same cohorts.

Table 8.6 Distribution of life expectancy at birth by marital status: white females, by birth cohort

Cohort	Total life expectancy at birth	Time spent in each marital status (in years)						
		Never-married	First marriage	Separated, formerly first married	Divorced	Widowed	Remarriage	Separated, formerly remarried
1940–1944	75.5	22.4	27.9	0.6	6.7	9.2	8.5	0.2
1935–1939	74.5	22.1	29.5	1.1	7.8	7.9	5.8	0.3
1930–1934	73.7	21.8	32.0	0.6	4.6	9.3	5.2	0.2
1925–1929	71.9	22.4	31.1	0.5	3.5	9.2	4.9	0.1
1920–1924	70.7	22.3	31.0	0.5	3.2	9.1	4.4	0.2
1915–1919	69.2	23.3	29.9	0.4	2.4	9.1	4.0	0.1
1910–1914	66.4	23.2	28.2	0.4	1.8	9.0	3.6	0.1
1905–1909	65.5	23.2	28.7	0.3	1.4	9.0	3.0	0.0
		Percentage distribution						
1940–1944	100.0	29.6	36.9	0.8	8.9	12.2	11.2	0.3
1935–1939	100.0	29.7	39.6	1.5	10.5	10.6	7.7	0.4
1930–1934	100.0	29.6	43.4	0.8	6.2	12.7	7.0	0.2
1925–1929	100.0	31.2	43.3	0.8	4.8	12.9	6.8	0.2
1920–1924	100.0	31.6	43.9	0.7	4.5	12.8	6.3	0.2
1915–1919	100.0	33.6	43.2	0.6	3.5	13.2	5.8	0.2
1910–1914	100.0	35.0	42.5	0.7	2.8	13.6	5.4	0.2
1905–1909	100.0	35.5	43.7	0.4	2.1	13.7	4.6	0.1

of first marriage is increasingly common. Rising probabilities of separation and divorce not only shorten the time white women spend in a first marriage but also contribute to an increase in the proportionate amount of time divorced. Finally, because of the increased incidence of divorce and the fact that remarriage rates following divorce have remained stable, white females are spending proportionately more time remarried. When first marriages are combined with remarriages, white women from these cohorts are likely to spend between 47 and 50 per cent of their total average lifetimes in the married state.

Data in Table 8.7 show that there has been an impressive increase in life expectancy at birth for black women from 51 years for the 1905–09 birth cohort to 72 years for the 1940–44 cohort. This increase has not meant, however, that more time on average is being spent by black women in each marital status category. In particular, the amount of total average lifetime expected to be spent in a first marriage initially increased to just over 20 years but subsequently fell back to approximately 15 years for the 1940–44 cohort. This recent decline reflects rising probabilities of marital separation. Rising probabilities of separation and divorce also lie behind both the absolute and the proportionate increases in the amount of time black women spend separated and divorced. The differences between black and white women in the time spent separated are particularly noteworthy and are due in large part to the lower propensity by black women to terminate a separation with a formal divorce. With the exception of the 1940–44 cohort, the average absolute amount of time black women spend remarried has remained relatively constant, but as a proportion of total life expectancy it has fallen as life expectancy rose. Thus time spent married, whether in a first marriage or in a remarriage, has for black females comprised a gradually dwindling fraction of total lifetime experience. Black women from the 1905–09 cohort devoted roughly 41 per cent of their total lifetimes to being married, but this proportion fell to just over 31 per cent for the 1940–44 cohort. Black females have consistently been below white women in terms of total time spent married, but the sharp declines in the fraction among more recent cohorts of black women have accentuated the differences between blacks and whites.

4 Conclusion

Our results on the marital behaviours of adult black and white women span birth cohorts from 1905–09 to 1940–44. For these women there is evidence of a decline in the age at first marriage, a decline that ended and then showed signs of reversing with the 1935–39 cohort of white females and even earlier for blacks. (We know from a separate analysis of period marital status life tables that the decline in the age at first marriage terminated sometime during the 1950s followed by a sustained increase up to at least 1980). In

Table 8.7 Distribution of life expectancy at birth by marital status: black females, by birth cohort

Cohort	Total life expectancy at birth	Never-married	First marriage	Separated, formerly first married	Divorced	Widowed	Remarriage	Separated, formerly remarried
							Time spent in each marital status (in years)	
1940–1944	71.9	25.8	15.4	6.5	8.6	7.8	6.3	1.4
1935–1939	70.4	24.5	17.9	8.4	7.4	7.3	4.3	0.5
1930–1934	68.6	23.0	19.8	7.2	5.6	8.8	3.8	0.3
1925–1929	66.1	22.8	20.3	4.9	4.3	8.6	4.2	1.1
1920–1924	63.0	22.9	20.4	3.1	3.5	8.2	4.4	0.4
1915–1919	60.1	22.0	20.4	2.5	3.2	7.3	4.1	0.8
1910–1914	55.8	20.7	17.9	1.6	2.5	7.2	5.4	0.4
1905–1909	50.8	19.5	16.6	1.0	2.1	7.0	4.4	0.4
							Percentage distribution	
1940–1944	100.0	35.8	21.5	9.1	12.0	10.9	8.7	2.0
1935–1939	100.0	34.8	25.4	11.9	10.5	10.4	6.1	0.8
1930–1934	100.0	33.6	28.9	10.5	8.2	12.8	5.5	0.5
1925–1929	100.0	34.5	30.7	7.5	6.5	12.9	6.3	1.6
1920–1924	100.0	36.3	32.3	4.9	5.6	13.1	7.0	0.7
1915–1919	100.0	36.6	33.9	4.1	5.3	12.1	6.8	1.3
1910–1914	100.0	37.2	32.0	2.9	4.6	12.9	9.7	0.7
1905–1909	100.0	38.3	32.6	1.9	4.1	13.8	8.6	0.7

addition, successive birth cohorts have been characterized by rising fractions of first marriages ending in separation or divorce. Probabilities of separating have usually been higher for blacks than for whites, but smaller fractions of separated black women subsequently divorce. For the 1940–44 birth cohort, blacks and whites exhibit roughly equal tendencies for first marriages to end in divorce. Total remarriage rates for white women have increased, but they have remained stable for blacks. This has meant a rising amount of total lifetime spent in remarriage for white women, whereas this total lifetime proportion for black women has gone down slightly. When white and black women are contrasted in the aggregate, the amount of total lifetime that cohorts of white women spend married has fluctuated between about 47 and 50 per cent. However, the corresponding proportion for black females has declined from 41 per cent for the 1905–09 cohort to about 31 per cent for the 1940–44 cohort.

Since we have not discussed the fertility patterns of these women, we cannot precisely delineate the implications of changes in adult marital status for the living arrangements of children. If all childbearing occurred within marriage and if only couples without children were prone to the risks of separation and divorce, then children's living arrangements would be relatively immune to the marital behaviours of adults. Neither of these assumptions is true, however. The presence of young children may decrease the probability of a parental separation or divorce, but it does not prevent marital disruption. Moreover, not all fertility is confined to marriage.

In the introduction we cited evidence that marital fertility rates have been declining in the United States, but nonmarital fertility rates have been increasing. We know, for example, that the proportion of all births that are nonmarital births has risen for both white and black women. Moreover, there is a growing tendency for women in general, but especially for black women, to spend larger fractions of their total lifetimes outside marriage. This information suggests that proportionately more children will experience a single-parent family at some point in their lives, that the amount of time these children can expect to spend in a single-parent family will increase, and that the experience of black children with single-parent families will continue to be greater than for white children. The following chapter by Sandra Hofferth takes up these issues in more detail.

References

Espenshade, T. J., (1983), 'Black-White Differences in Marriage, Separation, Divorce, and Remarriage', paper presented at the annual meetings of the Population Association of America, Pittsburgh, Pennsylvania.

National Center for Health Statistics (1970), 'Mortality from Selected Causes by Marital Status: United States — Parts A and B', *Vital and Health Statistics*, Series 20, Number 8, Public Health Service, Hyattsville, Maryland.

National Center for Health Statistics (1982), *Vital Statistics of the United States,*

1978, Vol. I Natality, Public Health Service, Hyattsville, Maryland.

National Center for Health Statistics (1983), 'Advance Report of Final Natality Statistics, 1981', *Monthly Vital Statistics Report*, Vol. 32, No. 9, Supplement, Public Health Service, Hyattsville, Maryland.

US Bureau of the Census (1983), 'Marital Status and Living Arrangements: March 1982', *Current Population Reports*, Series P-20, No. 380, US Government Printing Office, Washington, DC.

Willekens, F. and A. Rogers, (1978), *Spatial Population Analysis: Methods and Computer Programs*, RR-78-18, International Institute for Applied Systems Analysis, Laxenburg, Austria.

9 Recent Trends in the Living Arrangements of Children: A Cohort Life Table Analysis*

SANDRA L. HOFFERTH

National Institute of Child Health and Human Development, Bethesda, Maryland, USA.

Introduction

During the past two decades dramatic changes in marriage and childbearing have occurred in the United States. First-marriage and remarriage rates have declined among youth in their late teens and early twenties so that the average age at first marriage has risen (Williams and Kuhn, 1973; US Bureau of the Census, 1980a; Cherlin, 1981). The annual divorce total has more than tripled and the divorce rate has increased by 136 per cent over the same period (Plateris, 1978; US Bureau of the Census, 1980a, b; 1981b; National Center for Health Statistics, 1982).

In addition, patterns of childbearing have changed. Besides reducing family size, falling marital fertility has accentuated the importance of non-marital childbearing; the proportion of all births that occur outside marriage has risen markedly among whites and nonwhites and among all age groups (National Center for Health Statistics, 1981). Slightly more than 2 per cent of white children were born out of wedlock in 1960; by 1980 11 per cent of white children were born out of wedlock. Among nonwhites the proportion of all children born out of wedlock more than doubled, from 22 per cent in 1960 to 55 per cent in 1980.

A third important development is that of nonmarital cohabitation. Over the decade of the 1970s the number of unmarried couples tripled (US Bureau of the Census, 1981a). Slightly over one quarter of these couples have children. Although the actual incidence of cohabitation at any one time is small, involving about 4 per cent of all households (Spanier, 1983), the number of couples who have ever cohabitated is considerably larger. Data available for college students, indicate that about one quarter had ever coha-bited (Macklin, 1978). It is clear that nonmarital cohabitation has increased

* This research was supported by federal funds from the Center for Population Research, The National Institute of Child Health and Human Development, US Department of Health and Human Services, under contract number N01-HD-02849. The contents of this publication do not necessarily reflect the views or policies of the US Department of Health and Human Services. The helpful comments of Thomas Espenshade, Douglas Wolf, Robert Schoen, Arthur Campbell, and Elizabeth Stephen, the research assistance of Carolyn O'Brien, and the programming assistance of Roger Kohn, John Moore, and Thy Dao are much appreciated.

in importance in the United States, even though individual lifetime experience with it remains unknown.

As a result, over the past two decades the proportion of children living with both of their natural parents has fallen dramatically, while the proportion living with only their mother has more than doubled (US Bureau of the Census, 1981a). This trend has aroused considerable concern for a number of reasons; one of the most important is the large differential in economic well-being between children in two-parent and female-headed, single-parent families. The purpose of this chapter is to explore the implications of changes in adult marital behaviour for the lives of their children. Increased freedom of choice and movement for adults does not necessarily come without a price. That price may be the well-being of children. However, it is only when we know how, in fact, adult behaviours play out in the lives of children that we can make some attempt to define the solutions.

In contrast to the previous chapter, this chapter focuses, therefore, on the living arrangements of children. The objective is to describe the proportion of children who ever experience a given family type and the proportion of childhood spent in that type. Age, race, birth cohort, and family type at birth differences are emphasized. The common analytic tool is the multistate life table, a variant of the increment–decrement life table. Because of differences between the types of analysis in the two papers, particularly differences in focus — for example, marital status versus living arrangements — and in data — PSID versus CPS — which require slightly different analytic approaches, the unique methodological characteristics of this analysis are emphasized throughout.

Methods

Living Arrangements versus Marital Status of Parents

There are two basic approaches to describing the family experiences of children. The first describes the living arrangements of children at one point in time, using data from a cross-sectional survey (e.g., Glick, 1979). This approach can provide a snapshot of children at a series of time points; however, no dynamic perspective is possible. The second approach describes the movement of children between families of different types defined by the marital status of their parents. Data from this approach heretofore came from retrospective marital and fertility histories obtained, again, in a cross-sectional survey (e.g., Bumpass, 1979, 1984; Furstenberg *et al.*, 1983). This approach is dynamic in so far as dates of births, marriages, and divorces provide markers for critical events through childhood. Using such data, the child's experience is a mirror image of the parental marital experience, weighted by the number of children the mother has.

Although the results are interesting and informative, retrospective marital and fertility histories still do not provide a picture of children's living arrangements. In particular, children do not always reside with their mothers, separations may occur which are not followed by divorce, informal unions have become fairly common, and many children spend periods of time with other relatives or non-relatives without a parent present. Although conceivable, complete retrospective histories of living arrangements have not been obtained. However, concurrently or prospectively obtained data about individuals in families over a long period of time are available in the Panel Study of Income Dynamics, the data set chosen for this study.

Data

This report is based on data from the first 12 years (1968 through 1979) of the Panel Study of Income Dynamics (PSID). The data were obtained in annual interviews with members of a national probability sample of about 5000 families that have been followed longitudinally since 1968. Although 24 per cent of the originally selected sample could not be interviewed in the first year, panel losses in subsequent years have been small (about 3 per cent annually). Sixty-four per cent of the families interviewed in 1968 were still in the sample in 1979. In addition, whenever a member of an original panel family formed a separate family, that entire family was added to the sample. By 1979 a total of 3310 split-offs had been added to the survey. Thus because the number of split-offs exceeds the panel losses, the number of families continues to increase. There were a total of 6373 families in the survey in 1979.

The PSID has many advantages for the analysis of change in living arrangements. The major advantage is that an actual record of where a child is living each year is obtained, as well as information about other members of that household. Children born to sample members as well as children in the survey initially are followed throughout the panel years. Although the PSID has many advantages for the analysis of changes in living arrangements, it was not originally designed for demographic research. Thus there are also problems. The most important of these include lack of information on precise relationships among family members, lack of detailed information on parental marital experience, and lack of detailed information on sub-families. A computer program was developed to code living arrangements for most children; about 10 per cent were coded manually (see Hofferth, 1985, 75–112 for a more detailed description of the procedure followed).

Key Variables

Living arrangements/family types of children were defined in terms of five variables: number of parents, sex of parents, marital status of parents, relationship of child to parents (natural versus stepchild), and relationship of child to other family members (if not living with a parent), following

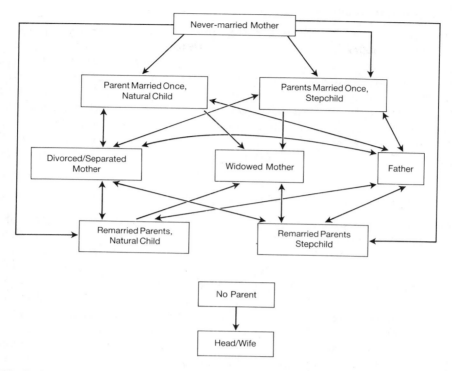

The direction of each arrow represents the direction of the transition; a two-headed arrow indicates possible return to state. The eight transitions to 'head/wife' and the eight to 'no parent' are included in the model. They were not represented in this figure in order to keep it readable.

Figure 9.1 Schematic representation of the family types which children experience and the potential transitions between them

Glick (1979). The ten family types are the following: (1) never-married mother, (2) two natural parents, both in first marriage, (3) one natural and one stepparent, both married once, (4) divorced or separated mother, (5) widowed mother, (6) two natural parents, one or both married more than once, (7) one natural and one stepparent, one or both married more than once, (8) father, (9) no parents, and (10) head/wife of own family.[1] The family types and the possible transitions between them are diagrammed in Figure 9.1. With the 10 family types there are 45 possible transitions (not including the 10 probabilities of remaining in the same state); the others are not logically possible.[2]

[1] Adoptive cannot be distinguished from natural parents with these data.

[2] 'Head/wife' of own family is assumed to be an absorbing state. Once in, a child cannot move to any other type. 'No parent' family is partially absorbing; children in a 'no parent' family can only become 'head/wife' of own family. These assumptions were made because of the large number of potential transitions out and the very small number of cases in each type.

Period versus Cohort Approaches

Since different birth cohorts are aggregated in the cross-section, compositional effects could mask substantial and rapid cohort change, thus limiting the researchers' ability to project future cohort experience. In this paper, children's experiences are analysed separately by actual birth cohort. Although this facilities interpretation of the results, it presents analytic problems; since only 12 years of data were available, all cohorts are censored either at the beginning or the end. In order to estimate the experience of early cohorts as well as recent cohorts of children, the unknown experience was projected using regression techniques.

Multiple versus Single State of Origin

One important distinction between the analysis of marital status and that of living arrangements is that there is only one initial state for the former — single — while there are multiple possible living arrangements for children at birth. In this study it was assumed that children begin life in only five of the 10 family types — never-married mother; two natural parents, both in their first marriage; divorced or separated mother; widowed mother; and two natural parents, one or both married more than once. The child is always assumed to be living with the natural mother at birth; if a mother is married at the time of a child's birth, that child is assumed to be living with both natural parents. The child may not be the natural child of the mother's husband, but that fact cannot be ascertained. In addition, it was assumed that if a never-married mother married within two years of a child's birth she married the father; otherwise she did not marry the child's natural father. Data presented in Furstenberg (1976) suggest that if the mother does not marry the father of the child within about two years, such a marriage is unlikely. Thus living arrangement life tables are more like tables of geographic mobility than like marital status or working life tables.

Applying the Multistate Life Table Approach to Children's Living Arrangements

The multistate life table is an increment–decrement life table that shows gross (not just net) flows of individuals into and out of discrete and mutually exclusive 'states'. Both exit from and entry (and re-entry) into states are permitted. The multistate life table displays the mortality and mobility history of a birth cohort, which in this case refers to a group of people born at the same moment in time and in the same region. By thinking of the family type in which children live as a 'state', this model can be adapted to a study of the living arrangements of children. This approach is described more fully in

Willekens and Rogers (1978) and in Espenshade and Braun (1982) and will not be discussed here.

The three basic inputs for calculating a multistate life table are the following:

1. mortality rates of children for each year of age by family type;
2. distribution of children born by family type; and
3. age-specific rates of moving from each family type to each alternative type by single year of age.

The sources of these inputs are first described, followed by a discussion of the summary statistics that form the basis of this paper.

Estimating Mortality Rates. Death rates for children by sex and race of child were obtained by interpolation from data from the National Center for Health Statistics for the years 1950 to 1978. Model life tables were also used to obtain death rates from one-year-olds. Death rates by family type are not available.

Recent birth cohorts have, of course, not yet reached age 18. To construct rates for incomplete cohorts, the natural logarithm of the death rate was regressed on age (linear), age (squared), race (black, white), and birth cohort (a set of five dummy variables for the six birth cohorts). Predicted values for incomplete experience were combined with actual rates to obtain predicted death rates for all ages, races, and birth cohorts.

Distribution of Children Born by Family Type. Estimates of the living arrangements of children at birth, by race and birth cohort, were obtained from the June 1980 Fertility and Marital History Supplement to the Current Population Survey (CPS).[3]

Estimating Transition Rates. Transition probabilities were calculated from the cross-classification of the living arrangements of children at age x and at age $x + 1$, by birth cohort and race. Using PSID data, however, this procedure gives complete estimates to age 17 for no birth cohort; all are censored either at the beginning or the end. In order to estimate the experience of early

---

[3] Estimates of the number of live births each year obtained from the Marital and Fertility History Supplement to the June 1975 Current Population Survey (CPS) were compared with estimates obtained from the National Center for Health Statistics (NCHS). Estimates from the CPS for the years 1950–74 (1975 was only one-half a year) show that live births to whites average 99.8 per cent of those reported by the NCHS. Live births to nonwhites average 80.8 per cent of those reported by the NCHS for 1950–72. Live births to nonwhites in 1973–74 are much lower — 65 per cent of the NCHS figures, on average. Of course, the CPS does not ask unmarried women under 18 their birth histories. Therefore, it will miss 1973–75 out-of-wedlock births to women who were under 18 years old in 1975. This was estimated to be 60 000 to 70 000 births per year for nonwhites. Adding these births to the total raises the coverage to a level similar to pre-1973 for non-whites. We conclude that CPS data are excellent for whites, somewhat less accurate, but still very good for non-whites. The 1980 CPS Marital and Fertility History Supplement was asked in the same way; the data quality is similar.

cohorts as well as recent cohorts of children, their incomplete experience has to be estimated. To do so the following procedure was used: the natural logarithm of each separate transition probability from each state, including the probability of remaining in the state, was regressed on age (an interval level variable), race (a dummy variable), and birth cohort (five dummy variables for the six birth cohorts 1950–54 to 1975–79). The regression was weighted by the number of cases in each category. Each model was examined individually. Nonlinearities were expressed as interactions or squared terms, where warranted, and the best model was identified for each transition. Predicted values of the transition probabilities were then obtained for all values of age, race, and birth cohort and normalized so that the transition probabilities in each row of the matrix (state at x by state at $x + 1$) summed to one. These normalized values were used to obtain transition rates for input into the life table procedure, in a procedure described by Ledent (1979) and by Schoen and Woodrow (1980:304).[4]

Estimating the Multistate Model. The distribution of children at birth, predicted death rates, and predicted transition rates for children aged 0 to 17 for the appropriate birth cohort (1950–54 to 1975–79) and race group (black, white) were input into a multistate life table programme developed by Willekens and Rogers (1978) to obtain estimates and projections of the experience of five-year cohorts of children born between 1950 and 1979. The predicted transition rates and death rates for the 1975 to 1979 birth cohort were combined with the actual distribution of children born between June 1979 and June 1980 to provide the projection of the experience of a child born in 1980 from birth to age 18.

Calculation of Summary Life Table Statistics. For ease of presentation and interpretation, the results of life table procedure were transformed into life status tables, described by Schoen and Nelson (1974). Because of the difficulty in interpreting the enormous amount of information produced, a set of tables that summarizes the results of the life table analyses over all initial statuses was created for each birth cohort: a summary table and the 10 associated tables each referring to a separate family type. These summary tables form the basis for the first part of the analysis. The results disaggregated by initial family type form the basis for the second part, analysis of the effect of children's family type at birth on family experiences to age 18.

Results

Transition of Children from a One-Parent to a Two-Parent Family

Table 9.1 shows the proportion whose mothers marry, by race, birth cohort,

---

[4] See Appendix for a discussion of the reasonableness of these projections.

Table 9.1 Proportion of children whose mothers marry or remarry, by race, birth cohort, and family type

Family type	Birth cohort						
	1980	1975–1979	1970–1974	1965–1969	1960–1964	1955–1959	1950–1954
White							
Single mother	.213	.213	.231	.148	.082	.197	.189
marries father	.145	.145	.166	.104	.046	.090	.159
marries other	.068	.068	.065	.044	.036	.107	.030
Divorced/Separated mother							
remarries	.914	.914	.922	.912	.912	.819	.577
reconciles	.016	.016	.010	.015	.026	.094	.314
Widowed mother	.567	.572	.595	.405	.514	.607	.801
Black							
Single mother	.406	.406	.422	.281	.182	.442	.300
marries father	.185	.185	.211	.130	.055	.110	.198
marries other	.221	.221	.211	.151	.127	.332	.102
Divorced/separated mother							
remarries	.923	.924	.925	.916	.915	.847	.613
reconciles	.011	.012	.008	.013	.021	.069	.285
Widowed mother	.249	.238	.254	.126	.172	.277	.505

and marital status of the mother. According to these data, about one out of five children born in 1980 of white single mothers can be expected to eventually move into two-parent families, compared with two out of five children of single black mothers. Among white children, the largest proportion will then be living with two natural parents; among black children about equal numbers will then be living with one natural and one stepparent as with two natural parents. The cohort trend is curvilinear among children of single mothers — the proportion falls, then rises. Among children of divorced and separated mothers, the trend is linear. An increase in the proportion moving into two-parent families occurs across cohorts. Nine out of ten white or black children born in 1980 and living with a divorced or separated mother are expected to eventually move into a two-parent family. Only a small proportion of this movement appears to be due to reconciliations (under 2 per cent). There is surprisingly little race difference in remarriage after divorce or separation. Finally, more than five out of ten white children of widowed mothers eventually live with two parents, more than two out of ten black children. The data suggest a decline across birth cohorts in movement into a two-parent family after living with a widowed mother.

Transition of Children from a Two-Parent to a One-parent Family

About three out of ten white children born in 1980 and in a first marriage, two-natural-parent family, can expect to experience a parental divorce or separation, four out of ten black children (Table 9.2). Across birth cohorts these figures have risen slightly, then fallen with more recent birth cohorts. The experience of divorce and separation, according to these figures, was highest among black children born in the 1960s and white children born in the early 1970s. These figures are much lower than could be expected. The reason is clear when the proportion whose father 'dies' is also considered. The proportion who move into a one-parent family due to the death of the father is very high — 35 per cent for blacks and 20 per cent for white children born in 1980 (data not presented here). The increase has also been marked since the birth cohort of 1950–54. The reason is probably over-reporting of deaths. In the Panel Study women with children who have, in fact, never been married often report that they are widows. In addition, there is considerable confusion in reporting of marital status for women who were divorced and whose ex-husband subsequently dies. Sometimes they report 'widowed,' sometimes 'divorced.' Thus deaths represent the breakup of a parental union, but it is unclear as to whether the father died or disappeared, and whether he was ever married to the mother in the first place. According to CPS data, the proportion of widowings is trivial in size — five

Table 9.2   Proportion of children whose mothers divorce or separate, by race, birth cohort, and family type

Family type	Birth cohort						
	1980	1975–1979	1970–1974	1965–1969	1960–1964	1955–1959	1950–1954
White							
First marriage, natural child	.304	.304	.319	.305	.306	.189	.037
First marriage, stepchild	.104	.104	.416	.270	.105	.063	.029
Remarriage, natural child	.909	.908	.981	.978	.978	.977	.968
Remarriage, stepchild	.931	.931	.932	.925	.938	.911	.885
Black							
First marriage, natural child	.411	.411	.467	.488	.502	.320	.059
First marriage, stepchild	.153	.153	.540	.362	.147	.096	.047
Remarriage, natural child	.943	.944	.973	.967	.966	.963	.960
Remarriage, stepchild	.938	.940	.937	.931	.940	.920	.903

Table 9.3   Proportion of children whose parents' marriage is dissolved by divorce or death of one parent, by race, birth cohort, and family type

Family type	Birth cohort						
	1980	1975–1979	1970–1974	1965–1969	1960–1964	1955–1959	1950–1954
White							
First marriage, natural child	.635	.635	.545	.378	.370	.269	.149
First marriage, stepchild	.104	.104	.416	.270	.105	.063	.029
Remarriage, natural child	.986	.986	.986	.984	.983	.983	.982
Remarriage, stepchild	.932	.932	.933	.926	.939	.912	.886
Black							
First marriage, natural child	.866	.866	.784	.615	.590	.462	.264
First marriage, stepchild	.153	.153	.540	.362	.147	.096	.047
Remarriage, natural child	.975	.975	.975	.971	.968	.967	.968
Remarriage, stepchild	.939	.941	.938	.931	.941	.921	.904

or six per cent. To obtain a more accurate picture of marital dissolutions, the proportion whose mother reported that her husband died and the proportion whose mother reported herself as divorced or separated should probably be summed. After this calculation (Table 9.3), it is clear that there has been an increase in the experience of breakup of parental unions with birth cohort, and that blacks experience higher levels than whites.

A substantial proportion of children are expected to go to live with their fathers — 11 per cent of black children, 13 per cent of white children born in 1980 (data not presented here). For whites this represents a doubling over the proportion born in the 1950s and 1960s who went to live with their father; it is about the same as it was for the 1950 cohort among blacks. In contrast, the proportion going to live with a nonrelative has been cut in half for recent cohorts of whites and blacks. These results suggest that children are staying with natural parents upon marital disruption more than in the past, and that one reason may be increased paternal participation in childrearing.

The first-marriage, one-natural and one-stepparent category is comprised of children who were born into a single-mother family and whose mother subsequently married, but not until two or more years after the birth of the child. Divorce and separation rates are relatively low; however, sample sizes are also relatively small. Divorce and separation rates are higher for blacks than for whites, though not by much. Trends indicate an increase in the late 1960s and early 1970s and a decline among more recent birth cohorts.

One surprising finding in this study is the very large proportion of children in remarriage families whose mother divorces or separates (Table 9.2). It does not seem to matter whether the child is a natural child or a stepchild. Rates are high for both races and all birth cohorts.[5] Nine out of ten children can be expected to move into a one-parent family from a remarriage family. There seems to be some decline in more recent birth cohorts in movement out of remarriage, natural-parent families, but rates are still high. There is, in contrast, a slight increase in movement out of remarriage, stepparent families; again, rates are high for both — nine out of ten children enter a single-parent family. Rates of movement into a widowed-mother category are small. Rates of movement into a father-only family have been increasing according to these data, with white or black children in a remarriage, two-natural-parent family born in 1980 more than five times as likely as children born in 1950–54 to go to live with their fathers (data not presented here).

Children's Experience with Different Types of Families

The transitions children make from one family type to another along with their initial distribution at birth determine their living arrangements at each age. In Table 9.4 is shown the proportion of children in each of ten living arrangements at ages 0 and 17 by birth cohort and race. The proportion living in each family type at age 0 represents the proportion of children in each family type at birth. For example, twice as many white children (6 per cent) in 1980 as in 1950–54 (3 per cent) were born to a never-married mother (Table 9.4). An additional 4 per cent were born in 1980 to a divorced or separated mother (compared to 2 per cent in 1950–54). Eighty per cent of white children were born to two natural parents both married once in 1980, compared to 90 per cent in 1950–54. Cohort trends are consistent. At any given age more recent birth cohorts are less likely to be living with two natural parents, and more likely to be living with a father, a divorced or separated mother, a widowed mother, or remarried parent and a stepparent (data not presented here).

Differences between black children and white children are great. Forty-three per cent of black children were born to a never-married mother in 1980, compared to 17 per cent in 1950–54. Thirteen per cent were born to a divorced or separated mother in 1980 (8 per cent in 1950–54), and an additional 1 per cent to a widowed mother. Thus a total of 58 per cent of black

---

[5] The several apparently idiosyncratic results obtained in this study, such as the high proportion of children in remarriage families whose mothers divorce or separate, is probably the result of a few unusual cases coupled with small sample sizes. The prediction of transition probabilities was highly sensitive to large values; in addition, continuity of observations (though not monotonicity) was assumed. Such an assumption may have been violated because of the small sample sizes. The large amount of data to be handled made it difficult to identify odd circumstances and correct them before running the final models. The problem of distinguishing between family types (such as widowed and divorced/separated mother families) may have been a contributing factor.

Table 9.4 Proportion of children living in family type at ages 0 to 17

Family type		Birth cohort						
		1980	1975–1979	1970–1974	1965–1969	1960–1964	1955–1959	1950–1954
White								
Single mother	0	.06	.06	.05	.04	.03	.03	.03
	17	.05	.05	.04	.04	.03	.03	.02
First marriage, natural child	0	.80	.81	.84	.87	.89	.90	.90
	17	.30	.31	.38	.54	.55	.70	.81
First marriage, stepchild	0	.00	.00	.00	.00	.00	.00	.00
	17	.01	.01	.02	.02	.04	.02	.01
Divorced/separated mother	0	.04	.05	.04	.04	.03	.02	.02
	17	.23	.23	.23	.17	.15	.08	.02
Widowed mother	0	.00	.00	.00	.00	.00	.00	.00
	17	.07	.07	.04	.02	.01	.01	.01
Remarriage, natural child	0	.09	.08	.06	.05	.05	.05	.05
	17	.00	.00	.00	.00	.00	.00	.00
Remarriage, stepchild	0	.00	.00	.00	.00	.00	.00	.00
	17	.24	.24	.24	.17	.15	.08	.02
Father	0	.00	.00	.00	.00	.00	.00	.00
	17	.08	.08	.02	.02	.03	.04	.06
Head/wife	0	.00	.00	.00	.00	.00	.00	.00
	17	.02	.02	.01	.01	.02	.03	.02
No parent	0	.00	.00	.00	.00	.00	.00	.00
	17	.01	.01	.01	.01	.01	.01	.02
Black								
Single mother	0	.43	.37	.33	.28	.19	.21	.17
	17	.25	.22	.19	.20	.16	.11	.12
First marriage, natural child	0	.40	.41	.49	.56	.66	.67	.70
	17	.06	.06	.11	.22	.26	.40	.62
First marriage, stepchild	0	.00	.00	.00	.00	.00	.00	.00
	17	.08	.07	.05	.05	.07	.09	.04
Divorced/separated mother	0	.13	.19	.14	.12	.11	.08	.08
	17	.20	.23	.26	.22	.22	.14	.04
Widowed mother	0	.01	.01	.01	.01	.01	.01	.01
	17	.14	.14	.10	.06	.03	.06	.05
Remarriage, natural child	0	.02	.03	.03	.04	.04	.04	.04
	17	.00	.00	.00	.00	.00	.00	.00
Remarriage, stepchild	0	.00	.00	.00	.00	.00	.00	.00
	17	.19	.22	.25	.21	.21	.13	.03
Father	0	.00	.00	.00	.00	.00	.00	.00
	17	.05	.05	.03	.02	.03	.04	.08
Head/wife	0	.00	.00	.00	.00	.00	.00	.00
	17	.01	.01	.01	.01	.01	.02	.02
No parent	0	.00	.00	.00	.00	.00	.00	.00
	17	.01	.01	.01	.01	.01	.01	.02

children were born to a mother who was not married, compared to 10 per cent of white children. Forty per cent of black children were born to two natural parents both married once in 1980, compared with 70 per cent in 1950–54.

As the children age and their parents marry, divorce, and remarry, the proportion living with an unmarried parent or two natural parents declines, while the proportion living with a divorced or separated mother, widowed mother, or one natural and one stepparent increases. Table 9.4 shows that although 80 per cent of all white children born in 1980 were born to two natural parents, both married once (the traditional family), by age 17 only 30 per cent are expected to still be in that family type. In contrast, among children born in 1950–54, the proportion living with natural parents declined only a small amount between birth and age 17 — from 90 to 80 per cent. Among black children the figures are similar, although fewer begin life in that family type. Forty per cent of black children were born to two natural parents both married once in 1980. By age 17 only 6 per cent of this birth cohort of children are expected to still be living in that family type. Of children born in 1950–54, in contrast, 70 per cent were born to two natural parents both married once and 62 per cent were still in such an arrangement at age 17. A relatively similar proportion of white and black children are projected by age 17 to be living with one natural parent and one stepparent, one or both remarried (24 and 19 per cent, respectively) or to be living with a divorced or separated mother (23 and 20 per cent, respectively). This contrasts sharply with the 1950–54 birth cohorts of whom 2 to 3 per cent were living with one natural parent and one stepparent at age 17. Eight per cent of white children are expected to be living with only their father, compared with five per cent of black children. Twice as many black children are expected to be living with a widowed mother (14 per cent) than white children (7 per cent) and five times more black (25 per cent) than white children (5 per cent) are expected to be living with a never-married mother. Only a small proportion (1 per cent) live with no parent or head their own families; there is no race difference.

Since once a child leaves a two-natural-parent family, he or she will never return (except for a few reconciliations), the proportion of children not living with two natural parents at each age represents the proportion of children that has ever lived with only one parent (either because of the breakup of a parental marriage or through an out-of-wedlock birth). The proportion of those not living with two natural parents at age 0 represents the proportion born out of wedlock. According to our estimates, by age 17, 19 per cent of white children born in 1950–54 had lived with only one parent. By age 17 almost 70 per cent of white children born in 1980 are projected to have lived with only one parent before they reach age 18. The comparable proportion was 48 per cent for black children born in 1950–54 and is projected to be 94 per cent among black children born in 1980. That is, seven out of ten white children and more than 9 out of 10 black children will have spent at least some time with one parent by the time they reach age 18.

One reason these figures are so high for recent birth cohorts is that a substantial proportion of children are born out of wedlock and, therefore, will by definition have lived for at least some time with only one parent — 10 per cent of the 1980 birth cohort of white children and 58 per cent of the 1980 birth cohort of black children. The differential between blacks and whites in the proportion starting life with only one parent may explain a large proportion of the difference between whites and blacks in children's experience with a one-parent family. If so, we would expect this black–white gap to disappear when differences in initial family type are controlled. To test this hypothesis the proportion of blacks and of whites who started out in a first-marriage, two-natural-parent family and who were still in such a family by age 17 was compared (results not presented here). This figure is 36 per cent of white children born in 1980 and only 11 per cent of black children born in the same year. Thus 64 per cent of white children born to two natural parents both in their first marriage, and 89 per cent of black children born to two natural parents both in their first marriage will have lived by age 17 for at least a short period with only one parent. The differential between the races (25 percentage points) is not affected at all by controlling for the differential proportion born out of wedlock. It appears to be primarily due to the greater probability that black children will move out of two-married-parent families as a result of parental separation and divorce.

The proportion living with only one parent shown here is substantially higher than that obtained by other researchers. Bumpass and Rindfuss (1979) estimated that one-third of white children and 59 per cent of black children would experience marital disruption. One reason the estimates presented here are higher is that out-of-wedlock childbearing is included. However, even when out-of-wedlock births are considered (e.g., Bumpass, 1984), the estimates from the PSID for children's experience with only one parent are higher for recent periods than those from other data sources.

A second reason our estimates differ is that they are cohort estimates, not period estimates. Period estimates should underestimate disruption experience consistently, especially during periods of rapid cohort change.

The third, and probably most important, reason these figures exceed those produced by other researchers (Bumpass, 1984; Furstenberg *et al*, 1983) is that they are based on actual living arrangements. One problem with the CPS, in particular, is that date of separation is only obtained for those who subsequently obtain a divorce. Thus periods of separation followed by reconciliation are not included in data obtained from the CPS. Other problems with using retrospective reports of the marital history of the mother rather than prospective reports of the living arrangements of the child are that informal unions are not included, nor temporary residence of the child with other relatives.

PSID data provide some confirmation that the amount of movement between and among living arrangements is much higher than estimates using marital and fertility history data. The probability of separation and divorce combined in the PSID is substantially higher than that estimated from the CPS (Hofferth, 1982), reflecting the additional transitions obtained by including separations followed by reconciliation. Surprisingly, the probability of reconciliation after separation is much lower than expected. This may be due more to the difficulty of determining whether the spouse is the same as before separation — that is, of determining whether separation is followed by marriage or reconciliation — rather than to a low rate of reconciliation. It may also be due to the mingling of cohabitation with marriage.

So far we have shown that using panel data on living arrangements, a multistate life table approach, and cohort rather than period analyses we obtain substantially higher estimates of the proportion of children who ever experience a one-parent family than have other researchers. The present analysis suggests the tremendous amount of actual movement of children among and between family types. However, to describe children's experiences, more information on their family structures and how they change over time than merely the cumulative proportion who will ever live with only their mother is needed. In particular, it is important to know the proportion of their childhood years spent in each different family type.

Proportion of Childhood Spent with Two Parents versus One Parent

Major changes have occurred in the proportion of their lives children spend in various family types (Table 9.5, 'Total' row). One of the most important is the sharp decline in the proportion of time spent with two parents and the associated sharp increase in the proportion of time spent with only one parent. White children born between 1950 and 1954 could expect to spend 92 per cent of their childhood with two parents, 78 per cent for black children. Of those children born in 1980, white children can be expected to spend 69 per cent of their childhood years with two parents, black children 41 per cent. Comparing the 1950–54 and 1980 birth cohorts, the years spent with two parents are increasingly comprised of time spent with one natural and one stepparent, rather than with two natural parents (results not presented here). For whites the large increase in time spent with one parent is due to increased time with a divorced mother; for blacks time spent with a divorced parent is important, but most important is the time spent with a never-married mother. For whites, but not blacks, the proportion of time spent with the father doubled between the 1950–54 and 1975–79 birth cohorts (from 2.5 to 5 per cent).

Thus, although it is clear that a majority of children will experience a single-parent family at some point, for white children for the most part these will be rather brief episodes. White children can be expected to spend most

Table 9.5 Proportion of first 18 years children are expected to spend with two parents, by birth cohort, family type at birth, and race

Family type at birth		1980	Birth cohort					
			1975–1979	1970–1974	1965–1969	1960–1964	1955–1959	1950–1954
Single mother	White	.144	.144	.162	.108	.056	.144	.158
	Black	.242	.242	.250	.187	.120	.315	.240
First marriage family	White	.752	.752	.803	.872	.862	.917	.940
	Black	.564	.564	.644	.765	.759	.842	.897
Divorced/separated mother	White	.550	.550	.542	.578	.618	.834	.910
	Black	.487	.487	.502	.526	.561	.717	.860
Widowed mother	White	.487	.487	.495	.427	.508	.708	.872
	Black	.211	.211	.235	.129	.195	.327	.680
Remarried mother and natural father	White	.530	.530	.556	.584	.618	.815	.900
	Black	.498	.498	.521	.540	.570	.703	.852
Total	White	.686	.687	.739	.813	.815	.888	.916
	Black	.411	.428	.488	.564	.606	.714	.777
Total N								
White: weighted			3211	9081	14853	17191	10906	3000
unweighted			2856	6522	9235	10302	6063	1552
Black: weighted			518	1551	2262	3255	2129	479
unweighted			2256	5535	8465	11205	6164	1376

of their childhood with two parents. Among black children the story is different. Almost all will live with one parent at some point and, in fact, the majority of their childhood years will be spent with only one parent. The proportion of time spent with no parent is small (less than 1 per cent) and has remained constant over time.

The Impact of the Family Type into Which a Child is Born

One important way the family status of the child at birth affects children is by affecting the paths which the child's life takes and the length of time spent in each path. For example, a child born to a never-married mother has only a small probability of living with two natural parents. Thus such a child's experience will be as different from that of a child who experiences a parental divorce as from a child who always lives with two natural parents. In addition, it doesn't really make much sense to speak of a child without considering his/her family type at birth. Table 9.4 showed the distribution of children at birth by family type, race, and birth cohort. These tables illustrated the enormous changes that have taken place in the distribution of children by family type at birth since 1950–54. In Table 9.5 the percentage of childhood spent with two parents is summarized by family status at birth for children born from 1950–54 to 1980, by five-year birth cohort.

Children born in 1980 to a never-married mother are expected to spend substantially less of their childhood (14 per cent for whites, 24 per cent for blacks) with two parents than those born to a married couple (75 per cent for whites, 56 per cent for blacks). The figures in the 1950–54 birth cohort were 16 per cent and 24 per cent for whites and blacks born into a never-married mother family and 94 per cent for whites and 90 per cent for blacks born into a first-marriage family. These differences exist in spite of the fact that many single mothers eventually marry and that many married couples later divorce. In fact, children born to a never-married mother spend a substantial period of time with her before she first marries. The black-white difference among children born to never-married mothers is due to the much lower proportion of white children of single mothers who move into two parent families. The black–white difference among children born into a first-marriage, natural-parent family is due to the higher rate of marital dissolution among blacks. Children born to a divorced or separated mother and children born to a remarried mother and a natural father are similar in length of time spent in two-parent families — about half their childhood. Children born to a widowed mother are similar to those born to a divorced or separated mother among whites — about half their time with two parents. In contrast children born to a widowed parent among blacks are much more like those of single (never-married) parents. Over 80 per cent of their lives is spent with only one parent.

Cohort trends are as expected. Among all initial statuses except never-married mother, with each succeeding birth cohort a smaller proportion of childhood is spent with two parents. The experience of children born to a single mother with two-parent families has been small over all birth cohorts.

It is clear that, in general, the proportion of childhood that can be expected to be spent with two natural parents has been rapidly declining, while the proportion of childhood expected to be spent with only one parent or with two remarried parents, one natural and one stepparent, has been increasing, regardless of the family type at birth. The family type at birth affects the overall proportion of childhood spent in each family type. For example, a child born to a first-marriage, natural-parent family can be expected to spend the largest proportion of childhood with two natural parents (over half for whites, under half for blacks); a child born to a widowed mother the least (none).

Summary and Conclusions

There are seven important findings for children:

1. First, a larger proportion of children than in the past will ever spend time with only one parent; by age 17, 19 per cent of white children born in 1950–54 had lived with only one parent. By age 17, 70 per cent of white children born in 1980 are projected to have spent at least some time with

only one parent before they reach age 18. The proportion was 48 per cent for black children born in 1950–54 and is projected to be 94 per cent for black children born in 1980.

2. A larger proportion of children's time will be spent with only one parent than in previous cohorts of children. White children born in 1950–54 could expect to spend 8 per cent of their childhood with only one parent, black children 22 per cent. Of those children born in 1980, white children can be expected to spend 31 per cent of their childhood years with only one parent, black children 59 per cent.

   a. Among those who live with only one parent, a growing proportion of time is spent with a never-married and with a divorced or separated mother compared with a widowed mother.

   b. Among those who live with two parents, a larger proportion of time is spent by recent cohorts in a remarriage family as opposed to a first marriage family.

3. There is a large amount of movement of children among family types. This is illustrated by the large proportion of white children who are expected to ever live with only one parent compared with the relatively small proportion of their childhood children can be expected to spend with that parent. (Blacks, however, spend over half of their childhood with only one parent).

4. The family type into which a child is born is critical to describing and understanding all later experiences. For example, white children born in 1980 to a never-married mother are expected to spend 86 per cent of their childhood with only one parent, compared with 25 per cent for white children born into a first-marriage family, and 45 per cent for white children born to a divorced or separated mother. Black children born in 1980 to a never-married mother are expected to spend 75 per cent with only one parent, compared with 44 per cent for black children born into a first-marriage family, and 51 per cent for black children born to a divorced or separated mother.

5. Compared to estimates by other researchers of children's family experience based upon marital and fertility histories of parents, the estimates obtained here show that a much larger proportion of children can be expected to ever live with only one parent. However, again compared to results using retrospective marital and fertility histories, a much larger amount of movement into as well as out of family types is shown, as well as a smaller actual number of years spent in a one-parent family.

6. Unfortunately with these data the impact of neither cohabitation nor marital separation could be separated from other family experiences. However, these results suggest that to understand children's actual living arrangements, non-marital arrangements and temporary separations must be considered.

7. Finally, black–white experiences have converged over the past several

decades. In particular, the experience of white children in one-parent families has been increasing faster than that of blacks; of course, the former started from a lower level. However, if trends continue, the family experiences of black and white children will be much more similar to each other than previously.

Appendix: Reasonableness of Projections

How reasonable are these projections? This is an important issue since all the results depend heavily on the methodology used to make them. The only way to really tell is to compare the results with those using other assumptions. The most reasonable alternative assumption is that the experience of current/recent birth cohorts of children is approximated by the experience of earlier birth cohorts of the same age. Thus, for example, the experience at age 15 of a child born in 1975–79 may be assumed to be the same as that of a child born in 1964 (or earlier). The problem, of course, is that the older the age at which the child's experience is to be estimated, the earlier the birth cohort with children who have completed that particular age year and, therefore, the more 'dated' that estimate becomes. This is likely to be especially troublesome in times of rapid social change, such as the 1960s and 1970s.

To explore the implications of our projection methodology, life tables were prepared from actual data from the entire sample of PSID children born between 1950 and 1979, pooled across birth cohorts. Based upon this synthetic cohort, by age 18 36 per cent of white children and 74 per cent of black children born between 1950 and 1979 would have spent or would be expected to spend some time with only one parent.[1] The projection methodology estimates that 70 per cent of white children born in 1980 and 94 per cent of black children born in 1980 will spend some time with only one parent before age 18. The difference projection makes over a synthetic cohort technique is 34 percentage points for whites, 20 percentage points for blacks. Thus projection from present trends gives us estimates that exceed those from a synthetic cohort constructed from the same data by 94 per cent for white children and 27 per cent for black children.

Based upon the synthetic cohort 1950–79, white children would spend or would have spent 14 per cent of their childhood with only one parent, black children 50 per cent. Estimates based on the projection of present and past trends tell us that 31 per cent of the childhood of white children and 59 per cent of the childhood of black children can be expected to be spent with one parent. That is, the projection method increased the estimate of the proportion of their childhood white children spend with one parent by 121 per cent, that of the proportion of childhood black children spend with one parent by 18 per cent.

Finally, from the synthetic cohort we show that white children born in 1950–79 into a first-marriage family could expect to spend 11 per cent of their childhood in a one-parent family, black children 31 per cent. The comparable figures based on a continuation of present trends are 25 per cent and 44 per cent for whites and blacks, respectively. Here projection based on current trends increased the estimates by 127 per cent for whites and 42 per cent for blacks.

[1] These figures are lower than those obtained by Bumpass (1984) using a similar methodology (42 per cent and 86 per cent for whites and blacks, respectively). Of the several possible sources of difference between the two estimates, one of the most important is that different periods are covered. Bumpass' figures are based on the years 1963 to 1979; ours include children born between 1950 and 1979. Thus ours include more years of very low divorce/separation rates compared with his.

Thus the projection of childhood experience based on current trends provides for a substantial increase in single-parent family experience for white children, a smaller increase for black children. These differences are consistent with current trends, which indicate that since 1950 rates of divorce and separation have been increasing faster among whites than among blacks (Espenshade, 1983). However, whether our projected rates will be close to the true rates depends on many factors, only some of which involve the reasonableness of the estimation procedure. Others depend on the extent to which trends continue unchanged into the future.

In any case, synthetic estimates represent a lower limit (see Bumpass, 1984 for example). The difference between the estimates utilizing a synthetic cohort and those using the projection methodology represents the implications of current trends and our best guess as to what the future will be. It is likely, of course, that the true value will be somewhere in-between the two estimates.

References

Bumpass, Larry L. (1984), 'Children and Marital Disruption: A Replication and Update', *Demography* 21(February) 71–82.

—— and Ronald R. Rindfuss (1979), 'Children's Experience of Marital Disruption', *American Journal of Sociology* 85(July) 49–65.

Cherlin, Andrew (1981), *Marriage, Divorce and Remarriage*, Harvard University Press, Cambridge, Mass.

Espenshade, Thomas and Rachel Braun (1982), 'Life course Analysis and Multistate Demography: An Application to Marriage, Divorce, and Remarriage', *Journal of Marriage and the Family* 44(November) 1025–36.

Espenshade, Thomas (1983), 'Black–White Differences in Marriage, Separation, Divorce and Remarriage', Paper presented at the Annual Meeting of the Population Association of America.

Furstenberg, Frank F., Jr. (1976), *'Unplanned Parenthood: The Social Consequences of Teenage Childbearing'*, The Free Press, New York.

——, Christine W. Nord, James L. Peterson, and Nicholas Zill (1983), 'The Life Course of Children of Divorce: Marital Disruption and Parental Contact', *American Sociological Review* 48(October) 656–68.

Glick, Paul C. (1979), 'Children of Divorced Parents in Demographic Perspective', *Journal of Social Issues* 35, 170–81.

Hofferth, Sandra L. (1982), 'Children's Family Experience to Age 18: A Cohort Life Table Analysis', Paper Presented at the Annual Meeting of the Population Association of America.

—— (1985), 'Children's Life course: Family Structure and Living Arrangements in Cohort Perspective', Glen H. Elder, Jr (Ed.), *Life Course Dynamics*, Cornell University Press, Ithaca.

Ledent, Jacques (1979), 'Multistate Life Tables: Movement versus Transition Perspectives', *Environment and Planning* 12, 533–62.

Macklin, Eleanor D. (1978), 'Nonmarital Heterosexual Cohabitation', *Marriage and Family Review* 1(March/April) 1–12.

National Center for Health Statistics (1981), 'Advance Report of Final Natality Statistics, 1979', *Monthly Vital Statistics Report* 30(6).

—— (1982), 'Advance Report of Final Natality Statistics, 1980', *Monthly Vital Statistics Report*, 31(8), Supplement.

Plateris, Alexander A. (1978), 'Divorces and Divorce Rates, United States', *Vital and Health Statistics* 21(29).

Schoen, Robert and Verne E. Nelson (1974), 'Marriage, Divorce and Mortality: A Life Table Analysis', *Demography* 11(May) 267–90.

—— and Karen Woodrow (1980), 'Labor Force Status Life Tables for the United States, 1972', *Demography* 17(August) 297–322.

Spanier, Graham B. (1983), 'Married and Unmarried Cohabitation in the United States: 1980', *Journal of Marriage and the Family* 45(May) 277–88.

U S Bureau of the Census (1980a), 'American Families and Living Arrangements', *Current Population Reports*, Series P-23, No. 104, May.

—— (1980b), 'A Statistical Portrait of Women in the United States: 1978', *Current Population Reports*, Series P-20, No. 365.

—— (1981a), 'Marital Status and Living Arrangements: March 1980', *Current Population Reports*, Series P-20, No. 365.

—— (1981b), *Statistical Abstract of the United States*, U S Government Printing Office, Washington, D.C.

—— (1982), 'Marital Status and Living Arrangements: March 1981', *Current Population Reports*, Series P-20, No. 372.

Willekens, Frans and Andrei Rogers (1978), *Spatial Population Analysis: Methods and Computer Programs*, RR-78-18, Laxenburg, Austria: International Institute for Applied Systems Analysis.

Williams, Kristen and Russell Kuhn (1973), 'Remarriages, United States', *Vital Statistics*, Series 21, No. 25.

10 The Projection of Family Composition over the Life Course with Family Status Life Tables

JOHN BONGAARTS

The Population Council, New York, USA.

Introduction

The intrinsic demographic complexity of families and households is probably the main reason why the study of these family units is still one of the least developed subdisciplines of demography. The unit of analysis in conventional demography is the individual whose characteristics are described with a limited number of variables such as age and sex. Detailed theories and models have been developed to describe how distributions of individual characteristics are determined by vital processes. In contrast, the family demographer has to deal with multi-dimensional families, households and kin groups. Not only does every individual in a family unit have an age, sex, and marital status, but family members are related to one another in a variety of ways. It is this network of relationships that makes families such important socio-economic units, but it poses a formidable problem to the demographer who tries to determine how these interrelated groups of individuals develop over time under the influence of vital processes.

The chapters in this volume demonstrate that a wide range of models and methodologies are now available to describe and analyse the structure of families, households and kin groups. Prominent among these different approaches is the multistate life table which has seen rapid development in recent years. Multistate life tables have their roots in the standard mortality life table in which only one state (living) and only one decrement (death) is recognized. The single decrement life table has led to the development of multiple decrement life tables, such as the net nuptiality table, and these in turn were the precursors of the multistate marital status life tables which allow both decrements from and increments to the various marital statuses (e.g., single, currently married, divorced, widowed). These increment–decrement life tables are thus able to provide a unique and detailed description of marital status distributions and transitions over the life course of a cohort of individuals (Schoen and Nelson 1974, Schoen 1975, Schoen and Land 1979, Espenshade and Braun 1982, Espenshade, and Hofferth, in this volume, Willekens *et al*. 1982, and Willekens in this volume).

The objective of the work described in this chapter is to construct and apply a family status life table. This technique takes the development of the multistate marital status life table the next logical step by adding a variety of maternal (or paternal) statuses in order to keep track of the number, age and sex of offspring of the life table cohort. State transitions in the family status life table therefore take place not only when marriages, divorces, or deaths of adults take place but also at the births, deaths, and departure from home of children. As a result, the family status life table can provide a detailed description of the number and composition of the nuclear families generated over the life course of a cohort. In addition, and perhaps more important for future applications, the family status life table models the links between family characteristics and their proximate determinants which include fertility, mortality, first marriage, divorce, remarriage, and children's departure from home.

Methodology

A family status life table is constructed with the same basic technique used in the calculation of other multistate life tables. A cohort of individuals is followed from its birth until its last member has died. Over the life course of the cohort individuals are at risk of dying and, while alive, they are at risk of transferring between various states. The life table records the distribution of individuals among states at successive exact ages as well as the number of deaths and transfers between states that occur during each age interval. From these 'stock' and 'flow' data a variety of summary measures such as the mean duration of stay in a state can then be calculated. In order to construct multistate life tables, it is necessary to provide as inputs the risks of dying and of transferring between states to which individuals are subjected. These risks usually differ by age and other characteristics of the individual. The life tables can be calculated either for males or for females, but to simplify the presentation of the family status life table, only the case of a female cohort will be discussed in this chapter.

In contrast to the marital status life table which typically only distinguishes between four states, the family status life table may contain several hundred family states. This increase in complexity is caused by the addition of so-called maternal states to describe the number, sex, age, and residential status of living children as well as the women's parity and fecundity status. A detailed account of the procedure for constructing a family status life table is presented next.

The marital status life table

The first step in the calculation of a family status life table is the production of a marital status life table. Of the different available approaches for constructing a marital status life table, the one proposed by Schoen (1975) has been selected here, because it is easiest to program on a computer. Schoen provides a set of simple equations to estimate the life table population, by age, in each of four marital states: (1) single, (2) currently married, (3) divorced and (4) widowed. Transitions between these states occur at the time of a first marriage, divorce, onset of widowhood, or remarriage, as summarized in the following diagram:

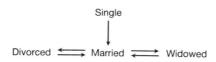

The number of surviving women in each marital state $m(m = 1, 2, 3$ or $4)$ at exact age x will be denoted by $1(x)^m$. The variable $1(x)^m$ as well as other life table measures are calculated directly from age and marital status-specific state transition rates such as first marriage, remarriage, divorce, widowhood, and death rates. A detailed description of this marital status life table methodology can be found elsewhere (Schoen, 1975) and it will therefore not be repeated here. Since single year age intervals are used in the family status life table, the underlying marital status table is calculated for one year age increments from $x = 0$ to $x = 90$.

The addition of parity and fecundity status

Maternal states representing different parity levels are relatively easy to add to the marital status life table. This is accomplished by dividing the population in each marital state into subgroups according to parity. A woman moves from one parity to the next when she gives birth but she stays at the same parity level when a marital status transition occurs. The rate of parity transitions is determined by age, parity and marital status specific fertility rates which are given as inputs. Unfortunately, such detailed input data are not available in many populations. Age and marital status specific fertility rates are more easily estimated, but using these as birth probabilities for women of all parities will in general produce inaccurate life tables except in natural fertility populations where there is, by definition, no parity-specific fertility control. However, in that case valid results can only be obtained if the cohort of women is stratified further by fecundity status to distinguish between sterile and fecund women. Parity transitions are, of course, only made by fecund women.

Let the superscripts m, p and f represent, respectively, marital status ($m = 1, 2, 3$ or 4), parity ($p = 0$ to, say, 20) and fecundity status ($f = 0$ for fecund and 1 for the sterile women), and let $1(x)^{m,p,f}$ denote the size of the life table population in the various states at exact age x. It is clear that the addition of new states has produced a more comlex life table. The total number of states to be distinguished equals the product of the numbers of marital, parity, and fecundity statuses, e.g. $4 \times 21 \times 2 = 168$, using the ranges of m, p and f just given. In addition, there are many more increments and decrements from each state compared with the simple marital status life table. For example, the following increments to and decrements from the state representing married fecund women of parity p are possible:

Increments ⟶	State ⟶	Decrements
First marriage	Married	Death
Remarriage (divorced)	Fecund	Divorce
Remarriage (widowed)	Parity p	Widowhood
Birth of order p if married		Onset of sterility
		Birth of order $p + 1$

The methodology for estimating the life table population $1(x)^{m,p,f}$ for a cohort of women is described in Appendix A.

The addition of family characteristics: the number of living children

The marital–parity–fecundity status life table cannot be considered a true family status life table because it makes no reference to the characteristics of children. To describe the family composition of women at a given age, it is necessary to keep track not only of martial, parity, and fecundity statuses, but also of the number, age, sex, and residential status of living children. In theory, one could consider constructing a family life table by stratifying the population further for each characteristic of each child. However, this approach is impractical because the number of states to be accounted for becomes prohibitively large. To accomplish the objective of projecting family composition over the life course of a cohort of women, it is therefore necessary to use a different approach.

To introduce children's characteristics, a special technique is used that calculates the final family status life table from a set of partial family status life tables. This technique is best described by giving a specific example. Let us take the family life table in which the number of currently living children is added as a maternal status. That is, within each marital, parity, and fecundity state, the life table population is further stratified according to the number of currently living children. Let $1(x)^{m,p,f,c}$ denote the size of the population of women in this life table, where c represents the number of currently living children. If the probability of a death of a child were independent of the child's age, then transitions from one c state to the next could be relatively easily calculated. However, child mortality varies greatly with age, a fact that cannot be ignored. The variation with age in child mortality can be taken into account by using the partial family status life table technique. The first step in this approach is to calculate a set of partial family status life tables from which the complete table will be constructed. The sole purpose of each partial table is to estimate the distribution of the population over $mxpxfxc$ states at one, and only one, exact age x of the cohort in the complete table. Let the variable x' represent the exact age of women in each partial family status life table and let $1(x', x)^{m,p,f,c}$ denote the population in the partial table that will produce the entries at exact age x in the complete family status life table. Within each partial table the variable c refers to the number of children that will be alive at exact age $x' = x$ and not to all currently living children at each age x'. From each partial table only the results at age $x' = x$ are used for the complete table. There are therefore as many partial tables as there are distinct x values. In a partial table a transition from state c to state $c + 1$ takes place at the birth of a child that will survive to age $x' = x$ of the mother. The probability of such an event is estimated by multiplying the appropriate fertility rate at age x' by the probability that the child will survive $x - x' - 0.5$ years from its birth to the mother's age x. If $p(a)$ denotes the probability that a child reaches its ath birthday alive, then a proportion $p(x - x' - 0.5)$ of women who give birth at age x' will advance from state c to $c + 1$. The remaining proportion of women with a birth at age x', $1 - p(x - x' - 0.5)$, will not have a change in their c status. To calculate a complete set of partial family status life tables, only one variable, $p(a)$, is needed in addition to the input variables required for the martial–parity–fecundity status life tables (if child mortality is assumed to be independent of the mother's status). Of course, $p(a)$ is easily obtained from a standard mortality life table. Once the partial life table populations $1(x', x)^{m,p,f,c}$ have been calculated, their values at $x' = x$ are combined to obtain the population $1(x)^{m,p,f,c}$ in the complete family status life table.

The addition of other characteristics of children

The partial life table technique for the estimation of $1(x)^{m,p,f,c}$, can be modified to also calculate family status life tables that include other characteristics of children.

Define

c = number of living children
cm = number of living sons
cf = number of living daughters
ch = number of children living with their mother
chm = number of sons living with their mother
chf = number of daughters living with their mother

Separate life tables for $1(x)^{m,p,f,cm}$, $1(x)^{m,p,f,cf}$, $1(x)^{m,p,f,ch}$, $1(x)^{m,p,f,chm}$, and $1(x)^{m,p,f,chf}$ can now be calculated with variants of the procedure used for the estimation of $1(x)^{m,p,f,c}$. As described in the preceding section, $1(x)^{m,p,f,c}$ is obtained with a partial life table technique in which a transition from c to $c + 1$ takes place among a proportion of women who give birth at age x'. This proportion is derived from the variable $p(a)$ which in the life table for $1(x)^{m,p,f,c}$ equals the probability of survival of a child from birth to exact age a. The populations $1(x)^{m,p,f,cm}$ etc, are estimated in the same way, except that the survival function $p(a)$ is modified to correctly measure the probability of transferring between the states cm (or cf, ch, chm, chf). The appropriate $p(a)$ functions are listed in the table shown.

Family Life Table Population	*Corresponding Variant of Survival Function p(a)*
$1(x)^{m,p,f,c}$	$p(a) = r \cdot S(a)^s + (1 - r) \cdot S(a)^d$
$1(x)^{m,p,f,cm}$	$p(a) = r \cdot S(a)^s$
$1(x)^{m,p,f,cf}$	$p(a) = (1 - r) \cdot S(a)^d$
$1(x)^{m,p,f,ch}$	$p(a) = r \cdot h(a)^s \cdot S(a)^s + (1 - r) \cdot h(a)^d \cdot S(a)^d$
$1(x)^{m,p,f,cmh}$	$p(a) = r \cdot h(a)^s \cdot S(a)^s$
$1(x)^{m,p,f,cfh}$	$p(a) = (1 - r) \cdot h(a)^d \cdot S(a)^d$

where

a = exact age of the child
r = proportion of births that is male
$S(a)^s$ = probability of survival from birth to age a for males
$S(a)^d$ = probability of surviving from birth to age a for females
$h(a)^s$ = probability that a living son lives with his mother at age a
$h(a)^d$ = probability that a living daughter lives with her mother at age a

This procedure for calculating different family status life table populations can be taken one step further to also yield age distributions of children of women in the cohort. This is accomplished by calculating a series of additional life tables, one for each age group of the children. The life table for each age group is obtained by a simple modification of the procedure already described. This modification consists of setting the functions $S(a)^s$ and $S(a)^d$ equal to zero outside the desired age groups of children. For example, let $1(x)^{m,p,f,cf(10-15)}$ be the life table population at age x of the cohort in marital, parity and fecundity status, m, p, and f, with cf daughters between exact ages 10 and 15. The population $1(x)^{m,p,f,cf(10-15)}$ is obtained by seting $S(a)^d$ equal to 0 for a > 15 and for a < 10 in the life table for $1(x)^{m,p,f,cf}$. By repeating this calculation for successive age groups of the children their age distribution can be obtained.

Estimating nuclear family size

Let n represent the nuclear family size of women in the life table cohort. The family size can be calculated directly from ch by adding the appropriate number of adults. That is for married women $n = ch + 2$ because there are two parents in these husband–wife nuclear families. For single, widowed, and divorced mothers $n = ch + 1$, if one assumes that children stay with their mothers when a marriage ends. Single, widowed, and divorced women without children at home do not have their own nuclear families. (These women may of course be living with their parents, but families of origin are not considered in this study.)

A computer program (FAMTAB) for calculating family status life tables

A full exploration of the extremely detailed results that would be available in a complete set of family status life tables is beyond the scope of this chapter. Instead, an initial exploratory analysis will be made here with the computer program FAMTAB. The task of calculating and presenting family life table results has been simplified in FAMTAB by using model schedules for input data and by providing only a subset of potentially available output tables. In addition, the following simplifying assumptions were made for the female life table population and its offspring:

1. Only currently married fecund women bear children. The fertility rates of these women are age- and parity-specific.
2. mortality risks are functions of age and sex only.
3. the risks of first marriage, remarriage, divorce, and widowhood are only functions of age and marital status.
4. At the time of a marital disruption, all children present in the family stay with their mother.
5. the proportion of children living with their mother is only a function of the children's age and sex.
6. a distinction is made between 4 marital, 2 fecundity, 3 parity $(0, 1, 2 +)$ and 20 maternal statuses, where maternal status is measured by either c, cm, cf, ch, cmh, or cfh (or their age-specific versions). The total number of possible states is therefore $4 \times 2 \times 3 \times 20 = 480$, but single women are assumed to have zero fertility so that only $3 \times 2 \times 3 \times 20 + 2 = 362$ states need to be distinguished.
7. the sex ratio at birth is a constant equal to 1.05 males per female birth.
8. multiple births are counted as single births.
9. the risk of onset of sterility is only a function of age.

Each of these assumptions can be changed or eliminated in future studies, but they have been incorporated in the present version of FAMTAB. A more detailed account of FAMTAB's inputs and outputs is provided next.

Model input schedules for FAMTAB

In order to calculate a family status life table, the transition risks from each possible state must be specified as inputs. In a complete model this would include age, sex, and marital and maternal status-specific fertility, mortality, first marriage, remarriage, divorce, widowhood and departure-from-home rates. Needless to say, such data are not available for any real population and even if they were available, it would be very cumbersome to use them. This problem is solved in FAMTAB by introducing the following model schedules which can be specified with a limited set of input parameters:

1. First marriage: The age-specific risks of first marriage are derived from the Coale–McNeill marriage model (Coale and McNeill 1972). This model can be estimated from three input parameters: the average age at first marriage, the initial age at marriage and the proportion ever marrying.

2. Remarriage and divorce: Age-specific remarriage rates for widowed and divorced women and the age-specific divorce rates for married women are derived from standard schedules. These standards are set equal to the US 1975 patterns estimated by Schoen (1983). The actual remarriage and divorce rates used in family status life tables are calculated from these standards by multiplying by an 'index' which is assumed to have the same value for all age groups. Specifying remarriage and divorce rates therefore requires three parameters: the index of remarriage for divorced women, the index of remarriage for widowed women and the index of divorce. Since US remarriage and divorce rates in 1975 are among the highest ever observed, the indexes of most other populations will fall between 0 and 1.0 but the indexes can exceed 1.0.

3. Sterility onset: the age-specific risk of becoming sterile is derived from the age-specific proportions sterile estimated by Henry (1965). This age-specific risk is used in all applications of FAMTAB presented here, because there is no evidence for large systematic differences in levels of natural sterility among populations (Bongaarts and Potter 1983). However, in some countries, e.g., in tropical Africa, the incidence of pathological sterility may be substantial and in those cases the sterility schedule has to be adjusted.

4. Fertility; Age- and parity-specific fertility rates for married fecund women are derived with a procedure described in Appendix B. Three parameters are required: the total fertility rate, the degree of marital fertility control (as defined in the Coale–Trussell fertility model) and an index for the change in fertility with increasing parity.

5. Mortality: age-specific mortality rates for males and females are taken from the Coale-Demeny model life tables (Coale and Demeny 1983) using interpolation as required. Input parameters are the male and female life expectancies at birth.

6. Widowhood: the age-specific rate of widowhood is set equal to the mortality rate of males whose age is a predetermined number of years

higher (or lower) than that of their female spouses. This age difference is an input parameter.

7. Children's departure from home: The age-specific proportions of sons and daughters living with their mothers are also estimated with the Coale McNeill model. Input parameters are the average and initial ages at departure and the proportion ever departing for both sons and daughters.

Output tables provided by FAMTAB

Once each of the input parameters is specified, the life table transition rates are calculated and these rates in turn make it possible to construct family status life tables. To list a complete set of life table results would involve hundreds of pages of detailed tabulations because stock and flow data as well as other statistics can be produced by the family life tables for each of the states. In FAMTAB this unmanageable volume of output is reduced in two ways. First, the output is limited to stock data. Second, only a subset of available stock data is produced. More specifically, parity and fecundity status information will be suppressed so that attention can be focused on the distribution of women in different marital and maternal states. For example, the number of women surviving to age x in marital status m with c living children equals

$$P(x)^{m,c} = \sum_p \sum_f l(x)^{m,p,f,c} \tag{10.1}$$

From $P(x)^{m,c}$ other summary statistics are readily calculated. Let $M(x)^c$, $D(x)^c$ and $E(x)^c$ denote the distributions of the number of living children among, respectively, currently married, previously married (i.e., widowed and divorced) and ever-married women at exact age x. Then:

$$M(x)^c = P(x)^{2,c} / \sum_c P(x)^{2,c} \tag{10.2}$$

$$D(x)^c = [P(x)^{3,c} + P(x)^{4,c}] / \sum_c [P(x)^{3,c} + P(x)^{4,c}] \tag{10.3}$$

$$E(x)^c = [P(x)^{2,c} + P(x)^{3,c} + P(x)^{4,c}] / \sum_c [P(x)^{2,c} + P(x)^{3,c} + P(x)^{4,c}] \tag{10.4}$$

Table 10.1 gives an example of a FAMTAB output table with these three distributions. The variables $E(x)^c$, $M(x)^c$, and $D(x)^c$ are presented respectively in the upper, middle and lower panel of Table 10.1. The input parameters used to obtain these results are given in the next to the last column of Table 10.2, which will be discussed later.

Other output tables of FAMTAB are produced with equations similar to (1), (2), (3) and (4) using the life table populations $l(x)^{m,p,f,cm}$, $l(x)^{mm,p,f,cf}$, $l(x)^{m,p,f,ch}$, $l(x)^{m,p,f,chm}$, $l(x)^{m,p,f,chf}$, and their variants which are specific for the

Table 10.1   Percent distribution of the number of living children by age and marital status of the women in family status life table cohort.

Ever-married women

Per cent distribution of number of living children, both sexes and all ages	15	20	25	30	35	40	45	50	55	60	65	70	75	80	85	90
0	85.6	44.6	20.2	10.9	7.5	6.5	6.4	6.5	6.8	7.1	7.4	7.9	8.6	9.6	11.0	13.5
1	13.5	34.0	26.1	15.6	9.6	7.2	6.7	7.0	7.4	7.9	8.6	9.4	10.4	11.9	13.9	16.9
2	0.8	15.4	24.2	20.1	14.2	10.7	9.8	10.1	10.7	11.4	12.2	13.1	14.3	15.8	17.7	19.8
3	0.0	4.8	16.2	19.7	17.1	13.8	12.6	12.9	13.5	14.1	14.8	15.6	16.4	17.3	18.1	18.4
4	0.0	1.1	8.3	15.3	16.8	15.3	14.2	14.4	14.7	15.1	15.4	15.7	15.9	15.8	15.3	14.0
5	0.0	0.2	3.4	9.7	13.9	14.5	14.1	14.0	14.0	14.0	13.9	13.6	13.1	12.3	10.9	8.9
6	0.0	0.0	1.1	5.1	9.7	12.0	12.2	12.0	11.7	11.4	10.9	10.2	9.4	8.2	6.7	4.8
7	0.0	0.0	0.3	2.3	5.8	8.7	9.4	9.1	8.7	8.2	7.5	6.	5.9	4.8	3.6	2.3
8	0.0	0.0	0.1	0.9	3.0	5.5	6.5	6.2	5.7	5.2	4.6	4.0	3.3	2.5	1.7	0.9
9	0.0	0.0	0.0	0.3	1.4	3.1	4.0	3.8	3.4	3.0	2.5	2.1	1.6	1.1	0.7	0.3
10	0.0	0.0	0.0	0.1	0.6	1.6	2.2	2.1	1.8	1.5	1.3	1.0	0.7	0.5	0.3	0.1
Total	100.0	100.0	100.0	100.0	100.0	100.0	100.0	100.0	100.0	100.0	100.0	100.0	100.0	100.0	100.0	100.0
% Cohort	13.3	59.1	70.6	70.9	68.7	65.9	62.9	59.5	55.2	49.9	42.9	34.4	24.4	14.2	6.1	1.6
Average	0.153	0.845	1.831	2.821	3.710	4.377	4.632	4.555	4.420	4.267	4.095	3.900	3.674	3.407	3.083	2.694

Currently married women

	15	20	25	30	35	40	45	50	55	60	65	70	75	80	85	90
0	85.6	43.9	18.7	9.2	6.0	5.1	5.1	5.4	5.7	6.1	6.5	6.9	7.6	8.5	9.9	12.2
1	13.5	34.2	25.8	14.5	8.2	5.6	5.3	5.7	6.3	6.8	7.5	8.4	9.5	11.0	13.1	16.1
2	0.8	15.6	24.7	20.0	13.4	9.5	8.6	9.1	9.8	10.5	11.4	12.5	13.7	15.3	17.3	19.7
3	0.0	4.9	16.9	20.4	17.2	13.3	12.0	12.4	13.0	13.7	14.5	15.4	16.4	17.4	18.3	18.9
4	0.0	1.1	8.7	16.2	17.6	15.6	14.3	14.4	14.8	15.3	15.7	16.0	16.3	16.3	15.8	14.6
5	0.0	0.2	3.6	10.4	14.8	15.4	14.7	14.6	14.6	14.6	14.4	14.2	13.7	12.9	11.5	9.4
6	0.0	0.0	1.2	5.5	10.5	13.0	13.1	12.8	12.5	12.1	11.5	10.9	9.9	8.7	7.1	5.2
7	0.0	0.0	0.3	2.5	6.4	9.6	10.3	10.0	9.4	8.8	8.1	7.3	6.3	5.2	3.8	2.5
8	0.0	0.0	0.1	1.0	3.4	6.2	7.2	6.9	6.3	5.7	5.0	4.3	3.5	2.7	1.8	1.0
9	0.0	0.0	0.0	0.3	1.6	3.5	4.5	4.3	3.8	3.3	2.8	2.3	1.8	1.3	0.8	0.4
10	0.0	0.0	0.0	0.1	0.6	1.8	2.5	2.4	2.1	1.7	1.4	1.1	0.8	0.5	0.3	0.1
Total	100.0	100.0	100.0	100.0	100.0	100.0	100.0	100.0	100.0	100.0	100.0	100.0	100.0	100.0	100.0	100.0
% Cohort	13.2	57.0	65.0	62.9	59.3	54.6	49.5	43.5	36.4	28.2	19.3	10.9	4.5	1.2	0.2	0.0
Average	0.153	0.857	1.887	2.946	3.902	4.639	4.912	4.802	4.634	4.459	4.267	4.056	3.816	3.531	3.192	2.792

	Previously married women (widowed and divorced)															
0	92.6	61.4	37.1	24.5	17.4	13.3	10.9	9.5	8.8	8.4	8.2	8.4	8.8	9.6	11.1	13.5
1	7.0	27.6	29.8	24.5	18.9	14.6	12.0	10.4	9.6	9.3	9.4	9.8	10.7	12.0	14.0	16.9
2	0.4	8.6	18.6	20.9	19.1	16.4	14.3	13.0	12.5	12.5	12.8	13.5	14.5	15.9	17.7	19.8
3	0.0	1.9	9.2	14.6	16.4	16.0	15.1	14.5	14.3	14.6	15.0	15.7	16.4	17.3	18.1	18.4
4	0.0	0.3	3.6	8.5	12.2	13.8	14.1	14.3	14.5	14.8	15.2	15.5	15.8	15.8	15.3	14.0
5	0.0	0.0	1.2	4.2	7.8	10.5	11.8	12.5	13.0	13.3	13.4	13.3	13.0	12.2	10.9	8.9
6	0.0	0.0	0.3	1.8	4.4	7.1	8.8	9.8	10.3	10.4	10.3	9.9	9.2	8.2	6.7	4.8
7	0.0	0.0	0.1	0.7	2.2	4.2	5.9	6.9	7.3	7.3	7.0	6.5	5.8	4.8	3.6	2.3
8	0.0	0.0	0.0	0.2	1.0	2.3	3.6	4.3	4.6	4.6	4.3	3.8	3.2	2.5	1.7	0.9
9	0.0	0.0	0.0	0.1	0.4	1.1	2.0	2.5	2.6	2.6	2.3	2.0	1.6	1.1	0.7	0.3
10	0.0	0.0	0.0	0.0	0.1	0.5	1.0	1.3	1.4	1.3	1.2	0.9	0.7	0.5	0.3	0.1
Total	100.0	100.0	100.0	100.0	100.0	100.0	100.0	100.0	100.0	100.0	100.0	100.0	100.0	100.0	100.0	100.0
% Cohort	0.1	2.2	5.7	7.9	9.4	11.3	13.3	16.0	18.8	21.7	23.7	23.6	19.8	13.0	6.0	1.6
Average	0.078	0.523	1.176	1.833	2.495	3.116	3.593	3.883	4.005	4.019	3.955	3.828	3.642	3.395	3.080	2.693

Stable population:

Average for ever-married women = 3.0149
  for currently married women = 2.9663
  for previously married women = 3.2228

Cohort:

Average for ever-married women = 3.4515
  for currently married women = 3.4378
  for previously married women = 3.4873

Model Input: TFR = 6.00/EXF = 50./AAM = 8.0/PEM = 0.99/IRMV = 0.50/IRMW = 0.50/IDV = 0.25/AADF = 18.0/AADM = 22.0/PPM = 1.000

age of children. These output tables contain distributions of the following variables:

number of living children by age and sex
number of children living at home by age and sex
nuclear family size

These distributions are available separately for each marital status and age of the cohort.

Although the unit of analysis in the family status life tables is the individual, these tables can also be used to describe the characteristics of the nuclear families generated over the life course of the cohort. This switch from individuals to families as units of analysis is possible in FAMTAB because the family characteristics of husband–wife nuclear families are equal to those of married women, and because the characteristics of previously married women with children represent those of female-headed nuclear families. Female-headed and husband–wife families can be combined to obtain the characteristics of all nuclear families.

Family composition over the life course: Illustrative application of the family status life table

As already noted, the results of a comprehensive analysis of a complete set of family status life tables would consist of a huge volume of output data that is difficult to summarize. Even the program FAMTAB, with its restrictions on inputs and outputs, produces 60 output tables similar to Table 10.1 for each set of input parameters. The findings presented in this section are therefore only a small sample of data taken from the output of a set of computer runs of FAMTAB.

To permit an admittedly rather crude analysis of changes in the family life cycle over the course of a demographic transition, three sets of input parameters were selected. These input data represent hypothetical populations at three different points in the demographic transition: (1) pre-transitional, (2) transitional and (3) post-transitional. The values of the parameters selected for each of the transition phases are presented in Table 10.2. Fertility and mortality are assumed to decline between the first and last phase of the transition and age at marriage as well as divorce and remarriage rates are assumed to increase. None of these three hypothetical populations is intended to represent any known real population; instead, they each have characteristics that are not atypical for populations in the three transition phases. (But the age at marriage is too low to represent the Western European experience in the first two phases). The population growth rate resulting from the vital processes summarized by the input parameters equals 0.1 for the pre-, 2.1 for the mid- and 0.0 for the post transitional phase.

Table 10.2   Input parameters for family status life table program FAMTAB for three hypothetical populations

Input parameters	Transition phase		
	1	2	3
First marriage			
average age	18	18	22.5
initial age	12	12	14
proportion ever marrying	0.99	0.99	0.95
Fertility			
total fertility rate	6	6	2.104
index of marital fertility control	0.0	0.0	2.0
index of parity progress trend	1.0	1.0	0.5
Mortality			
life expectancy, female	25	50	75
life expectancy, male	23	47	71
Divorce			
index of divorce	0.1	0.25	1.0
Widowhood			
age difference of spouses	4	4	3
Remarriage			
index of remarriage after divorce	0.25	0.5	1.0
index of remarriage after widowhood	0.25	0.5	1.0
Departure from home			
average age, sons	22	22	20
initial age, sons	14	14	14
proportion ever departing, sons	1.0	1.0	1.0
average age, daughters	18	18	20
initial age, daughters	12	12	14
proportion ever departing, daughters	1.0	1.0	1.0

Figure 10.1 plots the cohort's average nuclear family size, by type of family, in the three transition phases (family size for the cohort is estimated as the weighted average of the age-specific average family sizes of women in each type of family). As expected, husband–wife families are, on average, larger than female-headed families. This is largely due to the presence of an additional adult male in husband–wife families. Interestingly, the number of children in female-headed families is, on average, larger than in husband–wife families. The explanation for this finding lies in the fact that previously married women without children are not considered nuclear families. All female-headed families therefore have at least one child present. Husband–wife families on the other hand can have no children present. Figure 10.1 also indicates that average family size does not vary greatly over the course of the transition. Between phases 1 and 2 the average size of all families rises from 3.6 to 4.1. This is primarily due to the rise in life expectancy which increases the number of surviving children. Between phases 2 and 3 average family size declines, largely as a result of the change in

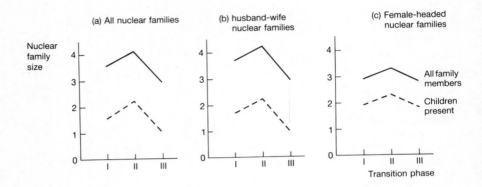

Figure 10.1   Average nuclear family size by family type and transition phase

the total fertility rate. This effect of declining fertility on family size is to some extent counteracted by a further rise in life expectancy.

A more detailed picture of trends in average family size over the cohort's life course is provided in Figure 10.2. Average size of all nuclear families rises from a little over 2.0 to a maximum at age 35 (40 in phase 2) and declines thereafter, approaching 2.0 in the oldest age groups. At all ages family size is largest in phase 2 and smallest in phase 3. The age pattern of family size of husband–wife and female-headed families is very similar to that of all families in Figure 10.2 (data not shown).

The next four figures focus on the characteristics of children of the women in the life table. The unit of analysis is changed from the family (as in Figures 10.1 and 10.2) to the ever-married woman to insure that widowed and divorced women without children are not excluded. Single women are not included because they have not been subjected to the risk of childbearing.

Figure 10.3 presents trends in the number of children ever born, currently living, and living at home, by age of the cohort. The number of children ever born per ever-married female reaches a maximum of slightly over 6.0 in phases 1 and 2 and slightly over 2.1 in phase 3 at the end of the reproductive years. These values are higher than the corresponding total fertility rates because a small percentage of women never marries. As expected from the declining level of mortality during the transition, the difference between the number of children ever born and currently living is largest in phase 1 and smallest in phase 3. The percentage of all living children that actually lives at home ranges from close to 100 for the youngest mothers to zero for women over age 70. As a consequence, the average number of children present first rises with age, but then declines after age 35 of the mother

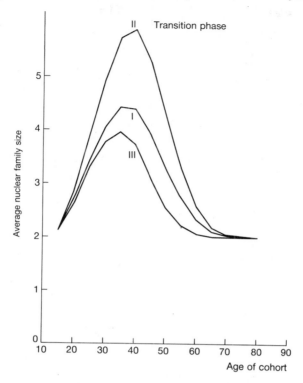

Figure 10.2 Average nuclear family size by age of cohort for three transition phases

as the rate of departure from home exceeds the rate of addition of new children.

The discussion up to this point has dealt strictly with averages of family sizes or of numbers of children. While these averages are useful for analytic purposes, they conceal a substantial amount of variation in these variables at the individual level. For individual women of a given age, the number of children (ever born, currently living, or living at home) may range from zero to more than twice the average. This variation can be measured with statistical indices such as the standard deviation or the coefficient of variation but further insights can be gained from an examination of distribution itself. Of special interest are the cases that deviate farthest from the average. For example, the upper panel of Figure 10.4 plots the proportion of ever-married women with no children present in the family by age of the cohort and transition phase. This proportion declines rapidly from near 1.0 among the youngest women to its minimum at age 35, the same age at which the average number of children present reaches its maximum (see Figure 10.3). By age seventy all children have either left home or died and the proportion with no children present then reaches again 1.0. For all ages this proportion is highest

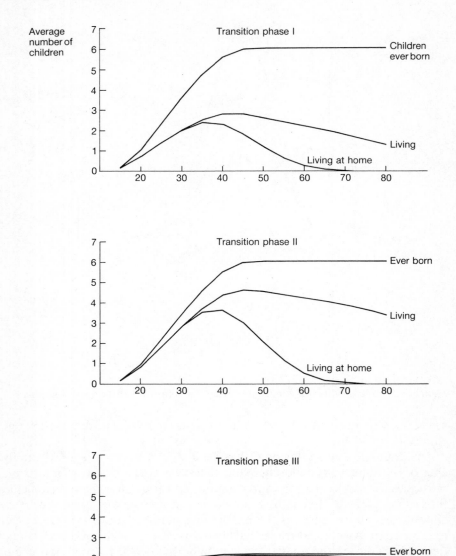

Figure 10.3 Average number of children ever born, currently living and living at home among ever-married women by age of the cohort and transition phase

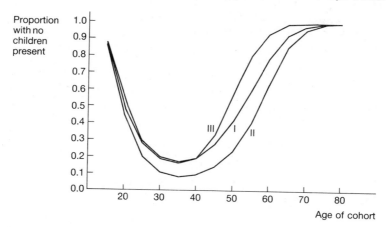

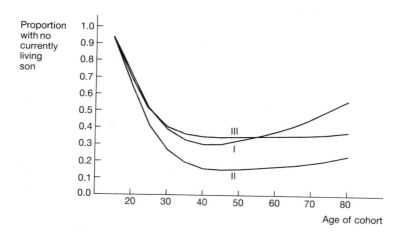

Figure 10.4 Proportion of ever-married women with no children present and with no currently living son by age of the cohort and transition phase

in phase 3 of the transition and lowest in phase 2. The lower panel of Figure 10.4 presents the proportion of ever-married women with no currently living son, again by age of the cohort and for each of the three transition phases. This variable reaches a minimum at age 40 in phase 1 when the proportion equals 0.30. For transition phases 2 and 3 the minima of, respectively, 0.15 and 0.34 are reached at age 45. After reaching its minimum the proportion with no currently living son rises slowly in all three phases. This rise is least rapid for phase 3 because it has the lowest level of mortality.

The family status life table as calculated by FAMTAB can also estimate the age distribution of children by age and marital status of the cohort. To

206 *John Bongaarts*

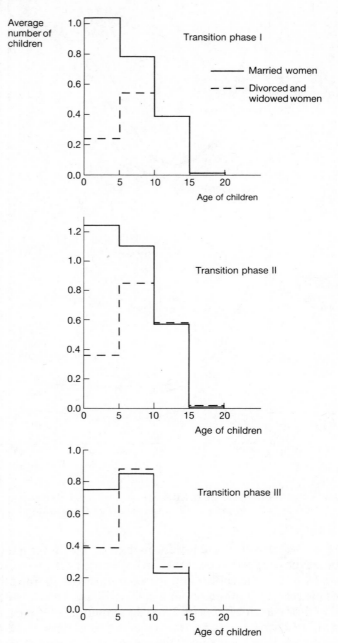

Figure 10.5 Average number of children among currently and previously married women at age 30 of the cohort by age of the child and transition phase

illustrate this application, Figure 10.5 presents the age distributions of children for married and previously married women at exact age 30. FAMTAB generates these distributions also for other ages of the cohort, but age 30 was selected because it produces interesting differences between women of these two marital statuses. The number of children under age 5 is smaller for the previously married than for married women in all transition phases. This is to be expected as currently widowed and divorced women are much more likely not to have been exposed to the risk of childbearing in the past few years compared with currently married women. Somewhat surprisingly, previously married women have more children between 10 and 15 than married women. This finding can be explained by the fact that women who are divorced or widowed at a given age have a slightly lower average age at marriage than women who are married at the same age. This is in turn the consequence of the direct relationship between duration of marriage and the cumulative risk of experiencing a marital disruption. The slightly lower age at first marriage among women who are divorced or widowed at age 30, implies that these women had higher fertility when they were aged 15–19. This excess of births compared with the later marrying women without a marital disruption yields the excess of 10 to 15 year-old children at age 30 of the cohort.

A final example of a FAMTAB result is provided in Figure 10.6 which plots the proportion of ever-married women with no children under age 5 by age of the cohort and transition phase. The general shape of these graphs are similar to those found in the upper panel of Figure 10.4, except that the minima are higher and are reached at age 25. In all transition phases more than half of the married women in the central childbearing age groups has at least one child under age five. In contrast, the majority of widowed or divorced women has no child under age 5 for all ages of the cohort. A notable finding in Figure 10.6 is that the difference between currently and previously married women diminishes as progress is made from transition phase 1 to phase 3. This is due to the higher divorce and remarriage rates in phase 3. With the relatively frequent transitions between currently married and previously married status, the characteristics of the families of women in different marital statuses differ less in phase 3 than in phase 1.

Conclusion

The preceding analysis has demonstrated the feasibility of constructing family status life tables. However, a substantial amount of further research is required before the full potential of this approach can be realized. An essential next step is the testing of the validity or adequacy of the assumption incorporated in the program FAMTAB. A preliminary test of a simple earlier version of this program with data from Pakistan was judged successful, because the model output distributions closely coincided with observed

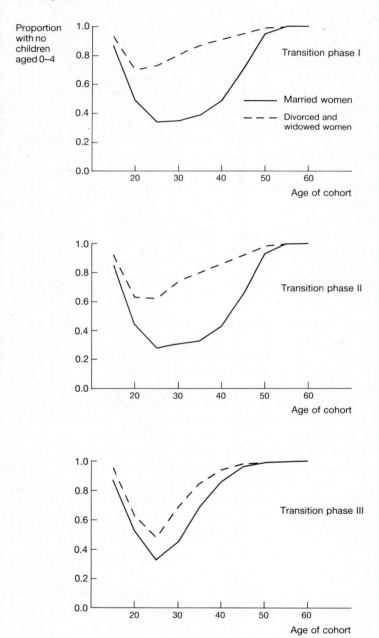

Figure 10.6 Proportion of currently and previously married women with no children aged 0–4 by age of the cohort and transition phase

patterns of family characteristics in this population (Bongaarts 1982). This is encouraging, but further tests are needed before one can have full confidence in the results of the family status life table. It is clear that FAMTAB has to be revised for application in most developed countries because the present version does not allow extra-marital fertility. If an option for extra-marital fertility is added to FAMTAB, it will provide more realistic distributions of family composition in developed countries, but other refinements such as parity specificity in divorce and remarriage rates may also be required. Testing of FAMTAB with or without refinements of course requires an extensive set of empirical input data for the population (cohort) in which the test is carried out. The lack of a complete and accurate set of such input data in existing populations makes a comprehensive test of family status life tables very difficult, and in most cases only partial tests can be made.

A wide range of applications of family status life tables is available. In this chapter only a sample of potentially available results were examined. In addition to the estimates of the proportion of the cohort in each family status, the family status life table can calculate the number of individuals transferring between states at different ages. The proportion of women that ever visits a state and the average duration in a state can also be estimated. Since these output variables are a direct function of the inputs, the family status life table can be used to make detailed analyses of the effects of various proximate determinants (fertility, mortality, marriage, divorce, etc.) on family composition and on the timing and quantity of life course events. Yet another practical application of the family status life table would be for projecting future trends in family size and composition. In sum, the family status life table has the potential for becoming an important new tool for demographers.

Appendix A: Procedure for calculating a marital–parity–fecundity status life table

Increments to or decrements from different states in the marital–parity–fecundity status life table take place at the time of each of the following events: first marriage, remarriage, divorce, widowhood, death, birth, and onset of sterility. The objective of the life table methodology described in this appendix is to calculate the life table population of females $1(x)^{m,p,f}$ from the risks of occurrence of each of these events. Starting from the birth of the cohort, the population $1(x)^{m,p,f}$ is calculated, one year at a time, for each exact single age x from $x = 0$ to $x = 90$. At each successive age $1(x+1)^{m,p,f}$ is derived from $1(x)^{m,p,f}$ by keeping track of the appropriate state transfers that accompany the occurrence of each event between x and $x + 1$.

The calculation of the life table population can be greatly simplified by assuming that particular events take place at one point in time rather than throughout the year between x and $x + 1$. More specifically, it is assumed here that women make transfers from the fecund to the sterile state at the beginning of year x and that transfers between marital states as well as deaths take place exactly in the middle of the year.

Define: $1(x)^{m,p,f}$ = life table population in marital status m, parity p, and fecundity status f at exact age x

$1(x1)^{m,p,f}$ = life table population at the beginning of year x but *after* the transfers between fecundity states have been made

$1(x2)^{m,p,f}$ = life table population in the middle of the year x *before* marital status transfers and deaths are taken into account (but after the parity and fecundity status transfers during the first half of the year)

$1(x3)^{m,p,f}$ = life table population in the middle of the year *after* marital status transfers and deaths have occurred

The procedure for calculation of $1(x+1)^{m,p,f}$ from $1(x)^{m,p,f}$ consist of four steps:

1) *Estimation of $1(x1)^{m,p,f}$ from $1(x)^{m,p,f}$.* Only transfers from the fecund to the sterile state are taken into account in this step so that

$$1(x1)^{m,p,0} = 1(x)^{m,p,0} (1 - s(x))^{m,p} \qquad (A1)$$

$$1(x1)^{m,p,1} = 1(x)^{m,p,1} + s(x)^{m,p} 1(x)^{m,p,0} \qquad (A2)$$

where $s(x)^{m,p}$ = proportion of fecund women in state m, p who become sterile at the beginning of year x

In the program FAMTAB, the variable $s(x)^{m,p}$ is assumed to be independent of marital and parity status and $s(x)$ is estimated from the average proportion currently fecund $F(x)$ (average between ages x and $x + 1$) with:

$$s(x) = (F(x-1) - F(x))/F(x-1) \qquad (A3)$$

The variable $F(x)$ is obtained, with interpolation, from estimates given by Henry (1965)

2) *Estimation of $1(x2)^{m,p,f}$ from $1(x1)^{m,p,f}$.* During the half year interval from $x1$ to $x2$ only transfers between parity states are made, yielding:

$$1(x2)^{m,p,0} = 1(x1)^{m,p,0} - 0.5 \times B(x)^{m,p} 1(x1)^{m,p,0} + 0.5 \times B(x)^{m,p-1} 1(x1)^{m,p-1,0} \qquad (A4)$$

$$1(x2)^{m,p,1} = 1(x1)^{m,p,1} \qquad (A5)$$

where $B(x)^{m,p}$ = age-specific fertility rate among fecund women at parity p in marital status m

A discussion of the procedure for deriving $B(x)^{m,p}$ from input parameters in FAMTAB can be found in Appendix B.

3) *Estimation of $1(x3)^{m,p,f}$ from $1(x2)^{m,p,f}$.* This step in the calculation of the marital–parity–fecundity life table is very similar to the calculation of a marital status life table, because it involves only transfers between marital states and deaths. The relevant equations were therefore directly taken from Schoen (1975). In the program FAMTAB the risks of moving between marital states are assumed to be

independent of parity and fecundity status, and mortality is age and sex but not marital status specific. This assumption can be modified easily in future versions of FAMTAB.

4) *Estimation of* $1(x+1)^{m,p,f}$ *from* $1(x3)^{m,p,f}$. To complete the estimation of $1(x+1)^{m,p,f}$ parity status transfers in the second half of the year have to be made in the life table. This is accomplished with the following equations which are similar to (A4) and (A5):

$$1(x+1)^{m,p,f} = 1(x3)^{m,p,f} - 0.5 \, B(x)^{m,p} \, 1(x3)^{m,p,0} + 0.5 \, B(x)^{m,p-1} \, 1(x3)^{m,p-1,0} \quad (A6)$$

$$1(x+1)^{m,p,l} = 1(x3)^{m,p,l} \quad (A7)$$

This four-step procedure is repeated for each single age increment over the life course of the cohort, yielding a complete life table population $1(x)^{m,p,f}$. The number of women transferring between different states at each age can also be calculated (with equations that are not provided here).

Appendix B: Estimating age and parity specific fertility rates for married fecund women

First, an age-specific marital fertility rate schedule is calculated with the Coale–Trussell model (Coale and Trussell, 1974). This model contains two parameters: one measures the degree of deliberate marital fertility control (which is provided as an input parameter in FAMTAB) and the other measures the overall level of marital fertility. The latter is adjusted so that the total fertility rate of the life table cohort is equal to the desired level as specified by another input parameter. Next, the age-specific marital fertility rate is divided by the age-specific proportions fecund, $F(x)$, to yield the age-specific fertility rate among married fecund women. The final step involves the introduction of parity specificity. To minimize the number of input parameters FAMTAB makes a distinction between only two parity levels: high parity (2 +) and low parity (0 and 1). This assumption implies that the age-specific fertility of married fecund women is the same for parities 0 and 1 and the same for parities 2 and higher. The ratio of the fertility rates of high to low parity women is provided as an input parameter. The age-parity-specific fertility of married fecund women is then obtained by inflating the age-specific marital fecund fertility rate for lower parities and by deflating it for higher parities until their ratio reaches the level specified.

References

Bongaarts, J. (1982), 'Simulation of the Family Life Cycle', *International Population Conference Manila 1981, Solicited Papers,* Vol. 3, International Union for the Scientific Study of Population, Liège.

Bongaarts, J., and R. Potter (1983), *Fertility, Biology and Behavior: An Analysis of the Proximate Determinants,* Academic Press, New York.

Coale, A. J., and P. Demeny (1983), *Regional Model Life Tables and Stable Populations,* Academic Press, New York.

—— and R. R. McNeill (1972), 'The Distribution by Age of the Frequency of First Marriage in a Female Cohort', *Journal of the American Statistical Association*, 67, 743–49.

Coale, J. A. and J. Trussell (1974), 'Model Fertility Schedule: Variations in the Structure of Childbearing in Human Populations', *Population Index*, 40, 185–258.

Espenshade, T. J. and R. E. Braun (1982), 'Life Course Analysis and Multistate Demography: An Application to Marriage, Divorce, and Remarriage', *Journal of Marriage and the Family* 44, 1025–36.

Henry, L. (1965), 'French Statistical Research in Natural Fertility', M. C. Sheps and J. C. Ridley, (eds.) *Public Health and Population Change*, University of Pittsburgh Press, Pittsburgh.

Schoen, R. (1975), 'Constructing Increment–Decrement Life Tables', *Demography*, 12, 313–24.

—— (1983), Personal communication.

—— and K. C. Land (1979), 'A General Algorithm for Estimating a Markov-Generated Increment–Decrement Life Table with Applications to Marital Status Patterns', *Journal of American Statistical Association*, 74, 761–76.

—— and V. E. Nelson (1974), 'Marriage, Divorce and Mortality: A Life Table Analysis', *Demography*, 11, 267–90.

Willekens, F. J., I. Shah, J. M. Shah and P. Ramachandran (1982), 'Multi-state Analysis of Marital Status Life Tables: Theory and Application', *Population Studies* 36, 129–144.

Part V

Kin Models and Simulation

11 Microsimulation of Household Cycles

KENNETH W. WACHTER

University of California Berkeley, California, USA

> War Ihr den Geist der Zeiten heisst
> Das ist im Grund der Herren eigner Geist
> In dem die Zeiten sich bespiegeln.
>
> *Goethe*, Faust I.

Faust's research assistant thought he could hope to capture the mental currents of the past. Faust rebuked him: 'What you all call the mind of former times is just at bottom your own mind, in which we find the times reflected.'

We who venture into simulation studies all no doubt first harbour a hope of capturing something as it was, is, or will be, of producing a copy as realistic as possible and more realistic than descriptive generalities can offer, of some process as it might happen. The word simulation itself connotes the making of a likeness. But the pursuit of realism through simulation is in fact a chimera, and a proper understanding of simulation and especially of demographic microsimulation begins with the assimilation of Faust's rebuke. What we make when we simulate is not a likeness of the operation of the world but a likeness of some set of our own ideas concerning the operation of the world.

Nothing will come of nothing. Conclusions from a simulation are only as trustworthy as the rates and rules which the simulation takes as given. Usually those rates which social scientists have estimated from firm empirical evidence come to a small number. Then there are those rates whose plausible range can be restricted, and a different simulation can be run with each combination of values of those rates. The multiplication of combinations would soon exhaust both budgets and patience, were the number of such rates not also small. There remain the rates which are sheer guesses. Conclusions which depend intimately on guesses are valueless. And so the only worthwhile simulations are either those which address such a narrow segment of experience that few rates need to be specified or those for which the model is sufficiently simple and scrutable that the guesses can be seen, on careful reflection, to have low impact on particular conclusions. The world being neither narrow, simple, nor scrutable, we are pushed toward the position that simulations serve to reveal the internal consequences of a simplifying theory rather than to mimic the world in its complexity.

Microsimulation of theories concerning household cycles is the subject of this general chapter. Setting microsimulation beside the companion approaches of analytic solution and macrosimulation, the early paragraphs discuss the kinds of problems amenable to simulation, the background literature, and the relative strengths and roles of the approaches. The testing of simulation programs is emphasized, and options for simulation design are reviewed. The later paragraphs consider hypotheses about household processes that have been tested in the recent past and that could be tested in the future, and reflect, finally, on the relationship between simulation and survey research.

Modes of simulation

Analytic solutions, macrosimulation, and microsimulation differ in the level at which calculations are actually performed. For analytic solutions, the unit is generally a whole population described by some function or equation of state, and the calculation consists of symbolic manipulation of formulas leading to closed-form expressions, as in chapter 14 by T. Pullum in this volume. The whole time period of interest is generally treated in one fell swoop, not step by step. Often, however, the formulas must be evaluated in specific cases by numerical integration or Monte Carlo sampling, blurring the distinction with the other approaches. For macrosimulations, the unit is a group, for instance an age and parity class or all households of a given type, and the calculations proceed iteratively, group by group and time period by time period, generally by means of transition matrix multiplication, as in the chapter by J. Bongaarts in this volume. For microsimulation, the unit is the individual, and the calculations proceed event by event, the changes in status of individuals determined sometimes by deterministic rules and more often by Monte Carlo realization of probability distributions, as in the chapters by J. Reeves, and J. Smith.

In this volume, the word 'household' denotes a co-resident domestic group. 'Household structure' refers to the age distribution and biological kinship relationships among members of a household, for whose classification one good reference is the introduction to Laslett and Wall (1972). Cycles in household structure occur as younger generations grow into the role positions of their predecessors. 'Family' remains a less precise word for kinship groups, construed either narrowly, as in 'nuclear family' or broadly, to encompass all a person's kith and kin, as in 'family demography'. The chapter by S. Kono is a household study; those by J. Smith and J. Reeves are kinship studies. Both household and kinship studies can be conducted through analytic, macro-, or microsimulation techniques.

The implementation of the calculations by any of these techniques, the programming, so to speak, on paper or computer, is generally mechanical and boring. The intellectual challenge is rather to be found in what all these techniques require in common. They all require the formulation of hypotheses for testing, the specification of the dynamics of the model, the definition of the inputs, provision of tests and checks and audits, and selection of statistics for output, all carried out in the face of constant tension between essential simplification and desired realism.

Theories which are too simple do not require simulations to expose their consequences. The questions amenable to simulation of any kind lie midway between the very simple and the very complicated. Questions of leverage are particularly well-suited to simulation. How much difference to the proportion of grandchildless elderly would a ten per cent rise in remarriage rates make, certain other things being constant? If everyone were trying to form stem-family households, how much difference to the proportion of stem-family households would a three year rise in brides' mean age at first marriage make, certain other things being constant? 'Certain other things being constant' is the phrase that gives meaning to findings in this domain, and simulation studies function in some respects as the social scientist's substitute for the natural scientist's controlled experiments under laboratory conditions. Hammel (1979) has called microsimulation studies of the past 'experimental history'.

Prospects are often bright for testing hypotheses by simulation experiments — does such and such a theory actually imply the consequences it is being invented to explain? Prospects are not always bright for estimating quantities by simulation. How many grandchildless elderly does the US have in 1984? How many years of their youth did average rural children spend in stem-family households in Hanoverian England? These survey-style questions for which we happen to lack surveys can be tackled in principle by simulation, but in practice they make heavy demands on our abilities to specify rates. A hundred years of US birth rates, death rates, and marriage age distributions can be pressed into giving an estimate of grandchildless elderly. But what correlation between the fertility of mothers and daughters are we to employ? What differentials and what intermarriage between native and foreign born? An exercise that starts as estimation often ends up as a test of how much the answers vary, holding constant or setting to zero such and such an intergenerational correlation or such and such an ethnic differential. Estimation often gives way to hypothesis testing, whatever our initial aims.

For complex processes the number of rates required for simulation grows so rapidly, because interactions involve two-way or many-way tables of rates, and table entries proliferate like the products of the individual factors. With five-year intervals, it takes perhaps ten numbers each to specify age distributions of brides and of grooms at first marriage. It takes a hundred numbers to specify the joint distribution, a thousand numbers to break it down by crude categories of income and of race. There are two modes of escape, to assume independence and condition the conclusions on this simplifying assumption, or to divert research into the development of a marriage model, until one has a model which generates the whole table from a few estimable parameters and which, in addition, the profession is ready to accept. This situation for marriage recurs with all the other demographic components of a simulation. Later paragraphs return in more detail to the specific options for various demographic components that can be entertained.

The literature of demographic simulation

Simulation studies in demography have, on the whole, chosen a path of caution, treating narrow questions and stating unashamedly the limitations of their assumptions. Work in areas of household and kinship is summarized throughout the present volume. Like this work, much of the demographic simulation research has developed with close ties to simulations in genetics and anthropology, well reflected at the outset in the collection by Dyke and MacCluer (1973) and continuing in studies in incest (cf. Hammel *et al.* (1979) and references and Le Bras 1980), in studies of small population dynamics (cf. Howell 1979, chapters 5, 11, 14), and in studies of effects of randomness on demographic estimators (cf. Wachter 1980, 105–8) and Hammel and McDaniel 1984). Dyke (1981) gives a recent summary. An equally active field of fertility–process simulation is summarized in Bongaarts and Potter (1983, 130–2). This demographic work has remained quite separate from the more extensive field of economic and policy simulation summed up by Sanderson (1980) and in the collection by Haveman and Hollenbeck (1980). Compared to the demographic simulations, the economic simulations tend to gain in scope and relevance at the expense of their greater dependence on rates which are guesses and on imputation of values to missing variables. A reaction against certain excesses is underway. Both the demographic and the economic simulation traditions are relevant to future research on household and family cycles, though the demographic tradition is the one in focus here.

These traditions have emphasized, and overemphasized, the distinction between analytic solutions, macrosimulation, and microsimulation. In fact, the thinking required about a problem is very much the same, whether one is carrying through analytic, macro, or micro calculations. Furthermore, the three approaches are far better used in tandem on a single problem than viewed as alternatives.

Occasionally, the choice among analytic, macro, and micro approaches may be swayed by the problem at hand. If the theory to be simulated specifies choices for individuals depending on their detailed circumstances, then it may be easiest to take the individual as the unit of analysis, opting for microsimulation. The alternatives would demand reasoning out beforehand the translation of the individual-level rules into transition rates for groups or their summarization into equations. For instance, hypotheses cast as rules determining which individuals remain in a household or form a new household depending on the configuration of relatives already present appeared easiest to test with microsimulation in the project of Wachter *et al.* (1978). If the outputs desired include measurements of random dispersion as well as central tendency, as in the case of small closed populations, microsimulations are indicated. If complex configurations of kin, step-nieces, half-sisters, the joint occurrence of siblingless, childless widows, etc., are of interest, then using individuals as the unit of analysis permits more flexibility. On the other hand, if a large number of different inputs or parameters are to be varied for the sake of broad-based sensitivity testing, macrosimulation has advantages of efficiency. If understanding of mechanisms generating qualitative regularities is the aim, there is no substitute for analytic solution.

But most problems do not fall into these categories. Most problems are amenable to treatment by any or all of the methods. Choice among methods, when choice is necessary, is most often a matter of convenience and of taste. What software and what expertise is locally available? For how much mathematics is one in the mood? What will prove easiest to document, to publish, and to explain? Journals are now often more receptive to reports of simulations than to analytic solutions. It appears easier to teach students entering demography from fields other than mathematics the techniques of microsimulation than to teach the mathematics required for analytic work or nonstandard macrosimulation. But training in conventional demographic projections facilitates macrosimulation just as training in microdemography facilitates microsimulation. To claim that any method is intrinsically best would be a mistake.

At best, on any problem, analytic, macro, and micro approaches should be used in tandem. Analytic work often demands simulations to check out the validity of approximations. Macrosimulation work often demands subsidiary microsimulations to justify amalgamation of certain groups or to supply missing transition rates, for instance when the splitting or amalgamation of parity groups is at issue. All simulation work demands analytic formulas for exact solutions on which to test the correct functioning of the simulation programs, as the next paragraph will discuss in more detail. Microsimulation, in its turn, demands macrosimulation for efficient tuning of input rates to match certain targets. For instance, Hammel, Wachter, and McDaniel (1981) use macrosimulation to obtain parity-specific rates to match published data on attained parities for early decades of the United States twentieth century. Reeves (1982) uses macrosimulation to interpolate between time periods and expand the sensitivity testing of a set of microsimulation experiments, an approach discussed further in chapter 12. The joint use of the techniques will surely be the pattern of the future.

Testing simulation programs

The testing of any program and the reporting of such tests are of paramount importance. Researchers only resort to simulation when models are complex, and thus when programs may malfunction without any obvious indications in the outputs. No study deserves to be taken on faith alone, nor can general remarks like 'the model was tested extensively' allay doubts. Here the use of different methods in tandem proves its worth. A micro-simulation can be programmed so that with special inputs and parameter settings it reduces to an essentially simpler model, so that its output should agree exactly with those of a simpler macrosimulation or with those of an analytic solution.

The simplest tests or audits draw on stable population theory. Suppose a program has been designed so that parity dependence and birth interval adjustments on deaths of previous infants can be suppressed and fertility rates set equal for married and unmarried women. Then with input rates unchanging over time and with an initial population whose ages correspond to the theoretical stable age pyramid, average population growth can be predicted exactly from stable population theory. With enough simulation runs with different random numbers governing the Monte Carlo realization of rates, even small discrepancies become statistically significant and can be recognized. Such tests are particularly effective at detecting individuals who might erroneously slip out of the pool of people at risk of giving birth or dying. Or the tests can reveal unclarities in delicate matters like the handling of twinning. Such a test for bias is illustrated by Hammel *et al.* (1976, 100–3).

There is a hierarchy of more complex tests. When parity and birth interval adjustments are in force, distributions of completed family size can be computed from renewal theory or from macrosimulation of birth processes and compared to microsimulation outputs. Household formation rules can be set to provide new households for every married couple, and the ratio of nuclear family households to solitaries can then be compared against predictions from a simple macrosimulation. Kinship microsimulations can be set to prohibit remarriage, and the expected number of direct lineal kin can be compared against exact predictions from stable theory from Goodman, Keyfitz, and Pullum (1974). In all tests, it is far better to have a model which reduces in the simple case to an exact match with the analytic or macro model, so that any statistically significant discrepancy is a signal for concern. If the expected match is only approximate, then the temptation to judge the fit 'quite good' is overwhelming and the value of the tests is vitiated.

Models are tested not only by comparison with the results of other models but also by examination of outputs for plausibility and agreement with empirical data. For this purpose it is important that there be an unambiguous quadripartite division of output statistics. First of four, there are output rates that match prespecified targets because the input rates have been tuned until the match is achieved. Marriage rates may be tuned to achieve a particular target for brides' mean age at first marriage. Second, there are output statistics that were unconstrained but turn out to match realistic targets, bolstering confidence in the simulations. The variance in completed family size or the husband's mean age at first marriage might be examples. In Hammel, Wachter, and McDaniel (1981, 20–2) the age structures and population sizes were checked through 1970 against empirical US values. Third, there are the output rates which were potentially free to wander and which may have wandered, but whose lack of agreement with reality can be seen or argued to be peripheral to the particular effects under investigation. In any simulation, the majority of outputs are perforce of this kind. Finally, there are the output rates which are generated as new information, proportions of types of households or person years lived in them or counts of living kin. Such outputs are not themselves answers. They are the raw material for graphical and statistical analysis, forming the evidential basis for maintaining or rejecting the hypotheses with which the simulations began.

Choices of models

This discussion is not the place to take up in detail the technical construction of microsimulation programs for studies of household structure. It is worth mentioning, however, some of the choices that must be made in algorithmic design. The most far-reaching choice of all is between an open and a closed model. In an open model, spouses for members of the existing population as simulated in the computer are created anew with certain characteristics in accordance with probability distributions. In a closed model, some or all marriages are arranged between individuals already in the population. Closed models are vastly more complex, but they are sometimes essential for small historical or contemporary populations or for certain kinds of complicated kinship tracking. Though open models need not ignore marriage squeeze phenomena, in practice it has been the closed models that have taken marriage squeezes most seriously.

Choice must also be made between on the one hand assigning the events in an individual's life course to him or her one after the other at the outset, in accordance with cohort rates, or, on the other hand, assigning the events that take place at a given time to the individuals alive at the time, in accordance with period rates. The former is more efficient, the latter more flexible in terms of the events like widowhood that depend on events to other individuals. Furthermore, output statistics can be computed as events occur in a simulation, period by period, or a census or register can be generated from which output statistics are recovered after the simulation is run.

There is a wide variety of levels of sophistication in the modelling of the

222 Kenneth W. Wachter

birth process. Should birth intervals be generated component by component, including amenorrheic intervals, conception waiting times, foetal wastage, and gestation, or should a probability model for the overall birth interval be employed? The former are more realistic, but for many purposes this realism is superfluous. The latter make more modest demands on empirical estimates. Similarly, there is choice as to whether to include migration in simulations, or to adjust for its likely effects after the experiment. There are choices as to whether to make divorce and remarriage depend both on duration and age or just on one or the other, a specific case of the general question of how specific each transition rate should be.

The component of microsimulation models most often in least satisfactory state is the marriage component for closed models. Models with single-sex dominance are unrealistic, but models with genuine two-sex structure exhibit instabilities. Perhaps the coming decade will solve this problem.

Microsimulation gives great scope to feedback mechanisms, for instance to homeostatic control of population growth or size, or to cohort modulations in fertility. Relatively little advantage of these possibilities appears to have been taken.

A final issue concerns assignment of individuals to households during their lives in the computer, genuine household cycle simulation, contrasted to computer generation of life course and kinship without residence, followed by residence assignments with a separate program operating on a kinship census. This latter stratagem is attractive, considering how hard it is to formulate full rules for household inclusion and fission over time. But it is no simple matter either to pass from tabulations of available kin, generated like those in chapters 12 to 14 of this volume, to estimates of attainable proportions of households of sundry types. A widowed mother who resides with one married child is preempted from residing with other married children, and may also preempt her child-in-law's mother from residing with the same couple. Either major simplifying assumptions must be made, or complicated analysis of the outputs from kinship simulation ensues, either through analytic solutions or further simulation. None the less the strategy may prove feasible, and some researchers are actively pursuing it.

The example of household kin composition

Attention now turns to examples of hypotheses about household and family demography that have been tested in previous studies or that would be worth testing in future studies. In the household area, the most extensive work up to now has focused on historical cases. The issue has taken the form: can certain levels or differences in demographic rates account for certain levels or differences in the occurrence of households of various types in a collection of communities? There are views, championed by Levy (1965), that demography imposes grave constraints on the kinds of households in which people can live, by limiting the available relatives alive to coreside. Whether such constraints have explanatory power in a particular setting depends on just how tight they are, relative to the breadth of demographic differences among communities being contrasted.

The hypothesis of this kind that has been most thoroughly tested is the hypothesis that demographic constraints were sufficiently tight in pre-census England to account for the low observed levels of stem-family households there, even if most opportunities to form stem-family households were being seized when they appeared. The full story of this test may be found in the first six chapters of Wachter *et al.* (1978). The tests involve implementing three alternative sets of detailed rules for household membership decisions. Each set is a version of stem family-forming behaviour. In one version the rules are designed more or less to maximize the time through the household cycle when the household would appear in cross-sectional data as a stem-family household, because the first-marrying child is the one chosen to bring the spouse into the household to co-reside. In a second version, the rules more or less minimize the time through the household cycle when the household appears of stem type, by forming stems through last-marrying heirs. Both versions are meant to be artificial, designed to put bounds on stem-family household proportions. A third version of rules modifies the extreme character of the first version in line with some key features of more realistic accounts of historical stem-family membership. There are numerous other assumptions, of course, including unchanging demographic rates and homogeneous communities, and a full understanding of the range of validity of the tests requires perusal of the full account.

It turns out that the differences between versions of stem-family formation behaviour are much greater than those that could be accounted for by differences in the demographic regimes tested. The demographic regimes involve nine combinations, with expectations of life between 25.4 and 40.2 years, brides' mean ages at marriage between 19.1 and 28.9 years, average completed parities between 3.37 and 4.91 and growth rates between −.006 and +.035. Under none of the household formation rules do the proportions of stem-family households fall to the observed English levels. Of the demographic influences, brides' mean age at first marriage exercises the most leverage; with the intermediate version of formation rules, a contrast between 19 and 25 years with heavy mortality corresponds to a contrast between 43 per cent and 30 per cent in the totals of multiple and extended family households.

The English pre-census setting thus provides an example where demographic constraints over household membership appear to be loose constraints and to have little explanatory power. At the extremes, the demography still matters. The Restoration English could scarcely have had percentages of extended and multiple households in the high 80s, like those Czap (1983,

119, 128–9) finds southeast of Moscow before 1858, without marriage ages dropping to the teens like the Russian demographic pattern. But in the middle range, the demography on its own explains little. Much more seems to hinge on detailed features of household formation behaviour itself. One reason appears to be that even in this most straightforward and best-thought-through example of a complex household formation process, the stem-family process, large numbers of households do not follow the supposed 'typical' path through the successive stages of the household cycle. A similar finding for nuclear family cycles has been emphasized in the review by Bongaarts (1983, 31). There are enough cases of deaths of heirs or their spouses, or failures to marry, or combinations of these eventualities, that a model of household formation needs to treat the non-standard circumstances with some care.

The stem-family microsimulation experiments reject their null hypothesis. They leave open the question of which other models of household formation behaviour would be compatible with the existing cross-sectional data. An effort to test another model is underway at the Cambridge Group for the History of Population and Social Structure. The model incorporates decisions in favour of nuclear family households except in hardship cases, such as aged widowed mothers. Can the level of potential hardship, suitably characterized, account for the observed level of household complexity?

The future: simulations and surveys

These historical studies could well serve as prototypes for relevant studies of contemporary household cycles. It is reasonable to conjecture that today's longer life expectancies imply even looser absolute constraints on the kinship composition of households than for pre-industrial England. But for sub-populations, like the elderly, the constraints might prove much tighter. Ages of women at marriage, especially at remarriage following divorce, have become more variable, while childbearing for the majority of women has become concentrated into a shorter span. For recent immigrant groups, relatives may be unavailable for coresidence not because of death but because of absence from the country. Successive generations of single-parent families may diminish opportunities for non-nuclear household formation. For some age groups the contrast between nuclear and solitary or non-family households may take the place, conceptually, which the contrast between extended or multiple and nuclear households holds in studies of the past. Therefore, a general view that demographic constraints on household structure are too loose in contemporary societies to merit examination would be misguided.

One example where demographic influences on contemporary household structure would be worth study may be given by way of illustration. There may well be a demographic component to the huge differentials in multigenerational households among various ethnic groups in the United States recently documented by Tienda and Angel (1982). Not death rates as such, but geographical mobility rates, immigration status of relatives, and ages at marital and non-marital childbearing might be important demographic determinants. Tienda and Angel themselves find economic factors insufficient to account for the differentials that they uncover. New group-specific information on entry into marriage and childbearing is becoming available, for instance from Michael and Tuma (1983), which might make simulation studies of ethnic differentials in multigenerational and extended households feasible.

Simulations need surveys. Do surveys need simulations? Would not national surveys with sufficiently rich retrospective kinship data and longitudinal panels with good kinship and residential tracking obviate the need for simulations?

Certainly, one use of simulation in the past has been to compensate for limited fine detail from surveys, detail needed to reconstruct subpopulations at risk of various transitions. Consider an example with widowhood. Suppose a cross-sectional survey reveals that some group with 10 per cent more three-generational households than average has 20 per cent more widows among mothers of working household heads. Suppose the survey is adequate to estimate completed family sizes greater than average, marriage ages later than usual, and a life table with heavier than usual male minority. But suppose it is not adequate to show directly how many widows have at the time of widowhood a married working child not already taking care of a mother-in-law, a child who might take the widow in. The simulation could use the estimates of demographic rates to predict the frequency of such circumstances for new widows. It could thus test whether the demographic causes of excess widowhood could be responsible for the whole 10 per cent differential in three-generational households, without any extra hospitability toward widowed mothers. On the other hand, if the survey were rich enough to determine a distribution of mothers' family circumstances on widowhood, simulation would appear unnecessary.

But this appearance would be deceptive. For, richer surveys mean deeper questions open to the asking. The questions are always likely to outstrip the detail in the surveys. In the widows' example, given distributions of circumstances, a next question might be whether among the demographic causes larger family size or heavier male mortality produced the main effect on household structure. Without simulation, one would need to find groups to survey similar in all other main respects and differing on this dimension. Better surveys do not remove the need for simulation. They extend it.

In this example, the simulation constitutes a model of transitions over time. It is a means for testing hypotheses about cycles of household change; it is also a means for estimating life-course statistics for individuals. Cross-sectional data do not reveal directly the time that individuals spend in different types of households or different conditions like marriage or employment. These are statistics that can, potentially, be read off simulation runs with ease. Regrettably, researchers have been slow to take up this opportunity to longitudinalize cross-sectional data through simulation. No simulation study has yet appeared as rich in life-course information as chapter 9 of this volume, culled by S. Hofferth directly from a longitudinal panel survey.

While surveys give a window on the world's complexity, simulations test the theories which abstract from this complexity a few simple regularities. In conjunction with longitudinal panel data in particular, simulations can help separate a few relevant interaction terms from a mass of irrelevant ones. Good panels may provide transition rates conditional on very fine breakdowns of circumstances. A rate for taking in widowed mothers might be calculated conditional on household head's age, number of children, number of married siblings, and income. A large enough sample size might make the differences among all these conditional rates statistically significant. But most differences in rates might be of little consequence for the particular cross-sectional statistics of interest, say for the proportion of multigenerational households. Pooling transition rates for households whose heads had different numbers of married siblings might yield effectively the same final outputs as treating these rates separately. For practical purposes, then, the interaction between propensity to take in a widowed mother and numbers of married siblings might be safely suppressed. Or it might turn out to be critical. In this context simulation can test the sensitivity of results implied by the transition rates estimated from longitudinal data, and lead to more parsimonious and trenchant accounts. This role is amplified when possible change in transition rates over time is being entertained.

Theories about social concomitants of cyclic household changes are difficult, at a basic level, because different households commonly pass through different sequences of stages. Time is 'many-fingered', as the physicists of general relativity call it. Households cannot be ordered uniquely by their position in a household cycle, and yet there is a cyclic progression taking place. Tabulations by age of household head or similar elementary strategies for identifying cyclic change lose their efficacy, because they lump together households going through different progressions and reaching different stages. With microsimulation, the principal differing paths through a household cycle can be treated separately, and the aggregate consequences tested and observed. Life of course offers more sports and variants of household change than any simulation can incorporate; full realism, as this chapter began by claiming, is not the goal. But an essential step toward realism, the step away from static models of household structure, to dynamic models of household cycles, is easier when techniques of microsimulation are at hand.

References

Bongaarts, John (1983), 'The Formal Demography of Families and Households: An Overview', *International Union for the Scientific Study of Population Newsletter* 17, 27–42.

—— and R. Potter (1983), *Fertility, Biology, and Behavior*, Academic Press, New York.

Czap, Peter (1983), 'A Large Family: The Peasant's Greatest Wealth', in Richard Wall, (ed.), *Family Forms in Historic Europe*, Cambridge University Press, 105–52.

Dyke, Bennett (1981), 'Computer Simulation in Anthropology', *Annual Review of Anthropology* 10, 193–207.

Dyke, Bennett, and J. MacCluer, (eds.) (1974), *Computer Simulation in Human Population Studies*, Academic Press, New York.

Goodman, Leo, N. Keyfitz, and T. Pullum (1974), 'Family Formation and the Frequency of Various Kinship Relationships', *Theoretical Population Biology*, 5, 1–27.

Hammel, Eugene A. (1979), 'Experimental History', *Journal of Anthropological Research*, 35.

——, D. Hutchinson, K. Wachter, R. Lundy, and R. Deuel (1976), *The SOCSIM Demographic-Sociological Microsimulation Program*, Institute of International Studies, University of California, Berkeley, Research Series Number 27.

Hammel, Eugene A., C. K. McDaniel, and K. W. Wachter (1979), 'Demographic Consequences of Incest Prohibitions', *Science*, 205, 972–77.

——, K. W. Wachter, and C. K. McDaniel (1981), 'The Kin of the Aged in the Year 2000', in S. Kiesler, Morgan, and Oppenheimer, (eds.) *Aging*, Academic Press, New York, 11–40.

—— and C. McDaniel (1984), 'A Kin-based Measure of *r* and an Evaluation of its Effectiveness', *Demography*, 21, 41–51.

Haveman, Robert, and K. Hollenbeck (1980), *Microeconomic Simulation Models for Public Policy Analysis*, (two volumes), Academic Press, New York.

Howell, Nancy (1979), *Demography of the Dobe !Kung*, Academic Press, New York.

Laslett, Peter, and R. Wall, Eds. (1972), *Household and Family in Past Time*, Cambridge University Press.

Le Bras, Hervé (1980), 'L'interdit de l'inceste', *La Recherche*, 107, 80–1.

Levy, Marion (1965), *Aspects of the Analysis of Family Structure*, Princeton University Press, 1–63.

Michael, Robert, and N. Tuma (1983), 'Entry in Marriage and Parenthood by Young Adults', National Opinion Research Center Discussion Paper 83–6, April 1983.

Reeves, Jaxk (1982), 'A Statistical Analysis and Projection of the Effects of Divorce on Future U.S. Kinship Structure', Ph.D. dissertation, University of California, Berkeley.

Sanderson, Warren (1980), *Economic–Demographic Simulation Models*, International Institute for Applied Systems Analysis, Laxenburg, Austria.

Tienda, Marta, and R. Angel (1982), 'Headship and Household Composition among Blacks, Hispanics, and Whites', *Social Forces* 61, 508–31.

Wachter, Kenneth (1980), 'The Sisters' Riddle', *Demography*, 17, 103–14.

——, E. A. Hammel, and P. Laslett (1978), *Statistical Studies of Historical Social Structure*, Academic Press, New York.

12 Projection of Number of Kin

JAXK H. REEVES
University of Georgia, Athens, Georgia, USA

This chapter discusses the problem of estimating the number of relatives of various types that persons in a population now have, have had, or will have in the future. Section 1 discusses the relevance and implications of kinship estimation, while Section 2 discusses the use of various simulation methods. In Section 3, useful new techniques for combining deterministic and simulation methods are explored. The chapter concludes with Section 4, presenting results of the above concepts applied to the US population.

1 Kin Calculation and Projection

Calculation and projection of expected number of kin serve many purposes. Historians and sociologists can use the results of such calculations to compare approximate household compositions between different societies, or between the same society of different eras. Public health officials or demographers can sometimes use kinship results to estimate a nation's vital statistics and vice versa. Administrators and government planners are frequently concerned with population projections in general, and projections of kin in particular.

Unfortunately, even today in well-developed countries, very few direct measures of living kin are recorded. For instance, one cannot go to any convenient reference book to find the average number of living brothers that a 30-year-old American male had in 1980. From the recorded demographic statistics (births, deaths, marriages, divorces, and immigrations) of a country, it is possible to estimate the expected number of kin of various types, but the process is rather complicated, as will be shown. Of course, if one does know (or has good estimates of) the kinship structure of a population at a particular point in time, it is possible to forward- or back-project the kinship structure of the population, provided one has estimates of the five demographic rates (see above) in the intervening years. It is not possible to determine uniquely demographic rates during a time period by observing changes in kinship structure over the period, but reasonable estimates and bounds can sometimes by obtained (Goldman, 1978; Wachter, 1980; McDaniel and Hammel, 1984).

The primary purpose of this chapter is to discuss techniques for making kinship projections into the future. The traditional analytic method for doing this is discussed by Pullum in chapter 14 of this volume. Unfortunately, those methods rely heavily on assumptions of stable populations and one-sex models, and are not applicable to our problem except in special cases. In Section 2 of this chapter, we will examine a stochastic simulation process which can be used to approximate a kinship distribution over time. Then, in Section 3, we will explore ways to combine the analytical formulae of chapter 14 with the simulation procedures of Section 2 to obtain improved estimates. These techniques are very useful in assessing the many possible errors which can occur in estimating kin by a complex procedure: initialization errors, errors in demographic rates, modelling errors, stochastic errors, and forecasting errors.

2 Simulation Methods

Upon reflection, it can be seen that all events determining the kinship structure of a population are contained in the following: births, deaths, marriages, divorces, and e/immigrations. If one had a complete list of these for a population throughout its history, one could find the number of kin of any type that each person had. The key ingredient necessary to do this would be some way of linking each vital event with its participants. If the information given in Table 12.1 were recorded for each event, kin calculations could be easily achieved. From such information a file could be created for each individual containing a record of his/her: sex, date of birth (or immigration), date of marriage(s), date of divorce(s), and date of death. Using this information, one could link to any relatives desired. To take a relatively complicated example, suppose one wanted to calculate the number of living first cousins which an individual had at time (t). One would first check the individual's birth record to find the identity of his/her parents. Then parents' parents' records would be located. The list of these four people's childbirths would be scanned, yielding (after deletion of the individual's parents) the parent's siblings and half-siblings, or aunts and uncles of the individual. These people's childbirth records would be scanned to yield first cousins. Finally, these cousin's records would be scanned to ascertain how many were alive at time (t).

Linking of records and computation of kin in the above manner is easily handled by a computer. The only problem with this procedure is that

Table 12.1   Vital events of kinship

Vital Event	Participants Involved	Other Information Needed
birth	infant, mother, father	date of event, sex of infant
death	deceased, spouse of deceased	date of event
marriage	bride, groom	date of event, marriage number
divorce	ex-bride, ex-groom	date of event, divorce number
immigration	immigrant, immigrant's relatives in country	date of event, sex of immigrant

individual vital statistics of the type needed are very unlikely to be available, except perhaps in small closed communities of interest to historical demographers. However, if one knows approximately the rates at which these vital events happen in a population, these events can be randomly simulated by a computer, and then, the counting of kin can be done as above. This is the essence of simulation methods of estimating kin.

To illustrate how simulation procedures can be used to project kin, a particular example (projecting the kin of the US White population in the year 2020) using a particular computer simulation package (SOCSIM) will be demonstrated at times during the remainder of this chapter. Other populations or simulation programs could be used, but they are all likely to have the general features shown in Table 12.2. Note that the initial population and past rates are not necessary for all simulations. They are necessary for kinship projections, since there are no directly available data on the kinship structure of any nation. If one had such data, or if one were merely trying to project and classify the population on the basis of race, age, sex, or marital status, one could obviously start in the present and project forward.

Table 12.2 Simulation flow chart

general procedure	example
initial population	US 1900 White population
↓	↓
Past vital rates	1900-1980 US vital rates
↓	↓
present population	US 1980 White population
↓	↓
future projected rates	1980–2020 projected vital rates
↓	↓
projection population	US 2020 White population

In general, one wants to choose the initial time to be sufficiently prior to the present so that the effects of misclassification of the initial population's kinship structure will have damped out by the time the simulation reaches the 'present.' Of course, if the initial time is too distant, there may be no reliable vital statistics for the intervening years. Similarly, one needs to consider how far into the future to make projections about kinship. If the fore-period is only a few years, then, even if the future projected rates are wrong, the kinship answers will still be approximately correct. If one tries to predict many years into the future, even perfect accuracy concerning past rates will not overcome the deleterious effects of incorrect guesses about future rates.

The remainder of this section will explain how a demographic microsimulation program works, with particular examples taken from the 1900→1980→2020 US White kinship simulation noted above. More details on this simulation, its input rates, and its results are given in Section

4. This particular simulation was performed using the SOCSIM package (Hammel *et al.*, 1976), but the outline given below should be applicable to other micro-simulation methods.

A demographic micro-simulation of a population into the future will consist of the following six steps:

1. One should create an initial computer population which is close to the real population (with respect to age, sex, and marital status structure) at some point in the past.
2. One should obtain the necessary age by sex by marital status by time-period specific rates of birth, death, marriage, divorce, and migration to project the population from the initial time to the present. These past rates must be estimated from available historical data.
3. Random number generation should be used to simulate the possible events of a person's life: birth (or immigration), marriage, parenthood, divorce, and death (or emigration). In micro-simulation models, each person's life path is simulated separately, but new possible events are generated for an individual each time his/her status with respect to age, marital status, or time-period changes. This process continues until the population has been simulated into the present.
4. The simulation program should be directed to store the individual records and link functions of the simulation population at various points in time. These data can then be analysed by kinship counting subroutines to determine the expected number of kin of various types which fall into certain categories. (For example, one could calculate the average number of living brothers of married women 40–45 years old in 1980 for a particular simulation population.)
5. Steps 2, 3 and 4 should be repeated a number of times, to yield different simulation populations which could result from applying the input rates stochastically to the initial population. If the initial population and input rates used are accurate reflections of the past, the average over the simulations of a particular kinship statistic should be a reasonable estimate of its true value.
6. One (or some) of the populations in step 5 should be chosen as 'the' current population to be simulated into the future, using some guesses or estimates about future rates. The output of these future simulations should be analysed as in step 4.

Many minor and several major difficulties arise in attempting to perform steps 1–6 above. Resolution of these problems is not a trivial matter, but detailed discussion of them would not be appropriate here. (For details, see Hammel, 1979 or Reeves, 1982). Some of the major concerns are the following:

a) The necessary age–sex–marital-specific rates needed for past time periods may be unavailable or unacceptably pooled.

b) The two-sex problem will rear its head, since no one has yet devised a completely satisfactory method of generating joint-sex processes (such as marriage) from separate male and female rates.

c) The subroutines needed to count the kin of a simulation population can become very complex, and error-prone, especially if one is dealing with relationships affected by divorce.

d) The simulation output for the 'present' time may turn out to be quite different from what is known to prevail. Various reasons for this occurring are errors in census counts, errors in vital rates statistics, undetected immigration–emigration, improper conditional rates, and stochastic errors. Determining which one(s) of the above are causing poor fits and remedying the problem is the most time-consuming task (along with obtaining past vital rates) involved in performing a kinship projection.

e) The estimation of future rates in step 6 above can become quite controversial, since no one knows what will happen in the future. Some suggestions on what to do about this are included in this section, with more concrete applications given in Section 4.

At this point, one is more than halfway done. A set of simulation populations now exist which should have, on the average, approximately the current kinship distribution of the population being studied. This in itself is quite useful information to many sociologists, demographers, and planners. What is frequently desired, however, are projections of the kinship distribution of this population at future points in time. To do this, one must do two things:

1. Choose one of the current simulation populations to be 'the' initial population for projections into the future, and
2. Guess or estimate vital rates for the future.

One might wonder why only one simulation population is chosen to start projections into the future. The reasons for not projecting all of them into the future is that this will increase the variance of the final estimates, by including populations which may have gone off course in earlier years of the simulation. It is a better strategy to choose from the candidates the one current simulation population that is 'best on the average'. What this means is left up to the projectionist. Typically one conducts χ^2-goodness-of-fit tests to see which simulation population comes closest to the average age-sex pyramid, or closest to the average female parity distribution. Of course, this depends on what kinship statistics of the future one is interested in. A person extremely concerned with sibling distributions of the future might want to pick the current simulation population whose distribution of expected siblings by age-group comes closest to that of the average over all current simulation populations.

The second consideration, choosing vital rates for the future, is tricky business. The natural first step is to run several simulations into the future with exactly the same rates as observed in the last time-period of the past-rate simulations. This will enable one to obtain estimates of how the kinship distribution will shift, even if vital rates stay exactly as they currently are. The next logical step is to experiment with raising and lowering the future vital rates about the current levels and seeing what effect this has on the kinship distribution. The easiest way to do this is by means of global multipliers which scale all fertility rates up by 10 per cent or mortality rates down by 5 per cent, for example. Of course, one can also experiment with changes in the actual shape of the distributions, such as lowering marriage rates for young women and raising them for older women, or increasing the illegitimacy rate.

The crucial question here, as with all projections, is: 'How confident can one be that the true future rates will fall within the High–Low band examined?' As Lee (1974) and other demographers have noted, demographic time series are very hard to predict. For instance, application of standard Box–Jenkins forecasting techniques to the crude birth rate (CBR) series (1917–1980) for married White US females will tell one with 95 per cent confidence that within the next 15 years the CBR will be in the range .060 to .163. This covers a range from lower than ever observed to as high as observed in the early 1960s. Obviously, this kind of possible variation in fertility rates will have a profound effect on kinship statistics as well.

Rather than giving huge confidence intervals for expected numbers of kin in the future, population projectionists would be more helpful if they gave tables presenting results of the form: 'An X per cent increase in fertility rates, with other rates held constant, would be expected to produce a Y per cent increase in kin of type (k).' Expected values and statements of this type for the 1980–2020 example are given in Section 4. A deeper analysis along these lines will even enable one to judge the relative impact of each of the major events on kinship distribution in the future. Not surprisingly, for most kinship statistics computed in the example simulations, fertility rates were extremely important determinants, first marriage rates were of moderate importance, and mortality, divorce, and remarriage rates had relatively little impact. Quantitative results of their respective effects can be seen in the tables of Section 4.

3 Combined Deterministic/Simulation Methods

Section 2 discussed kin calculations using simulation models. In this section, details on how to construct a reasonably realistic deterministic kinship projection model are investigated. In particular, this section examines the use of deterministic and simulation projections conjointly.

Using the same input rates as used in simulation, it is possible to project

234 Jaxk H. Reeves

deterministically the vital events of all cohorts of the population. The main reason for using simulation instead is that these deterministic equations can become quite complex, and because it is much harder to link cohorts than it is to link individuals. The procedure discussed next yields deterministic formulas which are manageable on a computer. Linking is still a problem for some kin relationships, but some useful results are noted.

Under micro-simulation the individual is the unit of measure, but for this procedure the cohort is the unit of measure. Each cohort can be thought of as 1.000 theoretical person starting off at age zero in marital status category single. As this cohort ages under the appropriate time-dependent age–sex–marital status-specific rates of birth, marriage, divorce, and death, fractions of this theoretical person flow into different demographic cells. Eventually, by age 100 or so, the person is back together again with mass 1.000 in the cell, 'dead'. Integrating over the cohort's life-span, one can find the number of person-years lived in each category by this cohort during its life, or during any period thereof. Simultaneous use of this information for several cohorts allows some kinship calculations to be made. This cohort integration procedure, while deterministic, is also called macro-simulation, to differentiate it from both the analytic formulas of chapter 14 and the micro-simulation methods of Section 2 of this chapter.

One purpose of the deterministic projection method is to duplicate the micro-simulation projection without randomness. If this were completely successful, and if kinship results could be disentangled from the output, there would be no need for simulation. This is not possible for most kinship variables, but the joint use of these deterministic results with micro-simulation results can be quite beneficial, as will be shown.

The main steps in performing deterministic kinship projection parallel the six steps given in the previous section. In other words, an initial population is projected from the past to the present and into the future. The major difference is that events happen deterministically to cohorts, rather than stochastically to individuals. Each cohort, which corresponds to an age-group changing over time, can be further partitioned by sex and marital status. Since almost all of the input rates depend on age, sex, and/or marital status, the cohorts can be deterministically projected through their lives. At any point in time, the joint distribution of the population by age-group, sex, and marital status can be attained exactly.

Of course, what is described in the previous paragraph is only moderately more sophisticated than the simple population projection exercises with which all demography students are familiar. The crucial elements insofar as kinship is concerned are the arrays binding one cohort to another. Some of the more important of these link arrays are those linking mothers' cohorts to childrens' cohorts (and vice versa), those linking husbands' cohorts to wives' cohorts (and vice versa), and those linking siblings' cohorts to one another. A brief discussion of each of these follows, but is should be remembered that the actual calculation and manipulation of these arrays to get kinship counts involves considerably more technical detail than shown here.

The link arrays are basically arrays which hold the conditional probabilities for various types of cohort interactions. For instance, the Husband-Wife link array could calculate, at any point in time, for all cohorts (*I*) and (*J*), the probability that a randomly chosen married man in cohort (*I*) had a wife in cohort (*J*). Similarly, one could calculate the links between parents cohorts and children's cohorts or between cohorts of siblings. Of course, since our deterministic procedure does not use parity-specific birthrates, calculation of these conditional probabilities can be quite complicated. One often-used procedure is to estimate means and variances for the birth distributions from the output of a simulation. Clearly, this will only work if one wants to run the deterministic projections after one has run some stochastic simulations. If one does not want to do this, estimates of the element of the link arrays are still possible, but they are highly variable. This is especially evident when one is dealing with counting lateral, rather than lineal, kin.

Once these estimates have been obtained, one can integrate and link over appropriate cohorts to form arrays which link siblings' cohorts to one another. This endeavour is confounded by the fact that the variance estimates are not too reliable, and by the radical changing of the variance during the early fertile years (15–30) of a female cohort's lifetime. If one is willing to use the results of these estimators along with those previously developed, one can also obtain estimates of lineal and lateral kin of the type shown in Table 12.3.

Table 12.3. Estimable lineal and lateral kinship variables

Variable	Parameters
expected number of living children	(age, sex, marital status)
expected number of living grandchildren	(age, sex, marital status)
probability of living mother	(age)
probability of living father	(age)
expected number of living parents	(age)
expected number of living grandparents	(age)
expected number of living in-laws	(age)
probability that parent's marriage has ended	(age)
probability that parent's marriage has ended by divorce	(age)
expected number of living siblings	(age, sex)
expected number older siblings	(age, sex)
expected number of younger siblings	(age, sex)
expected number of living aunts	(age)
expected number of living uncles	(age)
expected number of living nieces and nephews	(age)
expected number of living first-cousins	(age)
expected number of living siblings-in-law	(age)
expected number of immediate family	(age, sex, marital status)
expected number of dependents	(age, sex, marital status)

Once all the variables in Table 12.3 have been calculated, conditional on age, sex, marital status, and/or time-period, as appropriate, one would like to evaluate their accuracy. Theoretically, they should be as correct as the input rates, since they are being produced by a deterministic program. However, many of the formulas used above are only approximate, and, even if the formulas were all correct, programming errors could easily have occurred. One way of checking the program, as suggested throughout this section, is to use simulation in tandem with the deterministic projection program. If the deterministic program yields kinship results which are within the simulation's error bounds, then one can be 'fairly certain' that the two methods are conducting approximately the same projection process. In such cases, the deterministic answer is probably better than the simulation answers, since randomness has been eliminated.

If the deterministic kinship answers fall outside the error bounds, this is a sign that something may be wrong. The most likely cause is that the deterministic program is calculating kin incorrectly because of programming errors, misspecified rates, or poor approximations. It is also possible that the deterministic answer is correct and the simulation confidence intervals just happened not to cover the right answer for the variable being examined. An isolated case of this type is to be expected, but if the deterministic values for a variable are consistently (at all ages) over or under the simulation values for those ages, the deterministic process is probably in error.

Once one has achieved satisfactory agreement between the simulations and the deterministic program for a variable in years for which comparisons can be made, the deterministic program becomes even more useful. Recall from Section 2 that it is fairly expensive to dump simulation files and do linkages to count kin, so such counting is typically done only in selected 'snapshot' years. However, deterministic programs can easily be made to stop and print their results at any time. Thus, if one feels that the deterministic program and the simulation are yielding essentially the same answers for a variable at times T_1 and T_2, one can easily estimate the variable at times T, $T_1 < T < T_2$. This is useful for obtaining kinship distributions in non-snapshot years, or for tracing a particular cohort through its history.

Even if the deterministic calculation is too crude to fall within a simulation's error bounds, all is not lost. If the deterministic value is consistently high or low by approximately the same relative amount, then the deterministic results can be adjusted to match up more-or-less with the simulation values. The advantage of this is that better estimates (than those available by linear interpolation) could be obtained for these kinship variables in inter-snapshot years. Another potential use for these rough estimates is in trying to determine the effect of future rates on kinship variables. This will be illustrated further in Section 4.

Table 12.4 compares SOCSIM's output with that of a deterministic program for calculating kinship statistics for the US White population in

Table 12.4 Comparison of selected kinship statistics in 1960 and 1980

Variable	1960			1980		
	SOCSIM	(S.E. SOCS)	determin.	SOCSIM	(S.E. SOCS)	determin.
POP(20−)	.392	(.014)	.394	.315	(.012)	.304
POP(60+)	.141	(.005)	.136	.148	(.004)	.150
TOSIB(1015)	3.329	(.082)	3.309	2.659	(.054)	2.460*
TOSIB(3035)	3.708	(.097)	3.736	3.514	(.086)	3.490
TOSIB(5055)	2.865	(.088)	3.014	3.424	(.094)	3.559
LPAR(1015)	1.946	(.008)	1.941	1.953	(.006)	1.914*
LPAR(3035)	1.518	(.023)	1.527	1.567	(.020)	1.631
DVPAR(1015)	.115	(.011)	.117	.244	(.013)	.242
DVPAR(3035)	.130	(.013)	.147	.209	(.013)	.191
DVPAR(5055)	.063	(.012)	.112*	.149	(.014)	.158
BUMAR(1015)	.157	(.013)	.172	.280	(.013)	.284
BUMAR(3035)	.511	(.020)	.518	.417	(.016)	.480*
BUMAR(5055)	.935	(.012)	.935	.880	(.013)	.879
CHF(2025)	.711	(.051)	.695	.362	(.026)	.304*
CHF(3035)	2.529	(.081)	2.519	1.947	(.066)	1.792*
CHF(4045)	2.533	(.129)	2.592	2.481	(.104)	2.647
GCHF(5560)	4.376	(.364)	5.037	3.710	(.239)	4.046
GCHF(6570)	4.757	(.398)	5.557*	5.239	(.347)	5.687
ZPF(2025)	.586	(.030)	.556	.732	(.038)	.747
ZPF(3035)	.122	(.018)	.145	.182	(.021)	.205
ZPF(4045)	.170	(.022)	.131	.136	(.014)	.106*
ELDS(6570)	4.921	(.236)	5.416*	6.062	(.235)	5.592
IMMEF(2530)	2.716	(.071)	2.775	1.718	(.045)	1.636
IMMEF(4045)	2.960	(.095)	2.913	2.667	(.090)	2.651
SF(4045)	.070	(.017)	.048	.043	(.013)	.034
MF1(4045)	.739	(.025)	.707	.608	(.030)	.617
MF2(4045)	.131	(.019)	.149	.229	(.026)	.203
WF(4045)	.010	(.007)	.041*	.015	(.008)	.031*
DF1(4045)	.044	(.012)	.047	.083	(.017)	.092
DF2(4045)	.006	(.004)	.008	.021	(.009)	.024
EMF(4045)	.191	(.023)	.245*	.350	(.030)	.349
ERF(4045)	.138	(.020)	.158	.250	(.027)	.229

* = Deterministic value falls outside ± 2 standard error bound

1960 and 1980. The vital rates used from 1900 to 1980 in SOCSIM are described in Section 4. The deterministic program used the same input rates, and had the following rates derived from SOCSIM's output: age-specific female widowhood rate, age-specific female divorce rate, cohort–age-specific variance of parity distribution (σ^2), and female–male age distribution at marriage. In addition, age-specific zero–parity birthrates were included in the deterministic model, along with the general age-specific birth rates. The weights of the original cohorts of the deterministic model were set so as to yield cohorts which are distributed exactly the same as the cohorts used in the 1900 SOCSIM initial population. Neither method incorporated immigration into the projections, although SOCSIM can handle it.

In general, the agreement between the methods is good, especially for lineal kin. Even for the lateral kin shown, the disagreement is not too bad, although it is sometimes much worse for younger or older age-groups than those shown in Table 12.4. The table shows, for selected kinship variables of interest in 1960 and 1980, the SOCSIM estimate followed by its standard error (over the persons involved in 5 simulations), and the deterministic program's estimate. If the deterministic estimate falls outside a ± 2 Standard Error range about the SOCSIM estimate, it is followed by an asterisk (*).

One would expect asterisks to appear about 5 per cent of the time if the two programs were really doing the same thing. The larger discrepancy is due to inaccurate estimation of link functions in the deterministic program. Nevertheless, the two programs do seem to be giving answers which are fairly close to one another. Of course, some would argue that the deterministic program is not being tested fully, since it derives a number of its rates from SOCSIM. This is true for lateral kinship variables, but lineal kin would be counted about as accurately without SOCSIM. The beauty of using the two procedures conjointly, however, is that once the deterministic program has been adjusted to match up with some SOCSIM simulations, it can be used repeatedly to see what would happen if certain parameters were varied or if non-snapshot years (such as 1970, in the example) were to be investigated. This saves much time and money over what would be needed to run SOCSIM many times.

Table 12.5 explains what the acronym for each variable in Table 12.4 stands for. Each variable gives the expectation or probability for the age-

Table 12.5   Explanation of kinship variable names

Variable	Explanation
POP( )	The proportion of the population in the age-group specified (under 20 or over 60).
TOSIB	Expected number of Living Total Siblings (Natural Siblings plus Half-Siblings).
LPAR	Expected number of Living Parents.
DVPAR	The probability that one's parents' marriage has ended by divorce.
BUMAR	The probability that one's parents' marriage has broken up for any reason (divorce or death).
CHF	Expected number of natural children of females.
GCHF	Expected number of natural grandchildren of females.
ZPF	The proportion of Zero–Parity Females.
ELDS	The expected number of supporters of an elderly person. A supporter is defined to be any living brothers, sisters, spouses, children, or children's spouses over 21 and under 65.
IMMEF	The expected number of person's in a female's immediate family. Immediate family is defined to be husband (if married) and children or half-children under 18.
SF, MF1, MF2, WF, DF1, DF2	Proportions in Female Marital Status Groups (Single, First-Married, Remarried, Widowed, Divorced, Re-Divorced).
EMF	Proportion of Females whose marriage has ever ended.
ERF	Proportion of Females who have ever remarried.

group specified in parentheses behind the variable name, so, for example, TOSIB (3035) is the expected number of total siblings of those persons who are 30–35 years old. When examining the table, one should keep in mind that one is examining different cohorts at one snapshot in time (1960 or 1980), not following one cohort over its life. Most of these variables have been discussed previously, and most will be examined again in Section 4, where other aspects of this particular American population projection are examined.

The data in Table 12.4 are interesting in their own right, but they also illustrate certain points which will be of value in most kinship projections. The major purpose of running simulation and deterministic projection programs in tandem is to use one to verify the other or to decide when one method's results should supplant the other's. There are three general types of outcomes which can be observed when making kinship projections from these two methods:

(i) The two methods can agree quite well with one another.
(ii) The two methods can disagree significantly, but one knows the probable cause of the disparity.
(iii) The two methods can disagree significantly, but the reasons for the disagreement are unknown.

In the data of Table 12.4, most of the lineal variables seem to be of type (i), confirming the fact that the simulation and deterministic processes are conducting approximately the same projections. The sibling (TOSIB) and widowed female (WF) variables are examples of case (ii), where the disagreement is expected and most likely due to the inaccuracies in the link estimation of the deterministic program. The deterministic and simulation values of the living parents variables (LPAR) and the living grandparents variables (not shown) differ significantly at many ages, especially in 1980. This is a type (iii) situation in which there is no good explanation for the disagreement. It is suspected that the deterministic program used in this example incorrectly linked children's cohorts to their fathers' cohorts, but this has not been verified.

4 An Example From the US Population

The last section of this chapter provides more details of the 1900 → 1980 → 2020 projection of the US White population mentioned previously. It contains a brief description of how past and future rates were obtained or estimated. Much more could be written about the determination of these rates, but such material would be of little practical use to those trying to project other populations in other times. The rest of this section is devoted to analysing the kinship results which are projected for the US White population in the year 2020. These particular projections may be of limited interest, but the procedure for analysing effects of different rate schedules should be of general benefit.

The crucial data needed to find the current (1980) population kinship structure under both the simulation and deterministic models were the demographic rates of the US for the period 1900 to 1980. Each schedule of rates was changed decadally, so 8 different schedules, conditional on the parameters shown in Table 12.6, had to be found for each of the major demographic events: birth, death, marriage, and divorce. Immigration was not handled explicitly in these projections, because of lack of reliable data. For similar reasons, these projections apply only to the *White* population of the US from 1900 to 2020.

Table 12.6 Parameters of vital rates used in SOCSIM

Rate	Parameters
Birth	age-group, marital status, parity status
Death	age-group, sex, marital status
Marriage	age-group, marital status
Divorce	duration of marriage

The death rates from 1900 to 1980 were determined from Coale and Zelnick (1963) and from US Vital Statistics on mortality. The fertility schedules for the post–1916 period come from Heuser (1976+). The period from 1900–16 uses non-parity-specific birth rates given by applying a model of Sanderson (1978) to model marital fertility schedules of Coale (1971). Marriages rates from 1920 to 1960 were obtained from Graybill, Kiser, and Whelpton (1958), with some modifications necessary to mesh with the birth-rate schedules used. The marriage rates for the 1960s and 1970s were estimated from NCHS No. 21.21 (1978), and those for the period before 1920 by applying Sanderson's (1978) method to Coale and McNeil's (1972) marital model. Remarriage rates of widows and divorcees for the 1960s and 1970s come from NCHS publications. For decades prior to 1960, the remarriage rates were crudely estimated. Duration-specific divorce rates from 1921 onward were estimated based on the data in tables 2(p. 18) and 5(p. 21) in NCHS No. 21.34 (1978). The pre-1921 divorce estimates are based on crude divorce rates of Preston and McDonald (1979). For more details on all of the above rate estimation procedures, see Reeves (1982).

Future rates for the SOCSIM projections were obtained as outlined next. Sex–age-specific death rate projections for the future were obtained from Table B-2 of the US Current Population Reports (1976). Since these rates seemed rather stable, only one set of death projection rates was used. For birth, marriage, and divorce rates of the future, an attempt was made to obtain high, medium, and low projections of each. For birth rates, the projections of Table A.6 of page 78 of the 1976 Census Reports were used to give these three series. Of course, these series are age-specific, so adjustments had to be made to make them also parity-specific, as needed for SOCSIM. Medium age-specific first marriage projections were made by setting age 15–19 rates very low (1910–20 level), keeping age 20–24 rates at the 1970s level, and setting age 25–34 rates very high (post-World War II marriage rates). The high marriage projections were set a little higher than this (except for ages 25–34), and the low projections were set a little lower, but with the peak marriage age delayed somewhat. For divorce projections, the high rate schedule was the same as that observed in 1978, the medium rate was set at that of the early 1970s, and the low rate was that of the 1960s.

Once these rate schedules had been entered, the best-fitting 1980 simulation population (see Section 2) of SOCSIM was simulated 45 times from 1980 to 2020, with kinship calculations being made in the years 2000 and 2020. Five of these simulations were made with birth, marriage, and divorce rates all set at medium levels. Five more simulations were made of each of the eight (2 × 2 × 2) possible mixtures of high and low schedules of these rates (such as High Birth, Low Marriage, High Divorce) to yield the total of 45 simulations.

Table 12.7 Crude observed rates from SOCSIM runs 1980–2000

	Fertility	Marriage	Remarriage	Divorce
high (N = 20)	.10162	.10236	.12094	.02080
medium (N = 5)	.09204	.08916	.08886	.01945
low (N = 20)	.07887	.07346	.12094	.01390
range	(.86, 1.10)	(.82, 1.15)	(1.36, 1.36)	(.71, 1.07)

An objection to the method of projection used above is that the future rates are somewhat arbitrarily chosen. Furthermore, the high and low schedules are not bounds in any demographic or statistical sense. Table 12.7 shows the crude rates of birth, marriage, remarriage, and divorce which the high, medium, and low schedules produced in the 1980–2020 SOCSIM runs. Table 12.8 shows the ± 2 S.E. bounds which would be obtained by applying Box–Jenkins time-series projections to appropriately transformed series of these crude rates.

Table 12.8 Crude rates from time-series projections 1980–2020

	Fertility	Marriage	Remarriage	Divorce
high (+2 S.E.)	.17372	.15246	.12500*	.02256
medium (expected)	.09664	.09629	.08886	.01794
low (−2 S.E.)	.05591	.06063	.06500*	.01425
range	(.61, 1.89)	(.68, 1.71)	(.73, 1.41)	(.73, 1.14)

* = no time-series

In these tables, the fertility rate is the average annual birth rate for married women of child-bearing age (15–45). The marriage rate is the average annual rate of marriage for single (never-married) women 15–55. The divorce rate is the annual average divorce rate for married couples. The remarriage rate is the annual remarriage rate for widows and divorcees 15–55. The range shows what proportion of the medium SOCSIM rate was used in the high and low projections. In the SOCSIM runs, note that while fertility and nuptiality were approximately symmetrically distributed, remarriage was not varied, and divorce was skewed to the high side. More crucially, note that while the SOCSIM medium rates are near those of the time-series medium projections, the SOCSIM ranges are much smaller, especially for fertility and marriage rates. This difficulty is reexamined later in this section.

The Box–Jenkins (1976) methods are a well recognized statistical means of analysing time-series data. These methods attempt to discern trend and periodic variation amid the stochastic disturbances of any time series. Using these techniques, it frequently happens that a relatively simple model, using 3 or 4 parameters, can be found to explain the data adequately. Once such a model has been found, it can be used to make projections *and* provide error bounds for future values. In Table 12.8, a ± 2 standard error based about the projected values of each of the four crude rates is shown. Unfortunately, as is often the case with demographic time-series, the variability in the time-series projections (using Box–Jenkins methods) is much larger than that obtained from 'expert' projections of the future, such as those shown in Table 12.7. As noted by Lee (1974), we can explain demographic time-series much less well than we think.

From a statistical projection point of view, the ranges of crude fertility and first marriage rates shown in Table 12.7 are too narrow to give credible bounds in kinship in the future. This fact was not apparent until after the simulations into the future using SOCSIM had been performed, since the input rates were so category-specific that crude rates could not be easily estimated. (The crude rates shown in Table 12.7 are the crude rates observed as output after the simulations had been run.) One could completely scrap these results and try to adjust the category-specific input rates so as to get the wider ranges shown in Table 12.8, but that sort of manipulation is much easier and cheaper when done by a deterministic, rather than a simulation, program. A more resourceful use of the output of these simulations is the analysis of variance (ANOVA) decomposition described next.

Although the ranges of variability in the future projected rates of the simulation runs are less than the time-series bounds yield, they are large enough to give radically different answers to questions concerning kinship counts. To get an idea of the effect of these ranges of fertility, marriage, and divorce on kinship variables, an analysis of variance was performed. The 40 non-median simulations comprised a 2 × 2 × 2 design of High–Low Fertility by Marriage by Divorce, with 5 replications per cell. The dependent

Table 12.9 ANOVA results on kinship statistics: 2020

Variable	GM	√MSE	HF	HM	HD
POP0020	22.0%	1.4%	+ 4.2%*	+ 3.1%*	− 0.7%*
NS1015	1.600	.167	+ .231*	+ .076*	− .078*
NS3035	1.649	.121	+ .199*	− .004	− .048*
NS5055	2.313	.066	+ .017	− .001	+ .004
HS1015	.284	.083	+ .050*	+ .015	+ .059*
HS3035	.433	.083	+ .033*	+ .014	+ .028
HS5055	.372	.033	+ .004	− .006	− .005
TS1015	1.883	.193	+ .280*	+ .092*	− .019
TS3035	2.081	.137	+ .232*	+ .011*	− .020
TS5055	2.684	.079	+ .019	− .008	− .001
LGP1015	2.766	.061	+ .003	+ .065*	− .036
LGP3035	.799	.035	+ .021	+ .048*	+ .000
LD6570	4.403	.167	+ .083*	+ .076*	− .067*
LD7075	4.650	.167	+ .071*	+ .075*	− .065*
LD7580	4.328	.270	+ .025	+ .040	− .066
DP1015	.213	.044	+ .007	+ .002	+ .064*
DP3035	.301	.040	− .001	+ .003	+ .056*
DP5055	.379	.027	− .005	+ .001	+ .012*
BU1015	.254	.045	+ .003	+ .004	+ .056*
BU3035	.508	.045	+ .006	− .005	+ .052*
BU5055	.866	.023	− .007	− .001	+ .010*
DF2030	.040	.021	+ .003	+ .004	+ .010*
DF3040	.078	.026	+ .002*	+ .005	+ .021*
DF4050	.105	.028	− .003	− .006	+ .022*
DF5060	.126	.021	− .000	− .009*	+ .042*
ZF2025	.779	.071	− .026*	− .067*	+ .003
ZF3035	.318	.053	− .033*	− .061*	+ .004
ZF4045	.258	.041	− .038*	− .050*	+ .005
CF2025	.305	.078	+ .042*	+ .090*	+ .003
CF3035	1.412	.130	+ .195*	+ .162*	+ .003
CF4045	1.632	.152	+ .217*	+ .164*	− .036
GF4550	.384	.105	+ .115*	+ .150*	− .013
GF5560	1.646	.288	+ .370*	+ .363*	− .005
IF2530	1.577	.153	+ .068*	+ .212*	− .025
IF4045	2.166	.154	+ .190*	+ .121*	− .046*
IF5560	.758	.077	+ .012	+ .020	− .051*
SBF2530	.554	.053	+ .040*	+ .078*	− .004
SBF4045	1.248	.103	+ .099*	+ .064*	− .016
SBF5560	.521	.058	+ .006	+ .014	− .010

(* = Significantly different from zero at 2% level)

variables were the year 2020 kinship variables shown in Table 12.9.

The purpose of this decomposition is to show how much variation about the grand mean of a kinship variable is caused by high or low levels of a rate factor. Thus, the value of each kinship variable was decomposed into a grand mean plus contributions due to the effects of high or low birth, marriage, or divorce rates. The heading GM is for the grand mean for that variable. HF, HM, and HD stand respectively for the effects of High Fertility, High Marriage, and High Divorce rates, which are the negatives of the LF, LM, and LD values, because of the symmetric design. The $\sqrt{\text{MSE}}$ is the standard error, or the typical amount of unexplained error in a prediction, after accounting for the effects of fertility, marriage, and divorce. The variables shown here have all been defined, in less abbreviated form, in Table 12.5 with the exception of NSIB (Natural Siblings) and HSIB (Half-Siblings). Also, the variable SBF is a female support burden variable. It is the average number of dependent children which a women must support (along with her husband, if any) plus the average number of elderly persons she must support (along with her siblings, spouse, and spouse's siblings).

The asterisk (*) in Table 12.9 represents effects which are significantly different from zero at the 2 per cent level. Note that fertility seems to be the most significant effect for most variables, followed by marriage effects and divorce effects. If one believes that the levels of rates used in these projections are adequate to model the future, then one can compare the results shown here with the 1980 results of Table 12.4 to see how kinship is projected to change over the period from 1980 to 2020. Even if one feels that the range of rates is inadequate, the ANOVA decomposition allows one to see what the relative effects of certain rate assumptions on kinship projections are.

As mentioned above, an objection to the results of Table 12.9 is that they are based on rate schedules which may not display enough variability between high and low rates. To obtain a better quantitative idea of the effect of each major demographic rate on kinship variables in the year 2020, 21 projections into the future were made by using different values of the time-series rates as input into the deterministic program. These 21 projections were run at mixtures of different levels of rates to facilitate a regression analysis, as explained next.

Each of the 21 paths were obtained by choosing 4 independent normal (0,1) variates, and taking the associated rates from Table 12.8. For example, if the 4 variates chosen were $Z_F = -.623$, $Z_M = +1.315$, $Z_R = +0.587$, $Z_D = -.114$, the utilized rates for this path would be .623 SDs below the expected fertility rate, 1.315 SDs above the expected marriage rate, etc., yielding path values of $rf = .06789$, $rm = .13039$, $rr = .09781$, $rd = .01771$. This procedure seems to be a reasonable way of generating plausible design paths for the future, although one could argue that certain rate types (marriage and fertility, for instance) may not behave independently of one another.

Once the 21 design paths had been chosen, the deterministic program with appropriate multipliers was used to give approximately the desired crude rates. The year 2020 output for each of these 21 design paths was obtained, and values of the following 22 dependent variables were recorded for each trial: Population (P(20−), P(60+)), Female Marital Status (SF4045, MF4045, WF4045, DF4045, ED4045), Total Children (CF4045, CF3035,

CF2025), Zero–Parity Female Proportion (ZF3035, ZF4045), Grand-children (GF5560, GF6570, GF7580), Divorced Parents (DP1015, DP3035, DP5055), Immediate Family (IF2530, IF4045, IF5560), Elderly Supporters (LD6570).

Data for some variables, such as siblings, were not collected since the deterministic program is unreliable for those. Similarly, variables such as LPAR (living parents) were not included, since they depend primarily upon the death rate, which was not being varied in the design. The death rate in these regressions was not varied, since the variability associated with time-series projections of the death rate is very much smaller than that of the other vital rates.

Having done the above, each dependent variable (Y) was regressed jointly on the fertility rate (rf), marriage rate (rm), remarriage rate (rr), and the divorce rate (rd). The following three models were considered in performing these regressions:

(Model 1) $\quad \hat{Y} = b_0 + b_1 \cdot rf + b_2 \cdot rm + b_3 \cdot rr + b_4 \cdot rd \quad$ (Linear) (12.6)

(Model 2) $\ln(\hat{Y}) = b_0 + b_1 \cdot \ln(rf) + b_2 \cdot rm + b_3 \cdot rr + b_4 \cdot rd$

$$\text{(Log-linear) (12.7)}$$

(Model 3) $\ln(\hat{Y}) = b_0 + b_1 \cdot \ln(rf) + \dfrac{b_2}{rm} + b_3 \cdot rr + b_4 \cdot rd$

$$\text{(Demographic) (12.8)}$$

The rationale for these models will not be discussed here. However, it turns out that all three of the models yield very good explanations of the variables ($r^2 > .90$). This is partly due to the linear nature of many of the variables examined. Another reason for this is the assumption that the future rate schedules will all have the same age-specific shape, with levels being raised or lowered by a global multiplier. This is actually quite unlikely to happen. Table 12.10 displays the results of the regression for each variable. The results are consistent with those of Table 12.9, where comparisons can be made. The table gives the value of each regression coefficient under the best-fitting model ((i), (ii), or (iii), above), along with the proportion of explained variance, r^2. This information could be very useful to a person who wanted to make a quick *rough* projection about certain types of future American kin. Such a person would need only to specify the crude future rates of birth, marriage, remarriage, and divorce to obtain estimates. However, '*caveat emptor*' is good advice in this situation.

Since the results of Table 12.10 may be somewhat difficult to interpret, they are presented in a somewhat different form in Table 12.11. The latter table shows the medium level time-series prediction for each variable, along with the associated standard error of the regression prediction, $\sqrt{\text{MSE}}$. The next four columns show the expected effect of raising a particular crude demographic rate to the +1 S.E. level while keeping all other rates constant. For instance, the medium time-series projection for the expected number of

Table 12.10. Estimated regression coefficients for year 2020 kinship variables

Variable	Model	Intercept b_0	Fertility b_1	Marriage b_2	Remarriage b_3	Divorce b_4	r^2
P(60+)	1	.472	− 1.698	− .716	− .061	.716	.973
P(20−)	1	− .097	2.387	1.103	.091	− 1.109	.975
CF4045	3	3.555	1.142	− .045	2.348	− 5.668	.999
CF3035	3	3.423	1.193	− .049	4.433	− 5.893	.999
CF2025	3	2.419	1.188	− .077	0.100	− 3.948	.997
GF5560	3	6.278	1.948	− .089	0.857	− 10.528	.999
GF6570	3	4.903	1.425	− .049	0.654	− 7.717	.999
GF7580	3	3.900	0.897	− .038	0.500	− 5.830	.999
ZF4045	2	− 2.305	− .929	− 12.973	− 1.372	− 3.487	.970
ZF3035	2	− 1.921	− .783	− 11.473	− .885	− 3.038	.972
SF4045	2	− .027	− .011	− 30.178	0.014	0.119	.999
MF4045	3	− .092	.001	− .014	1.519	− 14.756	.989
WF4045	3	− 3.419	.001	− .019	1.034	− 12.850	.994
DF4045	3	− 1.373	.002	− .023	− 7.705	45.286	.976
ED4045	3	− .982	.002	− .031	0.085	35.545	.985
DP5055	1	.283	− .003	.001	− .010	6.124	.999
DP3035	1	.162	− .010	.131	− .084	17.509	.995
DP1015	1	.065	.133	.126	− .045	17.417	.993
IF5560	3	.150	.094	− .013	.338	− 16.751	.991
IF4045	3	2.985	.797	− .029	.886	− 9.178	.995
IF2530	1	− .275	11.777	10.043	.503	− 12.504	.977
LD6570	1	3.184	10.668	3.876	2.613	− 28.111	.994

children of females 40–45 (CF4045) is 1.670, but if the crude marriage rate were raised from the medium projection (.09629) to the + 1 SE level (around .12500), the expected number of children would be 1.670 + .184 = 1.854, or an 11 per cent increase.

The last column of the table, DIV.%, is shown to demonstrate the uses of tables of this type. It shows the percentage of a variable's value which would be affected by raising the divorce rate one standard error above its expected time-series value. Many of the outcomes are negative, since divorce would tend to lower the number of most types of kin. However, the interesting fact here is that the divorce rate seems to have remarkably little influence on most kinship variables. This is not to say that divorce will be uncommon in the future of the US, just that its effects on kinship will be much less severe than those caused by shifts in fertility or marriage rates. Of course, if this table contained step-siblings as a variable, that would undoubtedly be significantly affected by the divorce rate.

The purpose of this chapter has been to discuss projection of kin. The most important lessons to be gleaned from this discussion are:

1. Projection of future kin is very likely to include a significant amount of re-creation of the past.
2. Ideally, deterministic and simulation projection methods should be used

Table 12.11 Effect of + 1 S.E. change from medium time-series projecton on various kinship statistics in 2020

Variable	Med T–S	$\sqrt{\text{MSE}}$	Fertility	Marriage	Remarriage	Divorce	Div. %
P(60+)	.246	.012	− .065	− .020	− .001	.002	+ 0.8%
P(20−)	.228	.016	.092	.031	.002	− .003	− 1.3%
CF4045	1.670	.016	.778	.184	.020	− .021	− 1.3%
CF3035	1.500	.015	.736	.181	.013	− .021	− 1.4%
CF2025	0.288	.008	.141	.056	.000	− .003	− 1.0%
GF5560	1.963	.038	1.806	.451	.044	− .047	− 2.4%
GF6570	2.644	.048	1.616	.315	.046	− .047	− 2.4%
GF7580	3.822	.037	1.376	.454	.030	− .197	− 5.2%
ZF4045	.206	.018	− .055	− .062	− .007	.002	+ 1.0%
ZF3035	.262	.020	− .060	− .071	− .006	.002	+ 0.8%
SF4045	.055	.000	.000	− .036	.000	.000	0.0%
MF4045	.693	.006	.000	.023	.030	− .023	− 3.3%
WF4045	.024	.000	.000	.001	.001	− .001	− 4.1%
DF4045	.228	.003	.000	.012	− .033	.025	+11.0%
ED4045	.519	.005	.000	.039	.001	.044	+ 8.5%
DP5055	.398	.000	.000	.000	.000	.014	+ 3.5%
DP3035	.482	.003	.000	.004	.001	.040	+ 8.3%
DP1015	.401	.003	.005	.003	.000	.040	+10.0%
IF5560	0.625	.006	.020	.018	.030	− .024	− 3.8%
IF4045	2.038	.051	.623	.143	.041	− .021	− 1.0%
IF2530	1.643	.092	.452	.277	.020	− .029	− 1.8%
LD6570	4.351	.036	.410	.107	.066	− .065	− 1.5%

in conjunction. If only one is to be used, simulation is preferable, especially for calculating lateral or complex kin.

3. Time-series error bounds on most projected demographic rates are so large as to be practically useless. Tables such as 12.11 showing the relative effect of certain rates are much more useful.

4. If the American population examined is at all typical of other modern populations, it appears that fertility rates (and marriage rates to a lesser extent) are much more significant determinants of most types of kin than remarriage, divorce, or death rates.

References

Box, G. and G. Jenkins, (1976), *Time Series Analysis*, Holden-Day, San Francisco.

Coale, A. J. (1971), 'Age patterns of marriage', *Population Studies*, 25:193–214.

—— and D. McNeil, (1972), 'The Distribution by Age of the Frequency of First Marriage in a Female Cohort', *Journal of the American Statistical Association* 67:743–40.

—— and M. Zelnick, (1963), *New Estimates of Fertility and Population in the United States*, Princeton, N.J.: Princeton University Press.

Goldman, N. (1978), 'Estimating the Intrinsic Rate of Increase of a Population from the Average Number of Older and Younger Sisters', *Demography* 15:499–508.

Graybill, W. H., C.V. Kiser, and P. K. Whelpton, (1958), *The Fertility of American Women*, John Wiley and Sons: New York.

Hammel, E. A., D. W. Hutchinson, K. W. Wachter, R. T. Lundy, R. Z. Deuel, (1976), 'The SOCSIM Demographic-Sociological Microsimulation Program Operating Manual', University of California, Berkeley, Institute of International Studies Research Series, No. 27.

——, K. W. Wachter, C. K. McDaniel, (1979), 'The Kind of the Aged in the Year 2000', in E. S Morgan (ed.) *The Elderly of the Future*.

Heuser, R. (1976), Fertility Tables for Birth Cohorts by Color, U.S. 1917–1973, Washington, D.C.: Department of Health, Education, and Welfare, 76–1152.

Lee, R. D. (1974), 'Forecasting Births in Past-transition Populations: Stochastic Renewal with Serially Correlated Fertility', *Journal of the American Statistical Association* 69:607–17.

McDaniel, C. K. and E. A. Hammel, (1984), 'A Kin-based Measure of r and an Evaluation of its Effectiveness', *Demography* 21:41–52.

National Center for Health Statistics (NCHS) (1971), 'Vital Statistics of the United States, Vol. 2: Mortality', US Department of Health, Education, and Welfare (HEW).

—— (1977), 'Vital Statistics of the United States, Vol. 3: Marriage and Divorce: 1975', (HEW).

—— (1978), 'Vital Statistics of the United States, 21.21: Marriage by Cohort', (HEW).

—— (1979), 'Vital Statistics of the United States, 21.34: Divorce by Marriage Cohort', (HEW).

Preston S. H. and J. McDonald, (1979), 'The Incidence of Divorce within Cohorts of American Marriages Contracted since 1867', *Demography* 16:1–26.

Pollard, J. H. (1975), 'Modelling Human Populations for Projection Purposes — Some of the Problems and Challenges', *Australian J. of Statistics*, 17:63–65.

Reeves, Jaxk H. (1982), 'A Statistical Analysis and Projection of the Effects of Divorce on Future U.S. Kinship Structure', Ph.D. Dissertation, University of California, Berkeley, Statistics Department.

Sanderson, W. (1978), 'New Estimates of the Decline in the Fertility of White Women in the United States 1800–1920', Paper presented to the Stanford–Berkeley Colloquium in Historical Demography, May 24, 1978.

US Bureau of the Census (1970), 'Childspacing and Current Fertility', Subject reports.

—— (1975), 'Historical Statistics of the United States, Colonial Times to 1970', bicentennial edition.

—— (1976), 'Projections of the Population of the United States, 1977 to 2050', Current Population Reports, Series P-25, No. 704.

Wachter, K. W. (1980), 'The Sisters' Riddle and the Importance of Variance when Guessing Demographic Rates from Kin Counts', *Demography* 17:103–14.

13 The Computer Simulation of Kin Sets and Kin Counts

JAMES E. SMITH

Cambridge Group for the History of Population and Social Structure, University of Cambridge, United Kingdom

A kin count is a set of numbers expressing how many kin of various types exist for an individual at some time. In its simplest form a kin count is a single number, such as the number of that person's living brothers at his or her 65th birthday, or the number of children ever born to him or her during his or her lifetime. More complex kin counts may involve many numbers, such as a count of the number of various types of kin, according to their age and sex, which an individual has at death.

In principle, kin counts can be obtained by empirical enumeration using genealogical, survey, or census methods. But in practice it is often difficult or impossible to obtain kin counts by these methods. Genealogical research, even when done with the aid of computers, is labour intensive and requires extensive archival data. Censuses seldom include any information about kin who live outside ego's own household. Relevant surveys are hard to find, and to conduct special surveys is a very expensive proposition. All of these problems are compounded when we want kin counts for the past where genealogical and census data are even more sparse and surveys cannot be used.

In this chapter we introduce a method for producing what we shall call model kin counts. Our method is that of computer microsimulation. We will not undertake a comprehensive comparison of our method to other mathematical and simulation methods reviewed and illustrated in this volume, but several of the important similarities and differences will be noted. For convenience we refer to our method as the CAMSIM method because the computer software used for performing the microsimulations is so named. However, this term is only used for convenience and is not meant to imply that our method could only be implemented using CAMSIM or that the CAMSIM software is limited to this type of application.

Model Kin Counts

Model kin counts are those which are produced by some sort of modelling exercise rather than by empirical enumeration. They differ from empirical kin counts in the way in which they are obtained, and also in the uses to which they can be put. Most importantly, model kin counts are not usually legitimate substitutes for empirical kin counts in the sense of directly and literally standing in for missing empirical data. This point deserves some consideration by anyone using model kin counts.

If a kin count is obtained by some method of empirical enumeration it reflects the actual numbers of a person's kin, allowing for measurement error, as they exist in the real world. All the factors which determine the existence of kin, such as fertility, mortality, marriage, divorce, etc., are effectively 'taken into account' in an empirical kin count. In contrast, a model kin count only takes into account those factors which have been included in the model. Since there are always factors operating in the real world which are omitted from a model for one reason or another, it is not safe to assume that model kin counts are equivalent to those that would be obtained by empirical enumeration.

Rather than proposing our model kin counts as realistic substitutes for those that could, in principle, be obtained by empirical methods, we prefer to put them forward as useful fictions. Like model life tables, model stable populations, or model nuptiality schedules, our model kin counts have the form or appearance of the real things without pretending to be adequate substitutes for empirical data. But just as we may cautiously use a model stable population to help with the assessment and interpretation of empirical data, we may find model kin counts valuable aids to the evaluation and interpretation of empirical data. In other words, to say that model kin counts are useful fictions is not to say that they are pure fantasies. Like a good fictional story, a model kin count does not pretend to portray a specific instance of real-world happenings, but it does claim to be understandable in terms of the real world and to be useful in certain circumstances in shedding light on the operation of that world.

Of course there is a penumbral area between purely fantastic, and hence empirically useless, model kin counts and those which are more or less realistic, even to the point of being accurate substitutes for empirical data. It is the use to which a kin count will be put that will determine which of these extremes has the stronger pull on the modeller. But experience with scientific models in general, and computer simulation models in particular, has shown that attempts to produce more and more realistic results usually lead to unwieldy models which contain many *ad hoc* assumptions and which are impossible to verify and replicate.

Model Kin Sets

Although it is possible to discuss the production of model kin counts without dealing explicitly with kin sets, there is a great deal to be gained by not omitting this step. We define a kin set as a set of all of those people who at any time occupy any relevant kinship position relative to ego. A relevant kinship position is simply one that the modeller decides is relevant to his or her purposes. Having decided upon a list of relevant kinship positions, we construct a kin set by identifying every person who did, does, or ever will occupy any of those positions relative to the person whose kin set we are constructing.

A model kin set is a special type of kin set in which the people who are members of the set are created by the modeller, which is to say that certain information about each person in the kin set is produced from the model. Using CAMSIM, for example, we produce model kin sets in the form of computer files containing life history information about each person in an individual's kin set. The precise information recorded for each person in a model kin set will depend upon the nature of the model, but it is important to adhere as closely as possible to the general principle that all of the information which can be gleaned from the model about each person in the kin set is recorded.

Once a model kin set has been created it can be analysed and described like any other set of life history data for a sample of individuals. When doing this it is important to remember that a kin set is not the same thing as a random sample of individuals selected from a population. We will return to this point in a later section. For now we simply note that we may *describe* a kin set with whatever summary statistics we choose even though we are not yet sure how to make inferences from those numbers. One set of descriptive numbers is, in fact, a kin count — a tabulation of numbers of people in the kin set, according to their kinship positions, and perhaps other attributes, who live at some specified time or during some specified interval of time. Thus we see that the production of kin counts can be treated as an exercise in first generating kin sets and then processing those kin sets to yield kin counts.

There are at least two very important advantages in the kin set approach to producing kin counts which are worth special mention. One is that by giving explicit attention to the production of kin sets we are less likely to skip over the important task of verifying that our model is producing reasonable life histories for individuals. Unless the life histories of the individuals in the kin set are acceptable to us in all their features — ages at death, birth intervals, ages at marriage, proportions ever marrying, etc. — the kin counts which we produce, however reasonable they appear or however amenable to *post hoc* justification they are, do not deserve our confidence. Another advantage of focusing on kin sets is that of more efficient use of human and computer time. Once model kin sets have been produced they can be processed and reprocessed to produce many different types of kin counts without having to re-run the simulations. The savings in man and machine time are often great and often permit more detailed and extensive exploitation of simulation results than could be afforded otherwise.

The CAMSIM Algorithm for Producing Kin Sets

At the heart of every computer simulation model lies an algorithm, a group of procedural statements which specify the operations which are performed by the computer in generating the results. There is an unfortunate tendency to confuse algorithms with computer programs, and therefore to confuse computer simulation modelling with the task of writing computer programs. In fact, algorithms are to computer programs what mathematical equations are to arithmetic. Algorithms, like equations, utilize a special language for representing the subject being modelled. Computer programs, like arithmetic, must be added to generate results from a model once it is specified, and this is largely a mechanical task.

In the CAMSIM algorithm for generating kin sets each ego is treated as the central figure in a kinship system. The word 'kinship' is used here rather than 'kin' because we are talking about a system of positions rather than a system of people. These kinship positions are those which we called the 'relevant kinship positions' when we defined kin set earlier, and they are chosen by the modeller to meet his or her substantive purposes. The task of the algorithm, which is to say the simulation model, is to 'visit' each of these kinship positions and to generate the life history of each person who ever occupies each position. To do this we treat the kinship positions in groups, each group consisting of a female, all her spouses (if any), and all her children (if any).

The occupants of a group of kinship positions can be simulated by (1) creating a female at birth, (2) simulating her life course forward in time from her birth, (3) creating a spouse of the appropriate age whenever the female is scheduled to marry, and (4) creating a child at each point where the female is scheduled to give birth. Having completed these steps we have a completed life history for the female, a partial life history of each of her spouses (marriage date, marriage age), and a partial life history of each of her children (birth dates).

It is a simple matter to adjust our definition of a kinship group to refer to a male, all of his spouses (if any), and all of his children (if any). With a routine similar to that for females we can generate complete life histories for males, as well as partial life histories of their wives and children. Our CAMSIM algorithm includes both female and male routines so that a complete life history of either a man or woman, with partial life histories of spouses and children, can be produced.

Using the male and female simulation routines the simulation of a person and his or her descendants is straightforward. First, the kinship group consisting of that person, his or her spouses and children is simulated using the appropriate routine depending upon the sex selected for the person. Then for each child the appropriate routine is used to simulate the kinship group consisting of the child, his or her spouses (if any), and his or her children (if any). By continuing in this way we simulate the original person's descendants for as many generations as we want.

We come up against the first important limitation of our algorithm when considering spouses in more detail. Our algorithm effectively assumes a completely 'open' population in the sense that, when a person marries, his or her spouse is created *ex nihilo* and assigned whatever attributes, such as age, we desire. This means that we are not simulating a marriage market in which there is a constrained supply of spouses having various attributes, as there might be in a real population. However, provided that we do not intend to use the simulations to investigate marriage market dynamics, and provided that we assume that our people come from a large population and our rules for assigning attributes to spouses reflect whatever constraints exist in that population, we need not to be too concerned about our algorithm. Should we not want to make such assumptions, then we would have to build a different simulation algorithm, such as that of SOCSIM (see Reeves, chapter 12 in this volume), dealing with a closed population.

Another important limitation of our algorithm also has to do with spouses. Since each spouse is created *ex nihilo* at the time of marriage we have no information about the previous life history of the spouse. We do know, or rather assign, an age to the spouse so we can compute the spouse's birth date. However, we do not know whether the spouse had been married before or had children. The main effect of this limitation is to limit our ability to include step-children and step siblings in our kin sets — a limitation which will not occupy us further here but which can be 'worked around' in cases where it is of concern, such as when simulating populations with high divorce and/or widowhood rates.

The routines for simulating a kinship group can also be used to simulate ascending kin. To do this we think of the person as the child in a kinship group which consists of his or her parents, the person in question and his or her siblings. We must first decide whether we would prefer to have the complete life history of the person's mother or father, and then select the female or male simulation routine accordingly. Supposing that we decide upon the female routine, we then produce the complete life history of a female (the mother), and a partial life history of each of her spouses and children. Before executing this routine we do not know which child is the person chosen so we assign any arbitrary birth date to the person's mother when we run the routine. We also specify to the routine that the woman being simulated must have at least one child during her lifetime. Otherwise, of course, she could not be the mother. Various programming devices can be used to ensure that this condition can be met efficiently, although one could simply re-run the routine as many times as necessary to come up with a woman who has at least one child.

Having simulated the members of the kinship group we now insert the person chosen into that group as a child. We do this by randomly selecting a child from among those borne by the woman and we substitute our choice for that randomly selected child. In other words, we assume that the people we are simulating are a representative sample of children in terms of their birth orders. Having chosen which child of the mother our individual is to be, we take the difference between his or her birth date and the birth date of that child and call this difference the date adjustment factor. The date adjustment factor is then added to all dates in all of the life histories of the person's mother, her spouses, and her other children in order to 'move' them to the appropriate points in time relative to our chosen individual.

   This method of moving backward in time to simulate ascending kin can be applied repeatedly to simulate the person's mother's parents and siblings, father's parents and siblings, mother's mother's parents and siblings, etc. Of course, to obtain complete life histories of any of the siblings, parents, etc., would require that the appropriate male or female routine be applied to simulate their marital and fertility histories. The descendants of these siblings can be simulated to any depth to yield the person's lateral kin, such as first cousins, first cousins once removed, etc.

   A powerful feature of the CAMSIM algorithm is that it relies upon two basic routines, one for males and one for females, for simulating the person's ascending, descending, and lateral kin of all types, and to any distance in the past or future. In technical computer jargon these two routines are recursive, which means that while the female routine is simulating the person's mother, for example, it can interrupt its own execution to simulate his or her grandmother, for example, without losing its place. This recursive property leads to many computational and conceptual advantages, not the least of which is the fact that the computer program is highly modular with little redundancy. However, all of this is obtained at a price, and the price is non-trivial. Our rather facile movement forward and backward in time is only justified in the context of stable population assumptions. We now turn to this issue and other questions concerning the nature of the population which we are in fact simulating with the CAMSIM algorithm.

Kin Sets as Representative Samples

It is obvious that a kin set is not a random sample of individuals from a population. The person's parents must have had at least one child and this fact alone makes them unrepresentative of males and females in the population at large. Other types of statistical dependencies exist between individuals in a kin set, such as the fact that parents are always older than their children, so that no kin set can be treated as a random sample of individuals from a population.

   In what sense, then, can a kin set be said to be representative of anything more than itself? The answer to this question depends in part upon the specific simulation model, its algorithm and the various statistical dependencies which may be built into the model. Our answer to this very important question will be schematic and non-technical, partly because many of the technical issues remain unresolved, and partly because an introductory treatment ought to emphasize getting a 'feel' for the issues.

First we note that our approach to kin sets always starts with a person and works outwards to generate his or her kin set. Our first question about representativeness ought therefore to be about the persons chosen: of what population do they constitute a representative sample? Consider the case in which we want to produce kin sets for a sample of males each of whom lives to be at least 90 years old. This situation would arise if our aim were to produce kin counts for elderly males, for example. Rather than simulating a large number of males from birth, and then using only those few who happen to live to advanced ages, we gain in efficiency by being able to specify certain conditions in advance and then simulating only the relevant types of males. These persons are certainly not a representative sample of all males in the population, since the fact that they live to very old ages means, among other things, that they are guaranteed the opportunity to have more children than men who die younger.

What we can say about any group of people chosen with any attributes which we choose to set in advance is that they are representative of a population of chosen individuals having all the same pre-selected attributes and subjected to the same demographic rates included in our model. For example, a simulation of the life histories of 100 males all living to age 90 would yield results concerning their life histories, e.g. their marriage ages, numbers of children, etc., representative of the life histories of a population of males all of whom lived to 90 years of age. The term 'representative' is used here in the same way it is used in statistical sampling theory to mean that our 100 simulated persons can be treated as a simple random sample drawn from the population we have described.

The term 'population' is also used here in its statistical sampling sense and does not necessarily denote an empirically observed population at some point in time. It simply means an indefinitely large number of chosen individuals who experience exactly the same simulated conditions experienced by our sample of 100. But to make our kin sets and the kin counts derived from them into useful fictions rather than pure fantasies we ought to be able to think of them as somehow related to kin sets that would be found in some human population which does exist in time, has an age and sex structure, and so on, even if it is an idealized rather than an empirically observed population.

In demographic terms the population from which all members of our kin sets are drawn is a perfectly stable population. In other words, the demographic rates to which the individuals are subjected during the course of the simulation do not change with time. Although it would be relatively simple to create a kin set of descending kin of a chosen person under conditions of changing rates this could not be done for ascending kin with the current

CAMSIM algorithm. The difficulty is that the algorithm simulates the mother's (or father's) marital and fertility history before the precise temporal location of the people involved is known. Only after the date adjustment factor is computed and added to all dates is it possible to know precisely when the events in the mother's (or father's) marital and fertility history take place. Thus, it would be impossible to simulate using time-dependent demographic rates with this algorithm.

In addition to having time-independent demographic rates a stable population has a certain age structure which is determined by the demographic rates. This fact holds two implications for the creation of kin sets using our CAMSIM algorithm. Firstly, we have assigned the person as the nth child of his or her mother without regard for the age structure of a stable population which may cause there to be relatively more or fewer mothers of certain ages at any given point in time than our algorithm implies. Secondly, limitations on the numbers of people in various age groups in the stable population may imply a certain degree of overlap in the kin sets of different individuals, whereas we have so far assumed that no members of one person's kin set appear in another person's kin set.

As Le Bras (Le Bras and Wachter, 1978, p. 165) has shown, the probability of a newborn having a mother of age x in a stable population is given by:

$$A(x) = S(x)f(x)\exp(-rx)$$

where $S(x)$ is the probability of a female surviving from birth to age x, $f(x)$ is the fertility rate of women at age x, and r is the growth rate of the stable population. Using the CAMSIM algorithm, the implied value of $A(x)$, which we call $A^*(x)$ is shown in the Appendix to be:

$$A^*(x) = S(x)f(x)\exp(-rT)$$

where T is the mean age at maternity in the stable population. The degree to which the distribution of chosen individuals' mothers' ages obtained from CAMSIM departs from that of the stable population is given by the ratio:

$$A^*(x)/A(x) = \exp[r(x-T)]$$

from which we see that at younger ages (x less than T) $A^*(x)$ is lower than $A(x)$, or in other words the CAMSIM algorithm underrepresents younger mothers, and vice versa for older mothers. In Table 13.1 we present $A^*(x)$ and $A(x)$ for simulations under late eighteenth century English conditions where r is high (.010) and we see that the differences between the distributions are small, amounting to less than half a percentage point for most ages. In populations with slower rates of growth the differences are smaller still, converging to no difference when r is zero. Although it is possible to adjust CAMSIM results to compensate for this small bias, we have not done so in the results presented later in this chapter.

Table 13.1 Comparison of $A(x)$ and $A^*(x)$ under conditions of rapid population growth ($r = .010$)

x	A(x)	A*(x)
15	.0000	.0000
16	.0011	.0009
17	.0025	.0021
18	.0044	.0039
19	.0083	.0073
20	.0139	.0124
21	.0227	.0204
22	.0308	.0280
23	.0399	.0366
24	.0486	.0433
25	.0495	.0461
26	.0535	.0507
27	.0541	.0518
28	.0546	.0529
29	.0585	.0572
30	.0568	.0561
31	.0549	.0548
32	.0527	.0532
33	.0519	.0529
34	.0478	.0492
35	.0470	.0490
36	.0415	.0437
37	.0383	.0407
38	.0343	.0369
39	.0311	.0338
40	.0280	.0307
41	.0234	.0259
42	.0160	.0179
43	.0116	.0131
44	.0081	.0093
45	.0070	.0081
46	.0035	.0041
47	.0027	.0031
48	.0019	.0023
49	.0012	.0015
Total	1.0000	1.0000

The question of overlapping membership of the kin sets of different egos is a more serious one. An extreme example will illustrate the problem. Consider the simulation of 100 kin sets for 1000 egos with each kin set containing all relatives back ten generations, forward ten generations, and laterally as far afield as second cousins. Using the CAMSIM algorithm each kin set created for a given person consists of completely different individuals from those included in any kin set created for any other person. Each of the 1000 kin sets would, of course, be very large (too large to really simulate) with, for example, over one thousand different people for each group in the earliest generation of great-great-great . . . grandparents. This would imply that our 1000 egos were descended from over one million distinct ancestors ten generations back, and that none of the descendants of any of these ancestors ever married into the kin set of another of our individuals. Needless to say, all of this is very unlikely even in a very large population, and for small populations we are certainly in the land of fantasy.

Although it is clear that the creation of totally non-overlapping kin sets is unacceptable in such an extreme case, there is less need for concern in more limited applications of the CAMSIM algorithm. For example, in a large population the chance of randomly selecting two individuals who share a grandparent is very small, as is the chance of randomly selecting any two who share any near relatives. But the wider the range of relatives included in the kin sets and the larger the number of individuals which are simulated, the greater the chance that they share relatives. In cases where there is a non-negligible chance that kin sets of various individuals share relatives the CAMSIM algorithm will produce kin sets that overestimate the variance between kin sets in various features. Again, one resolution of this problem is to resort to a closed population simulation model, such as SOCSIM (Reeves, this volume). However, it is also possible to use kin sets produced by CAMSIM to construct populations with specified degrees of relatedness, although such an exercise leads beyond the limits of the present chapter.

CAMSIM Parameters

So far we have discussed the CAMSIM microsimulation model in terms of its algorithm for producing kin sets without making specific reference to the way in which fertility, mortality, and marriage are handled. We now turn to these three items, but with the reminder that the approaches taken to the modelling of fertility, mortality, and marriage in the present simulations are not necessarily the only approaches which can be taken when using CAMSIM to generate kin sets. Indeed, any approach which is consistent with stable population assumptions could be taken.

Mortality. The principal mortality parameters used by CAMSIM are distributions of death ages for men and for women. When a person is born, a death age for the person is drawn from the appropriate distribution. When a spouse is created a death age is drawn from the appropriate distribution with the constraint that the death age must be at least one month after the marriage age of the spouse. Since all timing is done on a monthly basis in CAMSIM it is easy to specify neo-natal and infant mortality by months rather than years of age. Where distributions are given by years of age CAMSIM interpolates to yield outputs in terms of months.

Fertility. Fertility is modelled with a set of parity progression ratios which express the probability that a woman of parity n is eligible to have another child. These parity progression ratios may be specified according to a woman's age or other characteristics, although this is not done in the present simulations. The duration of time between marriage and first birth, first and second birth, and subsequent births is determined by distributions of birth intervals. When a woman marries or gives birth the appropriate parity progression ratio is used to determine whether she is eligible to have another child. If so, the birth date of the next child is determined from the appropriate birth interval distribution. Provided that the woman lives to that date, and provided that her husband lives until at least 8 months prior to that date, the woman actually has a child at the computed date. Only married women are eligible to conceive a child, with the exception of first births. Only married women can actually bear a first child, but the birth interval distribution from marriage to first birth allows births prior to nine months after marriage thus permitting pre-marital conceptions to give rise to first births within marriage.

Marriage. When a person is born an appropriate probability of permanent celibacy is used to determine whether the person is eligible to ever marry. If so, the person is assigned a marriage date computed from a distribution of first marriage ages. If the person survives to that date, he or she will marry. At marriage a spouse is created and assigned an age drawn from a distribution of spouse ages appropriate to the age of the person. For the sake of simplicity, divorce is not included in the simulations presented here although other CAMSIM simulations do include divorce. In the present simulations only the death of one of the spouses ends a marriage. When a married person dies the surviving spouse may or may not become eligible for remarriage, depending upon the probability of remarriage parameter. If the widow or widower is eligible for remarriage, the date of remarriage is determined from a distribution of waiting times to remarriage appropriate to the age and sex of the widowed spouse. If he or she survives to the remarriage date then a marriage takes place to a spouse of an age drawn from the distribution of spouse ages appropriate for the age of the person who is remarrying. The remarriage continues in force until one of the partners dies, when the cycle of remarriage is again begun.

In Table 13.2 various input parameters relating to mortality, fertility, and remarriage are presented for two simulations, involving 300 female individuals each, under two different demographic regimes. One we call 'pre-industrial' because its parameters are set with reference to demographic conditions in late eighteenth-century England where the keynote features were high fertility and high mortality resulting in a high rate of population growth. The other regime we call 'modern' because its parameters are set with reference to demographic conditions in England today with the notable exception that divorce is not included in the simulation. Fertility is low, as is mortality, and the implied rate of population growth (the intrinsic *r*) is slightly negative in the 'modern' simulations. Although pre-marital

Table 13.2   Selected parameters, English 'pre-industrial' and 'modern' simulations

	'pre-industrial'	'modern'
Expectation of life at birth		
males	35.8	69.5
females	38.2	73.1
Infant mortality (per 1000)		
male	179.8	13.4
female	164.1	10.4
Proportion of first births within		
8 months of marriage	.274	.160
12 '' '' ''	.557	.230
24 '' '' ''	.822	.430
Proportion of second births within		
18 months of first birth	.257	.100
24 '' '' '' ''	.496	.260
48 '' '' '' ''	.901	.820
Mean age at first marriage		
males	27.5	23.4
females	25.6	21.3
Parity progression probabilities		
marriage to first birth	.950	.910
first to second birth	.900	.860
second to third birth	.890	.440
third to fourth birth	.873	.360
fourth to fifth birth	.836	.100
fifth to sixth birth	.797	.100
Proportions eligible to marry		
male and female	.940	.940
Median duration from spouse death to remarriage (in months)		
males	13.	13.
females	19.	19.

conceptions are allowed under both demographic regimes, no illegitimate fertility is allowed. Because of the exclusion of divorce and illegitimacy, as well as other things, from our simulations they should not be taken as statements about the way things were, or are, in England. Rather, the value of these simulations lies in what they tell us about differences in kin counts which are caused by a shift from a high fertility and high mortality regime to one of low fertility and low mortality, all other things being equal.

Kin Count Results

Using the CAMSIM algorithm and the parameters described above we have simulated 300 female egos under each demographic regime, i.e. the English 'modern' and the English 'pre-industrial' regimes. In Table 13.3 we present some of the more important fertility measures obtained from the model kin sets.

Table 13.3   Selected demographic measures computed from simulated 'pre-industrial' and 'modern' kin sets

Age of woman	'Pre-industrial'		'Modern'	
	ASBR	ASMFR	ASBR	ASMFR
15–19	23.3	559.6	7.3	146.6
20–24	129.1	349.4	98.2	185.8
25–29	250.7	357.7	147.0	178.4
30–34	272.4	322.2	83.2	93.8
35–39	221.3	248.3	38.2	41.4
40–44	112.4	123.6	16.8	17.8
45–49	23.8	26.2	5.6	6.0
Total fertility rate	5.108		1.981	
Gross reproduction rate	2.492		.967	
Total marital fertility rate	8.297		2.944	
Net reproduction rate	1.385		0.945	
Mean age of maternity	31.36		28.52	
Intrinsic r	0.0104		− 0.0020	

Notes: ASBR and ASMFR are age specific birth rate per 1000 woman years lived, and age specific marital fertility rate per 1000 married woman years lived, respectively.

Comprehensive tables presenting kin counts and other information, such as means and distributions of ages of kin, have been produced from the model kin sets, but these tables consume many pages of computer output and cannot be reproduced here. Because the model kin sets are stored as machine-readable files they can also be processed to produce special tabulations, such as cross tabulations of numbers of kin of various types, correlations between ages of kin of various types, etc. For our purposes we only illustrate some of the information which is contained on our 'standard' set of computer-produced tables.

Tables 13.4 presents mean numbers of kin, mean ages of those kin, and the percentage of individuals having no kin of the specified type for three different types of kin — parents (biological mother and father), children (by any spouse), and siblings (other children of the person's mother). The points chosen in the lifetime are birth (0th birthday), and subsequent birthdays at 11-year intervals until the 88th. A striking feature of these figures is the difference between the survivorship of parents in the two regimes. By age 33 a person under the 'pre-industrial' regime has less than half the number of surviving parents, on average, than a person under the 'modern' regime. Even more striking is the difference between proportions of chosen individuals having no parents at this age: only 3 per cent under 'modern' conditions and over 35 per cent under pre-industrial conditions.

Although the differences in parental survival in the two regimes are quite dramatic, there are marked similarities in some of the other figures. We note, for example, that while the high fertility of the 'pre-industrial' regime does cause there to be more children surviving per chosen individual at every

Table 13.4   Mean numbers and mean ages of near kin, English 'modern' and 'pre-industrial' simulations

				Age of chosen individual					
	0	11	22	33	44	55	66	77	88
'Modern'									
Parents									
mean number	2.00	1.95	1.91	1.74	1.39	0.66	0.11	—	—
mean age	29.9	40.7	51.7	62.0	72.0	81.0	90.0	—	—
percentage with none	0	0.3	0.7	3.0	12.7	49.0	89.0	100	100
Children									
mean number	—	—	0.14	1.45	1.84	1.85	1.86	1.81	1.68
mean age	—	—	1.5	6.3	15.1	25.7	36.6	47.6	58.5
percentage with none	100	100	88.3	27.3	19.7	18.7	18.7	19.3	21.7
Siblings									
mean number	0.67	1.32	1.33	1.32	1.30	1.23	1.03	0.66	0.22
mean age	4.5	11.3	22.0	33.0	43.9	54.7	65.4	75.5	83.8
percentage with none	51.7	16.3	16.3	16.7	17.3	19.7	26.3	48.3	80.3
'Pre-industrial'									
Parents									
mean number	1.99	1.63	1.24	0.83	0.40	0.07	—	—	—
mean age	32.1	43.0	53.4	63.1	72.0	80.8	—	—	—
percentage with none	0	4.0	14.3	35.7	66.0	93.0	100	100	100
Children									
mean number	—	—	0.19	2.05	3.14	2.97	2.60	2.30	1.82
mean age	—	—	1.7	5.3	12.0	22.5	33.5	44.4	54.8
percentage with none	100	100	86.7	27.7	17.7	16.3	18.7	21.3	27.0
Siblings									
mean number	1.68	2.89	2.81	2.55	2.14	1.72	1.13	0.53	0.12
mean age	6.4	11.9	21.7	32.4	43.4	53.7	63.1	70.9	76.0
percentage with none	36.0	11.3	14.0	15.3	19.3	25.3	40.0	62.3	91.3

age, the proportion of those individuals with no surviving children is about the same at most ages in the two regimes. Also similar are the percentages of those having no siblings in the ages 22 to 44 in the two regimes. But with siblings, as with children, the higher fertility of the 'pre-industrial' regime more than compensates for the higher mortality, resulting in mean numbers that are greater at every age.

Some suggestive inferences about such topics as burdens of familial support can be made from these simple figures, although more detailed analyses would have to be undertaken on our kin set files before drawing firm conclusions. If we take a 33-year-old person under 'modern' conditions we see that she has a 97 per cent chance of having at least one surviving parent $(100-3=97)$, 73 per cent chance of having at least one child

(100 − 27.3 = 72.7), and about an 83 per cent chance of having at least one surviving sibling (100 − 16.7 = 83.3). Her parents are, on average, 62 years old, and if the person is to assume responsibility for care or support of her parents she will have at least one other sibling who can share the burden in most cases. The presence of own children, who are about 6 years old on average, will no doubt place some restrictions on the support activities of that 73 per cent of individuals having at least one child.

In the 'pre-industrial' regime the average ages of parents of 33-year-old egos is about the same as in the 'modern' regime, but now instead of 97 per cent of egos having at least one surviving parent, the proportion is just under two-thirds (100 − 35.7 = 64.3 per cent). Still, about 73 per cent of these individuals will have their own young children to support, and more of them than under 'modern' conditions. However, there will also be more siblings to share the burden of support — nearly twice as many as under 'modern' conditions. One could surmise from these figures that at the level of the individual family the main potential difficulty of support of the elderly is that the elderly begin to require support and assistance precisely when their own children are burdened with dependent toddlers, and the lowered fertility of the 'modern' regime means that there are fewer adult children to share in helping their elderly parents.

In all discussions of this type about familial support systems, particularly when the data are raw demographic statistics, we must proceed with caution. Mean numbers and mean ages hide important information about variances, and relevant numbers such as the proportion of individuals with two elderly parents *and* at least one young child *and* no siblings to share the task of assisting the elderly need to be produced along with our simple numbers. Moreover, a great deal of attention needs to be given to the micro-economics of time, money, and other scarce resources within the family and kinship group. Without further work along these lines we are left with crude assumptions, such as that all people over some age are in need of assistance. Nevertheless, any more sophisticated analysis is likely to require kin counts and other information about expected numbers and distributions of various types of kin like those which we have illustrated here.

In Table 13.5 we present numbers like those in Table 13.4, but with reference to three different categories of kin: kin of previous generations (parents, grandparents, uncles, aunts), kin of following generations (children, grandchildren, nephews, nieces), and kin of an individual's own generation (siblings, first cousins). With these numbers we are prepared to make a few preliminary comments about the popular notion of a 'generation gap'. First we note that under both demographic regimes individuals have relatively large numbers of kin of the same generation, but under pre-industrial conditions the numbers are much larger than under modern conditions. For kin of previous generations the differences between the two demographic regimes are not so great, but for following generations we

Table 13.5.   Mean numbers and mean ages of kin of previous, following, and same
generation as chosen individual, English 'modern' and 'pre-industrial'
simulations

	Age of chosen individual								
	0	11	22	33	44	55	66	77	88
'Modern'									
Previous generations									
mean number	8.15	7.39	6.18	4.43	2.94	1.43	.26	.01	—
mean age	42.2	51.3	58.9	64.6	71.7	80.0	87.3	—	—
percentage with none	0	0	0	0.3	5.0	28.3	77.7	99.3	100
Following generations									
mean number	—	—	.48	3.07	4.21	5.63	7.33	7.88	7.62
mean age	—	—	2.8	6.8	14.7	20.3	25.2	33.3	43.1
percentage with none	100	100	71.3	10.3	5.3	4.0	4.0	4.0	4.7
Same generation									
mean number	3.15	5.66	6.34	6.41	6.19	5.72	4.82	3.16	1.37
mean age	7.7	13.2	22.2	32.6	43.2	53.6	63.3	71.6	78.4
percentage with none	15.0	1.0	1.0	0.7	0.7	1.0	3.3	10.7	38.3
'Pre-industrial'									
Previous generations									
mean number	8.66	6.66	4.86	3.13	1.54	0.43	0.05	—	—
mean age	37.5	45.6	53.2	61.1	68.6	75.4	75.0	—	—
percentage with none	0	1.0	1.3	8.0	32.3	71.0	95.7	100	100
Following generations									
mean number	—	0.18	1.54	6.29	10.01	11.86	14.61	16.14	14.69
mean age	—	3.14	4.50	7.0	12.7	19.3	22.8	27.5	35.0
percentage with none	100	93.0	50.7	8.0	4.7	3.7	4.0	4.0	4.3
Same generation									
mean number	10.14	15.74	17.04	15.92	13.49	10.56	7.26	3.80	1.35
mean age	8.8	13.7	21.4	30.8	41.0	50.6	59.1	65.9	70.8
percentage with none	6.0	0.7	0.3	0.3	0.3	1.7	4.7	14.0	49.0

again see very much larger mean numbers under pre-industrial conditions.
We might say that the pre-industrial regime implies kin numbers that are
much more weighted toward the present and the future than does the
modern regime. This point is further supported by the percentages of individuals with no kin in previous generations: only 5 per cent at age 44 under
modern conditions compared with over 32 per cent under pre-industrial
conditions.

It would seem that from these figures a case could be made for a greater
'generation gap' — at least in a purely demographic sense — in the past than
in the present. It is under modern demographic conditions that a person is

more likely to have surviving kin of previous generations alive, and more of them. Also, the average ages of these older kin are higher, making one's contact with elder kin reach further to the chronological past. Of course, most discussions of the highly charged term 'generation gap' are not about such bare demographic facts. But again we suggest that any thorough discussion will need to take into account the demographic facts, beginning with the simplest, like those we have presented, and moving to the more complex which are also available from simulated kin sets.

Here we are beginning to reach far beyond our aim of presenting the outline of one method for generating kin counts, and related information, through the computer microsimulation of kin sets, and we must leave off. Returning to our focus on methodology, we conclude with the observation that there is far more information contained in such fictional simulations of simple demographic situations than is usually exploited. For this reason, and for the reason that replication and verification of results are extremely important in simulation modelling, we encourage much more carefully documented and thoroughly analysed microsimulation modelling of kinship, preferably always giving explicit attention to kin sets.

Appendix

Let g be a generation index which is set to any arbitrary value for the chosen individual, and to the value $g-1$ for his or her mother. We define the probability that this person will be born to a mother of age x as the number of births to women of age x in generation $g-1$ divided by the total number of births to women of all ages in generation $g-1$:

$$A^*(x) = B(x,g-1)/B(g-1)$$

where $B(g-1)$ is simply the sum of $B(x,g-1)$ across all values of x.

The numerator of this equation can be rewritten as:

$$W(g-2)S(x)f(x)$$

where $W(g-2)$ is the number of *females* born to mothers in generation $g-2$. (i.e. the number of females who might have become mothers to our individual, $S(x)$ is the probability of a female surviving from birth to age x, and $f(x)$ is the probability that a woman of age x gives birth. Noting that the denominator of our original equation is simply the sum of the numerator across x, we rewrite the equation as:

$$A^*(x) = [W(g-2)S(x)f(x)]/[\int_x W(g-2)S(x)f(x)]$$

which reduces to

$$A^*(x) = [S(x)f(x)]/[\int_x S(x)f(x)].$$

The denominator of this equation is the net reproduction rate (*NRR*) of the stable population which can also be expressed:

$$NRR = \exp(rT)$$

where T is the mean age at maternity.

Substituting this back into the equation we have:

$$A^*(x) = S(x)f(x)\exp(-rT). \quad \text{q.e.d.}$$

Reference

Le Bras, Hervé and Kenneth W. Wachter (1978), 'Living Forbears in Stable Populations.' In K. W. Wachter, E. A. Hammel, P. Laslett (*et al.*), *Statistical Studies of Historical Social Structure*. Academic Press, New York, 163–88.

14 Some Mathematical Models of Kinship and the Family

THOMAS W. PULLUM

Population Research Center, University of Texas, Austin, Texas, USA

1 Introduction

Mathematical techniques and models have been used in a great variety of ways within the context of the study of kinship and the family. All the chapters in the present section of this volume, and many of those elsewhere in the volume, use mathematics to formalize a set of assumptions and to generate the implications of these assumptions. The value of mathematics in this context, as elsewhere in the social sciences, is essentially to provide a language with which abstract structures and processes can be described relatively unambiguously, as well as to provide techniques for manipulating those abstractions. This chapter will attempt to describe specific instances in which formal modelling of kinship, the family or the household has been useful and holds the possibility of further utility.

An excellent brief summary of the objective of mathematical modelling in the social sciences has been given by Herbert Simon (1957). A comprehensive inventory of the techniques in general use, with a number of social science applications, has been provided by Fararo (1973). More specialized models in population study have been described by Keyfitz (1968, 1977).

The minimal requirements for modelling are simply stated. First, there must be a set of units. These can be individual human beings, or abstractions such as household heads, families, households, relationships, lines of descent, and so on. Second, there must be a set of states, either discrete categories or continuous qualities, which differentiate those units. Sometimes the articulation between the units and the states they occupy can be problematic. For example, marital status is a classificatory property of individuals, but if the unit of analysis becomes the married couple, then the married state is a defining characteristic and not a variable. There is a trade-off between the use of characteristics to define units and their use to differentiate units. Generally, there is some gain in flexibility if units are defined as simply as possible, and characteristics are seen as variables rather than defining qualities.

A third required feature of almost all models is some process, mechanism, or dynamic by which the units can change from one state to another. There may be an explicit time dimension, as in the familiar Lotka model of population growth, or time may be implicit and unspecified, as in structural equations models, but there are generally some formalized statements about how change occurs or is caused. What are the likely elements of models in the area of family demography, as distinct from the demography of individuals? It might at first seem surprising that each of the models used as illustrations in this chapter takes the individual as the unit of analysis. It will be argued that compound units, such as the couple or the family, tend to be more difficult to manipulate because they can dissolve or recombine over time. The distinctive character of the family enters through the kinds of states or variables which are attributed to individuals. For example, the states can consist of different roles within the household, such as household head; marital or parental statuses, such as number of children ever born; length of time in a role or status; and so on. The individual can also be assigned properties which derive from an aggregate of which he or she is a member, such as the size of the household, occupation of the spouse, the influence of other family members, and so on. The third element of the models, the forces which describe or cause a change in states, are rooted in household dynamics and demand the greatest ingenuity. This can be implemented with a variety of techniques, which will depend for example upon the kinds of states, whether or not a time dimension is included, and the number of variables, but conceptual clarity is always the principal challenge.

This chapter will review a set of research traditions which formally represent kinship and the family, arranged to highlight structural features first, and then passing on to increasingly dynamic models. This sequence will also lead from the rather diffuse notion of kinship as a part of the general social environment toward the more immediate and integrated unit of the co-resident family. The starting point is the modelling of kinship by mathematical anthropologists.

2   Representation of kinship structures

Within the tradition of anthropological research, one of the most important tasks of the ethnographer is to record information on kinship relationships. Thus, the ethnographer lists the labels which are used for the various biological categories of kin and anticipates or calls attention to the social implications of these labels. In English, for example, one's (first) cousin is any person with whom one shares a grandparent, regardless of the gender not only of that person but also of the grandparents and of the intervening parents. It would be possible to distinguish four or even more different kinds of first cousins. That these distinctions are not made in English is correlated with the cultural fact that English-speaking countries, and Western cultures more generally, even in the historical past, do not distinguish their obligations to or their expectations from these potentially differentiable cousins. In fact, without exception, English kin terms are bilateral, distinguishing at most the gender of the kin category (e.g. son or daughter, father or mother) but never the gender of the intermediate kin.

Recognized or socially meaningful categories of kin arise from normative interpretations of biological relationships. During the past three decades, considerable effort has been invested by anthropologists in the development of formal models to describe structures within which there is a social equivalence of kin who are quite different in their biological relationships. These structures are built up from the following kinds of principles. First, individuals at their birth are assigned membership in one of a set of moieties, clans, etc. Second, individuals are assigned these memberships on the basis of memberships of one or both parents. Third, one's membership at birth is a determinant of whom one is eligible to marry.

These algebraic models are based on the individual as the unit of analysis, clan membership or identity as the attribute, and descent and marriage as the processes which determine these identities. The limitation on potential marriage partners is a consequence of one's identity but is also a system dynamic which leads to the birth and identity of subsequent individuals.

Overlaid on this structure is a set of terms which link a selected individual, male or female, to his or her kin. In a traditional culture with a clan structure, these terms involve an elaboration of the kinds of terms used in the West (more precisely, their linguistic equivalents), incorporating some of the distinctions which are suppressed in the West plus some distinctions related to clan identity. In cultures which employ or formerly employed these elaborate distinctions, they are the fundamental basis of social organization and role relationships.

We shall not describe these models in detail. They require specialized terminology and some familiarity with group theory. They also tend to be highly idealized. Relatively accessible presentations are given by White (1963), the highlights of which are given also by Fararo (1973, 525–45). Instead, we shall summarize succinctly some recent developments in this line of research which begin to link it with family demography. The contribution of this recent research rests upon its empirical basis — using data to compare actual terminology with the normatively expected terminology — and in the inclusion of preferred age at marriage as an influence on the differences between these two terminologies.

Denham, McDaniel, and Atkins (1979) represent an effort to determine whether an elaborate (by Western standards) normative structure of kin relations in the Alyawara tribe of Australian aborigines is actually followed in practice. This structure, a classic in the literature on kinship, has 22 distinct kinship terms which were specified by Radcliffe-Brown. Denham, having elicited biological genealogies for 264 informants, asked these informants to apply the correct Alyawara kinship term when presented with photographs of their kin. The expected term predicted by Radcliffe-Brown's classification failed to match the reported term for many of the intermediate and distant kin. For example, in a high proportion of cases, the term which should have been applied to the mother's brother's daughter (MBD), actually quite a close and important relation in this structure, was not used, but was replaced by another one.

The Alyawara were also found by early ethnographers to have two strong preferences regarding marriage (within the stipulation of exogamy). The first was for bilateral second cross-cousin marriage. That is, a male would prefer to marry his mother's mother's brother's daughter's daughter (MMBDD). Denham's data showed clearly that first cousins, especially matrilateral cross-cousins, are preferred to second cousins. Second, the Alyawara were claimed to prefer sibling exchange marriage, whereby a brother and sister would marry a sister and brother from another family. Among the 114 marriages in the data base, there were no instances of sibling marriage. In short, Denham *et al.* found that although 'the model is internally consistent, and it is compatible with Alyawara and Aranda ideology . . . it does not correlate well with actual Alyawara kinship term applications and marriage practices.' (1979, 16).

Denham *et al.* propose a modification to the original model which takes into account the preferred age difference between spouses. Hammel (1976) and a few other anthropologists since Rose (1960) have noted that if the husband is to be substantially older than the wife, then certain types of marriage rules are difficult to implement, if not impossible. In the case of the Alyawara, Denham's fieldwork found that the average age difference between spouses was 14 years. Moreover, since a mother is on the average 28 years older than her children, it followed that a father will on the average be 42 years older than his children. It is then easy to see that a male will on the average be 14 years older than his MBD first cousin, i.e. of the correct age difference for marriage, but he will on the average be 14 years younger than his FZD first cousin and 28 years older this his MMBDD second cousin, sharply reducing the acceptability of such marriages. Sibling exchanges will also be difficult to accomplish because they must be limited to pairs of siblings in which a brother is either much older or much younger than a sister.

Denham's co-author, Atkins, proposed a scheme by which these mean age differences can be incorporated into the lattice of a genealogy, taking it into the three-dimensional form of a double helix. In the case of the Alyawara, where the mean age difference between spouses is half the mean maternal age at childbearing, the diagram is relatively simple (although not simple enough to permit a detailed description here). The diagram shows that the age difference is responsible for the slippage in kin terminologies noted above, as well as for the rarity of MMBDD marriages. The MBD first cousin tends to be in the same age range as the individual's wife or his daughter, and it is their category labels which tend to be substituted for the proper one. Unfortunately, the Denham *et al.* study does not indicate whether the actual ages, of those individuals for whom the terms are misapplied, conform to the pattern of age deviations in the model, but this could be regarded as a hypothesis for future work. One might even seek evidence that in Western cultures and terminology, there will be a tendency to refer to a late-born aunt or uncle as a cousin, or to refer to a late-born cousin as a niece or nephew, or at least to behave toward them as if that were the role they occupied, even though fully aware of the actual biological relationship.

The impression should not be given that the specific research reviewed here in some detail is unique. In addition to Hammel (1976), a few other anthropologists such as Fredlund and Dyke (1976) have used analytic methods as well as computer simulation for such purposes. This line of research has also been extended by Tjon Sie Fat (1981). He presents a powerful algebraic model which subsumes a broad range of marriage and descent rules and has the possibility for even greater generalization.

At this point there exists no model which adequately incorporates age preferences with normative marriage preferences in these settings — at least, no analytical model, as distinguished from simulation. And, of course, the use of the mean age difference between husbands and wives is an extremely crude demographic consideration. The numbers of kin of the relevant types and their age distribution are important as well, and the distribution or at least the acceptable range of husband–wife age differences would be preferable to the mean.

This discussion has considered a type of modelling which may appear to have limited application to modern industrialized societies. Nevertheless, some of the fundamental features of these ethnographically-derived models remain central today. We are not now encouraged to marry first or second cousins, for example, but we may, for intervals of time, include kin in our households or in a larger network of regular interaction, exchange, and support. A general model which allows for the availability of kin for such relationships, through demographic variables, and also specifies a structure of preferred or socially mandated relationships, with some room for substitutions, is a potential consequence of this work by mathematical anthropologists. Family demographers have found ways to deal with the issues of whether kin are actually available, so to speak, for incorporation into a household or into regular interaction. The next section will describe some of this work. They have tended to ignore, at least in formal modelling, a normative structure corresponding in any way to the algebraic models to which we have alluded. Such a structure could prioritize the biological roles in terms of their importance for support and interaction after ego has reached maturity.

3 Numbers of kin

Analytical models for frequencies of kin are of two types. The first type is exemplified by the work of Le Bras (1973) and of Goodman, Keyfitz, and Pullum (1974, 1975). It concerns the expected number of kin, ever-born or still alive, at specific ages of an individual, in a population. This research has only taken a deterministic format, and has used fixed age-specific schedules of fertility and mortality.

The deterministic models began with Lotka (1931), who wished to calculate the probability that a randomly selected woman of specified age a, would have her mother still living, under specified schedules of mortality and fertility. He reasoned that this probability, $M_1(a)$, would be given by:

$$M_1(a) = \int_\alpha^\beta l(a+x)m(x)e^{-rx}dx,$$

where $l(x)$ = the probability of surviving from birth to age x,
 $m(x)dx$ = the probability of a daughter being born to a woman in the age interval $(x, x + dx)$,
 r = the intrinsic rate of natural increase, and
 (α,β) = the lower and upper age limits of childbearing.

The logic behind this formula is not difficult. The age of the mother at the time of the woman's birth is taken to be x, so that her age (if she still lives) when the respondent is age a, will be $a + x$. Let $M_1(a|x)$ be the probability that a woman now aged a, whose mother was aged x at the birth, will have a currently living mother; this will simply be $l(a + x)/l(x)$, the chance of a woman surviving from age x to $a + x$. The unconditional probability, $M_1(a)$, can then be obtained by multiplying $M_1(a|x)$ by the probability that a woman aged a, will have been born to a mother age x, and integrating over x. In a stable population this latter probability will not depend at all upon the value of a, and will simply be the product of the maternity function, $m(x)$, and the stable age distribution, $l(x)e^{-rx}$. The formula for $M_1(a)$ then follows. Lotka's orphanhood formula was used in reverse by Brass (1953). Vital rates can be estimated from orphanhood levels if the latter are available at several ages a and if the survivorship and maternity schedules can be parameterized.

Goodman *et al.* (1974) generalized Lotka's orphanhood formula in two major directions. First, they extended it to the probabilities of survivorship of more distant progenitors (Le Bras, 1973, dealt independently with grandparents), and the expected numbers of other close kin, ever-born and still alive, by age a, of the respondent. They showed, in principle, how a formula such as that for $M_1(a)$ can be developed to relate the individual to any category of kin whatsoever. Second, they moved away from the assumption of a stable population. Thus, the more general form of $M_1(a)$ is

$$M_1(a) = \int_\alpha^\beta l(a+x)/l(x)W(x|t-a)dx,$$

where $W(x|t-a)$ is the age distribution (at time $t-a$) of the women who gave birth to a daughter at time $t-a$. Goodman *et al.* also calculated the probabilities of surviving progenitors and the expected frequencies of other kin under illustrative stable population regimes.

The strength of such work lies in its analytical coherence, supplemented by the computational convenience of the computer program to implement the formulas. It is possible to estimate the sensitivity of the various expected numbers to changes in the schedules of survivorship and fertility. Also, emulating the applications by Brass (1953) of the orphanhood formula, it is possible to obtain indirect estimates of vital rates from the empirically observed numbers of kin. Goldman (1978), Wachter (1980), and McDaniel and Hammel (1984) have developed estimates of the intrinsic growth rate using the formulas for numbers of older sisters and younger sisters of the individual.

The weaknesses of the deterministic formulas arise from their simplifying assumptions, some of which were explored in Goodman *et al.* (1975). The most serious assumptions, in terms of explaining why the calculated numbers can deviate substantially from the true numbers, merit discussion here because they apply to most models of family building. Of the four most serious assumptions, the first is demographic stability. This requirement was relaxed in the Goodman *et al.* generalization, in that the age distribution is not required to be fixed, but even so the $1(x)$ and $m(x)$ functions are not indexed by time and are therefore not subject to change during the lifespans of pertinent kin. Even this limited kind of stability will have severe implications for relationships which are traced across more than one generation.

The second weakness of this approach is that it is not based on parity progression. It is assumed that a fertility rate — more precisely, the chance of having a child during an interval of time and age — does not depend upon the number of children a woman has already had. This is the basic assumption of a Poisson process. The more fertility is controlled by delayed marriage and contraception, the more serious this assumption becomes. In a controlled setting, fertility can be broadly dispersed across ages, yet with relatively little variation in completed family sizes. The formulas will imply a broader dispersion in numbers of children and all other kin than is empirically observed, and this will affect the estimated mean frequencies because of the complex linkages between kin categories.

Thirdly, the deterministic model assumes that the population is homogeneous. In reality, of course, it is stratified by fecundity and by fertility targets. The overall observed schedules are implicitly averaged across different strata, but the expected values produced by the formulas need not be the averages across these strata. The fourth major weakness is the limitation to a single sex: the individual, the kin of interest, and all intermediate kin must be females. However, most formal demographic modelling is limited to a single sex, and even if the so-called two-sex problem were solved conceptually, the necessary input data for a two-sex model would almost never be available.

Formally, it would be possible to extend the formulas of Goodman *et al.* to make the rates time-dependent, order-specific, and stratified. (A two-sex formulation would be difficult.) But if this were done, the data requirements would become immense, and in addition the heuristic or conceptual value of the model might be eroded. If more complex data are available, then one may wish to turn to simulation, as described by Reeves in chapter 12 of this volume.

The limitations listed above for the deterministic models, and other limitations for other formal models, must also be kept in perspective. A model is not intended to serve just as a computing algorithm or as an accounting scheme, although algorithms and schemes can be very useful. Rather, a model is an effort to explicate a process. Much of its value comes from simplifying a process to its most important features, and then using standard mathematical techniques to simulate behaviour. Almost every useful model then goes through subsequent revisions, adding complexities which utilize available relevant data, in order to replicate better the mechanisms by which inputs are transformed into outputs in the real world. The deterministic models of kin frequencies have not yet seen such revisions, largely because the output quantities which the model seeks to estimate, as well as more elaborate or detailed input data, are all unavailable empirically.

The second type of model here is stochastic. The defining feature of a stochastic model is that basic events, such as having a birth or dying at a specific age, occur randomly with specified probabilities. These probabilities imply full distributions of output quantities, such as numbers of children ever born, and not just the mean values of these distributions. In the present context, a stochastic model gives the distribution of kin of each type under stable population assumptions. Time is marked by the length of a generation rather than by years of time or age. The stochastic models do not extend to the distribution of the number of survivors in a specific kin category at each age of the individual, which would correspond to the expected values developed by Goodman *et al.* These models have been developed out of the theory of branching processes. We shall briefly review their basic structure and suggest how they may be extended and used.

The adaptation of branching processes appears to have been made only recently by Waugh (1981) and Joffe and Waugh (1982) and independently by Pullum (1982), even though the theory has been available for many years. The starting point is the 'reproduction' probability generating function (p.g.f.) of a randomly sampled woman at her birth. If p_i is the probability, defined at birth, that a woman will have exactly i female births during her lifetime, then this probability generating function is given by $f(x) = p_0 + p_1x + p_2x^2 + \ldots$. The moment of this distribution can be obtained from successive derivatives of $f(x)$ at $x = 0$. The first moment, the mean, $p_1 + 2p_2 + 3p_3 + \ldots$, is the Net Reproduction Rate.

The papers by Waugh (1981) and by Joffe and Waugh (1982) use the probability-generating function to yield the distributions of all kin in generation k for a woman sampled in generation n. For example, if the woman is sampled in generation 1, then there will be one person in generation 0 (her mother); she and her sister will comprise the set in generation 1; and her daughters and nieces will comprise the set in generation 2. If the woman is sampled in generation 2, then there will be one person in generation 0 (her mother's mother); her mother and aunts in generation 1; she, her sisters, and her cousins in generation 2; and so on. (This is stated as a one-sex model.) They give the formulas for the moments of these distributions and also the probabilities of each specific combination of numbers of kin in each generation. With the latter formulas, for example, it is possible to calculate the probability distribution of the number of daughters plus nieces, conditional on a specified number of sisters. Waugh (1981) considers the case of a large population with time-homogeneity and independence of individuals. Joffe and Waugh (1982) relax these assumptions, although the probability generating function $f(x)$ remains the same in each generation.

Pullum (1982) approaches essentially the same problem with reference to specific categories of kin, rather than entire generations, giving the probability-generating functions for sisters, aunts, nieces, cousins, etc., distinct from other kin. He also gives illustrations of these distributions in a hypothetical setting of replacement fertility. The distributions are of 'eventual' frequencies of kin, a generalization of the notion of reproductivity in the first generation. One obtains the probability of exactly n kin of a specified type, say, consisting of all those persons who will ever be born into this type, regardless of how long they may live or how long the individual may live. When mortality is high, there is a high probability that a woman will produce no births at all (because she will not herself survive to childbearing age) and a corresponding high probability that she will have no descendants of other more remote types. Of course, kin types which do not depend upon ego's survival will be less affected by mortality. When mortality is low, as in developed countries, the eventual frequencies of kin will not be a great deal higher than the number who are actually available for interaction, making reasonable allowances for generational differences.

Other related uses of branching processes deal with the extinction of kin lines, the probability of being a first born child (Jagers, 1982), and so on.

What is the value of these models? First, they have a complementary relationship to the structural models of the preceding section. With some information about reproductivity, one can actually attach frequencies to the nodes in the lattices of kin categories. These can be summed in various ways, corresponding to culturally recognized combinations of relationships, such as 'first cousin.' Numbers like these are the demographic component of kinship referred to at the end of the previous section. Second, they permit estimation of the numbers of kin who are available for participation in kin-based households or communication networks. An individual has a chance of living with or depending upon or communicating with a specific type of kin, which is approximately proportional to the number of living kin of that type. Third, the models allow estimation of the proportion of the population which have no or few kin of a specific type. This sub-population will have limited opportunities for certain kinds of socialization as children or limited opportunities for social support when they are older. When fertility is low, and as childlessness becomes more acceptable again in America and Europe, increasing proportions of people will have no descendants for support in their old age. Small families mean that fewer children will have siblings of the same sex and fewer will have siblings of the opposite sex. These models permit one to quantify such obvious implications of low fertility. Fourth, models permit one to estimate the sensitivity of these numbers to changes in the vital rates or reproduction p.g.f.

The available models actually fall short of these potential uses. As noted, the branching process models do not include age or mortality, and the models which include age and mortality are deterministic and do not produce probability distributions. A reconciliation of these approaches seems likely in the near future, however, at the very least through a hybridization.

A different kind of limitation is that these models characterize an aggregate and do not include any more substantive components. In the investigation of theoretical propositions about kin contact, for example — say, the null hypothesis that after marriage a couple will have equal contact with the wife's kin and the husband's kin, taking account of availability — both contact and availability must be measured empirically for a sample of individuals. A model could suggest how the distribution would look, and might permit some generalizations across broad sweeps of time or social groupings for which empirical data are incomplete, but it would be insufficient for the testing of such a hypothesis. To repeat, these models are primarily of descriptive value at an aggregate level and enable one to see the consequences of changes in vital rates, as mentioned above, but their present formulation does not allow inclusion of non-demographic variables.

4 Family size distributions

The preceding section referred to the reproduction probability-generating function as the basic source of the eventual frequencies of kin in a stable population. Apart from such a role, this function has interest in its own right. Particularly in developed countries, in which the nuclear family predominates and child mortality is low, the number of children per woman will be the foremost determinant of the size of the co-resident family.

The reproduction probability-generating function refers to the daughters ever born to a female, defined at the point of her own birth. We shall also consider the distribution of children ever born (sons and daughters) defined at the point when the woman reaches age 45, i.e. has completed and survived the childbearing period. The linkage between these two distributions is described briefly in Pullum (1982). If a woman has had k children, then the maximum size of her nuclear family at any point will be $k + 2$, including herself and her spouse. It will be smaller during those years before all the children were born, or after they begin to leave home, or as a result of parental or child mortality. Divorce and separation and other kinds of family decomposition and recomposition may also be important, but the distribution of children ever born will be the major source of variation in co-resident family size during the part of the family life cycle when most individuals are being socialized.

The completed parity distribution has undergone truly dramatic changes in recent generations in Western countries, and in the past decade or so in several developing ones. It is remarkable, in view of the extent of this change, that the distribution is so rarely described by anything other than its mean.

Table 14.1 gives the percentages of women who had 0, 1, 2, 3, or 4 or more children, out of those cohorts of American women who were age 45–59 in 1900, 1925, 1950, and 1975. Among the earlier cohorts, survivorship is certainly an important factor for any translation of these figures to household membership, and we shall not attempt to make such a translation here. However, there can be no doubt that some of the major features of these differences have had in impact on the co-resident family size.

Table 14.1   Children ever born to women cohorts (USA)

Age 45–59 in:	Number				
	0	1	2	3	4 or more
1900	14	11	13	12	50 percentage
1925	22	12	14	12	40
1950	20	22	22	14	22
1975	9	11	24	22	34

Particular attention is drawn to the changing frequency of no children or one child. These two parities accounted for about 44 per cent of the American women who completed their childbearing at the middle of this century, a figure which cannot be attributed to the Great Depression of the 1930s because it was part of a long-term trend. A major factor in the postwar baby boom was the sharp reduction of these two lowest parities, with two children becoming the effective minimum. There are indications, of course, that the lowest parities are again becoming relatively common, whether because of non-marriage or for voluntary reasons within marriage.

Mathematical models can be used to describe this distribution, how it varies from one setting to another, and how it changes over time. For example, these models show that the increasing concentration or lack of dispersion in the family size distribution in the United States is not simply a consequence of the decline in the mean; it is a manifestation of greater consensus — whether normative or circumstantial — that the number of children should occupy a narrow range: not too small and not too large. This concentration sharply contrasts with the great dispersion in parities which characterizes high fertility settings, both historically and at present in developing countries. When fertility is high, the number of children ever born as well as the number surviving to any specific age is always highly dispersed. The World Fertility Survey, in its survey of ever-married women in the Philippines in 1978, found a mean of 5.5 children ever born to women aged 40–44, but 12 per cent had 0–2 and 18 per cent had 8 or more. The 1976 Colombian survey of all women showed an even more dispersed distribution for women aged 40–44. Their mean was 5.1 children, but 18 per cent had 0–2 and 22 per cent had 8 or more. These are only illustrations from a larger set of distributions (Hodgson and Gibbs, 1980).

Mathematical models to describe these patterns can take different forms. Lotka (1939, 121–2) was one of the first demographers to model the reproduction distribution. He proposed a two-parameter function which could be written as follows: $p_0 = a$ and $p_i = br^i$. (Since these proportions must sum to unity, there are in effect only two free parameters.) This function implies that all successive pairs of family sizes have the same ratio 1:r, with the exception of p_0 and p_1 which have the ratio $a:b$. Waugh (1981) has noted that this function has some desirable properties for mathematical manipulation. However, it has a very weak behavioural interpretation and does not conform well to a broad range of available data. This distribution can only have a mode of $i = 0$ or $i = 1$ (daughters) and it is unable to describe real settings where fertility is much above replacement level.

Shifting again from reproductivity to completed childbearing, several demographers, notably Henry and Ryder, have advocated the transformation or representation of the distribution with parity progression ratios, the conditional probabilities of attaining successively higher parities. Ryder (1982) and Feeney (1983) have recently proposed refinements of the PPRs which incorporate lengths of birth intervals.

The present author has reviewed a large number of family size distributions under a variety of transformations. A particularly promising representation is based on an analogy between childbearing and survivorship in the usual life table. In this analogy, 'age' is marked by successive births, and the termination of childbearing, i.e. the failure to progress to the next higher parity, is the decrement. 'Survivorship' at parity i, say, is then measured by the proportion of women in a cohort who ever achieved parity

i, beginning with a radix of 1 for parity 0. This survivorship function declines monotonically until the highest parity achieved by the cohort, just as the life table function $l(x)$ declines monotonically up to the highest age at death. This representation has another desirable property, in that the 'survivorship' function can be calculated at any point in a cohort's experience, and it converges toward the final distribution at a rate which describes the tempo of childbearing.

Chiang and van den Berg (1982) have developed many of the implications of this analogy. There is evidence that this representation of childbearing can be reduced to very few parameters, capitalizing upon the research of Brass and others on mortality, e.g. through the relational logit transformation of the survivorship function. These parameters can be interpreted as statistical measures of the mean, the dispersion, and the skew, say. Preferably, they can be re-stated to have more substantive interpretations, regarding the normative acceptability of very low parities, the consensus about the most desirable parities, and so on.

Models which can summarize or reduce the information in the childbearing pattern, especially with the inclusion of timing components, have the potential for integration with models of the family as a whole. Brass, building upon earlier work of Burch (1970), has developed a model for family size which uses the age-specific fertility rates of an indexed woman in the household. It seems that a re-casting of such models, using parity progression as captured by a few interpretable parameters, is necessary if they are to be extended to include full distributions, not just the mean. This is because age-specific fertility rates can be used to calculate mean parity, completed or cumulative to a specific age, but they are not sufficient to estimate the distribution of parities. Krishnamoorthy (1979) has developed Poisson-type approximations to the parity distribution based on age-specific fertility rates, and although these approximations may be satisfactory in a setting of natural fertility, they are much too broad when fertility is controlled by contraception. The same point was made in the discussion of models of kin frequencies.

5 Family transitions

We have discussed some topics in the demography of kin which have narrowed the focus from the structure of kinship categories to the frequencies of any kind of kin and then to the frequency distributions of children. The final stage of this sequence is the co-resident family or domestic group, as contrasted with the larger set of blood relatives. One can, of course, conceptualize intermediate groupings which depend upon levels of dependency or communication, say, but they will lack the objective clarity of the two extremes, the kin structure and the co-resident family.

Several chapters in this volume, including those by Willekens and

Feichtinger present new models of family statuses and transitions from one status to another. With these authors, we prefer to treat the family in which an individual resides as a characteristic of that individual. An entity which is subject to the decomposition and recomposition that characterize the family can be an awkward choice, in itself, for the unit of analysis. There is no loss of information if one attaches to each individual, at each year (or some other interval) of age, the characteristics of his or her family, in as much detail as desired, and including the role of the individual (e.g. relation to head) within the larger unit. Such an approach admittedly duplicates much information. One variation is to identify a single individual within the family as the 'marker' to achieve a one-to-one correspondence between families and a subset of individuals. Brass (1983) has proposed the use of a marker, specifically an adult woman, and has ingeniously linked the life course of the family to this woman.

Without attempting to summarize these new approaches to the life course of the co-resident family, so to speak, one can indicate in broad terms the potential of such modelling. First, the specification of statuses or dimensions and their possible inter-connections will allow one to conceptualize transitions more clearly. Currently, Grady and McLaughlin (1983) are using the US Current Population Surveys of the 1970s to identify the sources of increases in the population living alone. Single-person families or households typically arise when, say, one member of an elderly couple dies; or a younger couple are divorced, and their children remain with one parent, so that one parent lives alone; or an adult child leaves home to live alone. There are other sources as well. One can apply the notion of risk: individuals have a chance of moving into the state of 'living alone' which depends upon their current state. The increase in living alone in the 1970s may have been due to a change in the size of the prior groups at risk or due to an increase in the rates of transition out of these risk groups. The distinction between these two sources of change involves a careful specification of the pathways between different family statuses.

Second, as in stable population theory and in much of multi-dimensional mathematical demography, one can generate synthetic or stable distributions which serve to summarize complex schedules of rates. This is precisely the character of the mean family sizes which Brass computes under alternative schedules of mortality and fertility. Such distributions should not be interpreted as projections, but by comparison with current observed means and distributions, inferences can be made about trends in transition rates.

Thirdly, such models allow one to investigate the sensitivity of the overall distribution to changes or disturbances, particularly hypothetical ones, in the underlying rates. Some of these rates are of the traditional demographic type, such as mortality rates; others pertain more specifically to household formation and change, such as the rates at which adult children leave the parental home and elderly parents move in with their children. By simulation or possibly by more analytic methods, a particular type of rate can be changed, by a plausible amount, with everything else held constant, and the impact on the synthetic or stable distribution can be evaluated.

At present, household models do not explicitly include a linkage to the larger network of kin. Heuristically, and with reference to the concluding comments in section 2, it would ideally be possible to take account of the number (and possibly age and accessibility) of kin who have some risk of joining the family. In a model for the Alyawara, say, it would be particularly important to incorporate kin categories which are allegedly favoured for marriage. Cultural preferences would be expressed by the actual rate at which persons were transferred to the 'spouse' category. Some kin, such as elderly parents, siblings, etc., are also at risk, not of marriage, but of co-residence. Here, as in the work of Grady and McLaughlin, one wishes to distinguish between the fact of availability, the 'denominator at risk', and the actual rate of transition, of joining the chosen individual's family. At a more practical level, such information is difficult to obtain empirically, particularly in developing countries where the extended family occurs with non-trivial frequency.

6 Conclusion

This chapter has not presented new models or empirical analyses, in contrast with most of the chapters of this volume. It has had the rather more modest objective of conveying, in a brief space, the character of formal modelling of kin networks and family formation. We have tried to indicate, with almost no explicit use of mathematics, a broad range of issues. These issues touch upon both the nature of modelling itself and, more importantly, the conceptual linkages between kinship structures, frequencies of kin, the child-bearing of individual women, and the formation of the co-resident household.

References

Bongaarts, J. (1983), 'The Formal Demography of Families and Households: an Overview', *Newsletter*, 17. International Union for the Scientific Study of Population, Liège.

Brass, W. (1953), 'The Derivation of Fertility and Reproduction Rates from Restricted Data on Reproductive Histories', *Population Studies* 7, 137–66.

—— (1983), 'The Formal Demography of the Family: An Overview of the Proximate Determinants', in *The Family, British Society for Population Studies, OPCS Occasional Paper*, No. 31, Office of Population Censuses and Surveys (OPCS), London, 37–49.

Burch, T. K. (1970), 'Some Demographic Determinants of Average Household Size: An Analytic Approach', *Demography* 7, 61–9.

Chiang, C. L., and B. J. van den Berg (1982), 'A Fertility Table for the Analysis of

Human Reproduction', *J. of Mathematical Biosciences* 62, 237–51.

Denham, W. W., C. K. McDaniel, and J. R. Atkins (1979), 'Aranda and Alyawara Kinship: A Quantitative Argument for a Double Helix Mode', *American Ethnologist* 6, 1–24.

Fararo, T. J. (1973), *Mathematical Sociology*, Wiley, New York.

Feeney, G. (1983), 'Population Dynamics Based on Birth Intervals and Parity Progression', *Population Studies* 37, 75–89.

Fredlund, E. V., and B. Dyke (1976), 'Measuring Marriage Preference', *Ethnology* 15, 35–45.

Goldman, N. (1978), 'Estimating the Intrinsic Rate of Increase of a Population from the Average Number of Older and Younger Sisters', *Demography* 15, 499–508.

Goodman, L. A., N. Keyfitz, and T. W. Pullum (1974), 'Family Formation and the Frequency of Various Kinship Relationships', *Theoretical Population Biology* 5, 1–27.

——, N. Keyfitz, and T. W. Pullum (1975), 'Addendum to Family Formation and the Frequency of Various Kinship Relationship', *Theoretical Population Biology* 8, 376–81.

Grady, W. R., and S. D. McLaughlin (1983), 'Living Arrangements Among the Never Married: Changes in the Propensity to Live Alone in the United States', presented at annual meetings of the Population Association of America.

Hammel, E. (1976), 'The Matrilateral Implications of Structural Cross-Cousin Marriage', in E. Zubrow (ed.), *Demographic Anthropology: Quantitative Approaches*, University of New Mexico Press, Albuquerque.

Hodgson, M., and J. Gibbs (1980), 'Children Ever Born', *Comparative Studies No. 12*, World Fertility Survey.

Jagers, P. (1982), 'How Probable is it to be First Born? And Other Branching-Process Applications to Kinship Problems', *J. of Mathematical Biosciences* 59, 1–15.

Joffe, A., and W. A. O'N. Waugh (1982), 'Exact Distributions of Kin Numbers in a Galton–Watson Process', *J. of Applied Probability* 19, 767–75.

Keyfitz, N. (1968), *Introduction to the Mathematics of Population*, Addison-Wesley, Reading, Mass.

—— (1977), *Applied Mathematical Demography*, Wiley, New York.

Krishnamoorthy, S. (1979), 'Family Formation and the Life Cycle', *Demography* 16, 121–9.

Le Bras, H. (1973), 'Parents, Grandparents, Bisaïeuls', *Population* 1, 9–38.

Lotka, A. J. (1931), 'Orphanhood in Relation to Demographic Factors: A Study in Population Analysis', *Metron* 9, 37–109.

—— (1938), Théorie Analytique des Associations Biologiques', Vol. 2. Hermann, Paris.

McDaniel, C. K., and E. A. Hammel (1984), 'A Kin-based Measure of r and an Evaluation of its Effectiveness', *Demography* 21, 41–51.

Pullum, T. W. (1982), 'The External Frequencies of Kin in a Stable Population', *Demography* 19, 549–65.

Rose, F. (1960), *Classification of Kin, Age Structure and Marriage Amongst the Groote Eylandt Aborigines*. Akademie Verlag, Berlin.

Ryder, N. B. (1977), 'Models of Family Demography', *Population Bulletin of the United Nations*, 9, United Nations, New York.

—— (1982), 'Progressive Fertility Analysis', *Technical Bulletin No. 8*, World Fertility Survey.

Simon, H. (1957), *Models of Man*, Wiley, New York.

Tjon Sie Fat, F. E. (1981), 'More Complex Formulae of Generalized Exchange', *Current Anthropology* 22, 377–90.

Wachter, K. W. (1980), 'The Sisters' Riddle and the Importance of Variance when Guessing Demographic Rates from Kin Counts', *Demography* 17, 103–14.

Waugh, W. A. O'N. (1981), 'Application of the Galton–Watson Process to the Kin Number Problem', *Advanced Applied Probability* 13, 631–49.

White, H. (1963), *An Anatomy of Kinship*, Prentice-Hall, Englewood Cliffs.

Part VI

Projection of Households

15 The Headship Rate Method for Projecting Households

SHIGEMI KONO

Institute of Population Problems, Tokyo, Japan

1 Introduction

This chapter reviews the headship rate method for household projections and suggests some extensions and improvements.

As is well known, the headship rate method has been the most commonly used method of household projection in recent years. If the basic population projections by sex and age are adequate, it can provide a reasonably accurate picture of the future number and composition of households. It is straight-forward and requires simple input data. It has some methodological advantages over other methods of household projections. Because it employs available population projections by sex and age (and sometimes by marital status) as its base, it can reflect underlying changes in population composition which have a large effect on the size and composition of house-holds and families. Since the population composition is determined by the past fertility and mortality, and migration, the method can indirectly reflect these three elements of population change.

On the other hand, however, it cannot take into account a dynamic aspect of formation, growth, contraction and dissolution of households and it cannot provide numerical figures of entries into and exits from the stock of households. This paper reviews the development of the headship rate method and illustrates our search for ways to expand the method, including an application of multiple decrement table techniques to headship.

The need for reasonable projections of the future number and composi-tion of households and families has been growing since the end of the Second World War. A quick survey of the literature indicates that in many countries, particularly in the developed ones, the demand for projections of the number and structure of households has been made by many government departments and sectors of private industry.

Traditionally, the biggest users of household and family projections have been the government agencies concerned with the planning of housing and building. Next are the government agencies and private industries planning the development of public utilities and the production and distribution of consumer durables such as electric appliances, furniture, and automobiles, for which the unit of consumption is household rather than individual.

Specifically, planners often want to know the future number of households, whether the future increase in households is likely to be greater or smaller than population growth, and how many new households will be formed in the next year, the next five years, etc. Interest has sometimes also centred on the future growth of the number of families, the number of married couples, and the distribution of families by type (for example, primary or secondary). Most recently, demand has also grown for projections of future households by size class, that is by one-person households, two-person households, three-person households, etc.

2 Development of the Headship Rate Method

Since the 1950 round of censuses, many countries have been collecting more detailed information on the demographic and socio-economic characteristics of families, households, and housing. The recent development of more detailed statistical data of improved quality has therefore enabled many countries for the first time to undertake projections of numbers of households and families. Based on these improved data, a host of European and North American countries started preparing household and family projections around 1950 (The Economic Commission for Europe, 1968). This was chiefly in response to the great demand arising from the post-war reconstruction and national economic development planning, particularly in the fields of housing and consumer durables.

The United States Bureau of the Census made its first attempt to project future household formation during the Second World War, when certain government agencies urgently needed such information to enable them to allocate material resources for industrial production. The task of these agencies was to assess minimum civilian needs for housing, household appliances, automobiles, etc. To facilitate this task, the Bureau in 1943 published its first set of household projections. From the beginning, they employed the headship rate method specific for sex and age of heads (Glick, 1957).[1]

This use of the headship method had been anticipated as early as 1938, when the United States National Resources Planning Committee published projections of the number of households up to 1980, using the headship rate method on the basis of the 1930 population census (US National Resources Planning Committee, 1938). In this series, future sex–age-specific headship rates were kept constant throughout.

The headship rate method requires the classification of the population by sex and age and, if possible, by marital status. For each class, projections are made for (a) the number of persons and (b) the ratio of the number of

---

[1] This set of projections was published by the United States Bureau of the Census, *Population — Special Reports*, Series p. 46, No. 4.

household heads to the number of persons, or the proportion who are heads, called a 'specific headship rate'. The projected number of households in the entire population is obtained by adding up over all classes the product (*a*) and (*b*) estimated separately for each class.

To clarify the headship rate method, it may be useful to express the steps by an algebraic equation. Let $P(i,j,t)$ be the population of sex i, age j and at time t, and let $H(i,j,t)$ be the number of heads of households or families by sex i, age j and time t. Then the headship rate specific for sex and age at time t, $h(i,j,t)$ is expressed by the following formula:

$$h(i,j,t) = \frac{H(i,j,t)}{P(i,j,t)}. \qquad (15.1)$$

The formula for projecting the number of households may be presented as follows. Suppose that for year $t + x$ (x years from the base year) the population projections by sex and age have already been prepared and the sex–age headship rates have been estimated, then the number of households for the year $t + x$ can be obtained by the following equation:

Total number of future households in year $t + x$

$$\sum_i \sum_j H(i,j,t + x) = \sum_i \sum_j P(i,j,t + x) \cdot h(i,j,t + x) \qquad (15.2)$$

The above equations simplify the situation in that they made no distinction between private ('family' or 'ordinary') and institutional ('collective' or 'quasi') households. If sex–age specific headship rates are also available for institutional households, then they can be incorporated in an obvious extension of equation 15.2.

3 Choices of Assumptions Regarding Prospective Changes in Headship Rates

In projections by the headship rate method, specific headship rates often are assumed to be constant, but for many countries changing headship rates would present a more realistic picture. This is particularly so in a situation as it is in Japan where the pace of economic development has been swift, and where massive migration of young workers to cities and metropolitan areas, increases in per capita income, and changes in the value system centering around the family and married life, are causing a rapid process of nucleation and formation of one-person households in both urban and rural areas. In this context, the main methodological problem is how to estimate accurately future levels of headship rates specific for sex and age or for sex, age, and marital status. The basic assumptions about future specific rates may be classified within the following four categories (United Nations, 1973):

1. Constant rate method;
2. Extrapolative method, using annual average change of rates in the past,

or applying a simple mathematical formula fitted to past trends;
3. Regression method, using either cross-sectional or subnational data on headship rates on the one hand, and economic and social indicators on the other;
4. Normative approach, using target rates based on the Government's housing policy and social and economic development programmes.

Although a detailed description of all of these approaches is beyond the scope of this chapter, the third and last categories, namely the 'regression approach' and the 'normative approach', being less familiar, require further discussion.

It is indeed likely that economic factors such as an increase in real income and in rents and mortgage rates, and social factors such as urbanization have large effects on changes in headship rates. The United Nations Manual on *Methods of Projecting Households and Families* illustrated how increasing per capita income in Sweden contributed to increasing headship rates in each sex–age–marital status group (United Nations, 1973). Pitkin indicated the overall importance of real income growth for household formation in postwar United States (Pitkin, 1982). Recent household projections for Japan, by the Institute of Population Problems, utilized regression coefficients between urbanization and sex–age headship rates (Institute of Population Problems, 1977). Masnick and Bane have made innovative household and family projections, using a cohort and regressing headship on economic factors including family income and labour force participation (Masnick and Bane, 1980).

The normative approach has been extensively used in the projections for the United Kingdom (Cullingworth, 1960; Needleman, 1961; Paige, 1965) and for Denmark (Ministry of Housing, Denmark, 1965) and Norway (Ministry of Municipal and Labour Affairs, Norway, 1965). Unlike the mathematical extrapolative method and the regression method, future headship rates are estimated by using the current headship rates, but adjusting to reflect probable future economic and social development and the Government's housing policy.

In Denmark, this normative approach underlay one of the variants of the projections, that based on so-called 'welfare headship rates'. It was assumed that a housing policy was established particularly to create opportunities for students and old people to form separate households. In this series, headship rates for all married men were assumed to be 1.0. Headship rates for other sex–marital status groups were assumed to be much higher than those observed in the 1960 census or those used in another variant, the 'economic headship rate' variant (in which headship rates were based on empirically derived income elasticities). The 'welfare headship rate' variant assumed that housing policy would raise headship rates substantially above 1960 levels, particularly for younger and older adults. In all marital status groups aged 25 to 70, headship rates were assumed to be above 0.8. The rates were at 0.9 for unmarried and previously married women aged 25-64.

The projections for Norway are similar to the 'economic' projections for Denmark. And the series of projections for the United Kingdom in the 1960s similarly uses normatively set goals, along with past and current headship levels, and to project future probable levels in relation to economic and social development.

The US Bureau of the Census uses the headship rate method for its most recent household projections. The Bureau employed sex–age–marital status-specific headship rates ('householder proportions' as they now call them) and in one series both marital status and householder proportions were projected by fitting an exponential curve to the past trends and extrapolating them into the future (Series B). In another series, weighted averages are calculated from the above curve-fitting results and the 1978 observed headship rates. The weights used to obtain the Series D proportions were 1/3 for Series B proportions and 2/3 for the 1978 proportions; to derive Series A, the weights were 2/3 for Series B proportions and 1/3 for the 1978 proportions (US Bureau of the Census, 1979).

So far the above discussion has referred to the headship rate method which has been employed strictly by the cross-sectional or period approach. As in analysis of fertility, however, the cohort approach was found useful in household projections, particularly when changes in headship rates are rapid among the young population and when the size of a certain cohort is quite different from its adjacent cohorts immediately before and after, as embodied in the postwar baby boomers. As Masnick and Pitkin (1983) demonstrated, the cohort approach can more adequately reflect a demographic change upon headship rate than the period approach does. That is to say, only the cohort approach can take into account appropriately the effect of different sizes of successive cohorts which results in an abrupt change in period headship rate. They have found, for example, that the baby boom children in the United States are more likely to move out of their parental homes and establish their own households because of the crowded situation in their parents' homes, and that for the same reason, grandparents are less likely to move in to live with their children in place of grandchildren. The method of projecting age-specific household headship by the cohort approach is particularly useful for the short and medium term. The limitation of the approach is, of course, that in young cohorts, headship rates are available only for recent years, thus creating uncertainty of estimating their future trends.

The Japanese Economic Planning Agency prepared household projections in September 1982, employing a comparatively new method. This method is, however, pretty close to the headship rate method described above, but, instead of using the headship rate as such, they contrived an 'index of household formation nucleus' in each household type. This index relates household to its constituting woman, instead of man, as a marker, if there is a woman available in each household type. When men are the only members of a household, then, of course, the index is related to a man as a marker.

First, in preparing household projections, the Japanese Economic Planning Agency categorized all households into nine types such as a household consisting of parents and their own children, one consisting of a father and his children only, one-person households, etc (Economic Planning Agency, 1982). As the second step, they calculated ratios of such marked people to the corresponding population cross-classified by sex, age, and marital status. For the projection purpose, the ratios were assumed to be constant for future years. The Economic Planning Agency, at the same time, prepared projections of population by sex, age and marital status. They, then, applied to them the specific household nucleus formation ratios mentioned above to obtain the number of households.

4 Extension of the Headship Rate Method to Project Households by Size Class

As already pointed out, recently there have been growing demands from government agencies and private companies in housing and consumer durables for projections of the number of households by *size class*. For example, housing construction agencies and private developers want to know local and national future demands for one-bedroom, two-bedroom, and three-bedroom apartments. Similarly, manufacturers of consumer durables want to know future demands for different types and sizes of consumer durables, which also depend partly on the number of households by size.

Although the concept of size class is simple, and although many countries provide current data, the methodology of projecting the future size distribution of households is not that simple because the distribution is determined by complex interactions of many factors such as declining fertility, increasing divorce, and the ageing of population, especially of women.

The conventional approach in preparing projections of households by size class is to utilize household projections by the headship rate method, and to break down the projected household heads for each age group into size classes. If the size class distribution in each age group can be kept the same as in the base year, the projections would be quite simple. But, in reality, the size class distribution in each age group has been changing rapidly in recent years, and it would be unrealistic to assume unchanging size class distributions for the future.

For example, Japanese censuses in 1965, 1970, and 1975 show well-marked trends in percentage distributions of households by size:

1. From 1965 to 1970 and to 1975, one-person households increased

rapidly. The sustained increases are noted both in young and advanced age groups. This conforms to recent European experience in this regard.[2]

2. Decreases are noted in size classes 5, 6, and 7 + : in these classes, in every age group, without exception. This trend is largely a consequence of the substantial decline in fertility since 1950, but undoubling of doubled-up households is also relevant.

3. Size classes 2, 3, and 4, on the other hand, exhibit complex trends, reflecting interactions of various factors influencing household size. For example, for size class 2, percentage shares have been decreasing in age groups 15–24, 25–34 and 35–44, whereas they have been increasing in age groups 45–54 and over.

There are fairly good reasons to believe that some portion of the recent increase in one-person households was related to decreases in size classes 2, 3, and 4 for young age groups, which in turn were associated with the recent delay in marriage and childbearing. On the other hand, the increases in the percentage shares of the middle and advanced age groups for size classes 2 to 4 are a consequence of the disappearance of high parity families and a decrease in doubled-up families.

Table 15.1 illustrates steps for calculating household projections by size class for Japan. To save space, we show the procedure only for one time interval. The first step involves the projection of percentage shares by size class for each age group. This was done by a modified exponential formula (Kono, 1981):

$$p(i,j,t+m) = 1 - [1 - p(i,j,t-n)] \cdot \left[\frac{1 - p(i,j,t)}{1 - p(i,j,t-n)} \right]^{\frac{(t+m)-(t-n)}{n}} \qquad (15.3)$$

where $p(i,j,t+m)$ denotes the percentage share of the households at age group i by size class j in year $t+m$, m years after the year t of the last census; $p(i,j,t)$ denotes the percentage share in year t, the year of last census; $p(i,j,t-n)$ denotes the percentage share in year $t-n$, n years before the last census. Such a percentage share, if multiplied by an age-specific headship rate, indicates an age-size specific headship rate. In many cases, m and n are identical, that is a census interval of 5 or 10 years. Extrapolated figures $p(i,j,t+m)$ in each age group were adjusted to sum to unity over all size classes. When the percentage share is increasing, the above formula is used; when it is decreasing the following alternative formula is applied:

$$p(i,j,t+m) = p(i,j,t-n) \cdot \left[\frac{p(i,j,t)}{p(i,j,t-n)} \right]^{\frac{(t+m)-(t-n)}{n}} \qquad (15.4)$$

---

[2] One of the salient features of the family formation in Europe is a continous and substantial increase in the number and proportion of the one-person household heads by young men and women. (See Hecht, 1976). In the United States, increases are also noted in old ages. (See Kuznets, 1978).

Table 15.1   Projections of households by size class for Japan, 1985: percentage distribution projected by modified exponential function

(1) Age group	(2)	(3)	(4)	(5)	(6)	(7)	(8)
	Projected percentage distribution of households by size class						
	1 person	2 persons	3 persons	4 persons	5 persons	6 persons	7 +
15–24	.789536	.110574	.085805	.013770	.000295	.000020	.000000
25–34	.219895	.145486	.229211	.309653	.071734	.017906	.006115
35–44	.069861	.068555	.132328	.471845	.180316	.055422	.021673
45–54	.084589	.171139	.263904	.340106	.093159	.030377	.016726
55–64	.157300	.335933	.263433	.124941	.047145	.041887	.029361
65 +	.230766	.406823	.148198	.060829	.044335	.063278	.045771

(1) Age group	(9) Projected number of households (000's)	(10)	(11)	(12)	(13)	(14)	(15)	(16)
		Projected number of households by size class (000's)						
		1 person (2)×(9)	2 persons (3)×(9)	3 persons (4)×(9)	4 persons (5)×(9)	5 persons (6)×(9)	6 persons (7)×(9)	7 + (8)×(9)
15–24	2 183	1 723.6	241.4	187.3	30.1	0.6	0.0	0.0
25–34	6 487	1 426.5	943.8	1 486.9	2 008.6	465.3	116.2	39.7
35–44	9 756	681.6	668.8	1 291.0	4 603.3	1 759.2	540.7	211.4
45–54	9 271	784.2	1 586.6	2 446.7	3 153.1	863.7	281.6	155.1
55–64	6 778	1 066.2	2 277.0	1 785.5	846.9	319.5	283.9	199.0
65 +	4 446	1 026.0	1 808.8	658.9	270.4	197.1	281.3	203.5
Age total	38 921	6 708.1	7 526.4	7 856.3	10 912.4	3 605.4	1503.7	808.7

Source: Projected percentage distribution:
Household projection: Tatsuya Itoh and Chizuko Yamamoto, 'Projections of the Number of Households for Japan, 1970–2000, Projected in January 1977', *Jinko Mondai Kenkyu*, No. 141, (January 1977), pp. 32–9.

The adjusted percentage shares are then multiplied by the corresponding age-specific projections of the number of households, given the results in columns (10) to (16) of Table 15.1.

The method is simple, but it has some advantages compared to other simple methods. First, it can utilize the already existing household projections by age group, which in turn were based on population projections by sex and age; hence, it can reflect changing age composition and produce projections specific for both age and size.

There are disadvantages, however. If extrapolation is done mechanically, the resulting percentage distribution of households by size can be absurd. For example, if the percentage share for a particular size class *j* decreases disproportionately faster than that for an adjacent class *j* + 1, the percentage share for class *j* might become smaller than that for the adjacent class *j* + 1, even though the percentage share for class *j* + 1 is normally smaller than that for class *j*. For example, in age group 15–24, the share for two-person households is normally larger than that for three-person households, but if the percentage share of three-person households decreased moderately between 1970 and 1975 while that of two-person households decreased rapidly during the same period, an unrealistic result may occur. In such a case, the decline in percentage share of two-person households may be decelerated, for example, taking the halfway point between the 1975 value and the initially extrapolated value.

5 Beyond the Cross-sectional Headship Rate Method

A. Gaps in the headship rate method

According to Bongaarts, the principal advantage of the headship rate method is its relative simplicity and the minimal data demands it makes (Bongaarts, 1983). A drawback of the method is that it is mechanical and does not specify the links between household size or distribution and their determinants: fertility, mortality, nuptiality, etc. These are useful remarks to start with in searching for alternative approaches.

One of the most serious limitations of the headship rate method is its incapacity to deal with the dynamics of family and household formation. It does not produce numerical estimates of additions to and subtractions from the stock of households, changes attributable to marriage, migration for jobs and higher education, and undoubling or doubling-up of households, and estimates of additions to households are what government and private enterprises have increasingly demanded for purposes of planning construction of houses and apartments, production and distribution of consumer durables, sales of newspapers, etc.

A rough approximation of net additions and subtractions of households may be obtained by comparing the projected number of heads for an age group with expected survivors based on actual census data for the base period and survival ratios. In Japan, however, the existence of many stem family households complicates the calculation since a transfer of headship from the older to younger generation within a household may take place without 'birth of a new household'.

Information of that kind requires a method such as Illing's or the vital statistics method, which adopts a stock-flow approach to household formation, taking account of new marriages, deaths of spouses, divorces, and net immigration of families, etc (Illing, 1968).[3] If such a stock-flow approach can be elaborated to deal with sex–age specificity, it would provide useful information. While this is theoretically possible, we have to find suitable input data, and Illing's calculations were not sex–age specific.

---

[3] Masnick and Pitkin's recent paper maintains that in the 1960s in the United States the pressure created by the presence of the baby boom generation on the ability of two generations of adults to share the same home also affected the chances that ageing parents would move in with their children, thus discouraging multigenerational households. This means that if the pressure was lessened and physical and social space was available, some of elderly parents might have moved in with their grown up children in lieu of grandchildren. (Masnick and Pitkin, 1983).

B. Issue of Co-residentiality with the Parents

In the West it is rare for adults to live with their parents, particularly after marriage. But, in the East, co-residence with the parents is common and this complicates household projections. Even in the West, however, some doubling-up occurs. If families bore a perfect one-to-one relation to households (except for one-person households which are not families), then household projections would be much less difficult, and advances in the demography of family formation could dictate how to prepare the household projections.

Consider the case of Japan. Let us assume that the doubling-up of households were minimum or close to minimum. Specifically, assume that headship rates were 100 per cent for married males at age groups 25–34 and over, and that the highest levels envisaged in the above-mentioned normative projections among the Scandinavian countries were to be realized in the other sex–age–marital status categories. Then, as Table 15.2 shows, the number of households estimated for 1980 would be far greater than the actual number, and average size of household would be only 2.47 persons, compared to 3.22 persons, the actual figure in the 1980 census.

Another demonstration of the relevance of doubling-up of married children and parents in Japan involves testing the validity of using birth parity data for estimating the size distribution of households. If a simply demographic approach can yield projections of households by size class, the parity distribution of fertility among the ever-married persons would seem to be of central importance in such an exercise. If demographic factors alone determine household formation, then families consisting of married couples or the widowed and divorced according to their birth parities (or size of own children) would largely determine the size-distribution of households.

In order to test this line of thinking, an attempt was made to calculate ratios between households by size according to sex, age, and marital status of heads and the corresponding number of currently married, widowed, and divorced women by birth parity. It is assumed that heads of households and the corresponding women, irrespective of whether they are heads themselves or the spouses of the heads, belong to the same age group. It is hypothesized that if there were no doubling up of kin, an approximate correspondence should exist between the household size and the parity distribution of women, that is, that the size distribution of households is determined largely by demographic factors. If there were no doubling-ups, for example, the number of the four-person households should be close to the number of the married couples with two children plus the number of widowed and divorced women with three children.

The results of this comparison in 1970 are shown in Table 15.3, but they are not very convincing. While the ratios between the number of heads of households by size and the number of women by parity are close to unity in age groups 35–39 and 40–44 in each category of comparable household

Table 15.2 Hypothetical estimates of the number of households assuming that doubling-up is minimum: Japan, 1980

(1)	(2)	(3)	(4)	(5)	(6)	(7)	(8)	(9)	(10)
Age group	Single population (000s)	Headship rate	Projected heads (000s) (2) × (3)	Married population (000s)	Headship rate	Projected heads (000s) (5) × (6)	Widowed and divorced	Headship rate	Projected heads (000s) (8) × (9)
Males									
15–17	2 614	0.00	0	0	0.90	2	0	0.80	0
18–24	5 214	0.45	2 346	333	0.95	316	20	0.90	18
25–34	3 670	0.90	3 303	6 177	1.00	6 177	120	0.95	114
35–44	589	0.90	530	7 962	1.00	7 962	203	1.00	203
45–54	199	0.90	179	7 128	1.00	7 128	253	1.00	253
55–64	62	0.90	56	4 157	1.00	4 157	238	0.95	226
65–74	26	0.85	22	2 662	1.00	2 662	373	0.90	336
75+	10	0.80	8	966	1.00	966	462	0.80	370
Total	12 384		6 444	29 387		29 370	1 669		1 520
Females									
15–17	4 492	0.00	0	6	0.00	0	0	0.75	0
18–24	4 531	0.35	1 586	881	0.00	0	19	0.85	16
25–34	1 563	0.80	1 250	8 058	0.00	0	225	0.90	203
35–44	440	0.90	396	7 894	0.00	0	834	0.95	792
45–54	342	0.90	308	6 531	0.00	0	837	0.95	795
55–64	169	0.90	152	3 923	0.00	0	1 529	0.90	1 376
65–74	60	0.80	48	1 790	0.00	0	2 076	0.85	1 765
75+	20	0.75	15	388	0.00	0	1 813	0.75	1 360
Total	9 617		3 755	29 471		0	7 333		6 307

Average size of household: 117 060/47 396 = 2.4698

Table 15.3   Comparison of the number of heads of households by size and the number of women by corresponding parity: Japan, 1970

(Numbers in all columns except for the ratios are in terms of 1000 household heads.)

(1) Age group	(2) Number of heads: household size: 1	(3) Status single house-holders	(4) Number of the widowed & divorced: parity 0	(5) (3)+(4)	(6) $\frac{(2)}{(5)}$	(7) Number of heads: household size: 2	(8) Number of women Married: parity 0	(9) Widowed & divorced: parity 1	(10) (8)+(9)	(11) $\frac{(7)}{(10)}$
15–19	161 715	159 405	4 610	164 015	0.986	25 690	46 685	5 095	51 780	0.496
20–24	733 645	724 925	9 985	734 910	0.998	342 055	672 530	12 375	684 905	0.499
25–29	459 085	432 605	22 350	454 955	1.009	666 435	590 875	31 210	622 085	1.071
30–34	201 995	162 235	26 880	189 115	1.068	383 675	240 330	44 160	284 490	1.349
35–39	142 645	89 615	34 900	124 515	1.146	251 175	201 915	57 270	259 185	0.969
40–44	140 230	61 910	45 530	107 440	1.305	265 650	200 110	73 470	273 580	0.971
45–49	153 145	39 645	56 845	96 490	1.587	310 400	179 965	99 475	279 440	1.111
50–54	167 090	23 460	62 380	85 840	1.947	352 285	147 125	110 805	257 930	1.366
55–59	179 505	16 655	70 765	87 420	2.053	408 975	123 525	94 575	218 100	1.875
60–64	171 090	11 580	75 725	87 305	1.960	399 980	94 310	83 935	178 245	2.244
65+	390 730	15 510	264 870	280 380	1.394	704 235	115 620	243 245	358 865	1.962

Source: Household: Bureau of Statistics, Office of the Prime Minister, *1970 Population Census of Japan*, Tokyo, 1973, Vol. 5, Part 1, Division 2, Table 40, pp. 394–396.
Fertility: Bureau of Statistics, Office of the Prime Minister, *1970 Population Census of Japan*, Tokyo, 1973, Vol. 5, Part 1, Division 1, Table 11, pp. 214–217.

Table 15.3 (continued).

(12) Age group	(13) Number of heads: household size: 3	(14) Number of women Married: parity 1	(15) Number of women Widowed & divorced parity 2	(16) (14)+(15)	(17) $\frac{(13)}{(16)}$	(18) Number of heads: household size: 4	(19) Number of women Married: parity 2	(20) Number of women Widowed & divorced: parity 3	(21) (19)+(20)	(22) $\frac{(18)}{(21)}$
15–19	6 710	22 320	1 760	24 080	0.279	4 320	7 115	1 080	8 195	0.527
20–24	153 425	602 325	3 130	605 455	0.253	42 495	142 400	2 070	144 470	0.294
25–29	815 545	1 454 900	11 610	1 466 510	0.556	392 555	1 327 180	2 175	1 329 355	0.295
30–34	917 605	699 275	32 025	731 300	1.255	1 190 705	1 996 005	8 590	2 004 595	0.594
35–39	571 460	497 330	55 730	553 060	1.033	1 484 135	1 781 495	23 715	1 805 210	0.822
40–44	529 830	370 630	76 280	446 910	1.186	1 243 830	1 168 405	48 585	1 216 990	1.022
45–49	532 555	238 695	96 900	335 595	1.587	842 135	627 095	80 920	708 015	1.189
50–54	519 655	147 295	117 675	264 970	1.961	618 965	275 700	108 920	384 620	1.609
55–59	498 085	112 855	109 900	222 755	2.236	473 895	146 560	120 870	267 430	1.772
60–64	367 555	79 650	88 645	168 295	2.184	281 215	92 850	101 465	194 315	1.447
65+	370 155	86 340	247 435	333 775	1.109	256 145	95 685	299 980	395 665	0.647

Table 15.3 (continued).

(23) Age group	(24) Number of heads: household size: 5	(25) Number of women Married: parity 3	(26) Number of women Widowed & divorced parity 4	(27) (25)+(26)	(28) $\frac{(24)}{(27)}$	(29) Number of heads: household size: 6	(30) Number of women Married: parity 4	(31) Number of women Widowed & divorced: parity 5	(32) (30)+(31)	(33) $\frac{(29)}{(32)}$
15–19	2 810	3 145	—	—	—	2 005	—	—	—	—
20–24	14 520	21 455	1 885	23 340	0.622	7 130	6 925	1 725	8 650	0.824
25–29	95 600	221 955	395	222 350	0.430	33 045	22 405	280	22 685	1.457
30–34	372 370	660 910	2 035	662 945	0.562	138 895	100 670	515	101 185	1.373
35–39	691 645	842 890	6 075	848 965	0.815	298 050	198 480	1 730	200 210	1.489
40–44	770 835	886 285	19 960	906 245	0.851	371 540	340 100	6 745	346 845	1.071
45–49	592 815	763 620	46 320	809 940	0.732	293 410	462 770	21 345	484 115	0.606
50–54	451 670	434 875	80 095	514 970	0.877	236 375	420 365	48 570	468 935	0.504
55–59	349 355	219 225	111 300	330 525	1.057	238 895	272 945	88 325	361 270	0.661
60–64	226 930	121 960	102 645	224 605	1.010	235 125	147 490	96 445	243 935	0.964
65+	288 650	124 435	310 630	435 065	0.663	393 710	145 795	327 795	473 590	0.831

size–parity combinations, the ratios are in general appreciably different from unity in the other age categories, suggesting that information on the age–parity distribution alone is of limited value for estimating households by size. Actually, it is conceivable that when heads (and their spouses) get old, most of their grown-up children leave home, thus making it difficult to keep the ratio at unity anyway. Hence, such a comparison in old age groups, say 50 years and over, may be meaningless. Inasmuch as the doubling-ups of families in households and parent–child co-residentiality are substantial, one may have to abandon any approach based solely on age, sex, marital status, fertility and mortality.

As far as heads aged 35–39 and 40–44 are concerned, there may be good reason to assume the co-residentiality with their parents is relatively rare, since their parents are likely to be still economically active and capable of living independently. Secondly, their children are less apt to be married, hence more likely to be still living with them. In this context, it should be noted that approximately in 1950–60, when those heads were married, the age at first marriage among the Japanese was already high: 26–27 years for men and 23–24 years for women. For these reasons, it is conceivable that in these age groups the ratios between the size of households and women's parity can correspond fairly closely.

6 Use of the Multiple Decrement Table: Construction of the Headship Life Table

One way to provide estimates of gross additions and subtractions to household stocks (estimates not given by the conventional headship rate method) is through an application of multiple decrement table methods. We can construct a 'headship life table', in which entries to and separations from headship status can be computed. Actually, separations or exits from the headship status take two forms, one due to mortality and the other due to relinquishment of headship because of doubling up with a household of their married son or daughter or of entering an institution. A household headship life table may be constructed by the following procedures, which are practically identical to those used in the construction of working life tables prepared by Wolfbein and Wool (1950) and Durand and Miller (1968).

Table 15.4 shows a headship life table for Japanese men in 1980. Explanation of each column in the Table is in order. Each concept of the headship life table is explained as follows:

Column (1), This column refers to age group.
Column (2), $_nh_x$. This column refers to the age-specific headship rate.
Column (3), $_nL_x$. As in a standard life table, this column refers to the stationary population, or the number of persons who would be living at any age interval out of 100 000 born alive.

Table 15.4 Household headship life table for the Japanese males, 1980[1]

(1)	(2)	(3)	(4)	(5)	(6)	(7)	(8)	(9)
Age group	Age-specific headship rates	Of 100 000 born alive living in years of age group			Of 100 000 born alive number living and in headship at the beginning of 5 years of age group	No. of person years in the headship remaining in the 5 years of age group and later years	Average remaining years of headship life for survivors in the headship at the beginning of 5 years	Expectation of life at the beginning of 5 years of age group
		In the population (stationary population)	In the headship (stationary population of household heads)					
	nh_x	nL_x	nLh_x	nLh_x^{*2}	lh_x^*	Th_x^*	$\mathring{e}h_x^*$	$\mathring{e}_x$
15–19	0.0494	492 369	24 323	466 323	98 627	5 233 935	53.07	59.45
20–24	0.2666	490 235	130 697	464 302	98 273	4 767 612	48.51	54.66
25–29	0.4836	488 012	236 003	462 196	97 823	4 303 310	43.99	49.90
30–34	0.7046	485 654	342 192	459 963	97 379	3 841 114	39.44	45.11
35–39	0.8356	482 552	403 220	457 025	96 859	3 381 151	34.91	40.34
40–44	0.8828	477 766	421 772	452 492	96 108	3 924 126	30.43	35.63
45–49	0.9166	469 939	430 746	445 079	94 898	2 471 634	26.05	31.05
50–54	0.9418	457 815	431 170	433 597	92 932	2 026 555	21.81	26.65
55–59	0.9471	440 331	417 037	417 037	90 020	1 592 958	17.70	22.43
60–64	0.9144	414 867	379 354	379 354	85 856	1 175 921	13.70	18.39
65–69	0.8571	375 577	321 907	321 907	79 660	796 567	10.00	14.61
70–74	0.7432	315 477	234 463	234 463	69 841	474 660	6.80	11.29
75–79	0.5959	235 509	140 340	140 340	55 656	240 197	4.32	8.50
80–84	0.4677	146 356	68 451	68 451	38 204	99 857	2.61	6.21
85+	0.3449	91 057	31 406	31 406	29 903	31 406	1.05	4.40

[1] For the ordinary households only, thus excluding the quasi-households.

[2] nLh_x^* is based on headship rate (nh_x) at age group 55–59 and stationary population (nL_x) at each age group.

Source: Headship rates: Bureau of Statistics, Office of the Prime Minister, *The 1980 Population Census of Japan*, Vol. 5, Division 1 and 2.
Life table: Institute of Population Problems, Ministry of Health and Welfare, *The 34th Abridged Life Tables* (April 1, 1980 to March 31, 1981), October 1981.

Table 15.4 (continued)

(10) Age group	(11) Mortality rate in 5 years of age group	(12) Accessions to the headship in 5 years of age group	(13) Rate of accessions to the headship in 5 years of age group	(14) Separations from the headship in 5 years of age group	(15) Rate of separations from the headship in 5 years of age group	(16)	(17)
					Due to all causes	Due to death	Due to doubling-up and due to entering institution
	$_nQ_x$	$_nA_x$	$_na_x$	$_nS_x$	$_nQ_x^s$	$_nQ_x^d$	$_nQ_x^i$
15–19	0.00433	106 479	0.21626	—	0.00433	0.00433	—
20–24	0.00453	105 898	0.21601	—	0.00453	0.00453	—
25–29	0.00483	107 329	0.21993	—	0.00483	0.00483	—
30–34	0.00639	63 215	0.13016	—	0.00639	0.00639	—
35–39	0.00992	22 552	0.04673	—	0.00992	0.00992	—
40–44	0.01638	15 883	0.03324	—	0.01638	0.01638	—
45–49	0.02580	11 537	0.02455	—	0.02580	0.02580	—
50–54	0.03819	—	—	14 133	0.07513	0.03830	0.03683
55–59	0.05783	—	—	37 683	0.11043	0.05686	0.05357
60–64	0.09471	—	—	57 447	0.17508	0.09189	0.08319
65–69	0.16002	—	—	87 444	0.27657	0.15031	0.12626
70–74	0.25348	—	—	94 123	0.40520	0.23200	0.17320
75–79	0.37855	—	—	71 889	0.56319	0.34734	0.21585
80–84	0.61646	—	—	37 045	0.89930	0.65000	0.24930
85+	1.00000	—	—	—	—	—	—

Column (4), $_nLh_x$. This column refers to the stationary male heads under the prevailing headship rates, or the number of males in the stationary population expected to be in the headship status at each age group.

It is computed by the formula:

$$_nLh_x = {}_nL_x \cdot {}_nh_x \qquad (15.5)$$

Column (5), $_nLh_x^*$. This column represents the number of males in the stationary population who would hypothetically be heads if the headship rate at each age under 55 years were the same as at age group 55–59, the maximum headship rate.

$$_nLh_x^* = {}_nL_x \cdot {}_5h_{55}. \qquad (15.6)$$

This column is required in calculating the average number of remaining headship life per headship survivor at ages under 55 in order to eliminate the effects of accessions to the household heads.

Column (6), $1h_x^*$. The number of male survivors at each exact age who would hypothetically be heads if the headship rate at each age under 55 years were the same as at age group 55–59.

$$1h_x^* = \frac{1}{10}({}_nLh_{x-n}^* + {}_nLh_x^*) \qquad (15.7)$$

Column (7), Th_x^*. This column represents the remaining years in the headship status at any age group including the hypothetical $_nLh_x^*$ values for ages under 55. It may be expressed as follows:

$$Th_x^* = \sum_{x=i}^{\omega} ({}_nLh_x^*) \qquad (15.8)$$

Column (8), $\overset{\circ}{e}h_x^*$. This column refers to the average remaining number of years of life for males in the headship status at a given age and it is computed from the values of Th_x^* and the number of survivors, including the hypothetical number at ages under 55 ($1h_x^*$), as follows:

$$\overset{\circ}{e}h_x^* = \frac{Th_x^*}{1h_x^*} \qquad (15.9)$$

However, for age group 55–59 and over

$$\overset{\circ}{e}h_x^* = \frac{Th_x^*}{1h_x} \qquad (15.10)$$

Column (9), $\overset{\circ}{e}_x$. As in the standard life table, this column represents the average number of years of life remaining at the beginning of the given age group.

Column (11), $_nQ_x$. This column represents the mortality rate for males living in the 5 years of age group. It is computed as follows:

$$_nQ_x = \frac{_nL_x - _nL_{x+n}}{_nL_x} \qquad (15.11)$$

This rate is in terms of the stationary population rather than the survivors at exact ages, as in the computation of a standard life table.

Column (12), $_nA_x$. This column represents net accessions to the male heads between successive years. This is the net increase in heads in the stationary population after allowing for mortality of household heads during the five years $(_nLh_x \cdot _nQ_x)$

$$_nA_x = _nLh_{x+n} - _nLh_x + _nLh_x \cdot Q_x \qquad (15.12)$$

Column (13), $_na_x$. This column refers to the rate of net accessions to the male heads between the successive years. It is expressed as follows:

$$_na_x = \frac{_nA_x}{_nL_x} \qquad (15.13)$$

Column (14), $_nS_x$. This column represents separations from the stationary male heads of households due to all causes and was computed as the difference between the stationary heads of household in successive years to the heads at age group x to $x + n$; or

$$_nS_x = _nLh_x - _nLh_{x+n} \qquad (15.14)$$

Column (15), $_nQ_x^s$.

$$_nQ_x^s = \frac{_nLh_x - _nh_{x+n}}{_nLh_x} \qquad (15.15)$$

For ages 15–54 it is assumed that death is the sole cause of headship relinquishment and, therefore,

$$_5Q_{15}^s \text{ to } _5Q_{50}^s = _5Q_{15} \text{ to } _5Q_{50} \qquad (15.16)$$

Column (16), $_nQ_x^d$. This column represents the rates of separation from the headship due to death under the assumption that the age-specific death rates for males in the headship status are the same as those for all males. $_nQ_x^d$ is derived from $_nQ_x$ and $_nQ_x^s$ as follows:

$$_nQ_x^d = \frac{_nQ_x (2 - _nQ_x^s)}{2 - _nQ_x} \qquad (15.17)$$

These rates differ from those in column (11) because deaths following headship relinquishment during the interval are excluded.

Column (17), $_nQ_x^r$. This column represents the rates of separation from the headship due to relinquishment of the household headship. $_nQ_x^r$ is obtained by subtracting the rate of separation by death from the total separation rate or,

$$_nQ_x^r = _nQ_x^s - _nQ_x^d \qquad (15.18)$$

The crux of this multiple decrement table is to calculate the number of heads under stationary conditions which are the product of age-specific headship rate and the stationary population. On the basis of stationary population of male heads, one can calculate average remaining years of headship life and the rates of entry into and exit from the headship status, the latter being further broken down by two major causes, one due to mortality and the other due to doubling-up (relinquishment of own household headship) or due to entering the institution.

The rates of accessions to and separations from the headship status are obtained from column (13), and columns (15), (16) and (17), respectively. The rates of accessions to and separations from the headship status may be used to estimate respectively the number of additions of new households and the number of exits due to death or due to doubling-up and entering the institution. Once rates of accessions and separations are obtained, the procedure for estimating numbers is similar to that of calculating the number of survivors in each age cohort in the population projections by using life table survival ratios.

7 Concluding Remarks

Despite several shortcomings, the headship rate method still has been the most widely used method for projecting households by governments and the private sector because of its simplicity and the ready availability of needed data. Since population composition factors account for a larger part of changes in the number of households (Kono, 1969), it is sensible to use available population projections as a base. By and large, headship rate method projections based on available population projections seem to provide adequate figures, although not perfect.

If the headship rate method were combined with other methods, such as micro-simulation to give better estimates of future headship rates, the value of this method would be enhanced. If the method can be expanded to make use of multiple decrement tables of headship life and micro-simulation, then the gaps inherent in the results of the conventional headship rate method would be filled in to some extent. Such a consolidated method would be able to provide more adequate and meaningful projections and generate richer output, containing more detailed information such as on the number of households by size class and by the number of co-resident children by age.

References

Bongaarts, John (1983), 'The Formal Demography of Families and Households: An Overview', *IUSSP Newsletter*, 17, 27–42.

Cullingworth, J. B. (1960), *Housing Needs and Planning Policy*, Routledge and Kegan Paul, London.

Denmark, Ministry of Housing (1965), 'Danish Housing Requirements, 1960–1980', Copenhagen.

Durand, John D. and Ann R. Miller (1968), *Methods of Analysing Census Data on Economic Activities of the Population*, United Nations Population Studies, No. 43, United Nations, New York.

Glick, Paul (1957), *American Families*, Census Monograph Series, John Wiley and Sons, New York.

Hecht, Alice (1976), 'Trends in the Size and Structure of Households in Europe, 1960–1970 and the Outlook for the Period 1970–2000', Paper presented at the Population Association of America Annual Meetings, Montreal, April 1976.

Illing, Wolfgang (1967), *Population, Family, Household and Labor Force Growth to 1980*, Economic Council of Canada, Ottawa. Staff Study No. 19.

Japan, Economic Planning Agency (1982), *Japan in the Year 2000*, Government Printing Office, Tokyo. In Japanese.

Japan, Institute of Population Problems (1977), Ministry of Health and Welfare, *Future Projections of Households*, Tokyo, Institute of Population Problems Research Series, No. 135. In Japanese.

Kono, Shigemi (1969), 'Changes in Households and Family Structure in Japan', IUSSP, *International Population Conference, London, 1969*, Vol. 3, 2223–33.

—— (1981), 'Further Contrivances on Methods of Household Projections with Special Attention to Size and Social Development Planning', in IUSSP, *International Population Conference, Manila 1981*, Solicited Papers, Vol. 3, 485–501.

Kuznets, Simon (1978), 'Size and Age Structure of Family Households: Exploratory comparisons', *Population and Development Review*, 4, 2, 187–223.

Masnick, George and Mary Jo Bane (1980), *The Nation's Families: 1960–1980*, Auburn House, Boston.

Masnick, George S. and John R. Pitkin (1983), 'The Baby Boom and the Squeeze on Multigenerational Households', presented at the Population Association of America Meetings, Pittsburgh, April, 14–16.

Needleman, L. (1961), 'A Long-term View of Housing', *National Institute of Economic Review*, London, No. 18, 15–37.

Norway, Ministry of Municipal and Labour Affairs (1965), 'Housing Situation and Housing Prospects in Norway', Oslo.

Paige, D. C. (1965), 'Housing', in: W. Beckerman *et al.* (eds.), *The British Economy in 1975*, Cambridge University Press, Cambridge, England, 366–403.

Pitkin, John R. (1982), 'Interactions among Population, Household Formation and Housing Consumption', Paper presented at the meeting of the American Real Estate and Urban Economics Association, New York.

United Nations, The Economic Commission for Europe (1968), *The Housing Situation and Perspectives for Long-term Housing Requirements in European Countries*, United Nations, Geneva.

United Nations (1973), Manual VII, *Methods of Projecting Households and Families*, United Nations, New York.

United States National Resources Planning Committee (1938), *The Problems of a Changing Population*, Government Printing Office, Washington, DC.

US Bureau of the Census (1979), *Current Population Reports*, Series P-25, No. 805,

'Projections of the number of households and families: 1979 to 1995', US Government Printing Office, Washington, DC.

Wolfbein, Seymore L. and Harold Wool (1950), *Tables of Working Life*, US Department of Labor, Bureau of Labor Statistics, Washington, DC., Technical Appendix.

16 The Relationship between Heads and Non-Heads in the Household Population: An Extension of the Headship Rate Method

JOHN R. PITKIN and GEORGE S. MASNICK

Joint Center for Housing Studies of MIT and Harvard University, Cambridge, Massachusetts, USA.

Introduction

The post-World War II period has witnessed a remarkable change in the number, size, and composition of households in the United States. Between the mid-1940s and 1986, the total number of households rose by 126 per cent, while adults living in households increased only 83 per cent. The number of persons per household fell from 3.63 to 2.67. The number of children under 18 per household declined from the post-war peak of 1.23 in 1964 to 0.71 in 1986, a fall of 42 per cent. The number of non-family households grew by 20.8 million over this period, an increase of 501 per cent. Single person households increased by 657 per cent, from only 2.8 million in 1947 to 21.2 million in 1986. Married couple households increased from 30.6 million to 50.9 million, but because of the tremendous increase in households headed by unmarried individuals, the married couple share of the total fell from 78.3 per cent to 57.6 per cent in 40 years. In 1947 the average occupied housing unit was more than eight times as likely to be headed by a family householder than by an unrelated individual. In 1986 this ratio had fallen to well under 3:1 (US Bureau of the Census, 1986).

It is not surprising that these dramatic changes in households have captured the attention of those concerned with such matters as child welfare, poverty, health care delivery, housing, education, social security, and consumer behaviour. What is being called for by analysts in both the public and private sectors is clearer understanding of the causes of these past trends, and some perception of what the future will be likely to bring. Such knowledge, however, has not been easy to provide. US Census Bureau household projections done in the early 1970s (US Bureau of the Census, 1972, 1975) were wide of the mark for both total number of households and the composition of households being formed over the remainder of the 1970s (Masnick, 1983). Even with the benefit of hindsight, efforts at modelling household trends have produced no generally accepted explanations about why households changed in the manner that they have over the last three decades, or about how they are likely to change in the future.

Three distinct themes pervade the now substantial volume of studies of this change in household behaviour. These themes centre on preferences, family structure, and economics. The preferences hypothesis holds that the taste for privacy has grown in the population at large (Beresford and Rivlin, 1966). The family structure hypothesis suggests that demographic shifts in fertility, mortality, and marriage patterns have altered family structures to favour living independently rather than in households with larger numbers of members (Burch, 1970; Kobrin, 1976). The economic hypothesis focuses on the affordability and costs of maintaining an independent household relative to living in a larger household. (Carliner, 1975; Ermisch, 1981; Pampel, 1983). Income growth, declining real rents, and falling economies of scale for the maintenance of larger households lead the list of suggested economic causes.

The three hypotheses do not necessarily exclude one another. Higher incomes, for example, may have permitted previously latent tastes for privacy to find expression in actual living arrangements (Michael *et al*. 1980; Burch *et al*. 1983). Changes in the ratios of older to younger adults in the population may have reinforced a growing preference for independent living among elderly widows.

Regardless of the sources of change that are emphasized, there is a strong tendency in empirical studies of household formation in recent United States history to treat headship exclusively as a result of the behaviour of individuals or nuclear family units.

In this paper, we argue that a greater understanding of trends, and a greater precision in projection of households, can be achieved if we give more attention to a dimension of the household formation process that has been almost entirely missing from most analyses and projections of household change. This dimension is the relationships between the demographic characteristics of non-heads and the characteristics of the households in which they are accommodated, and the heads of these households.

Household Formation and Headship Rates

The most basic approach to the analysis of household formation is founded on the identity linking population size, household size, and number of households. The number of households can be calculated by dividing the size of the population by the average household size. Projections of households can be accomplished from projections of these other two variables. The inverse of household size, or simply the ratio of households to population, can then be thought of as a gross aggregate headship rate. Total households equal population times this crude headship rate.

A simple refinement of the gross aggregate headship rate takes note of the fact that minors rarely head households. Since minors do not appear in the numerator of the headship rate, it is logical to exclude them from the denominator. The reciprocal of this definition of the headship rate is, of course, now the mean number of adults per household rather than the mean household size. By incorporating this simple refinement, we prevent changes in the ratio of children to adults in the population from distorting the measure of the propensity of the population to form independent households.

The next step in the refinement of headship rates stems from the variation in the propensity to form households over the life cycle. Cross-sectional data for many different periods in the United States, for example, show that headship rates increase rapidly during early adulthood. These rates continue to rise, but at a steadily decreasing rate at ages above 30, to a rather flat peak somewhere between 45 and 64 years (Kobrin, 1973). Post World War II cohort data, also for the US, indicate a generally similar pattern, but with a more gradual rise and a maximum significantly later in the life course (Masnick and Bane, 1980). Such life cycle variability in the propensity to head households motivated the further refinement of the headship rate approach to incorporate age-specific rates. Similar considerations lead to the incorporation of marital status and sex into the analysis of headship rates. Married couples have always had very high headship rates in the United States, and formerly marrieds have had higher headship rates than never marrieds of the same age and sex.

As with age differences in headship, historical US data showed great stability in marital status and sex–specific headship rates between 1890 and 1950 (Winnick, 1957). It was therefore suggested that the distribution of population by age, sex, and marital status, in conjunction with these headship rates, offered a stable basis for projecting the effects on the number of households of future shifts in the age distribution of household heads (US Bureau of the Census, 1953).

Table 16.1 shows that married couples in the US achieved almost universal household headship by 1960, while headship of unmarried adults has varied significantly by age, sex, and marital status. During the past two decades, headship rates for unmarried adults have increased dramatically. From the perspective of the ability to make reliable projections using the headship rate methodology, the large increases in headship rates of unmarrieds have posed new challenges to the utility of the method. Before a projected population can be turned into households, one must also now make estimates of future levels of age–sex–marital status-specific headship rates, which have lost their previous stability.

Even in the short term of one or two years, there is a potential for large swings in headship rates and gross levels of household formation. The recent experience of the US is instructive in this connection. During the 1970s, about 1.6 million new households were added per year to the stock on average. This figure averaged just under 1.3 million between 1980 and 1986,

Table 16.1   Headship rates by age and marital status, US: 1960, 1970, and 1980

Age Group	Currently Married Couples			Never Married Men and Women		
	1960	1970	1980	1960	1970	1980
15–19	.8356	.8690	.9157	.0064	.0103	.0191
20–24	.9467	.9616	.9687	.0885	.1592	.2441
25–29	.9760	.9860	.9858	.1954	.3397	.4747
30–34	.9841	.9925	.9926	.2662	.3931	.5659
35–39	.9884	.9946	.9953	.3194	.4152	.5625
40–44	.9908	.9958	.9962	.3657	.4468	.5672
45–49	.9902	.9954	.9958	.4293	.4964	.5776
50–54	.9905	.9947	.9952	.4834	.5316	.5956
55–59	.9892	.9928	.9942	.5101	.5970	.6504
60–64	.9832	.9909	.9919	.5606	.6257	.6594
65–69	.9772	.9873	.9908	.6015	.6501	.7091
70–74	.9695	.9847	.9899	.5913	.6559	.7128

Age Group	Female Widows			Other Previously Married Men and Women		
	1960	1970	1980	1960	1970	1980
15–19	.2953	.3395	.5556	.0939	.1408	.1813
20–24	.4894	.7132	.6144	.2763	.3873	.4148
25–29	.7137	.8136	.7400	.4556	.5961	.6117
30–34	.7996	.8486	.8342	.5554	.7015	.7254
35–39	.7917	.8942	.8977	.6309	.7313	.7826
40–44	.8134	.8936	.9017	.6543	.7531	.8020
45–49	.8089	.8836	.8989	.6758	.7652	.7984
50–54	.7919	.8602	.8911	.6804	.7521	.7958
55–59	.7576	.8411	.8876	.6803	.7619	.7918
60–64	.7120	.8168	.8820	.6774	.7609	.8009
65–69	.7019	.7978	.8699	.6575	.7594	.7948
70–74	.6551	.7711	.8528	.6521	.7537	.7936

Source: US Bureau of the Census, tabulations of 1960, 1970, and 1980, Census Public Use Sample microdata tapes.

and fell to only 391 thousand households added during the middle year of this period. This decline in household growth occurred at a time when the pool of potential heads (i.e., adult non-heads) continued to grow (US Bureau of the Census, 1983).

The first category of explanation usually offered to address these recent trends focuses on economic variables. Declining real income, high unemployment rates, high housing costs, and lack of confidence in the future all have been suggested as potentially important factors in this regard.

However, the explanations for these recent trends may also relate to a number of issues that have received little attention in recent analyses of headship rates. What are the living arrangements of adults who have chosen not to head their own households? What alternative living arrangements have been rejected by those who have recently decided to head a household? What are the factors that would make being accommodated in a household headed by someone else an attractive alternative to heading one's own household? To begin to address these questions we must look more closely at those adults who do not head households, and at the households in which they live. To the extent that this issue has been addressed in research on household formation, the focus has been on the role of kinship and family structure.

Family Structure and Headship

An observed relationship between population, age structure, and family composition led Kobrin (1976) to suggest an explanation of a change in one particular class of headship rates. Based on the rise in headship of older widowed women in the 1960s and 1970s, Kobrin inferred that the small number of offspring of these elderly women, or the 'mother–daughter' ratio, relative to the ratio for earlier cohorts, reduced the alternatives available to these older women to live in households headed by their offspring. Therefore, fewer were accommodated as non-head members, and more headed separate households.

It should be clear that 'mothers' who are no longer accommodated by their 'daughters' could, in theory, be accommodated in households headed by individuals in other population strata. For the change in the 'daughter' population to have a substantial direct effect on the headship of their 'mothers,' the number of the latter who are accommodated by other population groups must not increase as the number living with their children declines. This condition seems likely to be met: siblings, cousins, nieces, nephews, and nonrelatives, one assumes, are less inclined to accommodate them than the children they did not have would have been.

Census data for the US in 1970 support Kobrin's hypothesis: of all formerly married women age 75 to 79, 86.2 per cent of those who had given birth to no children headed their own household, while only 70.2 per cent of those who had borne one or more children did so (1970 Census Public Use tapes). Similar results have been obtained for Canada (Wister and Burch, 1983). Thus, substantial intercohort differences in fertility and childlessness could provide a direct linkage with trends in headship of the elderly.

If the parent generation–child-generation ratio correlates with the average family sizes of the parents, it must do so also for children: the more children per woman, the more siblings per child. This population ratio could also affect the headship of the children, although the effects would be observable at an earlier stage in the life course. Each child has exactly one set of natural parents, no matter how many siblings there are, so sheer availability of accommodation is not in question as it is for the elderly. Rather, what varies is the fraction of children that can comfortably be accommodated in their parents' households once they reach adulthood. Children of large families may therefore be more likely to head independent households than children of smaller families. Analytical models of the effects of the demographic transition on household composition (Coale, 1965; Burch, 1970) suggest a substantial increase in the size of household, resulting in crowding, which in turn would put pressure on increasing the likelihood that grown children would head their own household.

Although no direct empirical research analysing this effect on headship has come to our attention, we have found indirect evidence that is supportive. According to the 1970 US Census, there were an average of 0.143 'own children' living in the households of women age 60 to 64 who reported having ever borne exactly one child, and an average of 0.218 'own children' in the housenolds of women of the same age who reported having borne two or three children. Thus, roughly 14.3 per cent of only children were still living with parents, but only 8.7 per cent (assuming roughly equal numbers of mothers of two and three children) of the offspring of the larger families did so (1970 Census Public Use Sample data). More exact comparisons would require adjustments for survivorship and age distribution of the children, as well as corrections for errors in the reporting of childbearing history.

Absence from the parental household need not lead directly to household headship, since accommodations as a non-head may also be found in other households. But, the presumption must be that a significant share of such young adults will *not* find mutually acceptable accommodators outside their nuclear families, and therefore are more likely to head households.

This connection between family structure and headship rates differs qualitatively from the effect of the mother–daughter ratio. The effect does not follow from the existence or availability of a certain type of kin, but rather has to do with the number of potential competitors for space in the parental household. In the case of space for elderly parents, the existence of unused capacity might be of less importance, because the claim of a bereaved or possibly infirm parent for household space is strong. In other cases, though, the question of accommodating capacity becomes important, and in fact may be of overriding importance for the acceptance of nonnuclear kin and non-relatives into a household.

Household heads are averse to accommodating more than a certain number of non-head members. The number will vary across households. It depends, in part, on the size of the housing unit which the household occupies. Empirical evidence of this is found in the greater accommodation of non-nuclear adults by households in larger housing units than those in smaller units. For example, married couple households, with wife age 35 to 44 and with no children under the age of 15 present, were more than three times as likely in 1975 to include non-nuclear adult members if they lived in houses with seven or more rooms than if they lived in units with fewer than five rooms (tabulations from 1975 Annual Housing Survey data tape).

There are also indications that the capacity of households on average to accommodate non-head adults members is affected by the presence of children. Table 16.2 allows us to look more closely at recent trends in the households which accommodated adult non-head members age 15 and over, and breaks accommodating households down according to whether these adults are children of the head, other relatives of the head, or individuals unrelated to the head, called here 'secondary adults.' In 1975 almost one third of all US households contained non-heads age 15 and over (including children). This fraction had changed only slightly since 1960. Between 1960 and 1975, the proportion of households containing one or more related adults besides children declined from over 10 per cent to about 6.5 per cent. The proportion of all households that accommodated at least one secondary adult remained stable at approximately 3.5 per cent. Table 16.2 also shows that very few households contained secondary adults when there were also children present, other relatives being more common under those circumstances. Likewise, it was also rare to find households containing both other relatives and non-relatives. Households containing adult children, other relatives and secondary adults have become practically extinct. In light of the substantial growth in most indices of headship rates over this period, it is remarkable that the percentage of all households containing no adults other than the spouse of the head has remained nearly constant since 1960 at approximately two-thirds of all households. The increase in the fraction of households including adult children, from 22.9 to 24.7 per cent, resulted principally from the increase in birth rates in the late 1940s and 1950s, i.e., from changes in family structure. This larger number of children seems effectively to have helped displace other relatives and secondary adults from households.

We are therefore led to conclude that family structure is of very general importance in determining household membership and headship, and is not

Table 16.2   Households, by presence of adults other than head and spouse, 1960, 1970, 1975, USA

	1960	1970	1975
No other adults	66.72%	67.05%	67.62%
Adult children only	19.33	21.98	22.60
Other related adults only	7.36	5.35	4.47
Secondary adults only	2.66	2.68	3.09
Children and other relatives only	3.03	2.32	1.83
Children and secondary adults only	.45	.38	.26
Other relatives and secondary adults only	.33	.18	.11
All three	.10	.06	.02
TOTAL	100.00	100.00	100.00

Source: US Bureau of the Census, tabulations of 1960 and 1970 census 1:100 public use sample and 1975 Annual Housing Survey tapes.

limited to the issue of the availability of kin. The impacts are not confined to either nuclear or extended kin, since non-relatives' accommodation can also be affected. Because of the strong association of changes in population age structure with shifts in the structure of nuclear families, the age structure itself must be considered to have potentially significant influences on the headship rates of *all* strata. A general analytic framework for describing and analysing the relationships between heads and non-heads in different population age and marital status groups is required.

The Household Headship–Membership–Accommodation Matrix

The structure of living arrangements among the different demographic strata in the population can be usefully described by an extension of the familier headship rate method. Headship rates derive from a matrix which shows the division of each population subgroup being considered into heads and non-heads. If we define z age–sex–marital status strata, this matrix has z rows and 2 columns, heads and non-heads. (The population subgroups are arrayed in a single dimension to simplify the notation.) The headship rates are then the ratios of the counts of heads to the row sums, or stratum populations. This matrix can be expanded in a number of ways to describe the composition of households. The US Census Bureau (e.g., 1973, Table 204) since 1940 has published data on non-heads broken down according to their relationship to the head of the household in which they live: child, sibling, room-mate, etc. A different expansion of the column of non-heads, namely according to the population stratum of the head of the household in which they live, makes the relationships between population strata explicit. One column then becomes z columns, and the matrix goes from z by 2 to z by $z + 1$:

$$[\text{HMA}] = \begin{matrix} n_{11}n_{12}n_{13} \ldots n_{1z}h_z \\ n_{21}n_{22}n_{23} \ldots n_{2z}h_2 \\ . \\ . \\ . \\ n_{z1}n_{z2}n_{z3} \ldots n_{zz}h_z \end{matrix}$$

A similar formulation was proposed by Akkerman (1976) for a different purpose, and a simple version of such a matrix has recently been added to the tabulations of Current Population Survey data provided by the US Census Bureau (1983a). In the above notation, the rows are stratified by characteristics of the non-heads (n_{ij}) and the columns differentiate the characteristics of the head of the households in which the non-heads are accommodated. The sum of the elements in one row, $n_{i1} + n_{i2} + \ldots + n_{iz}$, is the total number of non-heads in stratum *i*. This sum plus h_i gives the total number of individuals in stratum *i*. The *stratum specific membership rate* is, therefore, the complement of the stratum specific headship rate.

From the extended headship matrix we can derive a measure of the frequency with which individuals in stratum *i* co-reside as non-heads with heads in any stratum *j*. This ratio can be termed an *intergroup membership rate*: the proportion of individuals in a particular age–sex–marital status category (stratum *i*) who reside as non-heads with heads in a particular age–sex–marital status category (stratum *j*). Besides headship and membership, the HMA matrix contains information about the accommodation of non-head members by households. In particular, we observe that any column sum gives the total number of non-heads that live in households headed by members of a particular population stratum *j*. The *stratum-specific accommodation rate* is given as the column sum ($n_{1j} + n_{2j} + \ldots + n_{zj}$) divided by the total number of persons in the *j*th stratum. It is the average number of non-heads accommodated per capita, not per household or per head. (Note that the denominator of the accommodation rate is individuals, not households, since household headship and the number of households will become the dependent variable determined by the system we are considering.) Just as the membership rate can be particularized to an individual element of the HMA matrix, so can the accommodation rate. The *intergroup accommodation rate* represents the mean number of non-heads of class *i* that are accommodated per capita in *j*.

With a simple stratification of the population by age only, an HMA matrix may contain as few as 64 cells. Allowing for full stratification by marital status, family size, and sex, the matrix may comprise up to 2500 elements, still a manageable size. As an illustration, an HMA matrix for the United States in 1970 is shown in Table 16.3, which also shows the intergroup and stratum specific membership and accommodation rates. We point out that this illustrative example is, unfortunately, incomplete in that teenagers are omitted both as heads and non-heads. Their omission, a result of the design of the work data set from which we tabulated the matrix, does not seriously distort the remainder of the matrix. The first row shows, for example, that of the people age 20 to 24 in the Census Public Use sample, 1 273 900 lived as non-head members of households headed by 35 to 44 year-olds. This number represents 9.2 per cent of the total number of 20 to 24 year-olds (the intergroup membership rate) and 5.6 per cent of the population age 35 to 44 (the intergroup accommodation rate). We have added a column which shows the total number of non-heads in each stratum, 8 160 100 in the case of 20 to 24 year-olds. Reading down the column of non-heads accommodated in households headed by 35 to 44 year-olds we see that the largest element, 6 029 700 is the diagonal, reflecting the large number of spouses accommodated as non-heads. Departing from Census convention, this table classifies married couples by the age of the wife, hence the number of 45 to 54 year-olds accommodated by this stratum is also relatively large.

Table 16.3   Headship–Membership Accommodation Matrix, 1970, US

Age of Non-head	Age of Head of Household Accommodating Non-heads								Non-heads	Household Heads	Total Population
	20–24	25–29	30–34	35–44	45–54	55–64	65–74	75-Plus			
			(populations in 100s)								
20 to 24 (1)	26 501	3724	1035	12 739	25 372	9589	1577	524	81 601	57 199	138 260
Membership rate	.192	0.027	.007	.092	.183	.069	.011	.004	.586	.414	1.000
Accommodation rate	.192	0.029	.009	.056	.112	.053	.013	.008			
25 to 29	18 870	26 647	3005	1993	7024	5696	1371	315	64 921	65 447	130 368
Membership rate	.145	0.204	.023	.015	.054	.044	.010	.002	.498	.501	1.000
Accommodation rate	.137	.204	.027	.009	.031	.031	.011	.005			
30 to 34	3028	19 140	20 565	3907	2183	3634	1517	308	54 282	58 103	112 385
Membership rate	.027	.170	.183	.035	.019	.032	.013	.003	.483	.517	1.00
Accommodation rate	.022	.147	.183	.017	.010	.020	.012	.004			
35 to 44	1210	5861	22 896	60 297	6816	4276	4196	1500	107 052	118 687	225 739
Membership rate	.005	.026	.101	.267	.030	.019	.019	.007	.474	.526	1.000
Accommodation rate	.009	.045	.204	.267	.030	.023	.034	.022			
45 to 54	657	1252	2246	30 032	58 399	6709	3164	2994	105 723	121 392	227 115
Membership rate	.003	.005	.010	.133	.257	.029	.014	.013	.465	.535	1.000
Accommodation rate	.005	.010	.020	.134	.257	.037	.026	.043			
55 to 64	462	897	1273	4529	28 322	41 283	4844	2652	84 262	98 289	182 551
Membership rate	.002	.005	.007	.025	.155	.226	.026	.014	.462	.538	1.000
Accommodation rate	.003	.007	.011	.020	.125	.226	.040	.038			
65 to 74	214	491	891	3475	5621	18 746	21 702	2664	53 804	68 046	121 850
Membership rate	.002	.004	.007	.028	.046	.154	.178	.022	.442	.558	1.000
Accommodation rate	.001	.004	.008	.015	.025	.103	.178	.039			
75 and over	122	199	381	2066	5407	5907	9350	8439	31 871	37 043	68 914
Membership rate	.002	.003	.005	.030	.078	.086	.136	.122	.462	.538	1.000
Accommodation rate	.001	.001	.003	.009	.024	.032	.077	.122			
Total number accommodated	51 064	58 211	52 292	119 308	139 144	95 840	47 721	19 396			
Sum of accommodation rates	.369	.446	.465	.528	.613	.525	.392	.281			

Note: Sample of population in households headed by individuals age 20 and over. A small number of cases were also omitted due to read errors on the computer tape.
(Source: 1970 Census Public Use Sample (1-in-100))

The column sums and the total accommodation rates for the strata appear in the bottom rows.

As shown here, the HMA matrix includes all non-head members age 20 and older, regardless of their relationship to the head of their household. The method can be extended by including only certain classes of relationships, e.g., all relatives and non-relatives except spouses, or including only nuclear family members (children and parents), only non-nuclear relatives or only non-relatives. In these variants, headship is no longer the exact complement of total membership.

Accommodation Rates and Accommodation as Behaviour

The reader will recall the definition of the stratum-specific accommodation rate as the number of non-head adult members in households headed by a given population stratum divided by the total number of persons in this stratum. Table 16.4 shows the stratum-specific rates of accommodation for four different classes of non-heads for the US in 1960, 1970, and 1975. The pattern of variation across the strata is quite different than that for membership rates (complement of headship rates), which are also shown, and which decline almost monotonically from early adulthood. In all three years accommodation rates for all members combined reached a clear maximum above 0.59 at age 45 to 54 with minima at both tails of the age range. Accommodation rates rose over the 15 year period for 45 to 54 year olds as the result of larger numbers of offspring reaching early adulthood. These rates were roughly stable in the adjoining age classes but fell substantially in both tails of the age distribution. Membership rates by contrast did not increase in any part of the age distribution over the period. This disparity lends support to a hypothesis that a shortage of (or squeeze on) accommodation casued some of the fall in membership (and rise in headship) rates during the 1960 to 1975 time span.

From the lower panel of Table 16.4 we can see that the age pattern of acommodation rates for non-relatives almost exactly reversed between 1960 and 1975, while the overall level remained roughly stable. There was a similar, though less extreme shift in the age pattern of membership with non-relative heads.

Accommodation rates, we believe, are not arbitrary constructs useful only insofar as they reflect influences of age structure on composition of residential families and households, but have at least as much behavioural significance as headship rates. The same forces that influence headship — preferences, economic situation, and family structure — may also bear upon the frequency with which people accommodate non-head members in their households. If, for example, higher incomes allow more people to express a preference for independent living by heading a house-

Table 16.4   Accommodation and membership rates, by relationship and age, 1960, 1970, 1975, US

Age	Accommodation Rates			Membership Rates		
	1960	1970	1975	1960	1970	1975
All members combined:**						
20–24 years	.404	.369	.321	.588	.586	.604*
25–29 years	.475	.446	.427	.521	.498	.476
30–34 years	.496	.465	.452	.503	.483	.459
35–44 years	.542	.528	.531*	.493	.474	.460
45–54 years	.595	.613	.648*	.493	.465	.455
55–64 years	.540	.525	.528	.491	.462	.452
65–74 years	.436	.392	.377	.496	.442	.418
75 years or more	.321	.281	.265	.548	.462	.413
Husbands:						
20–24 years	.359	.314	.261	.184	.180	.153
25–29 years	.421	.398	.354	.360	.360	.339
30–34 years	.434	.416	.411	.403	.401	.394
35–44 years	.433	.421	.416	.428	.412	.414
45–54 years	.399	.407	.409	.431	.409	.409
55–64 years	.338	.347	.355	.394	.394	.400
64–74 years	.245	.253	.265	.345	.336	.344
75 years or more	.119	.125	.133	.247	.245	.242
All relatives except husbands:						
20–24 years	.026	.018	.013	.363	.352	.394*
25–29 years	.040	.028	.023	.138	.116	.101
30–34 years	.050	.036	.024	.085	.069	.051
35–44 years	.095	.095	.103*	.062	.050	.037
45–54 years	.177	.191	.228*	.057	.044	.036
55–64 years	.176	.158	.160	.076	.054	.043
64–74 years	.157	.118	.099	.127	.089	.064
75 years or more	.164	.129	.117	.270	.198	.160
All non-relative members:						
20–24 years	.019	.037	.047	.042	.053	.057
25–29 years	.014	.020	.030	.023	.023	.035
30–34 years	.012	.012	.017	.015	.014	.014
35–44 years	.014	.012	.012	.012	.012	.009
45–54 years	.019	.014	.011	.015	.012	.010
55–64 years	.027	.019	.013	.021	.014	.009
64–74 years	.034	.022	.013	.024	.016	.010
75 years or more	.038	.027	.015	.032	.020	.011

Source: 1960 and 1970 Public Use Microdate (1-in-100) Samples and 1975 Annual Housing Survey (national) tapes.
* The Annual Housing Survey counts college students living in dormitories as living with their parents. As a result, this cell is biased upward slightly in comparison with 1960 and 1970.
** Married couples counted by wife's age; husbands as members.

hold, might they not also affect the number of non-heads that households desire to accommodate? This effect could be positive, in view of the rise in the number of households that could conveniently accommodate non-heads, but is more likely to be negative. Higher income reduces the economic incentive to share housing and increases the ability to afford privacy. Just as individuals with a strong taste for privacy or a shallow network of kin may be more likely than others to head a household, the people who move from membership to headship in response to an increase in income will be selected disproportionately from those with a strong preference for privacy. A negative elasticity of accommodation coupled with the sharp changes in distribution and level of real income among the elderly since 1960 may, for example, account for the steep decline in accommodation of non-relatives by this population group, from .038 to .015 by 1975 for the 75 and over age group.

Accommodation rates are also affected by factors whose influence on headship rates can be measured only indirectly, for example, characteristics of the housing units occupied by the household heads in a population stratum, the presence of minor children of different ages as well as the number and characteristics of adults in accommodator households. As a case in point, elderly widows who own large houses may willingly accommodate lodgers in rooms that would otherwise be empty, while widows who rent small apartments may accommodate almost none, lacking not only the space, but the frequently high fixed housing costs of utilities, property taxes and essential maintenance. In 1960, 7.6 per cent of the 75 year and older population who headed households occupied owned housing units with 7 rooms or more (tabulations from 1960 Census Public Use Sample tape). By 1975, in spite of improvements in income for this group, the proportion had fallen to 6.7 per cent (tabulations from 1975 Annual Housing Survey data tape). We surmise that this decline was caused by the strong demand for larger houses by the large families who produced the baby boom generation (Pitkin and Masnick, 1980). Whatever the cause, the changed housing circumstances of the elderly population may account for part of this group's disproportionate decline in accommodation of non-relatives.

Our attention has so far been focused on the headship–accommodation–membership relationships between different population age groups, as in Table 16.3, and for different types of relationships, as in Tables 16.2 and 16.4. Because age structure is correlated with family structure, age is probably the most important single dimension on which to stratify an HMA matrix, but a partition by sex and marital status may provide useful additional information, especially if there is a shift in marital and divorce patterns. To show how such a scheme can supplement a stratification by age alone, the accommodation rates for two classes of non-heads by sex and marital status groups are shown for the US in 1960, 1970, and 1975 in Table

Table 16.5   Accommodation of unrelated adults and related adults other than
spouses and children, by marital status and sex of head, 1960, 1970, 1975

Marital status and sex of head	Population age 15 and older	Accommodation rates	
		unrelated adults	related adults
1960			
Married, spouse present	40 466	.102	.021
Male, never married	11 750	.055	.023
Male, previously married	4 550	.096	.057
Female, never married	9 915	.054	.026
Female, previously married	11 607	.112	.060
Widowed	7 519	.117	.064
Other	4 088	.102	.053
Total	78 286	.090	.030
1970			
Married, spouse present	44 301	.069	.011
Male, never married	15 593	.038	.037
Male, previously married	5 522	.092	.080
Female, never married	13 984	.040	.033
Female, previously married	15 111	.089	.040
Widowed	9 125	.092	.037
Other	5 986	.084	.043
Total	94 511	.064	.027
1975			
Married, spouse present	48 008	.054	.008
Male, never married	18 871	.032	.053
Male, previously married	6 036	.083	.083
Female, never married	16 220	.031	.039
Female, previously married	17 151	.082	.035
Widowed	9 685	.085	.026
Other	7 446	.078	.046
Total	106 286	.053	.029

Source: 1960 and 1970 Census Public Use Microdata (1-in-100) Samples and 1975 Annual Housing Survey (national sample) tapes.

16.5 (Unlike Table 16.3, this table does not include own children with related adults).

Between 1960 and 1975, the fraction of couples and individuals who accommodated related (non-child) adults dropped, from 9.0 to 5.3 per cent, while accommodation of non-relatives declined only slightly. The 1960–75 fall in accommodation of relatives was distributed rather evenly across sex and marital status groups: the classes with the highest (widowed females) and lowest accommodation rates (never married females) were the same in 1975 as in 1960. The near-stability in overall accommodation of unrelated non-head members masks large compensating shifts among sex and marital status groups similar to those seen earlier among age groups. The rates fell substantially for married men. As a result of this shift, the fraction of all unrelated non-head members who lived with couples or widows fell from 58 per cent in 1960 to 21 per cent in 1975. These latter changes cannot simply be attributed to age effects, but conversely, these sex and marital status differences apparently do not account for all the differences in trends for various ages.

The trends and differences by age, sex, and marital status could, of course, be considered jointly in a single HMA matrix, which in this case would be (8 × 6 =) 48 rows by (48 + 1 =) 49 columns. As long as appropriate data are available, a matrix of this size poses no computational problems, but is difficult to display in standard printed formats. This larger matrix has the additional advantage of clarifying at least partially the relationship between membership and accommodation and the composition of actual households and families. It shows, for example, how many extra members are included in households that are headed by married couples.

In spite of the apparent significance of sex and marital status differences in accommodation and membership rates, the issues raised by large shifts in age structure seem to be of greater significance for post World War II trends in US household formation.

Our final empirical illustration shows the possible size of age-structure effects on household formation in the US. Here, we have made simple calculations of age-standardized rates for the US between 1940 and 1980. These calculations are shown in Table 16.6 and illustrate the potential for significant differences between the membership and accommodation

Table 16.6   Age-Standardized indices of household formation, US, 1940–1980[1]

	1940	1950	Year 1960	1970	1980[2]
Population age 20 and over, in households	83 563	94 407	106 620	121 972	149 785
Age-standardized members:					
From membership rates	40 881	45 841	51 361	59 327	72 982
From accommodation rates	40 893	46 196	52 419	59 327	71 391
Household heads:					
From membership rates	42 682	48 566	55 258	62 645	76 803
From accommodation rates	42 670	48 211	54 201	62 645	78 394
Actual households; head age 20 or over	34 461	41 638	52 201	62 645	79 931
Index of household formation					
From membership rates	80.7	85.7	94.6	100.0	104.1
From accommodatin rates	80.8	86.4	96.4	100.0	102.0

[1] Computed using age-specific rates of accommodation and membership and published age distributions of population in households.
[2] For 1980, age distribution of household population is estimated from the distribution for the total population, the distribution of the household population in 1970 and the reported 1980 total population in households; households with head age 20 and over estimated from Current Population Survey age distribution and Census count of total households.

approaches. (The reader should remember that the membership rate and headship rate approaches are necessarily equivalent since the two rates are complements of each other.) The second and third rows in this table show the 'expected' numbers of non-heads in the population given the actual changes in the age distribution and the hypothetically constant 1970 age-specific rates of accommodation and membership shown in Table 16.3. Between 1970 and 1980, the number of non-head members expected from holding membership constant at 1970 levels rose by about 1.6 million more than the number expected from holding accommodation rates constant. This imbalance implies that during the 1970s there was a squeeze on non-headship accommodations resulting purely from shifts in the age structure of the population.

The last two rows of Table 16.6 give the ratios of the actual households to those 'expected' from the two sets of rates; thus they are age-standardized indexes of household formation. They show that the membership standardized index increased by 4.1 per cent on average between 1970 and 1980, from 100.0 to 104.1. As much as half of the observed shift in headship during this decade could be attributed to scarcity of accommodation in households, for the accommodation standardized index rose only to 102.0.

It is not apparent on theoretical grounds whether households are best projected by simple membership or accommodation rate models, or indeed, whether there is any general rule that one model more closely replicates reality than the other. The membership method adopts one of the two possible simplest rules of thumb about the equilibration of households offering accommodation and non-heads seeking membership. There seems to be no *a priori* grounds to believe that the accommodation rate method might not be a more accurate simplification. Until we have a basis for choosing one method over another, a reasonable procedure for analysing and projecting trends in household formation would be to give equal weight to measures based on the accommodation rate and the membership rate.

A model of accommodation rates and behaviour can, in theory, serve as a replacement for a model of headship rates and behaviour: if we know which individuals from a given population are accommodated as members of households, we also know which ones are not, and that they therefore head households themselves. In practice, though, the accommodation approach complements the headship approach, for just as the pure headship approach is blind to the availability and qualities of individuals as accommodators, a pure accommodation approach is blind to the availability and qualities of individuals as potential household members. The two approaches have much greater power together than separately, because it is only by taking account of the relative numbers of potential members and accommodators that one can fully measure the effects of household size and crowding on headship and the number of households. This is analogous to the economic model of supply, demand, and market clearing, where the actual sales of a commodity are determined jointly by actors on both sides of a market.

References

Akkerman, A. (1976), 'The Household Composition Matrix and its Application to Migration Analysis and Population Projection', prepared for the Committee on Resources and the Environment, The University of Calgary, Alberta, Canada.

Beresford, J. C., and A. H. Rivlin (1966), 'Privacy, Poverty and Old Age', *Demography*, 3, 247–58.

Burch, T. K. (1970), 'Some Demographic Determinants of Average Household Size: An Analytic Approach', *Demography*, 7, 61–70.

——, *et al.* (1983), 'Changing Household Headship in the United States, 1900 to 1970: A Test of the Income Threshold Hypothesis', paper presented at the annual meetings of the Population Association of America, Pittsburgh, PA.

Carliner, G. (1975), 'Determinants of Household Headship', *Journal of Marriage and the Family*, 37, 28–38.

Coale, A. J. (1965), 'Appendix: Estimates of Average Size of Households', in A. Coale, *et al.*, (eds.), *Aspects of the Analysis of Family Structure*, Princeton University Press, Princeton.

Ermisch, J. F. (1981), 'An Economic Theory of Household Formation', *Scottish Journal of Political Economy*, 28, 1–19.

Kobrin, F. E. (1973), 'Household Headship and its Changes in the United States, 1940–1960, 1970', *Journal of the American Statistical Association*, 68, 793–800.

Kobrin, F. E. (1976), 'The Fall in Household Size and the Rise of the Primary Individual in the United States', *Demography*, 13, 127–38.

Masnick, G., and M. J. Bane (1980), *The Nation's Families: 1960–1990*, Auburn House, Boston.

Masnick, G. (1983), 'The Demographic Factor in Household Growth', Working Paper No. W83-3, MIT/Harvard Joint Center for Urban Studies, Cambridge, Mass.

Michael, R. T., V. Fuchs, and S. R. Scott (1980), 'Changes in the Propensity to Live Alone: 1950–1976', *Demography*, 17, 39–53.

Pampel, F. C. (1983), 'Changes in the Propensity to Live Alone: Evidence from Consecutive Cross Sectional Surveys, 1960–1976', *Demography*, 20, 433–47.

Pitkin, J. R., and G. Masnick (1980), *Projections of Housing Consumption in the U.S., 1980 to 2000, by a Cohort Method*, Annual Housing Survey Studies No. 9, Washington, DC: US Department of Housing and Urban Development, Office of Policy Development and Research.

Pitkin, J. R., and G. Masnick, (1981), 'Linking Projections of Households with Housing Consumption: An Exploration of Alternative Series', report to the US Department of Housing and Urban Development, Office of Policy Development and Research, Joint Center for Urban Studies of MIT and Harvard University, Cambridge, Mass.

US Bureau of the Census (no date), *Census of Population and Housing: 1960 Public Use (1-in-100) Sample*, computer tape; *Census of Population and Housing: 1970*

326   *John R. Pitkin*

Public Use (1-in-100) Sample, computer tape.

—— (1953), 'Projections of the Numbers of Households and Families, 1955 and 1960', *Current Population Reports*, Series P-20, No. 42.

—— (1972), 'Demographic Projections for the United States', *Current Population Reports*, Series P-25, No. 476.

—— (1973), *Census of Population: 1970*, 'Characteristics of the Population, United States Summary', Vol. 1, Pt. 1. Sec. 2.

—— (1975), 'Projections of the Number of Households and Families: 1975 to 1990', *Current Population Reports*, Series P-25, No. 607.

—— (1978), *Annual Housing Survey (National): 1975*, computer tape.

—— (1979), 'Projections of the Number of Households and Families: 1979–1995', *Current Population Reports*, Series P-25, No. 805.

—— (1983a), 'Households and Family Characteristics: March 1982', *Current Population Reports*, Series P-20, No. 381.

—— (1983b), 'Households, Families, Marital Status and and Living Arrangements: March 1983 (Advance Report),' *Current Population Reports*, Series P-20, No. 382.

—— (1986), 'Households, Families, Marital Status and Living Arrangements: March 1986 (Advance Report),' *Current Population Reports*, Series P-20, No. 382.

Winnick, L. (1957), *America's Housing and Its Use*, Wiley, New York.

Wister, A., and T. Burch (1983), 'Fertility and Household Status of Older Women in Canada, 1971.' *Canadian Studies in Population*, 10, 1–13.

17 Household Change and Housing Needs: A Forecasting Model*

INGVAR HOLMBERG

Demographic Research Institute, Göteborg, Sweden

General background

Social planning is often based mainly on information about individuals. This means that important subgroups such as families and households are not adequately considered in this context. This is unfortunate because many economically important decisions are household decisions. And household and family behaviour, as distinct from individual behaviour, also have important effects on society as a whole.

For example, in Sweden the relation between population growth and household changes became increasingly weaker during the 1970s. The yearly growth of the number of households varied between one and two per cent during the 1970s, while population growth has been only a quarter of one per cent.

Increasing formation of separate households lies behind these different trends. The distribution of households by size has shifted towards smaller households. Table 17.1 illustrates these changes in Sweden. The proportion of people in households with two or fewer persons has increased from 55 to 64 per cent. Average household size has, as a consequence, decreased from 2.6 to 2.3.

The changes in the number of families and households are of great importance to forecasting many types of demand for both goods and services. Traditional methods of household forecast are highly aggregated, and do not properly take into account the great structural changes (illustrated in the table) over the last ten years. Forecasts of this type may easily become misleading because households are different, the composition of

* The present work has been carried out under grant 790144-4 of the Swedish Building Research Council. Many people have been involved in different phases of the research. The original model was developed by Björn Hårsman and Bertil Marksjö, then at the Stockholm Master Planning Commission and Stockholm Office of Statistics respectively. Later Folke Snickars, at that time in the Research Group for Urban and Regional Planning, Royal Institute of Technology, Stockholm, joined in the work. They have all provided many valuable comments during the course of the work.

In the latest phase of the research Peter Dellgran as an economist and Paul Olovsson as a computer specialist, both with the Demographic Research Unit, have made many valuable contributions. I am grateful to them all, although the responsibility of the present paper remains solely mine.

Table 17.1   Percentage distribution of households by size 1970, 1975 and 1980: all
Sweden

Household size	Year		
	1970	1975	1980
1	25	30	33
2	30	31	31
3	19	17	15
4	16	15	15
5+	9	7	6
No. of households (1000s)	3 040	3 325	3 496
No. of people (1000s)	7 915	8 016	8 130

Source: Population census, 1970, 1975 and 1980.

dwelling units varies and the change of residence by individual households
must be related to migratory moves.

It is obvious that the changing household composition has great impact on
the quantitative aspects of housing planning, especially since housing units
have a very long length of life.

In Swedish housing planning — primarily compulsory municipal
programmes for the supply of housing — the analysis of demand is mostly
restricted to an estimate of the future number of households by the so-called
headship rate method, a technique which was largely developed during the
1930s and 1940s. There are only rare exceptions where household forecast
and the analysis of housing demand have not been dominated by pure demographic factors. The estimates of the distribution of households by size are
generally made rather schematically by means of simple trend extra-
polations. The methods used cannot be said to take into account the complexity of regional or national housing markets.

A forecasting system that takes all these facts into consideration is being
developed at the University of Göteborg. A preliminary version of the model
has been used for a national forecast of the Swedish housing market as a
whole; recently the system has also been used for making regional forecasts.

In this chapter we present the model which is being developed and applied
in Sweden for estimating the future number of households.

The chapter is organized in the following way: the next section deals with
concepts and definitions; the third section deals with methodological considerations, while the fourth describes one application of the model. The
chapter ends with some reflections on the potential for further development
of the model.

Concepts and definitions

The definition of a household used in the population censuses of Sweden is
based on the concept of individuals sharing the same dwelling unit. A
household is defined as a group of people who live in the same dwelling, or in

the same house. A *family*, on the other hand, is generally defined as a group of relatives sharing the same dwelling.

The distinction has some bearing on the type of statistical data available in Sweden. Statistical data on families are recorded in a population register called RTB (= register of the total population). A household in this register is either a married couple, or a single person (with or without children below the age of 16). Changes in family status are collected from data on vital events such as marriage or divorce, birth, and death. The register is updated weekly. This register is used as a basis for statistics on both population changes and families. Because of the large number of people living together without being formally married there are large differences between the family composition of the Swedish population and the household composition. The latter data, however, are only obtained in the censuses every fifth year. The differences between register data on families and census data on households are clearly seen in Table 17.2.

Table 17.2 Comparison of register data on families and census data on households; single women with 0, 1, or 2 children (family statistics). Census of 1975 — percentage distribution.

Type of family according to RTB (single women)	Type of household according to the census									Other households
	1 adult			2 adults			3 + adults			
	0	1	2 +[1]	0	1	2 +[1]	0	1	2 +[1]	
Number of children 0	52	0	0	23	1	0	12	3	1	8
1	.	41	0	.	48	1	.	7	0	2
2 +	.	.	47	.	.	46	.	.	6	1

[1] Number of children
Source: Population Census 1975.

Table 17.2 shows that only about half of the women, being single according to RTB, were actually living without a partner. Among single women with one child, 55 per cent belonged to households with at least two adults.

The completeness and coverage of the Swedish population census are generally excellent. However, in defining households certain errors are likely to occur; for example, if a two-family house is recorded by mistake as a single family house, the two households living in the house will be recorded as one large household. If this is a frequent error, the proportion of large households will be slightly exaggerated, as might have been the case in the 1980 census. However, on the whole, the reliability of the census data regarding households and household composition is extremely high.

Methodological considerations

Some points of departure

The forecasting of households/families may be based on different theoretical assumptions, but all methods must have a common behavioural basis. The *demographic approach* has been used for household forecasts for a very long time, primarily in the form of the so-called headship rate method. One of the prerequisites of this method is that there is a forecast of the population by marital status. In Sweden the change in marriage patterns during the last 10 years has made this method more and more uncertain. Other solutions have had to be sought. One alternative has been to make the calculations directly on the age–sex distribution, ignoring marital status entirely. Obviously a forecast made in this way will be uncertain.

The *economic approach* is mainly focused on housing demand and does not explicitly treat household changes. Disregarding some minor deviations, changes in housing demand can generally be regarded as equivalent to changes in the number of households. One advantage of macroeconomic models of housing demand in estimating future household changes is that various explanatory variables are easily introduced. In the Swedish long-term economic forecast, change in housing demand (and consequently change in the number of households) is expressed as a function of economic variables such as change in real income and relative cost of housing, and of the demographic variables population growth and change in the average age of the population.

The most serious objection to the use of macroeconomic models for estimating future household change is that the demographic relations are treated in such a crude way, but, on the other hand, it is difficult to include more elaborate demographic variables because of the highly aggregated character of the model.

The development of a new set of models for household and housing forecast was based on the following requirements:

(i) the model must be able to account for the household transformations now taking place;
(ii) the model must include both economic and demographic variables;
(iii) the model must be based on the use of available statistical data;
(iv) the result of the forecast must be highly disaggregated (e.g. by age, household size and type);
(v) it must be easy to link different sub-models.

The household flow model

Although methods for estimating household change used in Sweden today start from data that are easily obtained, that advantage is more than offset by inherent drawbacks. For example, they do not take into account structural changes in the household formation process and changes in the situation on the housing market.

Another problem is that it is very difficult to distinguish between labour market and housing market factors and between housing demand and housing supply. The demographic approach is almost useless in regions which are part of a larger housing or labour market, for example, municipalities in large urban regions. Moreover, for more detailed planning, information about the total number of households is not enough. Other distributions are required, such as households by size, the proportion of households with children and so on.

The work described here draws upon a model development that started at the statistical office of the City of Stockholm in 1975. The work resulted in the so-called household flow method. The method is based on the assumption that it is possible to observe the distribution of the population by household category at two different points of time, (for example, at two population censuses), and that it is possible to study how people change their household status during this time interval.

The starting point for the model is the individual, who is followed for a certain period of time (an intercensal period). Thus the households are not treated directly. The process involves the following distinct steps:[1]

1. For a given intercensal period a transition matrix is derived which describes the 'flow' of people between household categories. This means that each individual has to be identified at both the beginning and the end of the period and that his or her household status has to be recorded on both occasions.

2. A conventional population projection is carried out which shows not only the population by age, but also total number of births as well as number of deaths, immigrants and emigrants in each age-group.

3. The original transition matrix, which has given row and column sums, is adjusted to correspond to a new set of marginal sums. An outline of the transition matrix is given in Table 17.3.

Note that in the original transition matrix, summing by rows gives the number of people in each household category at the beginning of the period, while summing by columns gives corresponding distribution at the end of the period. In the set of constraints the row sums correspond to the known distribution of the population by household category at the beginning of the projection interval. The column sums are generally not known — only the projected population by age.[2] When the adjustment has been carried to a pre-determined accuracy, summing by columns will give the projected population by both age and household category.

4. Step 3 is then repeated as many times as the desired number of projection intervals. In each new projection step the transition matrix is adjusted to row sums that were column sums in a previous step.

[1] A formal mathematical presentation of the model is provided in the Appendix.
[2] Since the projection is generally made for 5-year age-groups, the only additional constraint is that the sum of all the elements in the transition matrix for a given age-group should equal the projected number of people for that specific age-group.

5. All calculations are made separately for each age-group and can also be made specific for region and sex sub-divisions.

So far this model is equivalent to a multiregional projection model with households corresponding to regions, although in this version of the model the transition probabilities are not explicitly calculated. In its most simple form the adjustment process is similar to iterative proportional fitting (sometimes known as RAS or Cross-Fratar).

An additional step after the first one may be included if one wishes to make alternative assumptions about household change patterns. In this case the transition matrix is constrained to adjust to a different but predetermined number of households at the end of the first intercensal period. This new transition matrix replaces the one used in Step 3 above. The rationale for making this alternative calculation is that the observed transition matrix corresponds to a given level of income and housing costs. It may therefore be of interest to study household changes for a different level of income and housing costs. In a recent application of the model this alternative number of households was calculated by means of a macro-economic model (see Appendix).

The data base

The central part of the model is the transition matrix described above (see also Table 17.3). This matrix is obtained by matching data from two consecutive censuses. The details of the classification of the population at the two censuses 1975 and 1980 is given in Table 17.6, which also gives the number of people in each category for Greater Göteborg.

A classification of the population as shown in this table may be done either for the total population, or separately for five-year age-groups.

Two classification principles form the basis of the matching procedure. One concerns the households, which are subdivided by size (1, 2, 3, 4, and 5+ members) and by presence or non-presence of children below the age of 15. The second principle concerns the individuals, which are characterized not only by age, but also by their being heads of households or not.

The construction of the data base was carried out in several stages:

1. Determination of household category for each individual at the two censuses 1975 and 1980.

2. Matching of the results of the two censuses. If a match is obtained the individual was living in the country both in 1975 and 1980.

3. Non-matches in 1975 may be assumed to have either died or emigrated during the five-year period. They are, therefore first matched with a death register which contains information on all deaths during the intercensal period. Those who still do not match are assumed to have emigrated.

Table 17.3.   Original transition matrix from matching the 1975 and 1980 censuses

Census 1975	Census 1980							
	Dwelling households (size)[1]				Non-dwelling households	Deaths 1976–1980	Emigrants 1976–1980	Total population 1975
	1	2	3	4	5+			
Dwelling households 1								
2								
3								
4								
5+								
Non-dwelling households								
Births 1976–1980								
Immigrants 1976–1980								
Total population 1980								

[1] A further subdivision by two characteristics (children/no children, head of household/not head of household) makes this a 20 by 20 matrix, i.e. 4 categories in each size class (in one-person households three of them contain functional zeros).

4. Non-matches in 1980 may either have immigrated or been born during the period. They are first matched against a birth register which gives information on all births. Those who do not match are assumed to have immigrated.

5. In matching against the birth and death registers, two additional types of non-matches are obtained. In the first case we have people who are in the death register, but were not counted in the 1975 census. We assume that they are immigrants who died during the period. Secondly we have persons in the birth register who were not in the 1980 census. We assume that they were born during the period, but emigrated before the census.

The data base described above was not matched against data on immigrants and emigrants during the intercensal period. This was partly for economic reasons, but also because we assumed that the gain in precision would be too insignificant to justify the higher cost. This means that we cannot get information about people who have immigrated during the five-year period and then re-emigrated before the census, or about people who emigrated and then re-immigrated. An estimate of the size of the first category may be obtained by a comparison with official statistics on immigration and emigration.

The final data base contains information not only on the household distribution of the population, but also other useful information such as place of residence. This means that we are able to make the transition matrices specific for various regional subdivisions of the country. This kind of data has been used in recent forecasts for counties and regions in Sweden.

Household change — a model application

An application referring to Greater Göteborg has been carried out in order to illustrate the use of the model for household forecast.

Before we present the results of the forecast we shall give a brief overview of the population development and household changes in the region. The following sub-section then presents the results of the model calculations.

Population and household changes in Greater Göteborg 1960–1980

The general trend in population development in Sweden during the last decades is clearly reflected in Greater Göteborg as is seen in Table 17.4.

The number of households increased by 2 per cent per year (1.5 per cent in the country) during the period 1960 to 1980, while the household population grew by only 1 per cent (0.25 per cent). The largest expansion took place during the 1960s when the number of households grew by more than 2.5 per cent per year on average and the total population by 1.7 per cent.

Table 17.4   Population and households in Sweden 1960–1980 (000s)

Year	Sweden				Greater Göteborg			
	Households		Household population		Households		Household population	
	No.	Index	No.	Index	No.	Index	No.	Index
1960	2 582	100	7 341	100	203	100	556	100
1965	2 778	108	7 624	104	226	111	604	109
1970	3 050	118	7 915	108	263	130	661	119
1975	3 325	129	8 016	109	286	141	670	121
1980	3 496	135	8 130	110	300	148	677	122

Source: Population and Housing Census 1960–1980.

The rapid growth in the number of households without a corresponding population increase has led to a decline in average household size. Table 17.5 shows this development in Greater Göteborg. The change towards smaller households is obvious: At the beginning of the period the proportion of one- and two-person households is below 50 per cent, but at the end of the period the share has increased to more than two-thirds of all households.

Table 17.5   Distribution of households by size: Greater Göteborg 1960–1980 (Percent)

Year	Number of persons					Number of households (000s)	Persons per household
	1	2	3	4	5 +		
1960	21	28	22	18	11	203	2.73
1965	24	27	21	18	10	226	2.67
1970	28	29	19	16	8	263	2.51
1975	32	30	16	15	16	286	2.34
1980	35	31	14	14	6	300	2.26

Source: Population Census 1960–1980.

After this cursory description of the household and population development in a longer time perspective, Table 17.6 gives a more detailed view of the development during the period 1975 to 1980.

Some interesting facts about the change in the household population is seen in this table. Of a total of 670 000 people in dwelling households in 1975, about 87 per cent were still in dwelling households in 1980.[3]

In Sweden that part of the population belonging to non-dwelling households is of some importance to the determination of housing needs. It manifests much larger turnover than the household population — the number of

[3] The term 'dwelling household' is used to stress the importance of the dwelling in the definition; it is synonymous to private household. Non-dwelling households, on the other hand, comprise both institutional households and other private households (i.e. people with residence unknown or registered in the parish, or on the premises).

Table 17.6   People in dwelling households and non-dwelling[1] households 1975 and
1980 according to the censuses: components of change: Greater
Göteborg

Dwelling households 1975 670 266	Belonging to dwelling households 1975 and 1980 583 183	Transferred to non-dwelling households 1980 9 323	Emigrated 1976–1980 49 357	Deceased 1976–1980 28 403
Non-dwelling households 1975 20 496	Transferred to dwelling households 1980 8 424	Belonging to non-dwelling households 1975 and 1980 3 769	Emigrated 1976–1980 4 318	Deceased 1976–1980 3 985
Born 1976–1980 41 969	Belonging to dwelling households 1980 37 350	Belonging to non-dwelling households 1980 401	Emigrated 1976–1980 3 933	Deceased 1976–1980 285
Immigrated 1976–1980 51 668	Belonging to dwelling households 1980 48 200	Belonging to non-dwelling households 1980 3 107	Emigrated 1976–1980 —	Deceased 1976–1980 361
Total	Dwelling households 1980 677 157	Non-dwelling households 1980 16 600	Emigrated 1976–1980 57 608	Deceased 1976–1980 33 034

[1] For definitions see footnote 3.

people remaining after 5 years is only about 20 per cent of the total number in
1975.

The population of Greater Göteborg increased by only about 4000 people
(0.4 per cent) during the whole 5-year period. This figure conceals a very
slow increase in the household population and an almost 20 per cent decrease
of the population in non-dwelling households. Within the household
population there was some increase in the number of people in households
without children (8 per cent), while the number of people in households with
children showed a decrease almost as large (7 per cent). A closer look at the
various size categories reveals a rather complex picture of both increase and
decrease (see Table 17.7).

A household projection for 1985

To illustrate the household flow method we have prepared a projection of
the number of people in different household categories in 1985. Since the
purpose is to illustrate the method only, different alternatives have not been
considered. The calculations are based on the observed transition matrix for

Table 17.7   Household composition 1975 and 1980: Greater Göteborg

| Household size and type | No. of persons | | Change |
	1975	1980	(1975 = 100)
1 NC**	93 080	106 107	114
2 C*	11 528	13 092	114
NC	160 391	170 356	106
3 C	79 428	69 737	88
NC	59 847	59 726	100
4 C	141 585	138 484	98
NC	26 488	30 435	115
5 + C	91 662	81 128	88
NC	6 257	8 067	129
Subtotal C	324 203	302 441	93
NC	346 063	374 691	108
Total	670 266	677 132	101
Non-dwelling households	20 496	16 600	81
Whole population	690 762	693 732	100

* C: Households with children (below 15 years)
** NC: Households without children.

the period 1975–80 and may be viewed as a trend projection. The outer frame for the projection is a forecast of the population in Greater Göteborg for the same period. According to this forecast the population will increase very slowly — the total increase being only about 5000 people until 1985.

Since the projection refers to the household population only we have assumed that the relation between this part of the population and the total population remains the same in all age-groups. This implies a total household population of about 682 000 in the year 1985.

To make the household projection we also need information about births, deaths, immigration, and emigration during the intervening period. This information is not separately accounted for in the population projection, but we have made an estimate of a probable level. A starting point for this estimation was the observed numbers in the 5-year period 1975–80 which were adjusted so as to obtain a consistent relation between the populations in 1980 and 1985.

Our calculations show that the total number of households will increase by about 10 000. This corresponds to a total increase of 3 per cent, which should be compared with an increase of 5 per cent between 1975 and 1980. The household composition according to the projection is shown in Table 17.8.

The results of this projection are in agreement with the development observed between 1975 and 1980. This is to be expected, since we use a constant transition matrix implying a trend projection. The difference in comparison with a pure trend extrapolation is that we take into account both the age-household structure at the beginning of the projection period *and* the age structure at the end. We find, for example, that the average household

Table 17.8   Number of households 1980 and 1985

Household size and type	1980		1985	
	Number	per cent	Number	per cent
1 NC**	106 107	35	114 944	37
2 C*	6 546	2	6 563	2
NC	85 179	28	88 771	29
3 C	23 247	8	23 109	7
NC	19 909	7	20 374	7
4 C	34 622	12	33 068	11
NC	7 609	3	7 955	3
5 C	15 307	5	13 960	4
NC	1 560	1	1 538	0
C	79 721	27	76 700	25
NC	220 364	73	233 582	75
Total	300 085	100	310 282	100

*C: Households with children (below 15 years).
**NC: Households without children.

size continues to decline and that the proportion of one- and two-person households increases from 65 per cent in 1980 to 68 per cent in 1985.

Some thoughts about future work

The development of the model for household forecast presented here has raised a large number of issues and conclusions regarding its potential development and future application. Some of these will be summarized below.

The model is a part of an integrated system of models for both household and housing forecast aiming at a total perspective including a micro-oriented and disaggregated approach. The different models and their relation to each other are formulated so as to capture real structures and conditions in regional housing markets.

The present model does not explicitly take into account the conditions on the housing market. This is done in the total system of models, where a housing market model is used to find the stable distribution of households over dwellings. That sub-model uses a programming approach in which the objective function is a consumer surplus. By an iterative process an equilibrium point is derived with a consistent distribution of households over dwellings in regions.

The data base which was developed at Statistics Sweden permits much greater detail in the analysis of household change, especially with regard to the regional distribution. A natural extension of the model would be to use it for analysing a regional housing market as a closed system where people not only change their household status, but also the location of their dwellings within the region. In other words the metropolitan region of Greater Göteborg, for example, would be divided into one central region comprising the city, one region closely surrounding the city and one suburban area at a large distance from the CBD.

A second line of development would be to derive births within the model. At present, all population changes are determined through a population forecast which is used as an outer frame for the household forecast.

At present, we have for the three largest metropolitan regions (Stockholm, Göteborg, and Malmö) transition matrices for the periods 1965–70, 1970–75, and 1975–80. When the census in 1985 is completed we plan to make a new matching for the period 1980–85. We will then be able to study time trends in household change patterns as one of the issues in our future research in this field.

Appendix

A mathematical presentation of the household flow model

On the basis of observations on transitions of people between household categories and the age–household structure of the population at the beginning of the period we can make a direct calculation of transition probabilities.[4]

In the application of the model this calculation is never carried out. The observed transition pattern is entered into an optimizing model, specified in the following way:

$$\text{Min} \sum \sum P_{ij}^x \ln(P_{ij}^x / Q_{ij}^x) \tag{A17.1}$$

Subject to:

$$\sum_j P_{ij}^x = P_{i.}^x$$

$$\sum_i \sum_j P_{ij}^x = P_{..}^x$$

P_{ij}^x = estimated number of people in age-group x belonging to household type i at the beginning of a projection period and to type j at the end of this period.

$P_{i.}^x$ = number of people in age-group x belonging to household category i at the beginning of the projection period.

$P_{..}^x$ = estimated age distribution at the end of the projection period.

Q_{ij}^x = observed number of people in age-group x who moved during an earlier time period from household type i to j (*a priori* distribution).

The following relation is thus valid:

$$\sum_i Q_{ij}^x = \sum_j P_{ij}^x \tag{A17.2}$$

which implies that the column sums of the *a priori* distribution are used as row constraints when the new transition matrix is calculated. A more detailed description of the properties of the model is given in Hårsman (1981), where the relation between this approach and approaches in terms of transition probabilities is also discussed.

If we wish to study alternative trends in household development, we must derive alternative *a priori* distributions which are based on different predetermined

---

[4] Alternatively we may calculate corresponding rates and transform them to probabilities, in which case we also need the population structure at the end of the period.

numbers of households. The above constraints are then supplemented by the following:

$$\sum_x \sum_i \omega_j P_{ij}^x = H_j \qquad (A17.3)$$

ω_j = weight which is the inverted value of the number of people in household category j

H_j = number of households in category j

The projection may result in certain inconsistencies with respect to the distribution by age of people in different household categories. Therefore the following constraints must be added:

$$\sum_{x\epsilon X_1} \sum_i {}^B P_{i2}^x = \sum_{x\epsilon X_2} \sum_i {}^B P_{i2}^x \qquad (A17.4)$$

$$\sum_{x\epsilon X_1} \sum_i {}^B P_{i3}^x \geq \sum_{x\epsilon X_2} \sum_i \omega_3\, {}^B P_{i3}^x \qquad (A17.5)$$

$$\sum_{x\epsilon X_1} \sum_i {}^B P_{i4}^x \geq \sum_{x\epsilon X_2} \sum_i \omega_4\, {}^B P_{i4}^x \qquad (A17.6)$$

$$\sum_{x\epsilon X_1} \sum_i {}^B P_{i5}^x \geq \sum_{x\epsilon X_2} \sum_i \omega_5\, {}^B P_{i5}^x \qquad (A17.7)$$

$X_1 = 0, 1, \ldots, 14$ years
$X_2 = 15, 16, \ldots, \omega$ years

${}^B P_{i2}^x$ = number of people belonging to household category i at the beginning of the period and to two-person households with children at the end of the period when they are x years of age.
${}^B P_{i3}^x$, ${}^B P_{i4}^x$, and ${}^B P_{i5}^x$ are similarly defined

ω_i = weight equal to the inverted value of the number of people in the household (i.e. $\omega_3 = 1/3$, $\omega_4 = 1/4$, and $\omega_5 = 1/85.25$).

The meaning of these constraints is that the number of children in two-person households with children under the age of 15 years must be equal to the number of adults in the same household category (equation A17.4); the number of children in three-, four-, and five-person households with children must be at least as large as the number of households in each category (equations A17.5, A17.6, and A17.7).

When making a forecast for example for the year 1985, we start by setting Q_{ij}^x equal to the observed transition pattern for 1975–1980, $P_{i.}^x$ is set to the distribution of people by age and household category according to the census in 1980 and P^x is set to the number of people by age only according to a population projection for the year 1985. With the given set of constraints (e.g. equations A17.1–2, and A17.4–7) a new transition matrix P_{ij}^x is estimated. By summing each column in this matrix we get the projected distribution of the population by age and household category:

$$P_{.j}^x = \sum_i P_{ij}^x \qquad (A17.8)$$

From this distribution the number of households are easily obtained.

Besides information on the population in different household categories we also need, in a complete forecast, information about the estimated number of births, deaths, immigrants, and emigrants. These data are represented as separate categories in the system of equations above.

When formulated in this way the model closely resembles the multiregional projection model of Rogers *et al*. Our transition matrix (with P_{ij}^x expressed as probabilities) corresponds to the generalized Leslie matrix with household categories as regions.[5] There is an important difference in the fact that the population by age at the end of the projection period is included as a constraint in the calculation.[6]

The same general model is used both for the household projections and for estimating alternative transition matrices, the only difference being the set of constraints used in the calculation.

In the present version of the model a macroeconomic model of change in housing demand is used to derive alternative number of households:

$$\Delta H = \gamma_0 + \gamma_1 \cdot \Delta P + \gamma_2 \cdot \Delta A + \gamma_3 \cdot \Delta I + \gamma_4 \cdot r \qquad (A17.9)$$

where

ΔH = per cent change in housing demand (equal to per cent change in the number of households provided there is a balanced housing market)
ΔP = per cent change in relative cost of housing
ΔI = per cent change in real income
ΔA = per cent change in the average age of the population
r = per cent growth of the population
γ_0 is a constant and γ_1, γ_2, γ_3, and γ_4 are elasticities of demand.

In some recent applications of the model, the following model specification was used:

$$\Delta H = \gamma_0 - 1.0 \cdot \Delta P + 0.5 \cdot \Delta A + 0.4 \cdot \Delta I + 1.0 \cdot r$$

The constant γ_0 was estimated as the ratio of the estimated number of households and the observed number for the most recent period.

References

Dellgran, P., I. Holmberg, and P. Olovsson, (1984), 'Hushållsbildning och bostadsefterfrågan. Utveckling och tillämpning av modeller för regional bostads-byggnadspalnering'. (Household Formation and Housing Demand. Development and Application of Models for Planning Regional Housing Construction. In Swedish), Demographic Research Unit, Department of Statistics, Report 16, University of Göteborg, Sweden.

Hårsman, B. (1981), 'Housing Demand Models and Housing Market Models for Regional and Local Planning', Swedish Council for Building Research, Document D13 (1981), Stockholm.

[5] There is another difference pertaining to the fact that geographical regions are fixed in size, while households change in different ways. There are, however, no theoretical objections in principle against this way of regarding the process.

[6] To construct the multiregional projection in accordance with the household flow model would amount to using the age-structure of a separate national forecast as a constraint on the regional projections.

Part VII

Directions of Development of Family Demography

18 Discussion

NORMAN B. RYDER

Office of Population Research, Princeton, New Jersey, USA.

If demography is defined broadly as the study of the determinants and consequences of population trends, then almost all work in family demography concerns the consequences for families of the joint operation of the various demographic processes. The classic formulation is Lotka's stable population model. In that model, the processual inputs were female fertility by age, and female and male mortality by age; the structural outputs were the distribution of the population by age and sex. Progress in the field, spurred particularly by the postwar rise in fertility in developed countries, raised many questions about this essentially biological orientation to the subject, questions which moved ideas about measurement, and about the appropriate design of population models, in the direction of a more sociocultural orientation. Family demography is implicit in the recognition that all human societies control procreation, and thus the formation and continuation of unions which may lead to procreation. That control is necessitated by the long period of childhood dependence and the consequent desirability of enduring relations between parent and child, and between husband and wife, generally accompanied by co-residence.

Three criticisms were directed at the stable population model in its classic form: it was oriented to one sex; the reproductive process was specific only for age; and the data used in its application were ordinarily derived from a period cross-section. These concerns remain central to model construction in family demography, as noted in Wachter's contribution to the present volume.

The one-sex model prevails, *faute de mieux*, because of failure to develop a procedure for analysing the marriage market. The issue of the level of specificity needed to describe the reproductive process is a major source of tension in the decisions of model-builders: each new dimension added to enrich the description comes at the cost of demands on the data system, with structural complexity inhibiting understanding of how the model works. It now seems desirable to extend specification at least to marital status and duration, and to parity and birth interval length. As for the mode of temporal aggregation — period or cohort — considerations of convenience prevail. Models tend to be formulated with a cohort orientation; measurements are most often drawn from temporal cross-sections. The challenge of determining how processual inputs of cohort nuptiality, fertility, and mortality become translated into consequences for family structure, period by period, has not been faced.

The products of family demography displayed in the present volume originate from consideration of the consequences of the operation of two or more of the basic demographic processes, supplemented by transitions particular to the family concept. Three dimensions characterize the family: the conjugal, the consanguineal, and the residential. One can develop the account by proceeding from the less to the more complex. The first subject is the conjugal relationship, i.e., the formation and dissolution of marital unions. Second is the consanguineal relationship, that between parents and children, identifying the distinctive contribution of kinship studies. Next comes the nuclear family, the simplest residential combination of the conjugal and the consanguineal. Finally, the account turns to households, i.e., groups, familial and nonfamilial, characterized by co-residence.

This classification gives a falsely tidy impression of the way family demographers work, yet it may serve as a judicious protocol. Given the considerable complexity of comprehensive simulation of the evolution of family structures, discretion is surely advised. The most effective directions of effort in the near future are likely to be those focused on circumscribed parts of the system.

The conjugal dimension

In the past several decades, a formal approach to the study of the formation and dissolution of marriages has been systematized as a particular application of what is called the multistate life table. In their contributions to this volume, Willekens summarizes the state of the art (Chapter 7), and Espenshade exemplifies the procedure for recent experience in the United States (Chapter 8).

The arithmetic of structure and process begins with a classification of persons by marital status at two time points, and a record of the transitions of persons from any state at the first time to any state at the second time. Once algorithms are developed to express the subsequent structure as a function of the prior structure and the transition matrix, outputs become available which are isomorphic with those of the prototype life table, and interpretable alternatively as cohort histories or as population cross-sections. Even in the absence of a record of transitions, the redundancy in the system can be exploited, as Preston shows in Chapter 3, to determine some probabilities of decrement transition merely from the initial and final distributions of persons among states.

The marital status life table is strictly applicable only to one or the other of the two genders, but not to both jointly. If $B(i)$ bachelors of age i, and $S(j)$ spinsters of age j contract $M(i,j)$ marriages in an observed situation, then the array of rates $M(i,j)/B(i)$ suffice to determine the number of marriages of spinsters age j, once some new number of bachelors is specified, but only by ignoring the fundamental demographic precept that the number of spinster marriages should also depend on whatever number of spinsters there may be in the new situation. A generally different outcome, equally cogent from a formal standpoint and similarly flawed, would ensue from developing the implications of the array of rates $M(i,j)/S(j)$. There is no obvious rule for resolving the discrepancy between the male-based and the female-based alternatives.

Should one attempt to resolve the conundrum by calculating some average of $B(i)$ and $S(j)$, such as the harmonic mean, to serve as a denominator for $M(i,j)$, dual results are avoided, although it is easy to devise situations in which more marriages would be prescribed for one sex than there are persons available in that sex. And there is a more basic flaw in any resolution achieved by a mechanical averaging of the sexes; The question of availability of spouses is interdependent with the question of male and female preferences for particular marital combinations. The number of bachelors, $B(i)$, and of spinsters, $S(j)$, available for marriages $M(i,j)$ are conditional on the preferences of males of class i for females in classes other than j, and similarly on the preferences of females of class j for males in classes other than i. The interaction between availability and preference permeates the entire matrix. In any model with a modicum of realism, far more inputs are required (to represent the matrix of preferences) than there are outputs available (in the form of observed frequencies of marriage in each combination) to solve for them.

This line of thought has implications for the choice between cohort and period orientations in the conduct of nuptiality analysis. (Cf. Ryder, 1981). The analytic presupposition behind choice of the cohort approach in the analysis of secular change in nuptiality is that there is a coherent temporal pattern to an individual's nuptiality experience, as well as structural continuity for the cohort of which that individual is a member, coherence and continuity which are conceptually independent of the circumstances prevailing in the periods through which the individual and the cohort pass.

The joint character of the marriage event implies that the nuptiality of any cohort of one sex varies directly with the nuptiality of adjacent cohorts of the other sex and inversely with the nuptiality of adjacent cohorts of the same sex. Moreover, since the market for spinsters includes postmarried men as well as bachelors, and the market for bachelors includes postmarried women as well as spinsters, it follows that the accounting is obliged to incorporate the incidence of marital dissolution and remarriage for the sequence of male and female cohorts. The consequent interpretation of the behaviour of adjacent cohorts of the respective sexes destroys the case for the analytic primacy of the cohort orientation to the study of nuptiality. Period-specific segments of the marriage histories of each cohort and sex are ineluctably manifestations of the historically evolving marriage market.

The problem of the marriage market has proven resistant to technical ingenuity, and it seems unlikely to be resolved by collecting new kinds of evidence. Since there are important consequences of the shape of the marriage market for the modelling of family histories, it is at least incumbent on demographers to expose the issue by developing isomorphic models for the sexes separately rather than conceal it behind a one-sex formulation. The discrepancy between the two outcomes will serve as a signal of the need for modesty in drawing inferences.

The consanguineal dimension

The family is most commonly defined as a group of co-resident kin. There can be co-residence without kinship, and kinship without co-residence: the family is the intersection of these two dimensions. In turn, kinship is broadly based on both conjugal and consanguineal bonds. Although most kinship models encompass relations by marriage as well as by birth, the latter are the subject of this section.

There is very little evidence on numbers of kin, i.e., counts for a respondent of the numbers of relatives of different types surviving at time of observation. On the other hand, the process of creation of consanguineal relationships may be directly inferred from fertility records: Each birth initiates a joint survival function of parent and child. Accordingly, much effort has been directed to the development of kinship records through models.

Three orientations to modelling are distinguished: analytic, microsimulation, and macrosimulation. The analytic model characterizes links between family structure and demographic process with mathematical functions. Where such constructions are feasible, they permit the maximum understanding of the system, but there are stringent limits on tolerable complexity. Work with analytic models, as presented in Pullum's contribution to this volume (Chapter 14), manifests continual tension between the number of variables required to approximate reality (especially the incorporation of temporal variation in the underlying processes) and the ambition to explicate the outcome.

This dilemma has provoked extensive resort to the tactic of microsimulation, exemplified by Chapters 12 and 13 by Reeves and by Smith. In a microsimulation model, each person's life path is simulated separately, on the basis of numerical specification of the rates at which significant events occur, conditional on the individual's status at the time. The calculations proceed, event by event, through the individual's history, typically by Monte Carlo simulation of probability distributions. For each individual a file is maintained of the extant consanguineal relationships, formed by parenthood and erased by death of either party. In this way, one may investigate the evolution of a kinship network in circumstances in which the behaviour rules are too complicated to permit the construction of an analytic model.

While there is no limit in principle to the complexity permitted with micro-simulation, there are substantial practical restrictions. The evidence required to specify the input processes often taxes the data base. There is continuing conflict between the cost of the operation, as measured by the size of the population simulated, and the sampling errors associated with the outputs. Such errors are particularly troublesome when one is interested in a small subdivision of the population. Models generally provide the attractive possibility of experimentation with a range of inputs of one or another kind. This sets the stage for sensitivity analysis, as a surrogate for the kinds of partial derivatives which would be yielded by mathematical analysis, were that feasible. With microsimulation, however, such experimentation tends to be prohibitively expensive.

A third alternative is to use deterministic processes (as in most analytic models) rather than stochastic processes, but with particularistic rather than generalized inputs. The procedure is designated as macrosimulation because the units for which operating characteristics are prescribed are cohorts rather than individuals. For kinship analysis, the crucial elements of a macrosimulation model are the arrays binding one cohort to another, e.g., the probability that a mother in cohort i has a child in cohort j. The complexity of deterministic equations required to manifest these linkages provokes Reeves, in Chapter 12, to utilize microsimulation and macro-simulation *in tandem*.

The principal liability of the deterministic approach as customarily applied is that, whereas microsimulation yields comprehensive output distributions, the outputs of macrosimulation are ordinarily measures of central tendency. On the other hand, this is not inherent in the macro-simulation strategy: it is both feasible and desirable to incorporate simple heterogeneity in both the inputs and outputs of such models.

In many cultures, the kinship system is centred on the individual. Four kinds of primary relative are distinguished: the parent and the sibling in an individual's family of orientation; the spouse and the child in the individual's family of procreation. The system is readily extended to kin of higher degree. Thus, secondary relatives are primary relatives of primary relatives who are not themselves primary relatives, and so forth. Most models designed to count kin are keyed to the individual as the central figure in a system of relevant positions. The consequence is that membership in any kinship group, bounded by degree of relationship, is particular to choice of ego.

In many other cultures, past and present, kinship groups can be ascribed an identity independent of any individual member. Consanguineal kin groups are entered by birth (to a member of the group) and exited only by death. Such groups have a theoretically identifiable membership roster at any time. The activities of this kind of descent group tend to be focused on the survival of the group in the long term, as an institutional structure, and on the conduct of a system of cooperation and insurance in times of duress. Such descent systems are the prototype of the ethnic group, sometimes coexistent with the nation, as distinguished from citizenship in the modern state — a comparable extension of the concepts of residence and community.

Kinship models can help explore questions of considerable practical and theoretical importance, such as those associated with intergenerational relationships. In every society, one has rights and responsibilities with respect to one's parents and one's children, which tend to follow a well-defined cyclical course as the ages of the respective parties change. One focus of intergenerational demography is the survival and reproduction of an individual's generation, in temporal conjuncture with the survival and reproduction of the generations of the parents and of the children of the chosen person. An individual life history may be characterized by the changing frequencies over time of the numbers of parents, siblings, and children. The relevance of the sibling count is that siblings share that person's rights and responsibilities *vis-à-vis* parents. A sibling distribution is immediately derivative from a parity distribution, suitably modified to accommodate joint survival.

The outcome of such a consanguineal history evidently depends on both the quantum and tempo of net fertility in two successive generations. For example, the number of coexisting generations varies directly with the length of life and inversely with the length of generation. Likewise the length of joint survival of any two relatives (siblings, parent and child, husband and wife) varies inversely with their difference in age.

Models to investigate such processes require the complexity of parity-specific fertility, and are rich in inferences only if the vital processes are allowed to vary from one generation to the next. Of particular interest is the extent of coincidence between the time in which ego may be obliged to support elderly dependents and the time in which ego is also supporting youthful dependents. Such questions are germane to the extent that the family remains central to the provision of welfare. But as societies move towards a collective support system, the relevance of the intergenerational distribution declines relative to that of the age distribution. Thus generations, in some socially meaningful sense, are replaced by cohorts.

The nuclear family

The nuclear family may be identified as the family of procreation of a married couple. This combines consideration of the conjugal and consanguineal dimensions, but restricts the number of co-residing generations to two. Implicit in the concept of the nuclear family is the stipulation of neolocality, separating residentially the individual's family of procreation from his or her family of orientation. The constructions required derive from the elementary demographic processes of marital formation and dissolution, fertility, and mortality, together with the event of passage implicit in the neolocality stricture.

The first attempt at modelling the family was the so-called family life cycle. It is generally represented as a sequence of dated events: marriage, first birth, last birth, first child passage, last child passage, first parental death. Despite this focus on the temporal dimension of a family history, it is evident that the sequence of dates is also contingent on the number of children born.

Passage is an important event in family history for which there is little evidence. It may be defined variously as the time of departure of the child from the residence of its family of orientation, or its time of entry into the labour force, or time of marriage, or time of attaining some arbitrary age of adulthood. The sense of passage is the change of the child from dependent to independent status. The multidimensionality of that transition suffices to explain the difficulty of documenting the process.

The pertinence of the classic family life cycle is attenuated by divorce and remarriage. Were divorce equivalent to the departure of one person from the family, it could be viewed from the standpoint of that family as analogous to the consequences of mortality, but where both spouses retain at least one child, two families become created out of one. Similarly, a remarriage in which no more than one of the couple is a parent is a special mode of increase in family size, whereas, if both are parents, two families become one. Such instances of family fission and fusion make the 'family' an awkward unit of analysis. Otherwise said, there are as many different possible family histories as there are egos in terms of which the history is written. Although a parent is generally the marker for a family history, the justification is less theoretical than pragmatic. It is clear from Hofferth's contribution to the present volume (Chapter 9) that some important questions require family structure to be viewed with the eyes of the child.

One is led by such considerations to formulate a model not for the family, somehow defined, but rather for the family history of an individual. Birth initiates for an individual a family relationship with parents and possibly with siblings; within that family of orientation, the individual faces competing risks of death and passage. Subsequent to passage, there may be a solo interval in which the competing risks are death and marriage; such intervals are becoming longer and more frequent in many societies. Marriage initiates the individual's family of procreation, in which the competing risks are parenthood, divorce, and death. The history so constructed may be depicted in terms of temporal change for the individual in the incidence of parents and siblings in the family of orientation, and of spouse and children in the family of procreation.

Even this kind of history fails to yield a tidy sequence of dates, such as envisaged in the classic family life cycle. The general problem is that the differences between average times of occurrence of events which change the family structure are interpretable only for those with comparable exposure to risk of competing events. Although one can specify clearly the lapse of time between two well-defined events, the sequence *in toto* lacks methodological credibility beyond some simple and rare scenarios, as exemplified in Feichtinger's contribution to this volume (Chapter 5).

Given the plethora of exigencies which produce noncomparability, as discussed in this volume by Höhn, it would seem futile to try to find a way out of the impasse by developing a family of family life cycles. The classic approach has served the discipline well by posing, albeit not answering, an important question. Now it would seem judicious, on intrinsic grounds, to abandon the concept, and seek to explore the tempo as well as the quantum of family histories in methodologically more defensible ways.

Although deft analytic constructions are capable of yielding interpretive insights, the general direction of effort which seems most likely to supersede the family life cycle as a demographic genre is the construction of macrosimulation models of the nuclear family history of an individual. For example, Bongaarts, in Chapter 10, uses a multistate life table format to encompass marriage formation, parity-specific fertility, passage, and mortality. The outputs take the form of a running account of family structure by number, age and gender of co-resident living children. Despite precautions taken to avoid complications by limiting the types of family to be considered, the enterprise remains continually at risk of spilling over the bounds of organizational and theoretical command.

While it is difficult to draft general recommendations for a strategy to incorporate necessary complexity and still maintain analytic control, there may be some clues from experience with the isomorphic task of effective fertility measurement. The present writer has developed a measurement system, entitled progressive fertility analysis. (Ryder, 1982). Two features suggest its adaptability to model construction. First, parity progression, generally recognized as essential in family demography models, is complemented by specificity with respect to the tempo of progression, in an economical manner. Second, the shape of the measurement system is directly derivative from the requirements for projection, and is thus appropriate for programming the evolution of a simulated population. Although the multidimensional arrays required for the task may be unwieldy in full detail, they do not seem resistant in principle to devices for collapsing them into a workable set of parameters.

Most contributors to this volume admit and regret the failure to characterize the marriage market. Some of the ramifications of the unresolved two-sex problem appear to be important. In Chapter 6 the present writer gives a model of a marriage market predicated on arbitrary but not unreasonable rules. If the preference system in the market, in interaction with availability, yields an age difference between spouses — a by-product in part of the extent of remarriage — then the numbers of male and female marriages is strongly dependent on the prevailing growth rate of the population. The simple reason is that the magnitude of the growth rate is the most important determinant of the relative numbers of persons of different age. The system is reflexive in the sense that the extent of marriage itself helps to determine the growth rate. Thus some resolution of the marriage market is intrinsic to determination of the growth rate, and thus the age distribution; that distribution is reflected variously in family structure.

Moreover there is ordinarily a marked differentiation between the experiences of males and females with parenthood. Given the sharp distinctions of roles by gender, as well as by age and marital status, in every society, the likely discrepancy between male-oriented and female-oriented family histories is of major theoretical importance. For this reason alone, and quite aside from the technical two-sex riddle, the development of models based on males as well as on females is strongly urged. Beyond that, it seems likely that changes in availability consequent upon increase in the growth rate will provoke reconsideration of marriage preferences; such new normative configurations may be an integral element in the process of social change.

Households

The focus of household analysis is the residential dimension of individual life. Although the nuclear family is an important subset of households, it is a long way from exhausting the category.

Household data exist in large volume, particularly since census and survey data are ordinarily collected that way. Such evidence lends itself to a straightforward comparison of successive cross-sections, and the development of transition matrices, quite apart from whether there are family relationships. Given the consequential form in which the data are produced, the analysis tends to proceed in reverse, working back from the outputs to infer the nature of inputs.

There is much demand for the outputs of household demography, because the household is for many purposes the meaningful production and consumption unit. Much statistical work is oriented to the task of projecting the distribution of households by size. Holmberg's contribution to this volume is intended to complement a purely demographic model with residential transitions (and, in due course, economic determinants).

Much of household demography can be considered in abstraction from family relationships. Every individual in the (non-institutional) population is a member of one or another household, and a head may be designated for every such household by some stipulated rule. This permits calculation of the probability that a person in a particular category, such as age and sex, is a head. For analysis, as in the work by Burch *et al.*, (Chapter 2) such rates can be weighted by some standard population distribution to provide

informative indices of headship propensity. Given the one-to-one relationship between households and heads, the scheme is evidently a basis for
projections.

The counterpart of headship is that all others in the household are non-
heads. In this volume, Pitkin and Masnick focus their attention on the
matrix of data obtained by cross-classifying heads of households by
nonheads, specific for various characteristics. This formulation implies that
the propensity for nonheadship as well as for headship is an alternative for
analysis and projection. As they comment: 'This is analogous to the
economic model of supply, demand and market clearing, where the actual
sales of a commodity are determined jointly by actors on both sides of a
market.' The same analogy applies, of course, to the marriage market. As
there, one generally obtains different outcomes from projections based on
characteristics of heads and nonheads respectively. There is evident
advantage to performing the exercise both ways, to expose incompatibility;
the supposition is that, as with the marriage market, the problem is
analytically irresoluble.

An important class of households can be modelled by extension of nuclear
family models. Two important exceptions to the nuclear family arise from
breaches of the neolocality principle. First, there may be vertical extension
through the family of procreation of one or more of the child generation in
the nuclear family. Second, there may be vertical extension through the
family of orientation of one or more of the parent generation in the nuclear
family. In some cultures these would be considered as deviations; in other
societies they are the form of preference. As a counterpoint to the general
drift in developing societies toward nuclearization of the family, the
extended family is frequently reconstituted in response to situations of convenience and need, because the generational bonds remain intact. In this
volume, Kono's projection of the households of Japan takes explicit
account of the incidence of three-generation households.

Vertical extensions of the nuclear family are particular manifestations of
kinship as an institutionalized design for matching dependents and providers. Such responsibilities, lodged in primary relationships, tend to persist
throughout the joint lives of each relevant pair, and coresidence is a frequent
practical and convenient consequence.

The modelling of links between the family of orientation and the family of
procreation of an individual need not exceed the bounds of tolerable
complexity. Many forms of household record provide relevant data, even
though specification of exposure to risk may often be problematic. There is
ambiguity in the generational location of headship in any three-generation
family, attributable to the various connotations of headship. (The sex issue
of headship, to which much attention has been paid, is, to the contrary,
essentially a straw man — or straw woman.)

If a family is thought of as a matched set of dependents and providers, it follows that there is justification for redistributing members among house-holds whenever, as a consequence of demographic exigency, particular families become too large in dependents or too small in providers. Simulations which incorporate heterogeneity provide clear evidence of the substantial incidence of families malformed in one or the other respect. The modelling of residential redistribution of kin, to match dependents with providers in ways more sensible than that ensuing from the combination of demography and residential norms, is complicated by the circumstance that the requisite goods and services may flow between as well as within house-holds. Because residential redistribution is responsive to transitory exigencies, such as the economic circumstances of the respective parties, residential transitions prove to be uncomfortable objects of demographic modelling.

Conclusion

An examination of the contributions to this volume produces the strong impression that family demography is crippled for want of evidence. Many of the requisite transitions and relations remain largely undocumented, especially for developing countries. In consequence, the scarce resources of imagination and energy are excessively diverted into judgemental exercises. Much of the evidence that is available is flawed, a particularly acute problem in family demography because so many of the central relationships have a normative dimension. As a generalization, the reliability of information tends to vary inversely with the extent to which it is subject to moral evaluation.

In directing efforts to determine the structural consequences for the family of the operation of demographic processes, there is a tendency to ignore the likely dependence of those individual processes on the family structure. For example it is highly unlikely that fertility and mortality in a child generation are independent of the same processes in the parent generation.

From a methodological standpoint, there is a rich array of alternative models, deterministic and stochastic, with individual or cohort as unit; no strong case can be made for exclusive choice among them in prescriptions for future progress. None of them has grasped the nettle of the two-sex problem. Its imperviousness to conventional demographic weaponry is insufficient justification for continuing to act as if it did not exist.

Demographers are now beginning to give the field of family demography the kind of attention its theoretical and social importance calls for. Any projection of the developments of the past decade would suggest that the discipline is not far from achieving maturity, although the complexity of the subject prohibits any expectation of imminent closure.

References

Bongaarts, J., (1983), 'The Formal Demography of Families and Households: An Overview', *IUSSP Newsletter* No. 17, 27–42.

CICRED, (1984), *Demography of the Family*, Inter-Center Cooperative Research Programme, Project No. 2, Final Report, Paris.

Ryder, N. B., (1971), 'Notes on Fertility Measurement', *Milbank Memorial Fund Quarterly* 49(4), Pt. 2: 109–27, October.

—— (1978), 'Methods in Measuring the Family Life Cycle', in: *International Population Conference Mexico 1977*, International Union for the Scientific Study of Population, Liège, Vol. 4, pp. 219–26.

—— (1981), 'Cohort and Period Orientations to Measurement of Marital Formation and Dissolution', in *International Population Conference Manila*, International Union for the Scientific Study of Population, Liège, Vol. 1, pp. 467–83.

—— (1982), *Progressive Fertility Analysis*, World Fertility Survey, Technical Bulletin, No. 8.

Name Index

Subject Index